THE WORLD'S CLASSICS

REFLECTIONS ON THE
REVOLUTION IN FRANCE

EDMUND BURKE (1729–97) was the dominant inter-
preter of politics in the last quarter of the eighteenth
century. For most of his life, he was a practising politician,
working within the Whig party of the Marquess of
Rockingham and Charles James Fox. He was an MP from
1765–94, and was briefly a junior minister in short-lived
governments. He therefore wrote about the theory of
politics from an experience of politics. His was a pragmatic
approach above all else. What impressed him about
political institutions was not their origins in speculative
theories, but their capacity, or failure, to meet the real
needs of men living in a political community. Some
upheavals, like the American Revolution, could be applauded because they sought to reaffirm the political
institutions that were peculiar to a particular society. Burke
wrote in support of Poles, Corsicans, and the peoples of
India for the same reason. Other revolutions, however,
notably the French, were damned for cutting a people off
from its roots. Always, Burke is responding to the events of
his time. His cautionary words on the management of
change, its potential benefits and vicious potentialities,
have a new relevance as Cold War certainties give way to
more protean politics.

LESLIE MITCHELL is Fellow in Modern History at
University College, Oxford. He was born and educated in
Oxford. He has written widely on the politics of the Whig
party in the late eighteenth and early nineteenth centuries,
and is the author of the biography *Charles James Fox*
(Oxford, 1992).

THE WORLD'S CLASSICS

EDMUND BURKE

Reflections on the Revolution in France

Edited with an Introduction by
L. G. MITCHELL

Oxford New York

OXFORD UNIVERSITY PRESS

1993

Oxford University Press, Walton Street, Oxford OX2 6DP
Oxford New York Toronto
Delhi Bombay Calcutta Madras Karachi
Kuala Lumpur Singapore Hong Kong Tokyo
Nairobi Dar es Salaam Cape Town
Melbourne Auckland Madrid
and associated companies in
Berlin Ibadan

Oxford is a trade mark of Oxford University Press

Editorial material © L. G. Mitchell 1993

First published as a World's Classics paperback 1993

British Library Cataloguing in Publication Data
Data available

Library of Congress Cataloging in Publication Data
Burke, Edmund, 1729–1797.
Reflections on the Revolution in France/Edmund Burke:
edited with an introduction by L. G. Mitchell.
p. cm.—(World's classics)
Includes bibliographical references.
1. France—History—Revolution, 1789–1799—Causes.
2. France—Politics and government—Revolution, 1789–1799.
I. Mitchell, L. G. (Leslie George) II. Title. III. Series.
DC150.B83 1993 944.04—dc20 92–275
ISBN 0–19–281844–9

1 3 5 7 9 10 8 6 4 2

Typeset by Cambrian Typesetters
Printed in Great Britain by
BPCC Hazells Ltd.
Aylesbury, Bucks.

CONTENTS

CONTENTS

INTRODUCTION

THE *Reflections on the Revolution in France* was published on 1 November 1790, and was an immediate best-seller. Within six months it had sold nineteen thousand copies. By September 1791 it had gone through eleven editions. Anchored in a particular, historical context, it has become one of the indispensable textbooks for the political theorist. Burke would have been happy with this outcome, but he never made any pretence of the fact that his book was as much for the instruction of his contemporaries as of posterity. In essence, the work was a reply to a letter. On 4 November 1789 a young French friend of the Burke family had written innocently to ask the great man's views on events in Paris. Rarely has such an enquiry been so thunderously answered. Burke replied at length and with such gravity because, at a dinner of the Revolution Society celebrating the memory of the Glorious Revolution of 1688, certain of the diners had seen fit to send a message of congratulation to the National Assembly in Paris on the discovery of their new-found freedoms. English and French politics thereby became enmeshed. Burke's book was intended as a cautionary tale for readers on both sides of the Channel.

That Burke should write about a French theme at all was remarkable. Unlike most members of the Whig party, Burke had shown very little interest in France or its politics. He may have crossed the Channel in 1757. He certainly spent two months there in 1773, but this was a poor record compared to that of the Whig grandees who were his patrons in politics. Even when he ventured into France, Burke unfashionably avoided Paris, preferring to spend his time among the provincial clergy and gentry of Auxerre. These people became his principal informants on French affairs. While Fox, Rockingham, and Grey spoke to Mirabeau, Talleyrand, and Lafayette, Burke listened to the views of men and women whose names are barely known to history. As a result, his intelligence was often seen as prejudiced and defective. Tom

Paine thought Burke 'very unacquainted with French affairs'. Sometimes, Burke claimed to know France 'pretty tolerably for a stranger'. In his more honest moments, he was acutely embarrassed by 'the very bad French which I speak'. All in all, he was of the opinion that the best view of France could be had 'from the Pier at Margate'.

None of this mattered too much if the book was immediately intended as a warning to the English. The French Revolution was only a scarecrow with which to frighten England into political sense. It was unimportant if the scarecrow's rags were described a little inaccurately. The general points about politics that Burke was trying to make would still come across. Unfortunately, this was not the case. Burke's description of what had happened in France in 1789 and 1790 was so at odds with the facts of the situation that he suffered humiliation and rejection. Never has a book been so widely read and so widely spurned. The general statements about political society and its management contained in the book were lost sight of, and the hundred or so pamphlets penned in response to the *Reflections* largely harped endlessly on the inaccuracy of its details and the overblown hyperbole of the style in which it was written.

Burke was rejected right across the political spectrum. It was inevitable that Radicals like Tom Paine and Mary Wollstonecraft would dislike the book, but Fox found it 'to be in very bad taste' and Pitt saw only 'rhapsodies in which there is much to admire and nothing to agree with'. Contemporaries struggled to find answers to two questions. First, why had Burke come out in opposition to the Revolution at all? He had after all supported national revolutions in America, Ireland, Corsica, and Poland. After reading the *Reflections*, Thomas Jefferson insisted that, 'The Revolution in France does not astonish me as much as the revolution in Mr. Burke.' Secondly, why had Burke been so perversely inaccurate in his description of French politics? The events of 1789 and 1790 had been widely witnessed, not least by Englishmen. As Burke was writing, the Revolution had become something of a tourist attraction. Information and views were widely available. Therefore, it was unforgivable to muddle the tax system with the system of local government, or to turn the attack on the Palace of Versailles on 5–6 October 1789 into pure melodrama. The sentinel on duty outside Marie Antoinette's bedroom had not been murdered, but was regaling English visitors in Paris with tales of his adventures.

So grave were these questions that many people simply turned away. Benjamin Vaughan, an eyewitness to events in Paris, decided that Burke was simply not worth answering and so made himself 'idle a fortnight'. The French Press were more condescending than outraged. One or two editors indulged in phrases like 'un insolent pamphlet'. Most dwelt on the eccentricities of the piece, the 'bizarreries de l'auteur'. The English were predictably more intrigued to discover why a man who was universally recognized as one of the foremost intellects of the day should have been tempted into writing a terrible caricature of the greatest event in politics of his lifetime.

For some, the answer was simply that Burke had changed his politics in return for a pension from George III, one of the few people to admire the *Reflections* unreservedly. Others took the view that the recurrent rumour that Burke was a crypto-Catholic must be true. His mother had been Catholic. He had always spoken in favour of religious toleration, and, most significantly of all, such an intepretation would account for the extraordinary amount of space in his book that was devoted to a defence of the French Church and its clergy. In the cartoons of the Revolutionary period, Burke was frequently represented as a Jesuit, in cassock and biretta, enshrining an enduring myth that he had been partly enducated at that Order's seminary at Saint-Omer.

Yet another group of readers unsentimentally concluded that Burke had finally gone mad. The exact state of Burke's mind had been a matter of speculation for some time. The line of division between genius and insanity was thought to be a thin one. Losses of temper, accusations of being abandoned or ignored, and a tendency to take argument way beyond its proper limits had long been thought to mark Burke's public life. In the 1790s, the word 'Burkism' was coined to describe exaggerated claims. Pamphlet critics began to call him 'the ingenious madman'. Cartoonists portrayed him as Don

Quixote, tilting at imaginary windmills, with sparks flying from his enfevered head. Close friends like Fox jokingly pronounced themselves pleased that Burke had come out against the Revolution, for, if he had supported it, his intemperance would certainly have led to him being hanged. The violence of the language in some parts of the *Reflections*, the depiction of the members of the National Assembly as men of no ability, and the belief in a French addiction to cannibalism all bespoke a disordered mind. Good points were lost in hyperbole. What wisdom there was in the book was only that which is sometimes spoken by the fool.

Those who knew Burke best and who yet found his views immoderate had one final explanation. The *Reflections* was a rather sad attempt by Burke to reimpose his intellectual authority on the Whig party. Ever since the death of his patron, the Marquess of Rockingham, in 1782, Burke had felt himself increasingly ignored. In the 1770s, he had been the acknowledged arbiter of Whiggery. In the 1780s, that situation changed, as first Fox and then Sheridan came to challenge for this role. As far as Burke was concerned, the first, as a former protégé, could be accommodated, but the latter was a man without integrity or intellectual depth. It was therefore galling to be publicly exposed as a man whose influence in politics was dribbling away. In the long years of the impeachment of Warren Hastings, Burke bitterly complained that he alone of the managers of the case bothered to attend the trial regularly and give the matter the attention it deserved. In the Regency Crisis of 1788–9, no one asked Burke's advice and no one listened when it was given. He complained openly of the 'disgust' he felt when confronted with this 'neglect'. Against this background, answering the question of why the *Reflections* had been written was easy. The book was nothing more than a personal manifesto to be used by Burke to recover his intellectual control of Whiggery. It was less a serious commentary on France than a statement about English politics.

In arguing that the motives for writing the *Reflections* bore on English rather than French politics, contemporaries both took the point and missed it. It was true that Burke sought to instruct the English. It was not true that he was principally concerned with re-establishing his own career. He had a much grander point to make. Basically, Burke believed that what had happened in France in 1789 could happen in England at some date in the 1790s. The *Reflections* was an attempt to shake the complacency of the political élite. He was trying to convince them that the French were not simply copying the modest English Revolution of 1688, but were offering the world something dramatically new. Long before French armies began to cross frontiers, Burke was clear that the Revolution's ideas were for export. Based on assumptions that had never before been tested in European politics, the Revolution threatened to undermine the very structure of that continent's civilization. The English were as much at risk as anyone else. As Burke frankly informed a friend; 'I published on the idea, that the principles of a new, republican, frenchified Whiggism was [*sic*] gaining ground in this Country.'

Burke's thesis rested on the assumption that all the factors that had made for a Revolution in France were also present in England in 1789. Many pages of the *Reflections* are devoted to identifying them. First, there was the religious dissenter, excluded from civil rights and therefore disaffected with the political establishment as a whole. It was not surprising that French Protestants and Jews should have supported the Revolution so enthusiastically, or that they should have been so prominent in the attack on the Catholic Church. When Burke uses quotations from Rabaut de St Étienne, he was aware that he was using the words of a Protestant pastor. There was a parallel situation in England. Dissenting ministers were prominent spokesmen in the reform movements of the 1780s. At the dinner of the Revolution Society, whose activities prompted Burke to act, the provocative, pre-dinner sermon had been given by the Revd Richard Price. He and his friend Joseph Priestley were the direct equivalents of Rabaut de St Étienne and the Abbé Sieyès. Either as nonconformist divines protesting against exclusion, or as renegade clergy within the established Church seeking to benefit from a redistribution of episcopal and monastic wealth, they were all prepared to peddle nonsense ideas about the rights of man.

In the reforming societies of late eighteenth-century England, which Burke calls 'the avowed enemies of the constitution', radical clerics rubbed shoulders with the second type of potential revolutionary, 'the political Man of Letters'. Burke had infinite contempt for amateur philosophers in England and for the more considerable writers in France who were their models. According to him, scribblers like Capel Loftt, Sir Brooke Boothby, and Horne Tooke aped the more considerable, but no less misguided, speculations of Condorcet and Rousseau. For the latter, Burke entertained a particular animus. What united them all was a determination to push 'a scheme of politics not adapted to the state of the world in which they live'. Their thinking was fundamentally flawed. Operating from first principles rather than empirical study, they became 'so taken up with their theories about the rights of man, that they have totally forgot his nature'. In this respect, too, the Channel operated as no effective barrier. The *philosophe* was an English phenomenon as well as a French one. Correspondences flowed between the philosophically minded before the Revolution. Letters of goodwill and congratulation passed between radical societies after the Revolution. France and England were locked into a network of subversion that Burke sought to expose.

Besides the radical cleric and the amateur *litterateur* stood a figure yet more sinister and more diabolical. In Burke's terminology, he might bear the name 'speculator' or 'stock-jobber', or the whole fraternity might be damned as 'the monied interest'. He was a man who might countenance a revolution in order to secure a share in the redistribution of property that such a revolution would inevitably bring. The pillaging of the French Church in 1789–90 was taken as a supreme example of his handiwork. He was a man who, having lent money to government, would do anything in politics to secure his investments. The public good was subordinated to private concern. So the property of a private corporation within the state, the Church, was pillaged to fund the French national debt and so to guarantee the state's creditors their loans. Institutions, which had proved their worth over centuries, would be sacrificed to the immediate demands of speculators, *rentiers*, and those with nothing to lose. Once again, since the size and funding of the English national debt was a matter of deep concern in the 1790s, the parallel between England and France was exact.

All of these factors illustrated what Burke termed 'the warfare between the noble ancient landed estate, and the new monied interest'. On the one hand was a system of politics predicated on the sanctity of property. It was a system that had served England well. Property owning gave a man a firm and immovable interest in the well-being of the society in which that property was held. It also guaranteed him the education and leisure that made his involvement in politics reasonable, and the fulfilment of the duties that went with property holding regular and informed. On the other hand, the French had handed the control of politics over to worried investors and greedy speculators, who masked their predatory policies with talk of natural rights.

If proof were wanting that the radical dissenter, the amateur *philosophe*, and the speculator existed in England, interconnected and mutually supportive, Burke offered his readers the group of friends who met, under the patronage of Lord Lansdowne, at Bowood in Wiltshire. No passage in the *Reflections* is more bitter than that which discusses these men. Lansdowne himself was a disappointed politician in serious financial trouble. In Burke's mind, therefore, he was the natural equivalent of the Duc d'Orléans or the Comte de Mirabeau. In Jeremy Bentham, there was an example of the iconoclast, sweeping away longstanding practices in the visionary pursuit of the greatest happiness of the greatest number. In Richard Price and Joseph Priestley, there was that ingredient of religious dissent that had proved so subversive in France. Collectively, they represented 'the revolt of the enterprising talents of a country against its property', which, famously, was Burke's definition of Jacobinism. As J. G. A. Pocock hs observed, Burke's 'villains were not . . . honest mechanics, but literate, speculators in public funds, bureaucrats, technicians'. The Bowood Circle neatly encapsulated all these types. Its very existence made credible the claim that the _Reflections_ was a parable for the English as much as for the French. In a real sense therefore, the title of this book was unfortunate. It narrowed the reader's attention to events in one country, whereas Burke had two systems very much in mind.

To limit a discussion of the _Reflections_ to the context of the 1790s, however, would be to do Burke a great disservice. So challenging were events in France, that, to comment on them, he had to go to the heart of politics and address the central questions of why men live in communities at all, and on what terms. His remarks firmly relate to certain historical events, but out of them may be distilled arguments that could be applied to any society at any time. The historical dimension of the _Reflections_ makes its format a little unusual for a text in political theory, but such a text it undoubtedly is. In cataloguing the crimes and errors of the French, Burke was compelled to reflect on what made a political society stable, on what made it just, and on what made it workable. It was typical of his pragmatic nature that he should choose to start with a great historical example and move on to general propositions, rather than vice versa.

Central to Burke's critique of the revolutionaries' behaviour was his denial that a discussion about politics should start with a discussion about man's rights. Following the practice of most writers associated with the Enlightenment, the French first issued a priori statements like the Declaration of the Rights of Man, and then contrived to build a state that would accommodate those rights. To Burke this was an insane way of proceeding. Abstract rights were nothing more than 'a mine that will blow up at one grand explosion all examples of antiquity'. Even if men could be brought to agree what basic rights actually were, and the National Assembly had no consensus on that point, how they were to be enshrined and safeguarded in politics was open to question. Burke prided himself, by contrast, on being 'influenced by the inborn feelings of nature, and not being illuminated by a single ray of this new-sprung modern light'. The venomous attack on Rousseau in the *Reflections* may be taken as symbolic of Burke's total alienation from the working methods of the Enlightenment, whose protagonists started with the ideal and descended to the practical.

Burke firmly believed that the only viable way of speculating about politics was first to describe the raw material of the subject, man himself. This complicated creature had been caricatured by French *philosophes* as philosophically inclined, aware of the rights which society owed him, and clear about the duties that bound him to his neighbour. He was capable of shouldering the burden of liberty, equality, and fraternity. To Burke, this was only half, or less than half, the story. Man was certainly capable of reasoning, but he was also capable of much else. He could be passionate and prejudiced. He could be superstitious and violent. Habit and daily routine contributed as much to his political psychology as notions of extended liberty. To write about man as the French did, therefore, was to present a one-dimensional picture. To legislate on the basis of that description was, predictably, to produce chaos and instability. In 1790, Burke could predict the Terror of 1792–4 because he was convinced that the Revolution was flawed from the beginning.

By contrast, Burke believed that, given the diversity of man's political character, any existing institution should be approached with reverence. Any practice that had shown itself capable of binding men together in political communion for any length of time was entitled to respect. As he put it in the *Reflections* itself; 'it is with infinite caution that any man ought to venture upon pulling down an edifice which has answered in any tolerable degree for ages the common purposes of society, or on building it up again, without having models and patterns of approved utility before his eyes'. Political institutions and practices were validated by prescription, that is the argument that they had proved their usefulness over time. Any system of politics which passed this test could be taken as encapsulating the political character of the citizens who lived under it. History was more important than philosophy in the study of politics. Without it, institutions were at the mercy of every new fad and fancy. Nothing would have solidity; 'Men would become little better than the flies of a summer'.

In this respect, nothing could be more different than the approach to politics offered by the English and the French. Englishmen argued from what was or what had been; Frenchmen from what might be. Burke was clear that part of the reason for his country's success and stability in the eighteenth century was the fact that it enjoyed a parliamentary system that was six hundred years old. Even Radicals like Horne Tooke and Capel Lofft argued for an extension of the franchise not on the basis of natural rights, but because they believed that their Anglo-Saxon forefathers had enjoyed this privilege. In other words, they were anxious to reassert old liberties, not to invent new ones. When a group of reformers adopted the name of Revolution Society, it was in part to emphasize the motion of the wheel in history, with old values coming round again in a circular motion. Men of conservative instincts like Burke and his Radical critics therefore both chose to conduct their debate in history rather than theory.

By contrast, the French had shown a complete contempt for all the accumulated wisdom and evidence in their political history. Burke knew that there was much in *ancien régime* France that was defective. He declared himself to be 'no stranger to the faults and defects of the subverted government of France'. In private correspondence, in contrast to passages in the *Reflections*, he had been highly critical of Marie Antoinette and Louis XVI. Change must be accommodated in any political system. There had to be a pruning to encourage new growth. The French, however, had gone far beyond this. They had decided to change everything at once in defiance of the prescription of history and the political character of the French. The monarchy was not remodelled so much as neutralized; the *Parlements* were abolished and the Church subverted. The French were to work ten-day weeks and to live in *départements* that were neat squares. Burke's scorn for Condorcet's attempts to transform politics into a branch of mathematics is infinite.

Predictably, the Revolution ran into trouble. The French

were not so philosophic that they saw the advantages of squares and rectangles over the irregular, but familiar, contours of their old provinces. Nor were they so rational that they were willing to accept a new priest in place of an old one, or to feel themselves secure without the protection of their old saints. They resisted the notion that the working week had been extended, and, when offered a vote, stubbornly refused to exercise it. Abstention was the response of most Frenchmen in every revolutionary election. All of this, according to Burke, fractured whatever consensus there was in the political community known as France. The Revolutionaries talked of making all things new, of creating 'un nouveau Adam'. Instead they set up tensions and antagonisms that would pull France apart. Burke predicted civil disorder and its resolution by some kind of military *coup d'état* on this basis.

Empirically, there was much to be said, in Burke's account, for a comparison between the stability of England's politics and the anarchy that characterized public life in France. The English not only lived with their history, but they also bowed before the idea that all politics was predicated on the principle of property-owning. In comparison, the French despised their past and attacked property-holding remorselessly. The long section in the *Reflections* devoted to a critique of the Church settlement of 1789–90 seeks to make this point. At one stroke, the property of the Church was declared to be 'at the disposal of the nation'. The Revolutionaries denied that the sanctity of property had been touched by arguing that the holdings of a corporation, like the Church, within a state was of a different order from property owned by an individual. To Burke, this was mere sophistry. To attack any property was to attack all property. The English were to be praised for having 'identified the estate of the church with the mass of *private property*, of which the state is not the proprietor, either for use or dominion, but the guardian only and the regulator'.

According to Burke, history and prescription had proved beyond all reasonable doubt that property, in its widest definition, was what brought men from the savage to the political state and was what kept them there. Property could be defined as the possession of certain things, the exercise of certain rights, or merely the value in the labour of a particular pair of hands. All these properties needed to be defined and guaranteed in law. Each needed to be accorded a particular worth. Without guarantees of this sort, man would revert to the barbaric. Intelligent men in the late eighteenth century were interested in the idea that men could regress as well as progress.

In the narrower sense of conferring political rights, property meant the possession of goods, and more particularly of land. Unlike the monied men whom Burke so much disliked, landed proprietors, whose estates were units of social living passing from generation to generation, had the greatest interest in the prosperity and stability of the country in which they lived. In another place, Burke denominated landowners as 'the great oaks' of the constitution. They deserved their pre-eminence and should not be challenged by any other claim;

Nothing is a due and adequate representation of a state, that does not represent its ability, as well as its property. But as ability is a vigorous and active principle, and as property is sluggish, inert, and timid, it never can be safe from the invasions of ability, unless it be, out of all proportion, predominant in the representation.

As a result, it was horrific to see the French attacking the corporate property of the Church and the individual property of the émigré nobility. What property of any description could be considered safe when the French taught lessons such as these?

Emancipated from the constraints of historical prescription and circumventing the defences erected around the property principle, the French had become wreckers. Within a year or so of the fall of the Bastille, there was little in France's former political traditions that had not been uprooted. The generation of 1789 arrogated to themselves the right to change everything. Burke denied any generation such a right. In the *Reflections*, he expended much ink in attacking Richard Price's claim that the English had somehow chosen a new king in 1688. No particular generation, according to Burke, could ever make such a choice. It was out of the question, because one generation merely inherited from its ancestors, in trustee-ship, ideas and institutions which it handed on to its heirs. Burke preferred to call 1688 a necessary, but temporary, deviation from this model. It was restorative rather than revolutionary. It confirmed the historical rule of property rather than undermining it.

What Burke saw in France in 1789 was of a quite different order. Without reference to history or commonsense, the French embarked on the experiment of constructing a society from scratch. A threatening national bankruptcy and dis-locations in Court politics at Versailles created the opportunity for this experiment to be tried. Visionaries like Robespierre and down-at-heel journalists like Brissot only achieve promin-ence in such circumstances. Worryingly, Burke saw a similar, political scenario in England and comparable men ready to take advantage of it. What was at stake was a profound disagreement about the nature of the state. Either it was a human construction that could be modified or demolished at will, or it was something at once more mystical and more based on commonsense, more defined by history and experi-ence, more related to the true nature of man. Burke's plea in the *Reflections* is clear. It was simply that

the state ought not to be considered as nothing better than a partnership agreement in a trade of pepper and coffee, callico or tobacco, or some other such low concern, to be taken up for a little temporary interest, and to be dissolved by the fancy of the parties. It is to be looked on with other reverence; because it is not a partnership in things subservient only to the gross animal existence of a temporary and perishable nature. It is a partnership in all science; a partnership in all art; a partnership in every virtue, and in all perfection. As the ends of such a partnership cannot be obtained in many generations, it becomes a partnership not only between those who are living, but between those who are living, those who are dead, and those who are to be born.

NOTE ON THE TEXT

THE text of the *Reflections on the Revolution in France* is that prepared by Professor W. B. Todd for Volume VIII of the Clarendon edition of Burke's collected writings and speeches (Oxford, 1989). The source is the 9th edition of the work, published by J. Dodsley (London, 1791).

Typographical misprints have been corrected, double quotation marks changed to single, and full points removed from Dr, Mr, and St. With these exceptions, variations and inconsistencies in the spelling and punctuation of the original have been preserved, including in translations from the French. Ligatures (œ etc.) appearing in the original text are not reproduced except in French, where their use continues to be standard typographical practice.

Numbered footnotes are Burke's original notes; an asterisk signals an explanatory note to be found after the text.

SELECT BIBLIOGRAPHY

THE definitive edition of Burke's correspondence is T. W. Copeland and others, *The Correspondence of Edmund Burke*, 9 vols. (Chicago and Cambridge 1958–70). For his other writings, reference must be made to P. Langford and others, *The Writings and Speeches of Edmund Burke* (Oxford, 1981–92).

1. Bibliographies
Gandy, C. I. and Stanlis, P. J., *Edmund Burke: A Bibliography of Secondary Studies to 1982* (New York, 1983).

Pendleton, G. T., *Bulletin of Research in the Humanities*, 85/1 (1982), 65–103.

Todd, W. B., *A Bibliography of Edmund Burke* (London, 1964).

2. Biographies
Cone, C. B., *Burke and the Nature of Politics* (Lexington, Ky., 1957 and 1964).

Magnus, Sir P., *Edmund Burke* (London, 1939).

3. Contemporary Criticism
The *Reflections* provoked the publication of well over 100 pamphlets defending or, more usually, attacking Burke's views. Among the most important are the following:–

Boothby, Sir B., *A Letter to the Right Honourable Edmund Burke* (London, 1791).

Christie, T., *Letters on the Revolution in France* (London, 1791).

Macaulay, C., *Observations on the Reflections of the Right Honourable Edmund Burke, on the Revolution in France* (London, 1790).

Mackintosh, J., *Vindiciae Gallicae* (London, 1791).

Paine, T., *The Rights of Man* (London, 1791–2).

Priestley, J., *Letters to the Right Honourable Edmund Burke* (Birmingham, 1791).

Wollstonecraft, M.; *A Vindication of the Rights of Men* (London, 1790)

4. Modern Criticism
Cobban, A., *Edmund Burke and the Revolt against the Eighteenth Century* (London, 1960).

Copeland, T. W., *Edmund Burke: Six Essays* (London, 1950).

Dreyer, F. A., *Journal of Modern History*, 50/3 (1978).

Dreyer, F. A., *Burke's Politics: A Study in Whig Orthodoxy* (Ontario, 1979).

Freeman, M., *Edmund Burke and the Critique of Political Radicalism* (Oxford, 1980).

Gauzin, M., *La Pensée Politique d'Edmund Burke* (Paris, 1972).

Kramnick, I., *The Rage of Edmund Burke* (New York, 1977).

Lock, F. P., *Burke's Reflections on the Revolution in France* (London, 1985).

O'Brien, C. C., *The Suspecting Glance* (London, 1972).

O'Gorman, F., *Edmund Burke: His Political Philosophy* (London, 1973).

Pocock, J. G. A., *Historical Journal*, 3/2 (1960).

—— *Historical Journal*, 25/2 (1982).

Stanlis, P. J., *Edmund Burke: The Enlightenment and the Modern World* (Detroit, 1967).

—— *The Relevance of Edmund Burke* (New York, 1964).

A CHRONOLOGY OF EDMUND BURKE

REFLECTIONS ON
THE REVOLUTION
IN FRANCE

REFLECTIONS ON THE
REVOLUTION IN FRANCE 1790

It may not be unnecessary to inform the Reader, that the following Reflections had their origin in a correspondence between the Author and a very young gentleman at Paris, who did him the honour of desiring his opinion upon the important transactions, which then, and ever since, have so much occupied the attention of all men. An answer was written some time in the month of October 1789; but it was kept back upon prudential considerations. That letter is alluded to in the beginning of the following sheets. It has been since forwarded to the person to whom it was addressed. The reasons for the delay in sending it were assigned in a short letter to the same gentleman. This produced on his part a new and pressing application for the Author's sentiments.*

The Author began a second and more full discussion on the subject. This he had some thoughts of publishing early in the last spring; but the matter gaining upon him, he found that what he had undertaken not only far exceeded the measure of a letter, but that its importance required rather a more detailed consideration than at that time he had any leisure to bestow upon it. However, having thrown down his first thoughts in the form of a letter, and indeed when he sat down to write, having intended it for a private letter, he found it difficult to change the form of address, when his sentiments had grown into a greater extent, and had received another direction. A different plan, he is sensible, might be more favourable to a commodious division and distribution of his matter.

DEAR SIR,

You are pleased to call again, and with some earnestness, for my thoughts on the late proceedings in France. I will not give you reason to imagine, that I think my sentiments of such value as to wish myself to be solicited about them. They are of too little consequence to be very anxiously either communicated or withheld. It was from attention to you, and to you only, that I hesitated at the time, when you first desired to receive them. In the first letter I had the honour to write to you, and which at length I send, I wrote neither for nor from any description of men; nor shall I in this. My errors, if any, are my own. My reptuation alone is to answer for them.

You see, Sir, by the long letter I have transmitted to you, that, though I do most heartily wish that France may be animated by a spirit of rational liberty, and that I think you bound, in all honest policy, to provide a permanent body, in which that spirit may reside, and an effectual organ, by which it may act, it is my misfortune to entertain great doubts concerning several material points in your late transactions.

You imagined, when you wrote last, that I might possibly be reckoned among the approvers of certain proceedings in France, from the solemn public seal of sanction they have received from two clubs of gentlemen in London, called the Constitutional Society, and the Revolution Society.*

I certainly have the honour to belong to more clubs than one, in which the constitution of this kingdom and the principles of the glorious Revolution, are held in high reverence: and I reckon myself among the most forward in my zeal for maintaining that constitution and those principles in their utmost purity and vigour. It is because I do so, that I think it necessary for me, that there should be no mistake. Those who cultivate the memory of our revolution, and those who are attached to the constitution of this kingdom, will take good care how they are involved with persons who, under the pretext of zeal towards the Revolution and Constitution, too frequently wander from their true principles; and are ready on every occasion to depart from the firm but cautious and deliberate spirit which produced the one, and which presides in the other. Before I proceed to answer the more material particulars in your letter, I shall beg leave to give you such information as I have been able to obtain of the two clubs which have thought proper, as bodies, to interfere in the concerns of France; first assuring you, that I am not, and that I have never been, a member of either of those societies.

The first, calling itself the Constitutional Society, or Society for Constitutional Information, or by some such title, is, I believe, of seven or eight years standing. The institution of this society appears to be of a charitable, and so far of a laudable, nature: it was intended for the circulation, at the expense of the members, of many books, which few others would be at the expence of buying; and which might lie on the hands of the booksellers, to the great loss of an useful body of men. Whether the books so charitably circulated, were ever as charitably read, is more than I know. Possibly several of them have been exported to France; and, like goods not in request here, may with you have found a market. I have heard much talk of the lights to be drawn from books that are sent from hence. What improvements they have had in their passage (as it is said some liquors are meliorated by crossing the sea) I cannot tell: But I never heard a man of common judgment, or the least degree of information, speak a word in praise of the greater part of the publications circulated by that society; nor have their proceedings been accounted, except by some of themselves, as of any serious consequence.

Your National Assembly* seems to entertain much the same opinion that I do of this poor charitable club. As a nation, you reserved the whole stock of your eloquent acknowledgements for the Revolution Society; when their fellows in the Constitutional were, in equity, entitled to some share. Since you have selected the Revolution Society as the great object of your national thanks and praises, you will think me excuseable in making its late conduct the subject of my observations. The National Assembly of France has given importance to these gentlemen by adopting them; and they return the favour, by acting as a committee in England for extending the principles of the National Assembly.* Henceforward we must consider them as a kind of privileged persons; as no inconsiderable members in the diplomatic body. This is one among the revolutions which have given splendour to obscurity, and distinction to undiscerned merit. Until very lately I do not recollect to have heard of this club. I am quite sure that it never occupied a moment of my thoughts; nor, I believe, those of any person out of their own

set. I find, upon enquiry, that on the anniversary of the
Revolution in 1688, a club of dissenters, but of what
denomination I know not, have long had the custom of
hearing a sermon in one of their churches; and that afterwards
they spent the day cheerfully, as other clubs do, at the tavern.
But I never heard that any public measure, or political system,
much less that the merits of the constitution of any foreign
nation, had been the subject of a formal proceeding at their
festivals; until, to my inexpressible surprize, I found them in a
sort of public capacity, by a congratulatory address, giving an
authoritative sanction to the proceedings of the National
Assembly in France.*

In the antient principles and conduct of the club, so far at
least as they were declared, I see nothing to which I could
take exception. I think it very probable, that for some
purpose, new members may have entered among them; and
that some truly christian politicians, who love to dispense
benefits, but are careful to conceal the hand which distributes
the dole, may have made them the instruments of their pious
designs. Whatever I may have reason to suspect concerning
private management, I shall speak of nothing as of a certainty,
but what is public.

For one, I should be sorry to be thought, directly or
indirectly, concerned in their proceedings. I certainly take my
full share, along with the rest of the world, in my individual
and private capacity, in speculating on what has been done, or
is doing, on the public stage; in any place antient or modern;
in the republic of Rome, or the republic of Paris: but having
no general apostolical mission, being a citizen of a particular
state, and being bound up in a considerable degree, by its
public will, I should think it, at least improper and irregular,
for me to open a formal public correspondence with the actual
government of a foreign nation, without the express authority
of the government under which I live.

I should be still more unwilling to enter into that correspondence, under any thing like an equivocal description,
which to many, unacquainted with our usages, might make
the address, in which I joined, appear as the act of persons in
some sort of corporate capacity, acknowledged by the laws of

this kingdom, and authorized to speak the sense of some part of it. On account of the ambiguity and uncertainty of unauthorized general descriptions, and of the deceit which may be practised under them, and not from mere formality, the house of Commons would reject the most sneaking petition for the most trifling object, under that mode of signature to which you have thrown open the folding-doors of your presence chamber, and have ushered into your National Assembly, with as much ceremony and parade, and with as great a bustle of applause, as if you had been visited by the whole representative majesty of the whole English nation. If what this society has thought proper to send forth had been a piece of argument, it would have signified little whose argument it was. It would be neither the more nor the less convincing on account of the party it came from. But this is only a vote and resolution. It stands solely on authority; and in this case it is the mere authority of individuals, few of whom appear. Their signatures ought, in my opinion, to have been annexed to their instrument. The world would then have the means of knowing how many they are; who they are; and of what value their opinions may be, from their personal abilities, from their knowledge, their experience, or their lead and authority in this state. To me, who am but a plain man, the proceeding looks a little too refined, and too ingenious; it has too much the air of a political stratagem, adopted for the sake of giving under an high-sounding name, an importance to the public declarations of this club, which, when the matter came to be closely inspected, they did not altogether so well deserve. It is a policy that has very much the complexion of a fraud.

I flatter myself that I love a manly, moral, regulated liberty as well as any gentleman of that society, be he who he will; and perhaps I have given as good proofs of my attachment to that cause, in the whole course of my public conduct. I think I envy liberty as little as they do, to any other nation. But I cannot stand forward, and give praise or blame to any thing which relates to human actions, and human concerns, on a simple view of the object, as it stands stripped of every relation, in all the nakedness and solitude of metaphysical abstraction. Circumstances (which with some gentlemen pass for nothing) give in reality to every political principle its distinguishing colour, and discriminating effect. The circumstances are what render every civil and political scheme beneficial or noxious to mankind. Abstractedly speaking, government, as well as liberty, is good; yet could I, in common sense, ten years ago, have felicitated France on her enjoyment of a government (for she then had a government) without enquiry what the nature of that government was, or how it was administered? Can I now congratulate the same nation upon its freedom? Is it because liberty in the abstract may be classed amongst the blessings of mankind, that I am seriously to felicitate a madman, who has escaped from the protecting restraint and wholesome darkness of his cell, on his restoration to the enjoyment of light and liberty? Am I to congratulate an highwayman and murderer, who has broke prison, upon the recovery of his natural rights? This would be to act over again the scene of the criminals condemned to the gallies, and their heroic deliverer, the metaphysic Knight of the Sorrowful Countenance.*

When I see the spirit of liberty in action, I see a strong principle at work; and this, for a while, is all I can possibly know of it. The wild *gas*, the fixed air* is plainly broke loose: but we ought to suspend our judgment until the first effervescence is a little subsided, till the liquor is cleared, and until we see something deeper than the agitation of a troubled and frothy surface. I must be tolerably sure, before I venture publicly to congratulate men upon a blessing, that they have really received one. Flattery corrupts both the receiver and the giver; and adulation is not of more service to the people than to kings. I should therefore suspend my congratulations on the new liberty of France, until I was informed how it had been combined with government; with public force; with the discipline and obedience of armies; with the collection of an effective and well-distributed revenue; with morality and religion; with the solidity of property; with peace and order; with civil and social manners. All these (in their way) are good things too; and, without them, liberty is not a benefit whilst it lasts, and is not likely to continue long. The effect of liberty to individuals is, that they may do what they please: We ought to see what it will please them to do, before we risque congratulations, which may be soon turned into complaints. Prudence would dictate this in the case of separate insulated private men; but liberty, when men act in bodies, is *power*. Considerate people, before they declare themselves, will observe the use which is made of *power*; and particularly of so trying a thing as *new* power in *new* persons, of whose principles, tempers, and dispositions, they have little or no experience, and in situations where those who appear the most stirring in the scene may possibly not be the real movers.

All these considerations however were below the transcendental dignity of the Revolution Society. Whilst I continued in the country, from whence I had the honour of writing to you, I had but an imperfect idea of their transactions. On my coming to town, I sent for an account of their proceedings, which had been published by their authority, containing a sermon of Dr Price, with the Duke de Rochefaucault's and the Archbishop of Aix's* letter, and several other documents annexed. The whole of that publication, with the manifest design of connecting the affairs of France with those of England, by drawing us into an imitation of the conduct of the National Assembly, gave me a considerable degree of uneasiness. The effect of that conduct upon the power, credit, prosperity, and tranquility of France, became every day more evident. The form of constitution to be settled, for its future polity, became more clear. We are now in a condition to discern, with tolerable exactness, that true nature of the object held up to our imitation. If the prudence of reserve and decorum dictates silence in some circumstances, in others prudence of an higher order may justify us in speaking our thoughts. The beginnings of confusion with us in England are at present feeble enough; but with you, we have seen an infancy still more feeble, growing by moments into a strength to heap mountains upon mountains, and to wage war with Heaven itself. Whenever our neighbour's house is on fire, it cannot be amiss for the engines to play a little on our own. Better to be despised for too anxious apprehensions, than ruined by too confident a security.

Sollicitous chiefly for the peace of my own country, but by no means unconcerned for your's, I wish to communicate more largely, what was at first intended only for your private satisfaction. I shall still keep your affairs in my eye, and continue to address myself to you. Indulging myself in the freedom of epistolary intercourse, I beg leave to throw out my thoughts, and express my feelings, just as they arise in my mind, with very little attention to formal method. I set out with the proceedings of the Revolution Society; but I shall not confine myself to them. Is it possible I should? It looks to me as if I were in a great crisis, not of the affairs of France alone, but of all Europe, perhaps of more than Europe. All circumstances taken together, the French revolution is the most astonishing that has hitherto happened in the world.* The most wonderful things are brought about in many instances by means the most absurd and ridiculous; in the most ridiculous modes; and apparently, by the most contempt-ible instruments. Every thing seems out of nature in this strange chaos of levity and ferocity, and of all sorts of crimes jumbled together with all sorts of follies. In viewing this monstrous tragi-comic scene, the most opposite passions necessarily succeed, and sometimes mix with each other in the mind; alternate contempt and indignation; alternate laughter and tears; alternate scorn and horror.

It cannot however be denied, that to some this strange scene appeared in quite another point of view. Into them it inspired no other sentiments than those of exultation and rapture. They saw nothing in what has been done in France, but a firm and temperate exertion of freedom; so consistent, on the whole, with morals and with piety, as to make it deserving not only of the secular applause of dashing Machiavelian politicians, but to render it a fit theme for all the devout effusions of sacred eloquence.

On the forenoon of the 4th of November last, Doctor Richard Price, a non-conforming minister of eminence, preached at the dissenting meeting-house of the Old Jewry,* to his club or society, a very extraordinary miscellaneous sermon, in which there are some good moral and religious sentiments, and not ill expressed, mixed up in a sort of porridge of various political opinions and reflections: but the revolution in France is the grand ingredient in the cauldron. I consider the address transmitted by the Revolution Society to the National Assembly, through Earl Stanhope,* as originating in the principles of the sermon, and as a corollary from them. It was moved by the preacher of that discourse. It was passed by those who came reeking from the effect of the sermon, without any censure or qualification, expressed or implied.* If, however, any of the gentlemen concerned shall wish to separate the sermon from the resolution, they know how to acknowledge the one, and to disavow the other. They may do it: I cannot.

For my part, I looked on that sermon as the public declaration of a man much connected with literary caballers, and intriguing philosophers;* with political theologians, and theological politicians, both at home and abroad. I know they set him up as a sort of oracle; because, with the best intentions in the world, he naturally *philippizes*, and chaunts his prophetic song in exact unison with their designs.

That sermon is in a strain which I believe has not been heard in this kingdom, in any of the pulpits which are tolerated or encouraged in it, since the year 1648, when a predecessor of Dr Price, the Reverend Hugh Peters,* made the vault of the king's own chapel at St James's ring with the honour and privilege of the Saints, who, with the 'high praises of God in their mouths, and a *two*-edged sword in their hands, were to execute judgment on the heathen, and punishments upon the *people*; to bind their *kings* with chains, and their *nobles* with fetters of iron.'[1] Few harangues from the pulpit, except in the days of your league in France, or in the days of our solemn league and covenant in England,* have ever breathed less of the spirit of moderation than this lecture in the Old Jewry. Supposing, however, that something like moderation were visible in this political sermon; yet politics and the pulpit are terms that have little agreement. No sound ought to be heard in the church but the healing voice of

[1] Psalm cxlix.

Christian charity. The cause of civil liberty and civil government gains as little as that of religion by this confusion of
duties. Those who quit their proper character, to assume what
does not belong to them, are, for the greater part, ignorant
both of the character they leave, and of the character they
assume. Wholly unacquainted with the world in which they
are so fond of meddling, and inexperienced in all its affairs, on
which they pronounce with so much confidence, they have
nothing of politics but the passions they excite. Surely the
church is a place where one day's truce ought to be allowed to
the dissensions and animosities of mankind.

This pulpit style, revived after so long a discontinuance, had
to me the air of novelty, and of a novelty not wholly without
danger. I do not charge this danger equally to every part of the
discourse. The hint given to a noble and reverend lay-divine,
who is supposed high in office in one of our universities,[1] and
to other lay-divines 'of *rank* and literature,' may be proper
and seasonable, though somewhat new.* If the noble *Seekers**
should find nothing to satisfy their pious fancies in the old
staple of the national church, or in all the rich variety to be
found in the well-assorted warehouses of the dissenting
congregations, Dr Price advises them to improve upon non-
conformity; and to set up, each of them, a separate meeting-
house upon his own particular principles.[2] It is somewhat
remarkable that this reverend divine should be so earnest for
setting up new churches, and so perfectly indifferent concerning the doctrine which may be taught in them. His zeal is of a
curious character. It is not for the propagation of his own
opinions, but of any opinions. It is not for the diffusion of
truth, but for the spreading of contradiction. Let the noble
teachers but dissent, it is no matter from whom or from what.

[1] Discourse on the Love of our Country, Nov. 4, 1789, by Dr Richard Price,
3d edition, p. 17 and 18.
[2] 'Those who dislike that mode of worship which is prescribed by public
authority ought, if they can find *no* worship *out* of the church which they
approve, *to set up a separate worship for themselves*; and by doing this, and
giving an example of a rational and manly worship, men of *weight* from their
rank and literature may do the greatest service to society and the world.' P. 18.
Dr Price's Sermon.

This great point once secured, it is taken for granted their religion will be rational and manly. I doubt whether religion would reap all the benefits which the calculating divine computes from this 'great company of great preachers.' It would certainly be a valuable addition of nondescripts to the ample collection of known classes, genera and species, which at present beautify the *hortus siccus** of dissent. A sermon from a noble duke, or a noble marquis, or a noble earl, or baron bold, would certainly increase and diversify the amusements of this town, which begins to grow satiated with the uniform round of its vapid dissipations. I should only stipulate that these new *Mess-Johns** in robes and coronets should keep some sort of bounds in the democratic and levelling principles which are expected from their titled pulpits. The new evangelists will, I dare say, disappoint the hopes that are conceived of them. They will not become, literally as well as figuratively, polemic divines, nor be disposed so to drill their congregations that they may, as in former blessed times, preach their doctrines to regiments of dragoons, and corps of infantry and artillery.* Such arrangements, however favourable to the cause of compulsory freedom, civil and religious, may not be equally conducive to the national tranquillity. These few restrictions I hope are no great stretches of intolerance, no very violent exertions of despotism.

But I may say of our preacher, *'utinam nugis tota illa dedisset tempora saevitiae.'*—All things in this his fulminating bull are not of so innoxious a tendency. His doctrines affect our constitution in its vital parts. He tells the Revolution Society, in this political sermon, that his majesty 'is almost the *only* lawful king in the world, because the *only* one who owes his crown to the *choice of his people.'* As to the kings of *the world*, all of whom (except one) this archpontiff of the *rights of men*, with all the plenitude, and with more than the boldness of the papal deposing power in its meridian fervour of the twelfth century, puts into one sweeping clause of ban and anathema, and proclaims usurpers by circles of longitude and latitude, over the whole globe, it behoves them to consider how they admit into their territories these apostolic missionaries, who are to tell their subjects they are not lawful kings. That is their concern. It is ours, as a domestic interest of some moment, seriously to consider the solidity of the *only* principle upon which these gentlemen acknowledge a king of Great Britain to be entitled to their allegiance.

This doctrine, as applied to the prince now on the British throne, either is nonsense, and therefore neither true nor false, or it affirms a most unfounded, dangerous, illegal, and unconstitutional position. According to this spiritual doctor of politics, if his majesty does not owe his crown to the choice of his people, he is no *lawful* king. Now nothing can be more untrue than that the crown of this kingdom is so held by his majesty. Therefore if you follow their rule, the king of Great Britain, who most certainly does not owe his high office to any form of popular election, is in no respect better than the rest of the gang of usurpers, who reign, or rather rob, all over the face of this our miserable world, without any sort of right or title to the allegiance of their people. The policy of this general doctrine, so qualified, is evident enough. The propagators of this political gospel are in hopes their abstract principle (their principle that a popular choice is necessary to the legal existence of the sovereign magistracy) would be overlooked whilst the king of Great Britain was not affected by it. In the mean time the ears of their congregations would be gradually habituated to it, as if it were a first principle admitted without dispute. For the present it would only operate as a theory, pickled in the preserving juices of pulpit eloquence, and laid by for future use. *Condo et compono quae mox depromere possim.** By this policy, whilst our government is soothed with a reservation in its favour, to which it has no claim, the security, which it has in common with all governments, so far as opinion is security, is taken away.

Thus these politicans proceed, whilst little notice is taken of their doctrines; but when they come to be examined upon the plain meaning of their words and the direct tendency of their doctrines, then equivocations and slippery constructions come into play. When they say the king owes his crown to the choice of his people, and is therefore the only lawful sovereign in the world, they will perhaps tell us they mean to say no

more than that some of the king's predecessors have been
called to the throne by some sort of choice; and therefore he
owes his crown to the choice of his people. Thus, by a
miserable subterfuge, they hope to render their proposition
safe, by rendering it nugatory. They are welcome to the
asylum they seek for their offence, since they take refuge in
their folly. For, it you admit this interpretation, how does
their idea of election differ from our idea of inheritance? And
how does the settlement of the crown in the Brunswick line
derived from James the first, come to legalize our monarchy,
rather than that of any of the neighbouring countries? At
some time or other, to be sure, all the beginners of dynasties
were chosen by those who called them to govern. There is
ground enough for the opinion that all the kingdoms of
Europe were, at a remote period, elective, with more or fewer
limitations in the objects of choice; but whatever kings might
have been here or elsewhere, a thousand years ago, or in
whatever manner the ruling dynasties of England or France
may have begun, the king of Great Britain is at this day king
by a fixed rule of succession, according to the laws of his
country; and whilst the legal conditions of the compact of
sovereignty are performed by him (as they are performed) he
holds his crown in contempt of the choice of the Revolution
Society, who have not a single vote for a king amongst them,
either individually or collectively; though I make no doubt
they would soon erect themselves into an electoral college, if
things were ripe to give effect to their claim. His majesty's
heirs and successors, each in his time and order, will come to
the crown with the same contempt of their choice with which
his majesty has succeeded to that he wears.

Whatever may be the success of evasion in explaining away
the gross error of *fact*, which supposes that his majesty
(though he holds it in concurrence with the wishes) owes his
crown to the choice of his people, yet nothing can evade their
full explicit declaration, concerning the principle of a right in
the people to choose, which right is directly maintained, and
tenaciously adhered to. All the oblique insinuations concerning
election bottom in this proposition, and are referable to it.
Lest the foundation of the king's exclusive legal title should

pass for a mere rant of adulatory freedom, the political Divine proceeds dogmatically to assert,[1] that by the principles of the Revolution the people of England have acquired three fundamental rights, all which, with him, compose one system, and lie together in one short sentence; namely, that we have acquired a right.

1. 'To choose our own governors.'
2. 'To cashier them for misconduct.'
3. 'To frame a government for ourselves.'*

This new, and hitherto unheard-of bill of rights, though made in the name of the whole people, belongs to those gentlemen and their faction only. The body of the people of England have no share of it. They utterly disclaim it. They will resist the practical assertion of it with their lives and fortunes. They are bound to do so by the laws of their country, made at the time of that very Revolution, which is appealed to in favour of the fictitious rights claimed by the society which abuses its name.

These gentlemen of the Old Jewry, in all their reasonings on the Revolution of 1688, have a revolution which happened in England about forty years before, and the late French revolution, so much before their eyes, and in their hearts, that they are constantly confounding all the three together. It is necessary that we should separate what they confound. We must recall their erring fancies to the *acts* of the Revolution which we revere, for the discovery of its true *principles*. If the *principles* of the Revolution of 1688 are any where to be found, it is in the statute called the *Declaration of Right*.* In that most wise, sober, and considerate declaration, drawn up by great lawyers and great statesmen, and not by warm and inexperienced enthusiasts, not one word is said, nor one suggestion made, of a general right 'to choose our own *governors*; to cashier them for misconduct; and to *form* a government for *ourselves*.'

This Declaration of Right (the act of the 1st of William and Mary, sess. 2. ch. 2.) is the cornerstone of our constitution, as

---

[1] P. 34, Discourse on the Love of our Country, by Dr Price.

reinforced, explained, improved, and in its fundamental principles for ever settled. It is called 'An act for declaring the rights and liberties of the subject, and for *settling* the *succession* of the crown.' You will observe, that these rights and his succession are declared in one body, and bound indissolubly together.

A few years after this period, a second opportunity offered for asserting a right of election to the crown. On the prospect of a total failure of issue from King William, and from the Princess, afterwards Queen Anne, the consideration of the settlement of the crown, and of a further security for the liberties of the people, again came before the legislature.* Did they this second time make any provision for legalizing the crown on the spurious Revolution principles of the Old Jewry? No. They followed the principles which prevailed in the Declaration of Right; indicating with more precision the persons who were to inherit in the Protestant line. This act also incorporated, by the same policy, our liberties, and an hereditary succession in the same act. Instead of a right to choose our own governors, they declared that the *succession* in that line (the protestant line drawn from James the First) was absolutely necessary 'for the peace, quiet, and security of the realm,' and that it was equally urgent on them 'to maintain a *certainty in the succession* thereof, to which the subjects may safely have recourse for their protection.' Both these acts, in which are heard the unerring, unambiguous oracles of Revolution policy, instead of countenancing the delusive, gypsey predictions of a 'right to choose our governors,' prove to a demonstration how totally adverse the wisdom of the nation was from turning a case of necessity into a rule of law.

Unquestionably there was at the Revolution, in the person of King William, a small and a temporary deviation from the strict order of a regular hereditary succession,* but it is against all genuine principles of jurisprudence to draw a principle from a law made in a special case, and regarding an individual person. *Privilegium non transit in exemplum.** If ever there was a time favourable for establishing the principle, that a king of popular choice was the only legal king, without all doubt it was at the Revolution. Its not being done at that time is a proof that the nation was of opinion it ought not to be done at any time. There is no person so completely ignorant of our history, as not to know, that the majority in parliament of both parties were so little disposed to any thing resembling that principle, that at first they were determined to place the vacant crown, not on the head of the prince of Orange, but on that of his wife Mary, daughter of King James, the eldest born of the issue of that king, which they acknowledged as undoubtedly his.* It would be to repeat a very trite story, to recall to your memory all those circumstances which demonstrated that their accepting King William was not properly a *choice*; but, to all those who did not wish, in effect to recall King James, or to deluge their country in blood, and again to bring their religion, laws, and liberties into the peril they have just escaped, it was an act of *necessity*, in the strictest moral sense in which necessity can be taken.

In the very act, in which for a time, and in a single case, parliament departed from the strict order of inheritance, in favour of a prince, who, though not next, was however, very near in the line of succession, it is curious to observe how Lord Somers,* who drew the bill called the Declaration of Right, has comported himself on that delicate occasion. It is curious to observe with what address this temporary solution of continuity is kept from the eye; whilst all that could be found in this act of necessity to countenance the idea of an hereditary succession is brought forward, and fostered, and made the most of, by this great man, and by the legislature who followed him. Quitting the dry, imperative style of an act of parliament, he makes the lords and commons fall to a pious, legislative ejaculation, and declare, that they consider it 'as a marvellous providence, and merciful goodness of God to this nation, to preserve their said majesties *royal* persons, most happily to reign over us *on the throne of their ancestors*, for which, from the bottom of their hearts, they return their humblest thanks and praises.'—The legislature plainly had in view the act of recognition of the first of Queen Elizabeth, Chap. 3d, and of that of James the First, Chap. 1st, both acts strongly declaratory of the inheritable nature of the crown;

and in many parts they follow, with a nearly literal precision, the words and even the form of thanksgiving, which is found in these old declaratory statutes.

The two houses, in the act of King William, did not thank God that they had found a fair opportunity to assert a right to choose their own governors, much less to make an election the *only lawful* title to the crown. Their having been in a condition to avoid the very appearance of it, as much as possible, was by them considered as a providential escape. They threw a politic, well-wrought veil over every circumstance tending to weaken the rights, which in the meliorated order of succession they meant to perpetuate; or which might furnish a precedent for any future departure from what they had then settled for ever. Accordingly, that they might not relax the nerves of their monarchy, and that they might preserve a close conformity to the practice of their ancestors, as it appeared in the declaratory statutes of Queen Mary[1] and Queen Elizabeth, in the next clause they vest, by recognition, in their majesties, *all* the legal prerogatives of the crown, declaring, 'that in them they are most *fully*, rightfully, and *intirely* invested, incorporated, united, and annexed.' In the clause which follows, for preventing questions, by reason of any pretended titles to the crown, they declare (observing also in this the traditionary language, along with the traditionary policy of the nation, and repeating as from a rubric the language of the preceding acts of Elizabeth and James) that on the preserving 'a *certainty* in the SUCCESSION thereof, the unity, peace, and tranquillity of this nation doth, under God, wholly depend.'

They knew that a doubtful title of succession would but too much resemble an election; and that an election would be utterly destructive of the 'unity, peace, and tranquillity of this nation,' which they thought to be considerations of some moment. To provide for these objects, and therefore to exclude for ever the Old Jewry doctrine of 'a right to choose our own governors,' they follow with a clause, containing a most solemn pledge, taken from the preceding act of Queen

---

[1] 1st Mary, Sess. 3. ch. I.

Elizabeth, as solemn a pledge as ever was or can be given in favour of an hereditary succession, and as solemn a renunciation as could be made of the principles by this society imputed to them. 'The lords spiritual and temporal, and commons, do, in the name of all the people aforesaid, most humbly and faithfully submit *themselves, their heirs and posterities for ever*, and do faithfully promise, that they will stand to, maintain, and defend their said majesties, and also the *limitation of the crown*, herein specified and contained, to the utmost of their powers,' &c. &c.

So far is it from being true, that we acquired a right by the Revolution to elect our kings, that if we had possessed it before, the English nation did at the time most solemnly renounce and abdicate it, for themselves and for all their posterity for ever. These gentlemen may value themselves as much as they please on their whig principles; but I never desire to be thought a better whig than Lord Somers; or to understand the principles of the Revolution better than those by whom it was brought about; or to read in the declaration of right any mysteries unknown to those whose penetrating style has engraved in our ordinances, and in our hearts, the words and spirit of that immortal law.

It is true that, aided with the powers derived from force and opportunity, the nation was at that time, in some sense, free to take what course it pleased for filling the throne; but only free to do so upon the same grounds on which they might have wholly abolished their monarchy, and every other part of their constitution. However they did not think such bold changes within their commission. It is indeed difficult, perhaps impossible, to give limits to the mere *abstract* competence of the supreme power, such as was exercised by parliament at that time; but the limits of a *moral* competence, subjecting, even in powers more disputably sovereign, occasional will to permanent reason, and to the steady maxims of faith, justice, and fixed fundamental policy, are perfectly intelligible, and perfectly binding upon those who exercise any authority, under any name, or under any title, in the state. The house of lords, for instance, is not morally competent to dissolve the house of commons; no, nor even to dissolve itself, nor to abdicate, if it would, its portion in the legislature of the kingdom. Though a king may abdicate for his own person, he cannot abdicate for the monarchy. By as strong, or by a stronger reason, the house of commons cannot renounce its share of authority. The engagement and pact of society, which generally goes by the name of the constitution, forbids such invasion and such surrender. The constituent parts of a state are obliged to hold their public faith with each other, and with all those who derive any serious interest under their engagements, as much as the whole state is bound to keep its faith with separate communities. Otherwise competence and power would soon be confounded, and no law be left but the will of a prevailing force. On this principle the succession of the crown has always been what it now is, an hereditary succession by law: in the old line it was a succession by the common law; in the new by the statute law, operating on the principles of the common law, not changing the substance, but regulating the mode, and describing the persons. Both these descriptions of law are of the same force, and are derived from an equal authority, emanating from the common agreement and original compact of the state, *communi sponsione reipublicae*, and as such are equally binding on king, and people too, as long as the terms are observed, and they continue the same body politic.

It is far from impossible to reconcile, if we do not suffer ourselves to be entangled in the mazes of metaphysic sophistry, the use both of a fixed rule and an occasional deviation; the sacredness of an hereditary principle of succession in our government, with a power of change in its application in cases of extreme emergency. Even in that extremity (if we take the measure of our rights by our exercise of them at the Revolution) the change is to be confined to the peccant part only; to the part which produced the necessary deviation; and even then it is to be effected without a decomposition of the whole civil and political mass, for the purpose of originating a new civil order out of the first elements of society.

A state without the means of some change is without the means of its conservation. Without such means it might even risque the loss of that part of the constitution which it wished the most religiously to preserve. The two principles of conservation and correction operated strongly at the two critical periods of the Restoration and Revolution, when England found itself without a king. At both those periods the nation had lost the bond of union in their antient edifice; they did not, however, dissolve the whole fabric. On the contrary, in both cases they regenerated the deficient part of the old constitution through the parts which were not impaired. They kept these old parts exactly as they were, that the part recovered might be suited to them. They acted by the ancient organized states in the shape of their old organization, and not by the organic *moleculae* of a disbanded people. At no time, perhaps, did the sovereign legislature manifest a more tender regard to that fundamental principle of British constitutional policy, than at the time of the Revolution, when it deviated from the direct line of hereditary succession. The crown was carried somewhat out of the line in which it had before moved; but the new line was derived from the same stock. It was still a line of hereditary descent; still an hereditary descent in the same blood, though an hereditary descent qualified with protestantism. When the legislature altered the direction, but kept the principle, they shewed that they held it inviolable.

On this principle, the law of inheritance had admitted some amendment in the old time, and long before the aera of the Revolution. Some time after the conquest great questions arose upon the legal principles of hereditary descent. It became a matter of doubt, whether the heir *per capita* or the heir *per stirpes* was to succeed;* but whether the heir *per capita* gave way when the heirdom *per stirpes* took place, or the Catholic heir when the Protestant was preferred, the inheritable principle survived with a sort of immortality through all transmigrations—*multosque per annos stat fortuna domus et avi numerantur avorum.** This is the spirit of our constitution, not only in its settled course, but in all its revolutions. Whoever came in, or however he came in, whether he obtained the crown by law, or by force, the hereditary succession was either continued or adopted.

The gentlemen of the Society for Revolutions see nothing in

that of 1688 but the deviation from the constitution; and they take the deviation from the principle for the principle. They have little regard to the obvious consequences of their doctrine, though they must see, that it leaves positive authority in very few of the positive institutions of this country. When such an unwarrantable maxim is once established, that no throne is lawful but the elective, no one act of the princes who preceded their aera of fictitious election can be valid. Do these theorists mean to imitate some of their predecessors, who dragged the bodies of our antient sovereigns out of the quiet of their tombs? Do they mean to attaint and disable backwards all the kings that have reigned before the Revolution, and consequently to stain the throne of England with the blot of a continual usurpation? Do they mean to invalidate, annul, or to call into question, together with the titles of the whole line of our kings, that great body of our statute law which passed under those whom they treat as usurpers? to annul laws of inestimable value to our liberties— of as great value at least as any which have passed at or since the period of the Revolution? If kings, who did not owe their crown to the choice of their people, had no title to make laws, what will become of the statute *de tallagio non concedendo?*— of the *petition of right?*—of the act of *habeas corpus?** Do these new doctors of the rights of men presume to assert, that King James the Second, who came to the crown as next of blood, according to the rules of a then unqualified succession, was not to all intents and purposes a lawful king of England, before he had done any of those acts which were justly construed into an abdication of his crown? If he was not, much trouble in parliament might have been saved at the period these gentlemen commemorate. But King James was a bad king with a good title, and not an usurper. The princes who succeeded according to the act of parliament which settled the crown on the electress Sophia* and on her descendants, being Protestants, came in as much by a title of inheritance as King James did. He came in according to the law, as it stood at his accession to the crown; and the princes of the House of Brunswick came to the inheritance of the crown, not by election, but by the law, as it stood at their several accessions of Protestant descent and inheritance, as I hope I have shewn sufficiently.

The law by which this royal family is specifically destined to the succession, is the act of the 12th and 13th of King William.* The terms of this act bind 'us and our *heirs*, and our *posterity*, to them, their *heirs*, and their *posterity*,' being Protestants, to the end of time, in the same words as the declaration of right had bound us to the heirs of King William and Queen Mary. It therefore secures both an hereditary crown and an hereditary allegiance. On what ground, except the constitutional policy of forming an establishment to secure that kind of succession which is to preclude a choice of the people for ever, could the legislature have fastidiously rejected the fair and abundant choice which our own country presented to them, and searched in strange lands for a foreign princess, from whose womb the line of our future rulers were to derive their title to govern millions of men through a series of ages?

The Princess Sophia was named in the act of settlement of the 12th and 13th of King William, for a *stock* and root of *inheritance* to our kings, and not for her merits as a temporary administratrix of a power, which she might not, and in fact did not, herself ever exercise. She was adopted for one reason, and for one only, because, says the act, 'the most excellent Princess Sophia, Electress and Dutchess Dowager of Hanover, is *daughter* of the most excellent Princess Elizabeth,* late Queen of Bohemia, *daughter* of our late *sovereign lord* King James the First, of happy memory, and is hereby declared to be the next in *succession* to the Protestant line,' &c. &c.; 'and the crown shall continue to the *heirs* of her body, being Protestants.' This limitation was made by parliament, that through the Princess Sophia an inheritable line, not only was to be continued in future but (what they thought very material) that through her it was to be connected with the old stock of inheritance in King James the First; in order that the monarchy might preserve an unbroken unity through all ages, and might be preserved (with safety to our religion) in the old approved mode by descent, in which, if our liberties had been once endangered, they had often, through all storms and struggles of prerogative and privilege, been preserved. They did well. No experience has taught us, that in any other course or method than that of an *hereditary crown*, our liberties can be regularly perpetuated and preserved sacred as our *hereditary right*. An irregular, convulsive movement may be necessary to throw off an irregular, convulsive disease. But the course of succession is the healthy habit of the British constitution. Was it that the legislature wanted, at the act for the limitation of the crown in the Hanoverian line, drawn through the female descendants of James the First, a due sense of the inconveniencies of having two or three, or possibly more, foreigners in succession to the British throne? No!—they had a due sense of the evils which might happen from such foreign rule, and more than a due sense of them. But a more decisive proof cannot be given of the full conviction of the British nation, that the principles of the Revolution did not authorize them to elect kings at their pleasure, and without any attention to the antient fundamental principles of our government, than their continuing to adopt a plan of hereditary Protestant succession in the old line, with all the dangers and all the inconveniencies of its being a foreign line full before their eyes, and operating with the utmost force upon their minds.

A few years ago I should be ashamed to overload a matter, so capable of supporting itself, by the then unnecessary support of any argument; but this seditious, unconstitutional doctrine is now publicly taught, avowed, and printed. The dislike I feel to revolutions, the signals for which have so often been given from pulpits; the spirit of change that is gone abroad; the total contempt which prevails with you, and may come to prevail with us, of all antient institutions, when set in opposition to a present sense of convenience, or to the bent of a present inclination: all these considerations make it not unadviseable, in my opinion, to call back our attention to the true principles of our own domestic laws; that you, my French friend, should begin to know, and that we should continue to cherish them. We ought not, on either side of the water, to suffer ourselves to be imposed upon by the counterfeit wares which some persons, by a double fraud, export to you in illicit bottoms, as raw commodities of British growth though wholly alien to our soil, in order afterwards to smuggle them back again into this country, manufactured after the newest Paris fashion of an improved liberty.

The people of England will not ape the fashions they have never tried; nor go back to those which they have found mischievous on trial. They look upon the legal hereditary succession of their crown as among their rights, not as among their wrongs; as a benefit, not as a grievance; as a security for their liberty, not as a badge of servitude. They look on the frame of their commonwealth, *such as it stands*, to be of inestimable value; and they conceive the undisturbed succession of the crown to be a pledge of the stability and perpetuity of all the other members of our constitution.

I shall beg leave, before I go any further, to take notice of some paltry artifices, which the abettors of election as the only lawful title to the crown, are ready to employ, in order to render the support of the just principles of our constitution a task somewhat invidious. These sophisters substitute a fictitious cause, and feigned personages, in whose favour they suppose you engaged, whenever you defend the inheritable nature of the crown. It is common with them to dispute as if they were in a conflict with some of those exploded fanatics of slavery, who formerly maintained, what I believe no creature now maintains, 'that the crown is held by divine, hereditary, and indefeasible right.'—These old fanatics of single arbitrary power dogmatized as if hereditary royalty was the only lawful government in the world, just as our new fanatics of popular arbitrary power, maintain that a popular election is the sole lawful source of authority. The old prerogative enthusiasts, it is true, did speculate foolishly, and perhaps impiously too, as if monarchy had more of a divine sanction than any other mode of government; and as if a right to govern by inheritance were in strictness *indefeasible* in every person, who should be found in the succession to a throne, and under every circumstance, which no civil or political right can be. But an absurd opinion concerning the king's hereditary right to the crown does not prejudice one that is rational, and bottomed upon solid principles of law and policy. If all the absurd theories of lawyers and divines were to vitiate the objects in which they are conversant, we should have no law, and no religion, left in the world. But an absurd theory on one side of a question forms no justification for alledging a false fact, or promulgating mischievous maxims on the other.

The second claim of the Revolution Society is 'a right of cashiering their governors for *misconduct*.' Perhaps the apprehensions our ancestors entertained of forming such a precedent as that 'of cashiering for misconduct,' was the cause that the declaration of the act which implied the abdication of King James, was, if it had any fault, rather too guarded, and too circumstantial.[1] But all this guard, and all this accumulation of circumstances, serves to shew the spirit of caution which predominated in the national councils, in a situation in which men irritated by oppression, and elevated by a triumph over it, are apt to abandon themselves to violent and extreme courses: it shews the anxiety of the great men who influenced the conduct of affairs at that great event, to make the Revolution a parent of settlement, and not a nursery of future revolutions.

No government could stand a moment, if it could be blown down with any thing so loose and indefinite as an opinion of '*misconduct*.' They who led at the Revolution, grounded the virtual abdication of King James upon no such light and uncertain principle. They charged him with nothing less than a design, confirmed by a multitude of illegal overt acts, to *subvert the Protestant church and state*, and their *fundamental*, unquestionable laws and liberties: they charged him with having broken the *original contract* between king and people. This was more than *misconduct*. A grave and overruling necessity obliged them to take the step they took, and took with infinite reluctance, as under that most rigorous of all laws. Their trust for the future preservation of the constitution was not in future revolutions. The grand policy of all their regulations was to render it almost impracticable for any future sovereign to compel the states of the kingdom to have

---

[1] 'That King James the second, having endeavoured to *subvert the constitution* of the kingdom, by breaking the *original contract* between king and people, and by the advice of jesuits, and other wicked persons, having violated the *fundamental* laws, and *having withdrawn himself out of the kingdom*, hath *abdicated* the government, and the throne is thereby *vacant*.'

again recourse to those violent remedies. They left the crown what, in the eye and estimation of law, it had ever been, perfectly irresponsible. In order to lighten the crown still further, they aggravated responsibility on ministers of state. By the statute of the 1st of king William, sess. 2d, called '*the act for declaring the rights and liberties of the subject, and for settling the succession of the crown*,'* they enacted, that the ministers should serve the crown on the terms of that declaration. They secured soon after the *frequent meetings of parliament*, by which the whole government would be under the constant inspection and active controul of the popular representative and of the magnates of the kingdom. In the next great constitutional act, that of the 12th and 13th of King William,* for the further limitation of the crown, and *better* securing the rights and liberties of the subject, they provided, 'that no pardon under the great seal of England should be pleadable to an impeachment by the commons in parliament.' The rule laid down for government in the Declaration of Right, the constant inspection of parliament, the practical claim of impeachment, they thought infinitely a better security not only for their constitutional liberty, but against the vices of administration, than the reservation of a right so difficult in the practice, so uncertain in the issue, and often so mischievous in the consequences, as that of 'cashiering their governors.'

Dr Price, in this sermon,[1] condemns very properly the practice of gross, adulatory addresses to kings. Instead of this fulsome style, he proposes that his majesty should be told, on occasions of congratulation, that 'he is to consider himself as more properly the servant than the sovereign of his people.' For a compliment, this new form of address does not seem to be very soothing. Those who are servants, in name, as well as in effect, do not like to be told of their situation, their duty, and their obligations. The slave, in the old play, tells his master, '*Haec commemoratio est quasi exprobratio*.'* It is not pleasant as compliment; it is not wholesome as instruction. After all, if the king were to bring himself to echo this new kind of address, to adopt it in terms, and even to take the

---

[1] P. 22, 23, 24.

appellation of Servant of the People as his royal style, how either he or we should be much mended by it, I cannot imagine. I have seen very assuming letters, signed, Your most obedient, humble servant. The proudest domination that ever was endured on earth took a title of still greater humility than that which is now proposed for sovereigns by the Apostle of Liberty. Kings and nations were trampled upon by the foot of one calling himself 'the Servant of Servants;' and mandates for deposing sovereigns were sealed with the signet of 'the Fisherman.'*

I should have considered all this as no more than a sort of flippant vain discourse, in which, as in an unsavoury fume, several persons suffer the spirit of liberty to evaporate, if it were not plainly in support of the idea, and a part of the scheme of 'cashiering kings for misconduct.' In that light it is worth some observation.

Kings, in one sense, are undoubtedly the servants of the people, because their power has no other rational end than that of the general advantage; but it is not true that they are, in the ordinary sense (by our constitution, at least) any thing like servants; the essence of whose situation is to obey the commands of some other, and to be removeable at pleasure. But the king of Great Britain obeys no other person; all other persons are individually, and collectively too, under him, and owe to him a legal obedience. The law, which knows neither to flatter nor to insult, calls this high magistrate, not our servant, as this humble Divine calls him, but '*our sovereign Lord the King*,' and we, on our parts, have learned to speak only the primitive language of the law, and not the confused jargon of their Babylonian pulpits.

As he is not to obey us, but as we are to obey the law in him, our constitution has made no sort of provision towards rendering him, as a servant, in any degree responsible. Our constitution knows nothing of a magistrate like the *Justicia* of Arragon;* nor of any court legally appointed, nor of any process legally settled for submitting the king to the responsibility belonging to all servants. In this he is not distinguished from the commons and the lords; who, in their several public capacities, can never be called to an account for their conduct;

although the Revolution Society chooses to assert, in direct opposition to one of the wisest and most beautiful parts of our constitution, that 'a king is no more than the first servant of the public, created by it, *and responsible to it.*'

Ill would our ancestors at the Revolution have deserved their fame for wisdom, if they had found no security for their freedom, but in rendering their government feeble in its operations, and precarious in its tenure; if they had been able to contrive no better remedy against arbitrary power than civil confusion. Let these gentlemen state who that *representative* public is to whom they will affirm the king, as a servant, to be responsible. It will be then time enough for me to produce to them the positive statute law which affirms that he is not.

The ceremony of cashiering kings, of which these gentlemen talk so much at their ease, can rarely, if ever, be performed without force. It then becomes a case of war, and not of constitution. Laws are commanded to hold their tongues amongst arms; and tribunals fall to the ground with the peace they are no longer able to uphold. The Revolution of 1688 was obtained by a just war, in the only case in which any war, and much more a civil war, can be just. 'Justa bella quibus *necessaria.*'* The question of dethroning, or, if these gentlemen like the phrase better, 'cashiering kings,' will always be, as it has always been, an extraordinary question of state, and wholly out of the law; a question (like all other questions of state) of dispositions, and of means, and of probable consequences, rather than of positive rights. As it was not made for common abuses, so it is not to be agitated by common minds. The speculative line of demarcation, where obedience ought to end, and resistance must begin, is faint, obscure, and not easily definable. It is not a single act, or a single event, which determines it. Governments must be abused and deranged indeed, before it can be thought of; and the prospect of the future must be as bad as the experience of the past. When things are in the lamentable condition, the nature of the disease is to indicate the remedy to those whom nature has qualified to administer in extremities this critical, ambiguous, bitter portion to a distempered state. Times and occasions, and provocations, will teach their own lessons. The wise will determine from the gravity of the case; the irritable from sensibility to oppression; the high-minded from disdain and indignation at abusive power in unworthy hands; the brave and bold from the love of honourable danger in a generous cause: but, with or without right, a revolution will be the very last resource of the thinking and the good.

The third head of right, asserted by the pulpit of the Old Jewry, namely, the 'right to form a government for ourselves,' has, at least, as little countenance from any thing done at the Revolution, either in precedent or principle, as the two first of their claims. The Revolution was made to preserve our *antient* indisputable laws and liberties, and that *antient* constitution of government which is our only security for law and liberty. If you are desirous of knowing the spirit of our constitution, and the policy which predominated in that great period which has secured it to this hour, pray look for both in our histories, in our records, in our acts of parliament, and journals of parliaments, and not in the sermons of the Old Jewry, and the after-dinner toasts of the Revolution Society.—In the former you will find other ideas and another language. Such a claim is as ill-suited to our temper and wishes as it is unsupported by any appearance of authority. The very idea of the fabrication of a new government, is enough to fill us with disgust and horror. We wished at the period of the Revolution, and do now wish, to derive all we possess as *an inheritance from our forefathers*. Upon that body and stock of inheritance we have taken care not to inoculate any cyon* alien to the nature of the original plant. All the reformations we have hitherto made, have proceeded upon the principle of reference to antiquity; and I hope, nay I am persuaded, that all those which possibly may be made hereafter, will be carefully formed upon analogical precedent, authority, and example.

Our oldest reformation is that of Magna Charta. You will see that Sir Edward Coke,* that great oracle of our law, and indeed all the great men who follow him, to Blackstone,*[1] are industrious to prove the pedigree of our liberties. They endeavour to prove, that the antient charter, the Magna

---

[1] See Blackstone's Magna Charta, printed at Oxford, 1759.

Charta of King John, was connected with another positive charter from Henry I,* and that both the one and the other were nothing more than a re-affirmance of the still more antient standing law of the kingdom. In the matter of fact, for the greater part, these authors appear to be in the right; perhaps not always: but if the lawyers mistake in some particulars, it proves my position still the more strongly; because it demonstrates the powerful prepossession towards antiquity, with which the minds of all our lawyers and legislators, and of all the people whom they wish to influence, have been always filled; and the stationary policy of this kingdom in considering their most sacred rights and franchises as an *inheritance*.

In the famous law of the 3d of Charles I. called the *Petition of Right*, the parliament says to the king, 'Your subjects have *inherited* this freedom,' claiming their franchises not on abstract principles 'as the rights of men,' but as the rights of Englishmen, and as a patrimony derived from their forefathers. Selden,* and the other profoundly learned men, who drew this petition of right, were as well acquainted, at least, with all the general theories concerning the 'rights of men,' as any of the discoursers in our pulpits, or on your tribune; full as well as Dr Price, or as the Abbé Seyes.* But, for reasons worthy of that practical wisdom which superseded their theoretic science, they preferred this positive, recorded, *hereditary* title to all which can be dear to the man and the citizen, to that vague speculative right, which exposed their sure inheritance to be scrambled for and torn to pieces by every wild litigious spirit.

The same policy pervades all the laws which have since been made for the preservation of our liberties. In the 1st of William and Mary, in the famous statute, called the Declaration of Right, the two houses utter not a syllable of 'a right to frame a government for themselves.' You will see, that their whole care was to secure the religion, laws, and liberties, that had been long possessed, and had been lately endangered. 'Taking[1] into their most serious consideration the *best* means for making such an establishment, that their religion, laws,

---

[1] I W. and M.

and liberties, might not be in danger of being again subverted,' they auspicate all their proceedings, by stating as some of those *best* means, 'in the *first place*' to do 'as their *ancestors in like cases have usually* done for vindicating their *antient* rights and liberties, to *declare*,'—and then they pray the king and queen, 'that it may be *declared* and enacted, that *all and singular* the rights and liberties *asserted and declared* are the true *antient* and indubitable rights and liberties of the people of this kingdom.'

You will observe, that from Magna Charta to the Declaration of Right, it has been the uniform policy of our constitution to claim and assert our liberties, as an *entailed inheritance* derived to us from our forefathers, and to be transmitted to our posterity; as an estate specially belonging to the people of this kingdom without any reference whatever to any other more general or prior right. By this means our constitution preserves an unity in so great a diversity of its parts. We have an inheritable crown; an inheritable peerage; and an house of commons and a people inheriting privileges, franchises, and liberties, from a long line of ancestors.

This policy appears to me to be the result of profound reflection; or rather the happy effect of following nature, which is wisdom without reflection, and above it. A spirit of innovation is generally the result of a selfish temper and confined views. People will not look forward to posterity, who never look backward to their ancestors. Besides, the people of England well know, that the idea of inheritance furnishes a sure principle of conservation, and a sure principle of transmission; without at all excluding a principle of improvement. It leaves acquisition free; but it secures what it acquires. Whatever advantages are obtained by a state proceeding on these maxims, are locked fast as in a sort of family settlement; grasped as in a kind of mortmain* for ever. By a constitutional policy, working after the pattern of nature, we receive, we hold, we transmit our government and our privileges, in the same manner in which we enjoy and transmit our property and our lives. The institutions of policy, the goods of fortune, the gifts of Providence, are handed down, to us and from us, in the same course and order. Our political system is placed in a just correspondence and symmetry with the order of the world, and with the mode of existence decreed to a permanent body composed of transitory parts; wherein, by the disposition of a stupendous wisdom, moulding together the great mysterious incorporation of the human race, the whole, at one time, is never old, or middle-aged, or young, but in a condition of unchangeable constancy, moves on through the varied tenour of perpetual decay, fall, renovation, and progression. Thus, by preserving the method of nature in the conduct of the state, in what we improve we are never wholly new; in what we retain we are never wholly obsolete. By adhering in this manner and on those principles to our forefathers, we are guided not by the superstition of antiquarians, but by the spirit of philosophic analogy. In this choice of inheritance we have given to our frame of polity the image of a relation in blood; binding up the constitution of our country with our dearest domestic ties; adopting our fundamental laws into the bosom of our family affections; keeping inseparable, and cherishing with the warmth of all their combined and mutually reflected charities, our state, our hearths, our sepulchres, and our altars.

Through the same plan of a conformity to nature in our artificial institutions, and by calling in the aid of her unerring and powerful instincts, to fortify the fallible and feeble contrivances of our reason, we have derived several other, and those no small benefits, from considering our liberties in the light of an inheritance. Always acting as if in the presence of canonized forefathers, the spirit of freedom, leading in itself to misrule and excess, is tempered with an awful gravity. This idea of a liberal descent inspires us with a sense of habitual native dignity, which prevents that upstart insolence almost inevitably adhering to and disgracing those who are the first acquirers of any distinction. By this means our liberty becomes a noble freedom. It carries an imposing and majestic aspect. It has a pedigree and illustrating ancestors. It has its bearings and its ensigns armorial. It has its gallery of portraits; its monumental inscriptions; its records, evidences, and titles. We procure reverence to our civil institutions on the principle upon which nature teaches us to revere individual men; on account of their age; and on account of those from whom they are descended. All your sophisters cannot produce any thing better adapted to preserve a rational and manly freedom than the course that we have pursued, who have chosen our nature rather than our speculations, our breasts rather than our inventions, for the great conservatories and magazines of our rights and privileges.

You might, if you pleased, have profited of our example, and have given to your recovered freedom a correspondent dignity. Your privileges, though discontinued, were not lost to memory. Your constitution, it is true, whilst you were out of possession, suffered waste and dilapidation; but you possessed in some parts the walls, and in all the foundations of a noble and venerable castle. You might have repaired those walls; you might have built on those old foundations. Your constitution was suspended before it was perfected;* but you had the elements of a constitution very nearly as good as could be wished. In your old states you possessed that variety of parts corresponding with the various descriptions of which your community was happily composed; you had all that combination, and all that opposition of interests, you had that action and counteraction which, in the natural and in the political world, from the reciprocal struggle of discordant powers, draws out the harmony of the universe. These opposed and conflicting interests, which you considered as so great a blemish in your old and in our present constitution, interpose a salutary check to all precipitate resolutions; They render deliberation a matter not of choice, but of necessity; they make all change a subject of *compromise*, which naturally begets moderation; they produce *temperaments*, preventing the sore evil of harsh, crude, unqualified reformations; and rendering all the headlong exertions of arbitrary power, in the few or in the many, for ever impracticable. Through that diversity of members and interests, general liberty had as many securities as their were separate views in the several orders; whilst by pressing down the whole by the weight of a real monarchy, the separate parts would have been prevented from warping and starting from their allotted places.

You had all these advantages in your antient states; but you chose to act as if you had never been moulded into civil society, and had every thing to begin anew. You began ill, because you began by despising every thing that belonged to you. You set up your trade without a capital. If the last generations of your country appeared without much lustre in your eyes, you might have passed them by, and derived your claims from a more early race of ancestors. Under a pious predilection for those ancestors, your imaginations would have realized in them a standard of virtue and wisdom, beyond the vulgar practice of the hour: and you would have risen with the example to whose imitation you aspired. Respecting your forefathers, you would have been taught to respect yourselves. You would not have chosen to consider the French as a people of yesterday, as a nation of low-born servile wretches until the emancipating year of 1789. In order to furnish, at the expence of your honour, an excuse to your apologists here for several enormities of yours, you would not have been content to be represented as a gang of Maroon slaves,* suddenly broke loose from the house of bondage, and therefore to be pardoned for your abuse of the liberty to which you were not accustomed and ill fitted. Would it not, my worthy friend, have been wiser to have you thought, what I, for one, always thought you, a generous and gallant nation, long misled to your disadvantage by your high and romantic sentiments of fidelity, honour, and loyalty; that events had been unfavourable to you, but that you were not enslaved through any illiberal or servile disposition; that in your most devoted submission, you were actuated by a principle of public spirit, and that it was your country you worshipped, in the person of your king? Had you made it to be understood, that in the delusion of this amiable error you had gone further than your wise ancestors; that you were resolved to resume your ancient privileges, whilst you preserved the spirit of your ancient and your recent loyalty and honour; or, if diffident of yourselves, and not clearly discerning the almost obliterated constitution of your ancestors, you had looked to your neighbours in this land, who had kept alive the ancient principles and models of the old common law of Europe meliorated and adapted to its present state—by following wise examples you would have given new examples of wisdom to the world. You would have rendered the cause of liberty venerable in the eyes of every worthy mind in every nation. You would have shamed despotism from the earth, by shewing that freedom was not only reconcileable, but as, when well disciplined it is, auxiliary to law. You would have had an unoppressive but a productive revenue. You would have had a flourishing commerce to feed it. You would have had a free constitution; a potent monarchy; a disciplined army; a reformed and venerated clergy; a mitigated but spirited nobility, to lead your virtue, not to overlay it; you would have had a liberal order of commons to emulate and to recruit that nobility; you would have had a protected, satisfied, laborious, and obedient people, taught to seek and to recognize the happiness that is to be found by virtue in all conditions; in which consists the true moral equality of mankind, and not in that monstrous fiction, which, by inspiring false ideas and vain expectations into men destined to travel in the obscure walk of laborious life, serves only to aggravate and imbitter that real inequality, which it never can remove; and which the order of civil life establishes as much for the benefit of those whom it must leave in an humble state, as those whom it is able to exalt to a condition more splendid, but not more happy. You had a smooth and easy career of felicity and glory laid open to you, beyond any thing recorded in the history of the world; but you have shewn that difficulty is good for man.

Compute your gains: see what is got by those extravagant and presumptuous speculations which have taught your leaders to despise all their predecessors, and all their contemporaries, and even to despise themselves, until the moment in which they became truly despicable. By following those false lights, France has bought undisguised calamities at a higher price than any nation has purchased the most unequivocal blessings! France has bought poverty by crime! France has not sacrificed her virtue to her interest; but she has abandoned her interest, that she might prostitute her virtue. All other nations have begun the fabric of a new government, or the reformation of an old, by establishing originally, or by enforcing with greater exactness some rites or other of religion. All other people have laid the foundations of civil freedom in severer manners, and a system of a more austere and masculine morality. France, when she let loose the reins of regal authority, doubled the licence, of a ferocious dissoluteness in manners, and of an insolent irreligion in opinions and practices; and has extended through all ranks of life, as if she were communicating some privilege, or laying open some secluded benefit, all the unhappy corruptions that usually were the disease of wealth and power. This is one of the new principles of equality in France.

France, by the perfidy of her leaders, has utterly disgraced the tone of lenient council in the cabinets of princes, and disarmed it of its most potent topics. She has sanctified the dark suspicious maxims of tyrannous distrust; and taught kings to tremble at (what will hereafter be called) the delusive plausibilities, of moral politicians. Sovereigns will consider those who advise them to place an unlimited confidence in their people, as subverters of their thrones; as traitors who aim at their destruction, by leading their easy good-nature, under specious pretences, to admit combinations of bold and faithless men into a participation of their power. This alone (if there were nothing else) is an irreparable calamity to you and to mankind. Remember that your parliament of Paris* told your king, that in calling the states together, he had nothing to fear but the prodigal excess of their zeal in providing for the support of the throne. It is right that these men should hide their heads. It is right that they should bear their part in the ruin which their counsel has brought on their sovereign and their country. Such sanguine declarations tend to lull authority asleep; to encourage it rashly to engage in perilous adventures of untried policy; to neglect those provisions, preparations, and precautions, which distinguish benevolence from imbecility; and without which no man can answer for the salutary effect of any abstract plan of government or of freedom. For want of these, they have seen the medicine of the state corrupted into its poison. They have seen the French rebel against a mild and lawful monarch, with more fury, outrage, and insult, than ever any people has been known to rise against the most illegal usurper, or the most sanguinary tyrant. Their resistance was made to concession; their revolt was from protection; their blow was aimed at an hand holding out graces, favours, and immunities.

This was unnatural. The rest is in order. They have found their punishment in their success. Laws overturned; tribunals subverted; industry without vigour; commerce expiring; the revenue unpaid, yet the people impoverished; a church pillaged, and a state not relieved; civil and military anarchy made the constitution of the kingdom; every thing human and divine sacrificed to the idol of public credit, and national bankruptcy the consequence; and to crown all, the paper securities of new, precarious, tottering power, the discredited paper securities of impoverished fraud, and beggared rapine, held out as a currency for the support of an empire, in lieu of the two great recognized species that represent the lasting conventional credit of mankind, which disappeared and hid themselves in the earth from whence they came, when the principle of property, whose creatures and representatives they are, was systematically subverted.*

Were all these dreadful things necessary? were they the inevitable results of the desperate struggle of determined patriots, compelled to wade through blood and tumult, to the quiet shore of a tranquil and prosperous liberty? No! nothing like it. The fresh ruins of France, which shock our feelings wherever we can turn our eyes, are not the devastation of civil war; they are the sad but instructive monuments of rash and ignorant counsel in time of profound peace. They are the display of inconsiderate and presumptuous, because unresisted and irresistable authority. The persons who have thus squandered away the precious treasure of their crimes, the persons who have made this prodigal and wild waste of public evils (the last stake reserved for the ultimate ransom of the state) have met in their progress with little, or rather with no opposition at all. Their whole march was more like a triumphal procession than the progress of a war. Their pioneers have gone before them, and demolished and laid every thing level at their feet. Not one drop of *their* blood have they shed in the cause of the country they have ruined. They have made no sacrifices to their projects of greater consequences than their shoe-buckles,* whilst they were imprisoning their king, murdering their fellow citizens, and bathing in tears, and plunging in poverty and distress, thousands of worthy men and worthy families. Their cruelty has not even been the base result of fear. It has been the effect of their sense of perfect safety, in authorizing treasons, robberies, rapes, assassinations, slaughters, and burnings throughout their harrassed land. But the cause of all was plain from the beginning.

This unforced choice, this fond election of evil, would appear perfectly unaccountable, if we did not consider the composition of the National Assembly; I do not mean its formal constitution, which, as it now stands, is exceptionable enough, but the materials of which in a great measure it is composed, which is of ten thousand times greater consequence than all the formalities in the world. If we were to know nothing of this Assembly but by its title and function, no colours could paint to the imagination any thing more venerable. In that light the mind of an enquirer, subdued by such an awful image as that of the virtue and wisdom of a whole people collected into a focus, would pause and hesitate in condemning things even of the very worst aspect. Instead of blameable, they would appear only mysterious. But no name, no power, no function, no artificial institution whatsoever, can make the men of whom any system of authority is composed, any other than God, and nature, and education, and their habits of life have made them. Capacities beyond these the people have not to give. Virtue and wisdom may be the objects of their choice; but their choice confers neither the one nor the other on those upon whom they lay their ordaining hands. They have not the engagement of nature, they have not the promise of revelation for any such powers.

After I had read over the list of the persons and descriptions elected into the *Tiers Etat*, nothing which they afterwards did could appear astonishing. Among them, indeed, I saw some of known rank; some of shining talents; but of any practical experience in the state, not one man was to be found. The best were only men of theory. But whatever the distinguished few may have been, it is the substance and mass of the body which constitutes its character, and must finally determine its direction. In all bodies, those who will lead, must also, in a considerable degree, follow. They must conform their propositions to the taste, talent, and disposition of those whom they wish to conduct: therefore, if an Assembly is viciously or feebly composed in a very great part of it, nothing but such a supreme degree of virtue as very rarely appears in the world, and for that reason cannot enter into calculation, will prevent the men of talents disseminated through it from becoming only the expert instruments of absurd projects! If what is the more likely event, instead of that unusual degree of virtue, they should be actuated by sinister ambition and a lust of meretricious glory, then the feeble part of the Assembly, to whom at first they conform, becomes in its turn the dupe and instrument of their designs. In this political traffick the leaders will be obliged to bow to the ignorance of their followers, and the followers to become subservient to the worst designs of their leaders.

To secure any degree of sobriety in the propositions made by the leaders in any public assembly, they ought to respect, in some degree perhaps to fear, those whom they conduct. To be led any otherwise than blindly, the followers must be qualified, if not for actors, at least for judges; they must also be judges of natural weight and authority. Nothing can secure a steady and moderate conduct in such assemblies, but that the body of them should be respectably composed, in point of condition in life, of permanent property, of education, and of such habits as enlarge and liberalize the understanding.

In the calling of the states general of France, the first thing which struck me, was a great departure from the antient course. I found the representation for the Third Estate composed of six hundred persons.* They were equal in number to the representatives of both the other orders. If the orders were to act separately, the number would not, beyond the consideration of the expence, be of much moment. But when it became apparent that the three orders were to be melted down into one, the policy and necessary effect of this numerous representation became obvious. A very small desertion from either of the other two orders must throw the power of both into the hands of the third.* In fact, the whole power of the state was soon resolved into that body. Its due composition became therefore of infinitely the greater importance.

Judge, Sir, of my surprize, when I found that a very great proportion of the Assembly (a majority, I believe, of the members who attended) was composed of practitioners in the law. It was composed not of distinguished magistrates, who had given pledges to their country of their science, prudence, and integrity; not of leading advocates, the glory of the bar; not of renowned professors in universities;—but for the far greater part, as it must in such a number, of the inferior, unlearned, mechanical, merely instrumental members of the profession. There were distinguished exceptions; but the general composition was of obscure provincial advocates, of stewards of petty local jurisdictions, country attornies, notaries, and the whole train of the ministers of municipal litigation, the fomentors and conductors of the petty war of village vexation. From the moment I read the list I saw distinctly, and very nearly as it has happened, all that was to follow.

The degree of estimation in which any profession is held becomes the standard of the estimation in which the professors hold themselves. Whatever the personal merits of many individual lawyers might have been, and in many it was undoubtedly very considerable, in that military kingdom, no part of the profession had been much regarded, except the highest of all, who often united to their professional offices great family splendour, and were invested with great power and authority. These certainly were highly respected, and even with no small degree of awe. The next rank was not much esteemed; the mechanical part was in a very low degree of repute.

Whenever the supreme authority is invested in a body so composed, it must evidently produce the consequences of supreme authority placed in the hands of men not taught habitually to respect themselves; who had no previous fortune in character at stake; who could not be expected to bear with moderation, or to conduct with discretion, a power which they themselves, more than any others, must be surprized to find in their hands. Who could flatter himself that these men, suddenly, and, as it were, by enchantment, snatched from the humblest rank of subordination, would not be intoxicated with their unprepared greatness? Who could conceive, that men who are habitually meddling, daring, subtle, active, of litigious dispositions and unquiet minds, would easily fall back into their old condition of obscure contention, and laborious, low, unprofitable chicane? Who could doubt but that, at any expence to the state, of which they understood nothing, they must pursue their private interests, which they understood but too well? It was not an event depending on chance or contingency. It was inevitable; it was necessary; it was planted in the nature of things. They must *join* (if their capacity did not permit them to *lead*) in any project which could procure to them a *litigious constitution*; which could lay open to them those innumerable lucrative jobs which follow in the train of all great convulsions and revolutions in the state, and particularly in all great and violent permutations of property. Was it to be expected that they would attend to the stability of property, whose existence had always depended upon whatever rendered property questionable, ambiguous, and insecure? Their objects would be enlarged with their elevation, but their disposition and habits, and mode of accomplishing their designs, must remain the same.

Well! but these men were to be tempered and restrained by other descriptions, of more sober minds, and more enlarged understandings. Were they then to be awed by the super-eminent authority and awful dignity of an handful of country clowns who have seats in that Assembly, some of whom are said not to be able to read and write? and by not a greater number of traders, who, though somewhat more instructed, and more conspicuous in the order of society, had never known any thing beyond their counting-house? No! both these descriptions were more formed to be overborne and swayed by the intrigues and artifices of lawyers, than to become their counterpoise. With such a dangerous dispro-portion, the whole must needs be governed by them. To the faculty of law was joined a pretty considerable proportion of the faculty of medicine. This faculty had not, any more than that of the law, possessed in France its just estimation. Its professors therefore must have the qualities of men not habituated to sentiments of dignity. But supposing they had ranked as they ought to do, and as with us they do actually, the sides of sick beds are not the academies for forming statesmen and legislators. Then came the dealers in stocks and funds, who must be eager, at any expence, to change their ideal paper wealth for the more solid substance of land. To these were joined men of other descriptions, from whom as little knowledge of or attention to the interests of a great state was to be expected, and as little regard to the stability of any institution; men formed to be instruments, not controls. Such in general was the composition of the *Tiers Etat* in the National Assembly; in which was scarcely to be perceived the slightest traces of what we call the natural landed interest of the country.

We know that the British house of commons, without shutting its doors to any merit in any class, is, by the sure operation of adequate causes, filled with every thing illustrious in rank, in descent, in hereditary and in acquired opulence, in cultivated talents, in military, civil, naval, and politic distinction, that the country can afford. But supposing, what hardly can be supposed as a case, that the house of commons should be composed in the same manner with the Tiers Etat in France, would this dominion of chicane be borne with patience, or even conceived without horror? God forbid I should insinuate any thing derogatory to that profession, which is another priesthood, administering the rites of sacred justice. But whilst I revere men in the functions which belong to them, and would do, as much as one man can do, to prevent their exclusion from any, I cannot, to flatter them, give the lye to nature. They are good and useful in the composition; they must be mischievous if they preponderate so as virtually to become the whole. Their very excellence in their peculiar functions may be far from a qualification for others. It cannot escape observation, that when men are too much confined to professional and faculty habits, and, as it were, inveterate in the recurrent employment of that narrow

circle, they are rather disabled than qualified for whatever
depends on the knowledge of mankind, on experience in
mixed affairs, on a comprehensive connected view of the
various complicated external and internal interests which go
to the formation of that multifarious thing called a state.

After all, if the house of commons were to have an wholly
professional and faculty composition, what is the power of the
house of commons, circumscribed and shut in by the
immoveable barriers of laws, usages, positive rules of doctrine
and practice, counterpoized by the house of lords, and every
moment of its existence at the discretion of the crown to
continue, prorogue, or dissolve us? The power of the house of
commons, direct or indirect, is indeed great; and long may it
be able to preserve its greatness, and the spirit belonging to
true greatness, at the full; and it will do so, as long as it can
keep the breakers of law in India* from becoming the makers
of law for England. The power, however, of the house of
commons, when least diminished, is as a drop of water in the
ocean, compared to that residing in a settled majority of your
National Assembly. That Assembly, since the destruction of
the orders, has no fundamental law, no strict convention, no
respected usage to restrain it. Instead of finding themselves
obliged to conform to a fixed constitution, they have a power
to make a constitution which shall conform to their designs.
Nothing in heaven or upon earth can serve as a control on
them. What ought to be the heads, the hearts, the dispositions,
that are qualified, or that dare, not only to make laws under a
fixed constitution, but at one heat to strike out a totally new
constitution for a great kingdom, and in every part of it, from
the monarch on the throne to the vestry of a parish? But—
'*fools rush in where angels fear to tread.*'* In such a state of
unbounded power, for undefined and undefinable purposes,
the evil of a moral and almost physical inaptitude of the man
to the function must be the greatest we can conceive to happen
in the management of human affairs.

Having considered the composition of the third estate as it
stood in its original frame, I took a view of the representatives
of the clergy. There too it appeared, that full as little regard
was had to the general security of property, or to the aptitude

of the deputies for their public purposes, in the principles of their election. That election was so contrived as to send a very large proportion of mere country curates to the great and arduous work of new-modelling a state; men who never had seen the state so much as in a picture; men who knew nothing of the world beyond the bounds of an obscure village; who, immersed in hopeless poverty, could regard all property, whether secular or ecclesiastical, with no other eye than that of envy; among whom must be many, who, for the smallest hope of the meanest dividend in plunder, would readily join in any attempts upon a body of wealth, in which they could hardly look to have any share, except in a general scramble.* Instead of balancing the power of the active chicaners in the other assembly, these curates must necessarily become the active coadjutors, or at best the passive instruments of those by whom they had been habitually guided in their petty village concerns. They too could hardly be the most conscientious of their kind, who, presuming upon their incompetent under-standing, could intrigue for a trust which led them from their natural relation to their flocks, and their natural spheres of action, to undertake the regeneration of kingdoms. This preponderating weight being added to the force of the body of chicane in the Tiers Etat, compleated that momentum of ignorance, rashness, presumption, and lust of plunder, which nothing has been able to resist.

To observing men it must have appeared from the beginning, that the majority of the Third Estate, in conjunction with such a deputation from the clergy as I have described, whilst it pursued the destruction of the nobility, would inevitably become subservient to the worst designs of individuals in that class. In the spoil and humiliation of their own order these individuals would possess a sure fund for the pay of their new followers. To squander away the objects which made the happiness of their fellows, would be to them no sacrifice at all. Turbulent, discontented men of quality, in proportion as they are puffed up with personal pride and arrogance, generally despise their own order. One of the first symptoms they discover of a selfish and mischievous ambition, is a profligate disregard of a dignity which they partake with others. To be

attached to the subdivision, to love the little platoon we
belong to in society, is the first principle (the germ as it were)
of public affections. It is the first link in the series by which we
proceed towards a love to our country and to mankind. The
interests of that portion of social arrangement is a trust in the
hands of all those who compose it; and as none but bad men
would justify it in abuse, none but traitors would barter it
away for their own personal advantage.

There were, in the time of our civil troubles in England (I do
not know whether you have any such in your Assembly in
France) several persons, like the then Earl of Holland,* who
by themselves or their families had brought an odium on the
throne, by the prodigal dispensation of its bounties towards
them, who afterwards joined in the rebellions arising from the
discontents of which they were themselves the cause; men
who helped to subvert that throne to which they owed, some
of them, their existence, others all that power which they
employed to ruin their benefactor. If any bounds are set to the
rapacious demands of that sort of people, or that others are
permitted to partake in the objects they would engross,
revenge and envy soon fill up the craving void that is left in
their avarice. Confounded by the complication of distempered
passions, their reason is disturbed; their views become vast
and perplexed; to others inexplicable; to themselves uncertain.
They find, on all sides, bounds to their unprincipled ambition
in any fixed order of things. But in the fog and haze of
confusion all is enlarged, and appears without any limit.

When men of rank sacrifice all ideas of dignity to an
ambition without a distinct object, and work with low
instruments and for low ends, the whole composition becomes
low and base. Does not something like this now appear in
France? Does it not produce something ignoble and inglorious?
a kind of meanness in all the prevalent policy? a tendency in
all that is done to lower along with individuals all the dignity
and importance of the state? Other revolutions have been
conducted by persons, who whilst they attempted or effected
changes in the commonwealth, sanctified their ambition by
advancing the dignity of the people whose peace they
troubled. They had long views. They aimed at the rule, not at

the destruction of their country. They were men of great civil, and great military talents, and if the terror, the ornament of their age. They were not like Jew brokers contending with each other who could best remedy with fraudulent circulation and depreciated paper the wretchedness and ruin brought on their country by their degenerate councils. The compliment made to one of the great bad men of the old stamp (Cromwell) by his kinsman, a favourite poet of that time, shews what it was he proposed, and what indeed to a great degree he accomplished in the success of his ambition:

> Still as *you* rise, the *state*, exalted too,
> Finds no distemper whilst 'tis chang'd by *you*;
> Chang'd like the world's great scene, when without noise
> The rising sun night's *vulgar* lights destroys.*

These disturbers were not so much like men usurping power, as asserting their natural place in society. Their rising was to illuminate and beautify the world. Their conquest over their competitors was by outshining them. The hand that, like a destroying angel, smote the country, communicated to it the force and energy under which it suffered. I do not say (God forbid) I do not say, that the virtues of such men were to be taken as a balance to their crimes; but they were some corrective to their effects. Such was, as I said, our Cromwell. Such were your whole race of Guises, Condés, and Colignis.* Such the Richlieus,* who in more quiet times acted in the spirit of a civil war. Such, as better men, and in a less dubious cause, were your Henry the 4th and your Sully,* though nursed in civil confusions, and not wholly without some of their taint. It is a thing to be wondered at, to see how very soon France, when she had a moment to respire, recovered and emerged from the longest and most dreadful civil war that ever was known in any nation. Why? Because, among all their massacres, they had not slain the *mind* in their country. A conscious dignity, a noble pride, a generous sense of glory and emulation, was not extinguished. On the contrary, it was kindled and inflamed. The organs also of the state, however shattered, existed. All the prizes of honour and virtue, all the rewards, all the distinctions, remained. But your present confusion, like a palsy, has attacked the fountain of life itself. Every person in your country, in a situation to be actuated by a principle of honour, is disgraced and degraded, and can entertain no sensation of life, except in a mortified and humiliated indignation. But this generation will quickly pass away. The next generation of the nobility will resemble the artificers and clowns, and money-jobbers, usurers, and Jews, who will be always their fellows, sometimes their masters. Believe me, Sir, those who attempt to level, never equalize. In all societies, consisting of various descriptions of citizens, some description must be uppermost. The levellers therefore only change and pervert the natural order of things; they load the edifice of society, by setting up in the air what the solidity of the structure requires to be on the ground. The associations of taylors and carpenters, of which the republic (of Paris, for instance) is composed, cannot be equal to the situation, into which, by the worst of usurpations, an usurpation on the prerogatives of nature, you attempt to force them.

The chancellor of France at the opening of the states, said, in a tone of oratorial flourish, that all occupations were honourable.* If he meant only, that no honest employment was disgraceful, he would not have gone beyond the truth. But in asserting, that any thing is honourable, we imply some distinction in its favour. The occupation of an hair-dresser, or of a working tallow-chandler, cannot be a matter of honour to any person—to say nothing of a number of other more servile employments. Such descriptions of men ought not to suffer oppression from the state; but the state suffers oppression, if such as they, either individually or collectively, are permitted to rule. In this you think you are combating prejudice, but you are at war with nature.[1]

---

[1] Ecclesiasticus, chap. xxxviii, verse 24, 25. 'The wisdom of a learned man cometh by opportunity of leisure: and he that hath little business shall become wise.'—'How can he get wisdom that holdeth the plough, and that glorieth in the goad; that driveth oxen; and is occupied in their labours; and whose talk is of bullocks?'

Ver. 27. 'So every carpenter and work-master that laboureth night and day.' &c.

Ver. 33. 'They shall not be sought for in public counsel, nor sit high in the

I do not, my dear Sir, conceive you to be of that sophistical captious spirit, or of that uncandid dulness, as to require, for every general observation or sentiment, an explict detail of the correctives and exceptions, which reason will presume to be included in all the general propositions which come from reasonable men. You do not imagine, that I wish to confine power, authority, and distinction to blood, and names, and titles. No, Sir. There is no qualification for government, but virtue and wisdom, actual or presumptive. Wherever they are actually found, they have, in whatever state, condition, profession or trade, the passport of Heaven to human place and honour. Woe to the country which would madly and impiously reject the service of the talents and virtues, civil, military, or religious, that are given to grace and to serve it; and would condemn to obscurity every thing formed to diffuse lustre and glory around a state. Woe to that country too, that passing into the opposite extreme, considers a low education, a mean contracted view of things, a sordid mercenary occupation, as a preferable title to command. Every thing ought to be open; but not indifferently to every man. No rotation; no appointment by lot; no mode of election operating in the spirit of sortition or rotation, can be generally good in a government conversant in extensive objects. Because they have no tendency, direct or indirect, to select the man with a view to the duty, or to accommodate the one to the other, I do not hesitate to say, that the road to eminence and power, from obscure condition, ought not to be made too easy, nor a thing too much of course. If rare merit be the rarest of all rare things, it ought to pass through some sort of probation. The temple of honour ought to be seated on an eminence. If it be open through virtue, let it be remembered

---

congregation: They shall not sit on the judges seat, nor understand the sentence of judgement: they cannot declare justice and judgment, and they shall not be found where parables are spoken.'

Ver. 34. 'But they will maintain the state of the world.'

I do not determine whether this book be canonical, as the Gallican church (till lately) has considered it, or apocryphal, as here it is taken. I am sure it contains a great deal of sense, and truth.

too, that virtue is never tried but by some difficulty, and some struggle.

Nothing is a due and adequate representation of a state, that does not represent its ability, as well as its property. But as ability is a vigorous and active principle, and as property is sluggish, inert, and timid, it never can be safe from the invasions of ability, unless it be, out of all proportion, predominant in the representation. It must be represented too in great masses of accumulation, or it is not rightly protected. The characteristics essence of property, formed out of the combined principles of its acquisition and conservation, is to be *unequal*. The great masses therefore which excite envy, and tempt rapacity, must be put out of the possibility of danger. Then they form a natural rampart about the lesser properties in all their gradations. The same quantity of property, which is by the natural course of things divided among many, has not the same operation. Its defensive power is weakened as it is diffused. In this diffusion each man's portion is less than what, in the eagerness of his desires, he may flatter himself to obtain by dissipating the accumulations of others. The plunder of the few would indeed give but a share inconceivably small in the distribution to the many. But the many are not capable of making this calculation; and those who lead them to rapine, never intend this distribution.

The power of perpetuating our property in our families is one of the most valuable and interesting circumstances belonging to it, and that which tends the most to the perpetuation of society itself. It makes our weakness subservient to our virtue; it grafts benevolence even upon avarice. The possessors of family wealth, and of the distinction which attends hereditary possession (as most concerned in it) are the natural securities for this transmission. With us, the house of peers is formed upon this principle. It is wholly composed of hereditary property and hereditary distinction; and made therefore the third of the legislature; and in the last event, the sole judge of all property in all its subdivisions. The house of commons too, though not necessarily, yet in fact, is always so composed in the far greater part. Let those large proprietors be what they will, and they have their chance of being amongst the best, they are at the very worst, the ballast in the vessel of the commonwealth. For though hereditary wealth, and the rank which goes with it, are too much idolized by creeping sycophants, and the blind abject admirers of power, they are too rashly slighted in shallow speculations of the petulant, assuming, short-sighted coxcombs of philosophy. Some decent regulated pre-eminence, some preference (not exclusive appropriation) given to birth, is neither unnatural, nor unjust, nor impolitic.

It is said, that twenty-four millions ought to prevail over two hundred thousand. True; if the constitution of a kingdom be a problem of arithmetic. This sort of discourse does well enough with the lamp-post for its second:* to men who *may* reason calmly, it is ridiculous. The will of the many, and their interest, must very often differ; and great will be the difference when they make an evil choice. A government of five hundred country attornies and obscure curates is not good for twenty-four millions of men, though it were chosen by eight and forty millions; nor is it the better for being guided by a dozen of persons of quality, who have betrayed their trust in order to obtain that power. At present, you seem in every thing to have strayed out of the high road of nature. The property of France does not govern it. Of course property is destroyed, and rational liberty has no existence. All you have got for the present is a paper circulation, and a stock-jobbing constitution: and as to the future, do you seriously think that the territory of France, upon the republican system of eighty-three independent municipalities (to say nothing of the parts that compose them) can ever be governed as one body, or can ever be set in motion by the impulse of one mind? When the National Assembly has completed its work, it will have accomplished its ruin. These commonwealths will not long bear a state of subjection to the republic of Paris. They will not bear that this one body should monopolize the captivity of the king, and the dominion over the assembly calling itself National. Each will keep its own portion of the spoil of the church to itself; and it will not suffer either that spoil, or the more just fruits of their industry, or the natural produce of their soil, to be sent to swell the insolence, or pamper the luxury of the mechanics of Paris. In this they will see none of the equality, under the pretence of which they have been tempted to throw off their allegiance to their sovereign, as well as the antient constitution of their country. There can be no capital city in such a constitution as they have lately made. They have forgot, that when they framed democratic governments, they had virtually dismembered their country. The person whom they persevere in calling king, has not power left to him by the hundredth part sufficient to hold together this collection of republics. The republic of Paris will endeavour indeed to compleat the debauchery of the army, and illegally to perpetuate the assembly, without resort to its constituents, as the means of continuing its despotism. It will make efforts, by becoming the heart of a boundless paper circulation, to draw every thing to itself; but in vain. All this policy in the end will appear as feeble as it is now violent.

If this be your actual situation, compared to the situation to which you were called, as it were by the voice of God and man, I cannot find it in my heart to congratulate you on the choice you have made, or the success which has attended your endeavours. I can as little recommend to any other nation a conduct grounded on such principles, and productive of such effects. That I must leave to those who can see further into your affairs than I am able to do, and who best know how far your actions are favourable to their designs. The gentlemen of the Revolution Society, who were so early in their congratulations, appear to be strongly of opinion that there is some scheme of politics relative to this country, in which your proceedings may, in some way, be useful. For your Dr Price, who seems to have speculated himself into no small degree of fervour upon this subject, addresses his auditory in the following very remarkable words: 'I cannot conclude without recalling *particularly* to your recollection a consideration which I have *more than once alluded to*, and which probably your thoughts have *been all along anticipating*, a consideration with which my *mind is impressed more than I can express*. I mean the consideration of the *favourableness of the present times to all exertions in the cause of liberty.*'

It is plain that the mind of this *political* Preacher was at the time big with some extraordinary design; and it is very probable, that the thoughts of his audience, who understood him better than I do, did all along run before him in his reflection, and in the whole train of consequences to which it led.

Before I read that sermon, I really thought I had lived in a free country; and it was an error I cherished, because it gave me a greater liking to the country I lived in. I was indeed aware, that a jealous, ever-waking vigilance, to guard the treasure of our liberty, not only from invasion, but from decay and corruption, was our best wisdom and our first duty. However, I considered that treasure rather as a possession to be secured than as a prize to be contended for. I did not discern how the present time came to be so very favourable to all *exertions* in the cause of freedom. The present time differs from any other only by the circumstance of what is doing in France. If the example of that nation is to have an influence on this, I can easily conceive why some of their proceedings which have an unpleasant aspect, and are not quite reconcileable to humanity, generosity, good faith, and justice, are palliated with so much milky good-nature towards the actors, and borne with so much heroic fortitude towards the sufferers. It is certainly not prudent to discredit the authority of an example we mean to follow. But allowing this, we are led to a very natural question;—What is that cause of liberty, and what are those exertions in its favour, to which the example of France is so singularly auspicious? Is our monarchy to be annihilated, with all the laws, all the tribunals, and all the antient corporations of the kingdom? Is every land-mark of the country to be done away in favour of a geometrical and arithmetical constitution? Is the house of lords to be voted useless? Is episcopacy to be abolished? Are the church lands to be sold to Jews and jobbers; or given to bribe new-invented municipal republics into a participation in sacrilege? Are all the taxes to be voted grievances, and the revenue reduced to a patriotic contribution, or patriotic presents? Are silver shoe-buckles to be substituted in the place of the land tax and the malt tax, for the support of the naval strength of this kingdom? Are all orders, ranks, and distinctions to be confounded, that out of universal anarchy, joined to national bankruptcy, three or four thousand democracies should be formed into eighty-three, and that they may all, by some sort of unknown attractive power, be organized into one? For this great end, is the army to be seduced from its discipline and its fidelity, first, by every kind of debauchery, and then by the terrible precedent of a donative in the encrease of pay? Are the curates to be seduced from their bishops, by holding out to them the delusive hope of a dole out of the spoils of their own order? Are the citizens of London to be drawn from their allegiance, by feeding them at the expence of their fellow-subjects? Is a compulsory paper currency to be substituted in the place of the legal coin of this kingdom? Is what remains of the plundered stock of public revenue to be employed in the wild project of maintaining two armies to watch over and to fight with each other?—If these are the ends and means of the Revolution Society, I admit they are well assorted; and France may furnish them for both with precedents in point.

I see that your example is held out to shame us. I know that we are supposed a dull sluggish race, rendered passive by finding our situation tolerable; and prevented by a mediocrity of freedom from ever attaining to its full perfection. Your leaders in France began by affecting to admire, almost to adore, the British constitution; but as they advanced they came to look upon it with a sovereign contempt. The friends of your National Assembly amongst us have full as mean an opinion of what was formerly thought the glory of their country. The Revolution Society has discovered that the English nation is not free. They are convinced that the inequality in our representation is a 'defect in our constitution so *gross and palpable*, as to make it excellent chiefly in *form and theory*.'[1] That a representation in the legislature of a kingdom is not only the basis of all constitutional liberty in it, but of '*all legitimate government*; that without it a *government* is nothing but an *usurpation*;'—that 'when the representation is *partial*, the kingdom possesses liberty only *partially*; and if extremely partial it gives only a *semblance*; and if not only

[1] Discourse on the Love of our Country, 3d edit. p. 39.

extremely partial, but corruptly chosen, it becomes a *nuisance*.'
Dr Price considers this inadequacy of representation as our
fundamental grievance; and though, as to the corruption of
this semblance of representation, he hopes it is not yet arrived
to its full perfection of depravity; he fears that 'nothing will be
done towards gaining for us this *essential blessing*, until some
great abuse of power again provokes our resentment, or some
great calamity again alarms our fears, or perhaps till the
acquisition of a *pure and equal representation by other
countries*, whilst we are *mocked* with the *shadow*, kindles our
shame.' To this he subjoins a note in these words. 'A
representation, chosen chiefly by the Treasury, and a *few*
thousands of the *dregs* of the people, who are generally paid
for their votes.'

You will smile here at the consistency of those democratists,
who, when they are not on their guard, treat the humbler part
of the community with the greatest comtempt, whilst, at the
same time, they pretend to make them the depositories of all
power. It would require a long discourse to point out to you
the many fallacies that lurk in the generality and equivocal
nature of the terms 'inadequate representation.' I shall only
say here, in justice to that old-fashioned constitution, under
which we have long prospered, that our representation has
been found perfectly adequate to all the purposes for which a
representation of the people can be desired or devised. I defy
the enemies of our constitution to shew the contrary. To detail
the particulars in which it is found so well to promote its ends,
would demand a treatise on our practical constitution. I state
here the doctrine of the Revolutionists, only that you and
others may see, what an opinion these gentlemen entertain of
the constitution of their country, and why they seem to think
that some great abuse of power, or some great calamity, as
giving a chance for the blessing of a constitution according to
their ideas, would be much palliated to their feelings; you see
why they are so much enamoured of your fair and equal
representation, which being once obtained, the same effects
might follow. You see they consider our house of commons as
only 'a semblance,' 'a form,' 'a theory,' 'a shadow,' 'a
mockery,' perhaps 'a nuisance.'

These gentlemen value themselves on being systematic; and not without reason. They must therefore look on this gross and palpable defect of representation, this fundamental grievance (so they call it) as a thing not only vicious in itself, but as rendering our whole government absolutely *illegitimate*, and not at all better than a downright *usurpation*. Another revolution, to get rid of this illegitimate and usurped government, would of course be perfectly justifiable, if not absolutely necessary. Indeed their principle, if you observe it with any attention, goes much further than to an alteration in the election of the house of commons; for, if popular representation, or choice, is necessary to the *legitimacy* of all government, the house of lords is, at one stroke, bastardized and corrupted in blood. That house is no representative of the people at all, even in 'semblance or in form.' The case of the crown is altogether as bad. In vain the crown may endeavour to screen itself against these gentlemen by the authority of the establishment made on the Revolution. The Revolution which is resorted to for a title, on their system, wants a title itself. The Revolution is built, according to their theory, upon a basis not more solid than our present formalities, as it was made by an house of lords not representing any one but themselves; and by an house of commons exactly such as the present, that is, as they term it, by a mere 'shadow and mockery' of representation.

Something they must destroy, or they seem to themselves to exist for no purpose. One set is for destroying the civil power through the ecclesiastical; another for demolishing the ecclesiastick through the civil. They are aware that the worst consequences might happen to the public in accomplishing this double ruin of church and state; but they are so heated with their theories, that they give more than hints, that this ruin, with all the mischiefs that must lead to it and attend it, and which to themselves appear quite certain, would not be unacceptable to them, or very remote from their wishes. A man amongst them of great authority, and certainly of great talents,* speaking of a supposed alliance between church and state, says, 'perhaps *we must wait for the fall of the civil powers* before this most unnatural alliance be broken.

Calamitous no doubt will that time be. But what convulsion in the political world ought to be a subject of lamentation, if it be attended with so desirable an effect?' You see with what a steady eye these gentlemen are prepared to view the greatest calamities which can befall their country!

It is no wonder therefore, that with these ideas of every thing in their constitution and government at home, either in church or state, as illegitimate and usurped, or, at best as a vain mockery, they look abroad with an eager and passionate enthusiasm. Whilst they are possessed by these notions, it is vain to talk to them of the practice of their ancestors, the fundamental laws of their country, the fixed form of a constitution, whose merits are confirmed by the solid test of long experience, and an increasing public strength and national prosperity. They despise experience as the wisdom of unlettered men; and as for the rest, they have wrought underground a mine that will blow up at one grand explosion all examples of antiquity, all precedents, charters, and acts of parliament. They have 'the rights of men.' Against these there can be no prescription; against these no agreement is binding; these admit no temperament, and no compromise: any thing withheld from their full demand is so much of fraud and injustice. Against these their rights of men let no government look for security in the length of its continuance, or in the justice and lenity of its administration. The objections of these speculatists, if its forms do not quadrate with their theories, are as valid against such an old and beneficent government as against the most violent tyranny, or the greenest usurpation. They are always at issue with governments, not on a question of abuse, but a question of competency, and a question of title. I have nothing to say to the clumsy subtilty of their political metaphysics. Let them be their amusement in the schools.—'Illa *se jactet in aula—Aeolus, et clauso ventorum carcere regnet.*'*—But let them not break prison to burst like a *Levanter,** to sweep the earth with their hurricane, and to break up the fountains of the great deep to overwhelm us.

Far am I from denying in theory; full as far is my heart from withholding in practice (if I were of power to give or to withhold) the *real* rights of men. In denying their false claims of right, I do not mean to injure those which are real, and are such as their pretended rights would totally destroy. If civil society be made for the advantage of man, all the advantages for which it is made become his right. It is an institution of beneficence; and law itself is only beneficence acting by a rule. Men have a right to live by that rule; they have a right to justice; as between their fellows, whether their fellows are in politic function or in ordinary occupation. They have a right to the fruits of their industry; and to the means of making their industry fruitful. They have a right to the acquisitions of their parents; to the nourishment and improvement of their offspring; to instruction in life, and to consolation in death. Whatever each man can separately do, without trespassing upon others, he has a right to do for himself; and he has a right to a fair portion of all which society, with all its combinations of skill and force, can do in his favour. In this partnership all men have equal rights; but not to equal things. He that has but five shillings in the partnership, has as good a right to it, as he that has five hundred pound has to his larger proportion. But he has not a right to an equal dividend in the product of the joint stock; and as to the share of power, authority, and direction which each individual ought to have in the management of the state, that I must deny to be amongst the direct original rights of man in civil society; for I have in my contemplation the civil social man, and no other. It is a thing to be settled by convention.

If civil society be the offspring of convention, that convention must be its law. That convention must limit and modify all the descriptions of constitution which are formed under it. Every sort of legislative, judicial, or executory power are its creatures. They can have no being in any other state of things; and how can any man claim, under the conventions of civil society, rights which do not so much as suppose its existence? Rights which are absolutely repugnant to it? One of the first motives to civil society, and which becomes one of its fundamental rules, is *that no man should be judge in his own cause*. By this each person has at once divested himself of the first fundamental right of uncovenanted man, that is, to judge for himself, and to assert his own cause. He abdicates all right to be his own governor. He inclusively, in a great measure, abandons the right of self-defence, the first law of nature. Men cannot enjoy the rights of an uncivil and of a civil state together. That he may obtain justice he gives up his right of determining what it is in points the most essential to him. That he may secure some liberty, he makes a surrender in trust of the whole of it.

Government is not made in virtue of natural rights, which may and do exist in total independence of it; and exist in much greater clearness, and in a much greater degree of abstract perfection: but their abstract perfection is their practical defect. By having a right to every thing they want every thing. Government is a contrivance of human wisdom to provide for human *wants*. Men have a right that these wants should be provided for by this wisdom. Among these wants is to be reckoned the want, out of civil society, of a sufficient restraint upon their passions. Society requires not only that the passions of individuals should be subjected, but that even in the mass and body as well as in the individuals, the inclinations of men should frequently be thwarted, their will controlled, and their passions brought into subjection. This can only be done *by a power out of themselves*; and not, in the exercise of its function, subject to that will and to those passions which it is its office to bridle and subdue. In this sense the restraints on men, as well as their liberties, are to be reckoned among their rights. But as the liberties and the restrictions vary with times and circumstances, and admit of infinite modifications, they cannot be settled upon any abstract rule; and nothing is so foolish as to discuss them upon that principle.

The moment you abate any thing from the full rights of men, each to govern himself, and suffer any artifical positive limitation upon those rights, from that moment the whole organization of government becomes a consideration of convenience. This it is which makes the constitution of a state, and the due distribution of its powers, a matter of the most delicate and complicated skill. It requires a deep knowledge of human nature and human necessities, and of the things which facilitate or obstruct the various ends which are to be pursued by the mechanism of civil institutions. The state is to have recruits to its strength, and remedies to its distempers. What is the use of discussing a man's abstract right to food or to medicine? The question is upon the method of procuring and administering them. In that deliberation I shall always advise to call in the aid of the farmer and the physician, rather than the professor of metaphysics.

The science of constructing a commonwealth, or renovating it, or reforming it, is, like every other experimental science, not to be taught *à priori*. Nor is it a short experience that can instruct us in that practical science; because the real effects of moral causes are not always immediate; but that which in the first instance is prejudicial may be excellent in its remoter operation; and its excellence may arise even from the ill effects it produces in the beginning. The reverse also happens; and very plausible schemes, with very pleasing commencements, have often shameful and lamentable conclusions. In states there are often some obscure and almost latent causes, things which appear at first view of little moment, on which a very great part of its prosperity or adversity may most essentially depend. The science of government being therefore so practical in itself, and intended for such practical purposes, a matter which requires experience, and even more experience than any person can gain in his whole life, however sagacious and observing he may be, it is with infinite caution that any man ought to venture upon pulling down an edifice which has answered in any tolerable degree for ages the common purposes of society, or on building it up again, without having models and patterns of approved utility before his eyes.

These metaphysic rights entering into common life, like rays of light which pierce into a dense medium, are, by the laws of nature, refracted from their straight line. Indeed in the gross and complicated mass of human passions and concerns, the primitive rights of men undergo such a variety of refractions and reflections, that it becomes absurd to talk of them as if they continued in the simplicity of their original direction. The nature of man is intricate; the objects of society are of the greatest possible complexity; and therefore no simple disposition or direction of power can be suitable either to man's nature, or to the quality of his affairs. When I hear the simplicity of contrivance aimed at the boasted of in any new political constitutions, I am at no loss to decide that the artificers are grossly ignorant of their trade, or totally negligent of their duty. The simple governments are fundamentally defective, to say no worse of them. If you were to comtemplate society in but one point of view, all these simple modes of polity are infinitely captivating. In effect each would answer its single end much more perfectly than the more complex is able to attain all its complex purposes. But it is better that the whole should be imperfectly and anomalously answered, than that, while some parts are provided for with great exactness, others might be totally neglected, or perhaps materially injured, by the over-care of a favourite member.

The pretended rights of these theorists are all extremes; and in proportion as they are metaphysically true, they are morally and politically false. The rights of men are in a sort of *middle*, incapable of definition, but not impossible to be discerned. The rights of men in governments are their advantages; and these are often in balances between differences of good; in compromises sometimes between good and evil, and sometimes, between evil and evil. Political reason is a computing principle; adding, subtracting, multiplying, and dividing, morally and not metaphysically or mathematically, true moral denominations.

By these theorists the right of the people is almost always sophistically confounded with their power. The body of the community, whenever it can come to act, can meet with no effectual resistance; but till power and right are the same, the whole body of them has no right inconsistent with virtue, and the first of all virtues, prudence. Men have no right to what is not reasonable, and to what is not for their benefit; for though a pleasant writer said, *Liceat perire poetis*, when one of them, in cold blood, is said to have leaped into the flames of a volcanic revolution, *Ardentem frigidus Aetnam insiluit,** I consider such a frolic rather as an unjustifiable poetic licence, than as one of the franchises of Parnassus; and whether he were poet or divine, or politician that chose to exercise this kind of right, I think that more wise, because more charitable thoughts would urge me rather to save the man, than to preserve his brazen slippers as the monuments of his folly.

The kind of anniversary sermons, to which a great part of what I write refers, if men are not shamed out of their present course, in commemorating the fact, will cheat many out of the principles, and deprive them of the benefits of the Revolution they commemorate. I confess to you, Sir, I never liked this continual talk of resistance and revolution, or the practice of making the extreme medicine of the constitution its daily bread. It renders the habit of society dangerously valetudinary: it is taking periodical doses of mercury sublimate, and swallowing down repeated provocatives of cantharides* to our love of liberty.

This distemper of remedy, grown habitual, relaxes and wears out, by a vulgar and prostituted use, the spring of that spirit which is to be exerted on great occasions. It was in the most patient period of Roman servitude that themes of tyrannicide made the ordinary exercise of boys at school—*cum perimit saevos classis numerosa tyrannos.** In the ordinary state of things, it produces in a country like ours the worst effects, even on the cause of that liberty which it abuses with the dissoluteness of an extravagant speculation. Almost all the high-bred republicans of my time have, after a short space, become the most decided, thorough-paced courtiers; they soon left the business of a tedious, moderate, but practical resistance to those of us whom, in the pride and intoxication of their theories, they have slighted, as not much better than tories. Hypocrisy, of course, delights in the most sublime speculations; for, never intending to go beyond speculation, it costs nothing to have it magnificent. But even in cases where rather levity than fraud was to be suspected in these ranting speculations, the issue has been much the same. These professors, finding their extreme principles not applicable to cases which call only for a qualified, or, as I may say, civil and legal resistance, in such cases employ no resistance at all. It is with them a war or a revolution, or it is nothing. Finding their schemes of politics not adapted to the state of the world in which they live, they often come to think lightly of all public principle; and are ready, on their part, to abandon for a very trivial interest what they find of very trivial value. Some indeed are of more steady and persevering natures; but these are eager politicians out of parliament, who have little to tempt them to abandon their favourite projects. They have some change in the church or state, or both, constantly in their view. When that is the case, they are always bad citizens, and perfectly unsure connexions. For, considering their speculative designs as of infinite value, and the actual arrangement of the state as of no estimation, they are at best indifferent about it. They see no merit in the good, and no fault in the vicious management of public affairs; they rather rejoice in the latter, as more propitious to revolution. They see no merit or demerit in any man, or any action, or any political principle, any further than as they may forward or retard their design of change: they therefore take up, one day, the most violent and stretched prerogative, and another time the wildest democratic ideas of freedom, and pass from the one to the other without any sort of regard to cause, to person, or to party.

In France you are now in the crisis of a revolution, and in the transit from one form of government to another—you cannot see that character of men exactly in the same situation in which we see it in this country. With us it is militant; with you it is triumphant; and you know how it can act when its power is commensurate to its will. I would not be supposed to confine those observations to any description of men, or to comprehend all men of any description within them—No! far from it. I am as incapable of that injustice, as I am of keeping terms with those who profess principles of extremes; and who under the name of religion teach little else than wild and dangerous politics. The worst of these politics of revolution is this; they temper and harden the breast, in order to prepare it for the desperate strokes which are sometimes used in extreme occasions. But as these occasions may never arrive, the mind receives a gratuitous taint; and the moral sentiments suffer not a little, when no political purpose is served by the depravation. This sort of people are so taken up with their theories about the rights of man, that they have totally forgot his nature. Without opening one new avenue to the understanding, they have succeeded in stopping up those that lead to the heart.

They have perverted in themselves, and in those that attend to them, all the well-placed sympathies of the human breast.

This famous sermon of the Old Jewry breathes nothing but this spirit through all the political part. Plots, massacres, assassinations, seem to some people a trivial price for obtaining a revolution. A cheap, bloodless reformation, a guiltless liberty, appear flat and vapid to their taste. There must be a great change of scene; there must be a magnificent stage effect; there must be a grand spectacle to rouze the imagination, grown torpid with the lazy enjoyment of sixty years security, and the still unanimating repose of public prosperity. The Preacher found them all in the French revolution. This inspires a juvenile warmth through his whole frame. His enthusiasm kindles as he advances; and when he arrives at his peroration, it is in a full blaze. Then viewing, from the Pisgah* of his pulpit, the free, moral, happy, flourishing, and glorious state of France, as in a bird-eye landscape of a promised land, he breaks out into the following rapture:

'What an eventful period is this! I am *thankful* that I have lived to it; I could almost say, *Lord, now lettest thou thy servant depart in peace, for mine eyes have seen thy salvation.*—I have lived to see a *diffusion* of knowledge, which has undermined superstition and error.—I have lived to see the *rights of men* better understood than ever; and nations panting for liberty which seemed to have lost the idea of it.—I have lived to see *Thirty Millions of People*, indignant and resolute, spurning at slavery, and demanding liberty with an irresistible voice. *Their King led in triumph, and an arbitrary monarch surrendering himself to his subjects.*'[1]

Before I proceed further, I have to remark, that Dr Price seems rather to over-value the great acquisitions of light which he has obtained and diffused in this age. The last

[1] Another of these reverend gentlemen,* who was witness to some of the spectacles which Paris has lately exhibited—expresses himself thus, '*A king dragged in submissive triumph by his conquering subjects* is one of those appearances of grandeur which seldom rise in the prospect of human affairs, and which, during the remainder of my life, I shall think of with wonder and gratification.' These gentlemen agree marvellously in their feelings.

century appears to me to have been quite as much enlightened. It had, though in a different place, a triumph as memorable as that of Dr Price; and some of the great preachers of that period partook of it as eagerly as he has done in the triumph of France. On the trial of the Rev Hugh Peters for high treason, it was deposed, that when King Charles was brought to London for his trial, the Apostle of Liberty in that day conducted the *triumph*. 'I saw,' says the witness, 'his majesty in the coach with six horses, and Peters riding before the king *triumphing*.' Dr Price, when he talks as if he had made a discovery, only follows a precedent; for, after the commencement of the king's trial, this precursor, the same Dr Peters, concluding a long prayer at the royal chapel at Whitehall, (he had very triumphantly chosen his place) said, 'I have prayed and preached these twenty years; and now I may say with old Simeon, *Lord, now lettest thou thy servant depart in peace, for mine eyes have seen thy salvation*.'[1] Peters had not the fruits of his prayer; for he neither departed so soon as he wished, nor in peace. He became (what I heartily hope none of his followers may be in this country) himself a sacrifice to the triumph which he led as Pontiff. They dealt at the Restoration, perhaps, too hardly with this poor good man. But we owe it to his memory and his sufferings, that he had as much illumination, and as much zeal, and had as effectually undermined all *the superstition and error* which might impede the great business he was engaged in, as any who follow and repeat after him, in this age, which would assume to itself an exclusive title to the knowledge of the rights of men, and all the glorious consequences of that knowledge.

After this sally of the preacher of the Old Jewry, which differs only in place and time, but agrees perfectly with the spirit and letter of the rapture of 1648, the Revolution Society, the fabricators of governments, the heroic band of *cashierers* of *monarchs*, electors of sovereigns, and leaders of kings in triumph, strutting with a proud consciousness of the diffusion of knowledge, of which every member had obtained so large a share in the donative, were in haste to make a generous

---

[1] State Trials, vol. ii. p. 360, p. 363.

diffusion of the knowledge they had thus gratuitously received. To make this bountiful communication, they adjourned from the church in the Old Jewry, to the London Tavern, where the same Dr Price, in whom the fumes of his oracular tripod were not entirely evaporated, moved and carried the resolution, or address of congratulation, transmitted by Lord Stanhope to the National Assembly of France.

I find a preacher of the gospel prophaning the beautiful and prophetic ejaculation, commonly called '*nunc dimittis*,' made on the first presentation of our Saviour in the Temple, and applying it, with an inhuman and unnatural rapture, to the most horrid, atrocious, and afflicting spectacle, that perhaps ever was exhibited to the pity and indignation of mankind. This '*leading in triumph*,' a thing in its best form unmanly and irreligious, which fills our Preacher with such unhallowed transports, must shock, I believe, the moral taste of every well-born mind. Several English were the stupified and indignant spectators of that triumph. It was (unless we have been strangely deceived) a spectacle more resembling a procession of American savages, entering into Onondaga,* after some of their murders called victories, and leading into hovels hung round with scalps, their captives, overpowered with the scoffs and buffets of women as ferocious as themselves, much more than it resembled the triumphal pomp of a civilized martial nation;—if a civilized nation, or any men who had a sense of generosity, were capable of a personal triumph over the fallen and afflicted.

This, my dear Sir, was not the triumph of France. I must believe that, as a nation, it overwhelmed you with shame and horror. I must believe that the National Assembly find themselves in a state of the greatest humiliation, in not being able to punish the authors of this triumph, or the actors in it; and that they are in a situation in which any enquiry they may make upon the subject, must be destitute even of the appearance of liberty or impartiality. The apology of that Assembly is found in their situation; but when we approve what they *must* bear, it is in us the degenerate choice of a vitiated mind.

With a compelled appearance of deliberation, they vote

under the dominion of a stern necessity. They sit in the heart, as it were, of a foreign republic: they have their residence in a city whose constitution has emanated neither from the charter of their kind, nor from their legislative power. There they are surrounded by an army not raised either by the authority of their crown, or by their command; and which, if they should order to dissolve itself, would instantly dissolve them. There they sit, after a gang of assassins had driven away some hundreds of the members;* whilst those who held the same moderate principles, with more patience or better hope, continued every day exposed to outrageous insults and murderous threats. There a majority, sometimes real, sometimes pretended, captive itself, compels a captive king to issue as royal edicts, at third hand, the polluted nonsense of their most licentious and giddy coffee-houses. It is notorious, that all their measures are decided before they are debated. It is beyond doubt, that under the terror of the bayonet, and the lamp-post, and the torch to their houses, they are obliged to adopt all the crude and desperate measures suggested by clubs composed of a monstrous medley of all conditions, tongues, and nations. Among these are found persons, in comparison of whom Catiline would be thought scrupulous, and Cethegus* a man of sobriety and moderation. Nor is it in these clubs alone that the publick measures are deformed into monsters. They undergo a previous distortion in academies, intended as so many seminaries for these clubs, which are set up in all the places of publick resort. In these meetings of all sorts, every counsel, in proportion as it is daring, and violent, and perfidious, is taken for the mark of superior genius. Humanity and compassion are ridiculed as the fruits of superstition and ignorance. Tenderness to individuals is considered as treason to the public. Liberty is always to be estimated perfect as property is rendered insecure. Amidst assassination, massacre, and confiscation, perpetrated or meditated, they are forming plans for the good order of future society. Embracing in their arms the carcases of base criminals, and promoting their relations on the title of their offences, they drive hundreds of virtuous persons to the same end, by forcing them to subsist by beggary or by crime.

The Assembly, their organ, acts before them the farce of deliberation with as little decency as liberty. They act like the comedians of a fair before a riotous audience; they act amidst the tumultuous cries of a mixed mob of ferocious men, and of women lost to shame, who, according to their insolent fancies, direct, control, applaud, explode them; and sometimes mix and take their seats amongst them; domineering over them with a strange mixture of servile petulance and proud presumptuous authority. As they have inverted order in all things, the gallery is in the place of the house. This Assembly, which overthrows kings and kingdoms, has not even the physiognomy and aspect of a grave legislative body—*nec color imperii, nec frons erat ulla senatus.** They have a power given to them, like that of the evil principle, to subvert and destroy; but none to construct, except such machines as may be fitted for further subversion and further destruction.

Who is it that admires, and from the heart is attached to national representative assemblies, but must turn with horror and disgust from such a profane burlesque, and abominable perversion of that sacred institute? Lovers of monarchy, lovers of republicks, must alike abhor it. The members of your Assembly must themselves groan under the tyranny of which they have all the shame, none of the direction, and little of the profit. I am sure many of the members who compose even the majority of that body, must feel as I do, notwithstanding the applauses of the Revolution Society.—Miserable king! miserable Assembly! How must that assembly be silently scandalized with those of their members, who could call a day which seemed to blot the sun out of Heaven, 'un beau jour!'[1] How must they be inwardly indignant at hearing others, who thought fit to declare to them, 'that the vessel of the state would fly forward in her course towards regeneration with more speed than ever,'* from the stiff gale of treason and murder, which preceded our Preacher's triumph! What must they have felt, whilst with outward patience and inward indignation they heard of the slaughter of innocent gentlemen in their houses, that 'the blood spilled was not the most

[1] 6th of October, 1789.

pure?'* What must they have felt, when they were besieged by complaints of disorders which shook their country to its foundations, at being compelled coolly to tell the complainants, that they were under the protection of the law, and that they would address the king (the captive king) to cause the laws to be enforced for their protection; when the enslaved ministers of that captive king had formally notified to them, that there were neither law, nor authority, nor power left to protect? What must they have felt at being obliged, as a felicitation on the present new year, to request their captive king to forget the stormy period of the last, on account of the great good which *he* was likely to produce to his people; to the complete attainment of which good they adjourned the practical demonstrations of their loyalty, assuring him of their obedience, when he should no longer possess any authority to command?

This address was made with much good-nature and affection, to be sure. But among the revolutions in France, must be reckoned a considerable revolution in their ideas of politeness. In England we are said to learn manners at second-hand from your side of the water, and that we dress our behaviour in the frippery of France. If so, we are still in the old cut; and have not so far conformed to the new Parisian mode of good-breeding, as to think it quite in the most refined strain of delicate compliment (whether in condolence or congratulation) to say, to the most humiliated creature that crawls upon the earth, that great public benefits are derived from the murder of his servants, the attempted assassination of himself and of his wife, and the mortification, disgrace, and degradation, that he has personally suffered. It is a topic of consolation which our ordinary of Newgate* would be too humane to use to a criminal at the foot of the gallows. I should have thought that the hangman of Paris, now that he is liberalized by the vote of the National Assembly, and is allowed his rank and arms in the Herald's College of the rights of men, would be too generous, too gallant a man, too full of the sense of his new dignity, to employ that cutting consolation to any of the persons whom the *leze nation** might bring under the administration of his *executive powers*.

A man is fallen indeed, when he is thus flattered. The

anodyne draught of oblivion, thus drugged, is well calculated to preserve a galling wakefulness, and to feed the living ulcer of a corroding memory. Thus to administer the opiate potion of amnesty, powdered with all the ingredients of scorn and contempt, is to hold to his lips, instead of 'the balm of hurt minds,' the cup of human misery full to the brim, and to force him to drink it to the dregs.

Yielding to reasons, at least as forcible as those which were so delicately urged in the compliment on the new year, the king of France will probably endeavour to forget these events, and that compliment. But history, who keeps a durable record of all our acts, and exercises her awful censure over the proceedings of all sorts of sovereigns, will not forget, either those events, or the aera of this liberal refinement in the intercourse of mankind. History will record, that on the morning of the 6th of October 1789, the king and queen of France, after a day of confusion, alarm, dismay, and slaughter, lay down, under the pledged security of public faith, to indulge nature in a few hours of respite, and troubled melancholy repose. From this sleep the queen was first startled by the voice of the centinel at her door, who cried out to her, to save herself by flight—that this was the last proof of fidelity he could give—that they were upon him, and he was dead. Instantly he was cut down. A band of cruel ruffians and assassins, reeking with his blood, rushed into the chamber of the queen, and pierced with an hundred strokes of bayonets and poniards the bed, from whence this persecuted woman had but just time to fly almost naked, and through ways unknown to the murderers had escaped to seek refuge at the feet of a king and husband, not secure of his own life for a moment.*

This king, to say no more of him, and his queen, and their infant children (who once would have been the pride and hope of a great and generous people) were then forced to abandon the sanctuary of the most splendid palace in the world, which they left swimming in blood, polluted by massacre, and strewed with scattered limbs and mutilated carcases. Thence they were conducted into the capital of their kingdom. Two had been selected from the unprovoked, unresisted, promiscuous slaughter, which was made of the gentlemen of birth and family who composed the king's body guard. These two gentlemen, with all the parade of an execution of justice, were cruelly and publickly dragged to the block, and beheaded in the great court of the palace. Their heads were stuck upon spears, and led the procession; whilst the royal captives who followed in the train were slowly moved along, amidst the horrid yells, and shrilling screams, and frantic dances, and infamous contumelies, and all the unutterable abominations of the furies of hell, in the abused shape of the vilest of women. After they had been made to taste, drop by drop, more than the bitterness of death, in the slow torture of a journey of twelve miles, protracted to six hours, they were, under a guard, composed of those very soldiers who had thus conducted them through this famous triumph, lodged in one of the old palaces of Paris,* now converted into a Bastile for kings.

Is this a triumph to be consecrated at altars? to be commemorated with grateful thanksgiving? to be offered to the divine humanity with fervent prayer and enthusiastick ejaculation?—These Theban and Thracian Orgies,* acted in France, and applauded only in the Old Jewry, I assure you, kindle prophetic enthusiasm in the minds but of very few people in this kingdom; although a saint and apostle, who may have revelations of his own and who has so completely vanquished all the mean superstitions of the heart, may incline to think it pious and decorous to compare it with the entrance into the world of the Prince of Peace, proclaimed in an holy temple by a venerable sage, and not long before not worse announced by the voice of angels to the quiet innocence of shepherds.

At first I was at a loss to account for this fit of unguarded transport. I knew, indeed, that the sufferings of monarchs make a delicious repast to some sort of palates. There were reflexions which might serve to keep this appetite within some bounds of temperance. But when I took one circumstance into my consideration, I was obliged to confess, that much allowance ought to be made for the Society, and that the temptation was too strong for common discretion; I mean the circumstance of the Io Paean* of the triumph, the animating cry which called 'for *all* the BISHOPS to be hanged on the lamp-posts,'[1] might well have brought forth a burst of enthusiasm on the foreseen consequences of this happy day. I allow to so much enthusiasm some little deviation from prudence. I allow this prophet to break forth into hymns of joy and thanksgiving on an event which appears like the precursor of the Millenium, and the projected fifth monarchy,* in the destruction of all church establishments. There was, however (as in all human affairs there is) in the midst of this joy something to exercise the patience of these worthy gentlemen, and to try the long-suffering of their faith. The actual murder of the king and queen, and their child, was wanting to the other auspicious circumstances of this *'beautiful day.'* The actual murder of the bishops, though called for by so many holy ejaculations, was also wanting. A groupe of regicide and sacrilegious slaughter, was indeed boldly sketched, but it was only sketched. It unhappily was left unfinished, in this great history-piece of the massacre of innocents. What hardy pencil of a great master, from the school of the rights of men, will finish it, is to be seen hereafter. The age has not yet the compleat benefit of that diffusion of knowledge that has undermined superstition and error; and the king of France wants another object or two, to consign to oblivion, in consideration of all the good which is to arise from his own sufferings, and the patriotic crimes of an enlightened age.[2]

[1] Tous les Eveques à la lanterns.

[2] It is proper here to refer to a letter written upon this subject by an eye-witness. That eye-witness was one of the most honest, intelligent, and eloquent members of the National Assembly, one of the most active and zealous reformers of the state. He was obliged to secede from the assembly; and he afterwards became a voluntary exile, on account of the horrors of this pious triumph, and the dispositions of men, who, profiting of crimes, if not causing them, have taken the lead in public affairs.

EXTRACT of M. de Lally Tollendal's* Second Letter to a Friend.

'Parlons du parti que j'ai pris; il est bien justifié dans ma conscience.—Ni cette ville coupable, ni cette assemblée plus coupable encore, ne meritoient que je me justifie; mais j'ai à cœur que vous, et les personnes qui pensent comme vous, ne me condamnent pas.—Ma santé, je vous jure, me rendoit mes fonctions impossibles; mais meme en les mettant de coté il a eté au-dessus de mes forces de supporter plus long-tems l'horreur que me causoit ce sang,—ces têtes,—cette reine *presque egorgée,*—ce roi,—amené *esclave,*—entrant à Paris,

Although this work of our new light and knowledge, did not go to the length, that in all probability it was intended it should be carried; yet I must think, that such treatment of any human creatures must be shocking to any but those who are made for accomplishing Revolutions. But I cannot stop here. Influenced by the inborn feelings of my nature, and not being illuminated by a single ray of this new-sprung modern light, I confess to you, Sir, that the exalted rank of the persons

au milieu de ses assassins, et precedé des tetes de ses malheureux gardes.—Ces perfides jannissaires, ces assassins, ces femmes cannibales, ce cri de, TOUS LES EVEQUES A LA LANTERNE dans le moment ou le roi entre sa capitale avec deux eveques de son conseil dans sa voiture. Un *coup de fusil*, que j'ai vu tirer dans un *des carosses de la reine*. M. Bailley appellant cela *un beau jour*. L'assemblé ayant declaré froidement le matin, qu'il n'etoit pas de sa dignité d'aller toute entiere environner le roi. M. Mirabeau* disant impunement dans cette assemblée, que le vaisseau de l'état, loins d'etre arrêté dans sa course, s'élanceroit avec plus de rapidité que jamais vers sa régeneration. M. Barnave,* riant avec lui, quand des flots de sang couloient autour de nous. Le vertueux Mounier[1] echappant par miracle à vingt assassins, qui avoient voulu faire de sa tete un trophée de plus.

'Voila ce qui me fit jurer de ne plus mettre le pied *dans cette caverne d'Antropophages* [the National Assembly] où je n'avois de force d'élever la voix, ou depuis six semaines je l'avois elevée en vain. Moi, Mounier, et tous les honnêtes gens, ont le dernier effort à faire pour le bien étoit d'en sortir. Aucune idée de crainte ne s'est approachée de moi. Je rougirois de m'en defendre. J'avois encore reçû sur la route de la part de ce peuple, moins coupable que ceux qui l'ont enivré de fureur, des acclamations, et des applaudissements, dont d'autres auroient été flattés, et qui m'ont fait fremil. C'est à l'indignation, c'est à l' horreur, c'est aux convulsions physiques, que se seul aspect du sang me fait eprouver que j'ai cedé. On brave une seule mort; on la brave plusieurs fois, quand elle peut être utile. Mais aucune puissance sous le Ciel, mais aucune opinion publique ou privée n'ont le droit de me condamner à souffrir inutilement mille supplices par minute, et à perir de désespoir, de rage, au milieu des *triomphes*, du crime que je n'ai pu arrêter. Ils me proscriront, ils confisqueront mes biens. Je labourerai la terre, et je ne les verrai plus.—Voila ma justification. Vous pourez la lire, la montrei, la laisser copier; tant pis pour ceux qui ne la compredront pas; ce ne sera alors moi qui auroit eu tort de la leur donner.'

This military man had not so good nerves as the peaceable gentleman of the Old Jewry.—See Mons. Mounier's narrative of these transactions,* a man also of honour and virtue, and talents, and therefore a fugitive.

[1] N.B. Mr Mounier was then speaker of the National Assembly. He has since been obliged to live in exile, though one of the firmest assertors of liberty.

suffering, and particularly the sex, the beauty, and the amiable qualities of the descendant of so many kings and emperors, with the tender age of royal infants, insensible only through infancy and innocence of the cruel outrages to which their parents were exposed, instead of being a subject of exultation, adds not a little to my sensibility on that most melancholy occasion.

I hear that the august person, who was the principal object of our preacher's triumph, though he supported himself, felt much on that shameful occasion. As a man, it became him to feel for his wife and his children, and the faithful guards of his person, that were massacred in cold blood about him; as a prince, it became him to feel for the strange and frightful transformation of his civilized subjects, and to be more grieved for them, than solicitous for himself. It derogates little from his fortitude, while it adds infinitely to the honour of his humanity. I am very sorry to say it, very sorry indeed, that such personages are in a situation in which it is not unbecoming in us to praise the virtues of the great.

I hear, and I rejoice to hear, that the great lady, the other object of the triumph, has borne that day (one is interested that beings made for suffering should suffer well) and that she bears all the succeeding days, that she bears the imprisonment of her husband, and her own captivity, and the exile of her friends, and the insulting adulation of addresses, and the whole weight of her accumulated wrongs, with a serene patience, in a manner suited to her rank and race, and becoming the offspring of a sovereign distinguished for her piety and her courage; that like her she has lofty sentiments; that she feels with the dignity of a Roman matron; that in the last extremity she will save herself from the last disgrace, and that if she must fall, she will fall by no ignoble hand.

It is now sixteen or seventeen years since I saw the queen of France, then the dauphiness, at Versailles; and surely never lighted on this orb, which she hardly seemed to touch, a more delightful vision.* I saw her just above the horizon, decorating and cheering the elevated sphere she just began to move in,— glittering like the morning-star, full of life, and splendor, and joy. Oh! what a revolution! and what an heart must I have, to contemplate without emotion that elevation and that fall! Little did I dream when she added titles of veneration to those of enthusiastic, distant, respectful love, that she should ever be obliged to carry the sharp antidote against disgrace concealed in that bosom; little did I dream that I should have lived to see such disasters fallen upon her in a nation of gallant men, in a nation of men of honour and of cavaliers. I thought ten thousand swords must have leaped from their scabbards to avenge even a look that threatened her with insult.—But the age of chivalry is gone.—That of sophisters, oeconomists, and calculators, has succeeded; and the glory of Europe is extinguished for ever. Never, never more, shall we behold that generous loyalty to rank and sex, that proud submission, that dignified obedience, that subordination of the heart, which kept alive, even in servitude itself, the spirit of an exalted freedom. The unbought grace of life, the cheap defence of nations, the nurse of manly sentiment and heroic enterprize is gone! It is gone, that sensibility of principle, that chastity of honour, which felt a stain like a wound, which inspired courage whilst it mitigated ferocity, which ennobled whatever it touched, and under which vice itself lost half its evil, by losing all its grossness.

This mixed system of opinion and sentiment had its origin in the antient chivalry; and the principle, though varied in its appearance by the varying state of human affairs, subsisted and influenced through a long succession of generations, even to the time we live in. If it should ever be totally extinguished, the loss I fear will be great. It is this which has given its character to modern Europe. It is this which has distinguished it under all its forms of government, and distinguished it to its advantage, from the states of Asia, and possibly from those states which flourished in the most brilliant periods of the antique world. It was this, which, without confounding ranks, had produced a noble equality, and handed it down through all the gradations of social life. It was this opinion which mitigated kings into companions, and raised private men to be fellows with kings. Without force, or opposition, it subdued the fierceness of pride and power; it obliged sovereigns to submit to the soft collar of social esteem, compelled stern authority to submit to elegance, and gave a domination vanquisher of laws, to be subdued by manners.

But now all is to be changed. All the pleasing illusions, which made power gentle, and obedience liberal, which harmonized the different shades of life, and which, by a bland assimilation, incorporated into politics the sentiments which beautify and soften private society, are to be dissolved by this new conquering empire of light and reason. All the decent drapery of life is to be rudely torn off. All the superadded ideas, furnished from the wardrobe of a moral imagination, which the heart owns, and the understanding ratifies, as necessary to cover the defects of our naked shivering nature, and to raise it to dignity in our own estimation, are to be exploded as a ridiculous, absurd, and antiquated fashion.

On this scheme of things, a king is but a man; a queen is but a woman; a woman is but an animal; and an animal not of the highest order. All homage paid to the sex in general as such, and without distinct views, is to be regarded as romance and folly. Regicide, and parricide, and sacrilege, are but fictions of superstition, corrupting jurisprudence by destroying its simplicity. The murder of a king, or a queen, or a bishop, or a father, are only common homicide; and if the people are by any chance, or in any way gainers by it, a sort of homicide much the most pardonable, and into which we ought not to make too severe a scrutiny.

On the scheme of this barbarous philosophy, which is the offspring of cold hearts and muddy understandings, and which is as void of solid wisdom, as it is destitute of all taste and elegance, laws are to be supported only by their own terrors, and by the concern, which each individual may find in them, from his own private speculations, or can spare to them from his own private interests. In the groves of *their* academy, at the end of every visto, you see nothing but the gallows. Nothing is left which engages the affections on the part of the commonwealth. On the principles of his mechanic philosophy, our institutions can never be embodied, if I may use the expression, in persons; so as to create in us love, veneration, admiration, or attachment. But that sort of reason which banishes the affections is incapable of filling their place. These public affections, combined with manners, are required sometimes as supplements, sometimes as correctives, always as aids to law. The precept given by a wise man, as well as a great critic, for the construction of poems, is equally true as to states. *Non satis est pulchra esse poemata, dulcia sunto.** There ought to be a system of manners in every nation which a well-formed mind would be disposed to relish. To make us love our country, our country ought to be lovely.

But power, of some kind or other, will survive the shock in which manners and opinions perish; and it will find other and worse means for its support. The usurpation which, in order to subvert antient institutions, has destroyed antient principles, will hold power by arts similar to those by which it has acquired it. When the old feudal and chivalrous spirit of *Fealty*, which, by freeing kings from fear, freed both kings and subjects from the precautions of tyranny, shall be extinct in the minds of men, plots and assassinations will be anticipated by preventive murder and preventive confiscation, and that long roll of grim and bloody maxims, which form the political code of all power, not standing on its own honour, and the honour of those who are to obey it. Kings will be tyrants from policy when subjects are rebels from principle.

When antient opinions and rules of life are taken away, the loss cannot possibly be estimated. From that moment we have no compass to govern us; nor can we know distinctly to what port we steer. Europe undoubtedly, taken in a mass, was in a flourishing condition the day on which your Revolution was compleated. How much of that prosperous state was owing to the spirit of our old manners and opinions is not easy to say; but as such cases cannot be indifferent in their operation, we must presume, that, on the whole, their operation was beneficial.

We are but too apt to consider things in the state in which we find them, without sufficiently adverting to the causes by which they have been produced, and possibly may be upheld. Nothing is more certain, than that our manners, our civilization, and all the good things which are connected with manners, and with civilization, have, in the European world of ours, depended for ages upon two principles; and were indeed the result of both combined; I mean the spirit of a gentleman, and the spirit of religion. The nobility and the clergy, the one by profession, the other by patronage, kept learning in existence, even in the midst of arms and confusions, and whilst governments were rather in their causes than formed. Learning paid back what it received to nobility and to priesthood; and paid it with usury, by enlarging their ideas and by furnishing their minds. Happy if they had all continued to know their indissoluble union, and their proper place! Happy if learning, not debauched by ambition, had been satisfied to continue the instructor, and not aspired to be the master! Along with its natural protectors and guardians, learning will be cast into the mire, and trodden down under the hoofs of a swinish multitude.[1]

If, as I suspect, modern letters owe more than they are always willing to own to antient manners, so do other interests which we value full as much as they are worth. Even commerce, and trade, and manufacture, the gods of our oeconomical politicians, are themselves perhaps but creatures; are themselves but effects, which, as first causes, we choose to worship. They certainly grew under the same shade in which learning flourished. They too may decay with their natural protecting principles. With you, for the present at least, they all threaten to disappear together. Where trade and manu-factures are wanting to a people, and the spirit of nobility and religion remains, sentiment supplies, and not always ill supplies their place; but if commerce and the arts should be lost in an experiment to try how well a state may stand without these old fundamental principles, what sort of a thing must be a nation of gross, stupid, ferocious, and at the same time, poor and sordid barbarians, destitute of religion, honour, or manly pride, possessing nothing at present, and hoping for nothing hereafter?

I wish you may not be going fast, and by the shortest cut, to that horrible and disgustful situation. Already there appears a poverty of conception, a coarseness and vulgarity in all the

[1] See the fate of Bailly and Condorcet, supposed to be here particularly alluded to. Compare the circumstances of the trial, and execution of the former with this prediction. [1803]

proceedings of the assembly and of all their instructors. Their liberty is not liberal. Their science is presumptuous ignorance. Their humanity is savage and brutal.

It is not clear, whether in England we learned those grand and decorous principles, and manners, of which considerable traces yet remain, from you, or whether you took them from us. But to you, I think we trace them best. You seem to me to be—*gentis incunabula nostrae.** France has always more or less influenced manners in England; and when your fountain is choaked up and polluted, the stream will not run long, or not run clear with us, or perhaps with any nation. This gives all Europe, in my opinion, but too close and connected a concern in what is done in France. Excuse me, therefore, if I have dwelt too long on the atrocious spectacle of the sixth of October 1789, or have given too much scope to the reflections which have arisen in my mind on occasion of the most important of all revolutions, which may be dated from that day, I mean a revolution is sentiments, manners, and moral opinions. As things now stand, with every thing respectable destroyed without us, and an attempt to destroy within us every principle of respect, one is almost forced to apologize for harbouring the common feelings of men.

Why do I feel so differently from the Reverend Dr Price, and those of his lay flock, who will choose to adopt the sentiments of his discourse?—For this plain reason—because it is *natural* I should; because we are so made as to be affected at such spectacles with melancholy sentiments upon the unstable condition of mortal prosperity, and the tremendous uncertainty of human greatness; because in those natural feelings we learn great lessons; because in events like these our passions instruct our reason; because when kings are hurl'd from their thrones by the Supreme Director of this great drama, and become the objects of insult to the base, and of pity to the good, we behold such disasters in the moral, as we should behold a miracle in the physical order of things. We are alarmed into reflexion; our minds (as it has long since been observed) are purified by terror and pity; our weak unthinking pride is humbled, under the dispensations of a mysterious wisdom.—Some tears might be drawn from me, if such a spectacle were exhibited on the stage. I should be truly ashamed of finding in myself that superficial, theatric sense of painted distress, whilst I could exult over it in real life. With such a perverted mind, I could never venture to shew my face at a tragedy. People would think the tears that Garrick formerly, or that Siddons* not long since, have extorted from me, were the tears of hypocrisy; I should know them to be the tears of folly.

Indeed the theatre is a better school of moral sentiments than churches, where the feelings of humanity are thus outraged. Poets, who have to deal with an audience not yet graduated in the school of the rights of men, and who must apply themselves to the moral constitution of the heart, would not dare to produce such a triumph as a matter of exultation. There, where men follow their natural impulses, they would not bear the odious maxims of a Machiavelian policy, whether applied to the attainment of monarchical or democratic tyranny. They would reject them on the modern, as they once did on the antient stage, where they could not bear even the hypothetical proposition of such wickedness in the mouth of a personated tyrant, though suitable to the character he sustained. No theatric audience in Athens would bear what has been borne, in the midst of the real tragedy of this triumphal day; a principal actor weighing, as it were in scales hung in a shop of horrors,—so much actual crime against so much contingent advantage,—and after putting in and out weights, declaring that the balance was on the side of the advantages. They would not bear to see the crimes of new democracy posted as in a ledger against the crimes of old despotism, and the book-keepers of politics finding democracy still in debt, but by no means unable or unwilling to pay the balance. In the theatre, the first intuitive glance, without any elaborate process of reasoning, would shew, that this method of political computation, would justify every extent of crime. They would see, that on these principles, even where the very worst acts were not perpetrated, it was owing rather to the fortune of the conspirators than to their parsimony in the expenditure of treachery and blood. They would soon see, that criminal means once tolerated are soon preferred. They present a shorter cut to the object than through the highway of the moral virtues. Justifying perfidy and murder for public benefit, public benefit would soon become the pretext, and perfidy and murder the end; until rapacity, malice, revenge, and fear more dreadful than revenge, could satiate their insatiable appetites. Such must be the consequences of losing in the splendour of these triumphs of the rights of men, all natural sense of wrong and right.

But the Reverend Pastor exults in this 'leading in triumph,' because truly Louis XVIth was 'an arbitrary monarch;' that is, in other words, neither more nor less, than because he was Louis the XVIth, and because he had the misfortune to be born king of France, with the prerogatives of which, a long line of ancestors, and a long acquiescence of the people, without any act of his, had put him in possession. A misfortune it has indeed turned out to him, that he was born king of France. But misfortune is not crime, nor is indiscretion always the greatest guilt. I shall never think that a prince, the acts of whose whole reign were a series of concessions to his subjects, who was willing to relax his authority, to remit his prerogatives, to call his people to a share of freedom, not known, perhaps not desired by their ancestors; such a prince, though he should be subject to the common frailties attached to men and to princes, though he should have once thought it necessary to provide force against the desperate designs manifestly carrying on against his person, and the remnants of his authority; though all this should be taken into consideration, I shall be led with great difficulty to think he deserves the cruel and insulting triumph of Paris, and of Dr Price. I tremble for the cause of liberty, from such an example to kings. I tremble for the cause of humanity, in the unpunished outrages of the most wicked of mankind. But there are some people of that low and degenerate fashion of mind, that they look up with a sort of complacent awe and admiration to kings, who know to keep firm in their seat, to hold a strict hand over their subjects, to assert their prerogative, and by the awakened vigilance of a severe despotism, to guard against the very first approaches of freedom. Against such as these they never elevate their voice. Deserters from principle, listed with fortune, they never see any good in suffering virtue, nor any crime in prosperous usurpation.

If it could have been made clear to me, that the king and queen of France (those I mean who were such before the triumph) were inexorable and cruel tyrants, that they had formed a deliberate scheme for massacring the National Assembly (I think I have seen something like the latter insinuated in certain publications*) I should think their captivity just. If this be true, much more ought to have been done, but done, in my opinion, in another manner. The punishment of real tyrants is a noble and awful act of justice; and it has with truth been said to be consolatory to the human mind. But if I were to punish a wicked king, I should regard the dignity in avenging the crime. Justice is grave and decorous, and in its punishments rather seems to submit to a necessity, than to make a choice. Had Nero, or Agrippina, or Louis the Eleventh, or Charles the Ninth, been the subject; if Charles the Twelfth of Sweden, after the murder of Patkul, or his predecessor Christina,* after the murder of Monaldeschi, had fallen into your hands, Sir, or into mine, I am sure our conduct would have been different.

If the French King, or King of the French,* (or by whatever name he is known in the new vocabulary of your constitution) has in his own person, and that of his Queen, really deserved these unavowed but unavenged murderous attempts, and those subsequent indignities more cruel than murder, such a person would ill deserve even that subordinate executory trust, which I understand is to be placed in him; nor is he fit to be called chief in a nation which he has outraged and oppressed. A worse choice for such an office in a new commonwealth, than that of a deposed tyrant, could not possibly be made. But to degrade and insult a man as the worst of criminals, and afterwards to trust him in your highest concerns, as a faithful, honest, and zealous servant, is not consistent in reasoning, nor prudent in policy, nor safe in practice. Those who could make such an appointment must be guilty of a more flagrant breach of trust than any they have yet committed against the people. As this is the only crime in which your leading politicians could have acted inconsistently,

I conclude that there is no sort of ground for these horrid insinuations. I think no better of all the other calumnies.

In England, we give no credit to them. We are generous enemies: We are faithful allies. We spurn from us with disgust and indignation the slanders of those who bring us their anecdotes with the attestation of the flower-de-luce on their shoulder.* We have Lord George Gordon fast in Newgate;* and neither his being a public proselyte to Judaism, nor his having, in his zeal against Catholick priests and all sort of ecclesiastics, raised a mob (excuse the term, it is still in use here) which pulled down all our prisons, have preserved to him a liberty, of which he did not render himself worthy by a virtuous use of it. We have rebuilt Newgate, and tenanted the mansion. We have prisons almost as strong as the Bastile, for those who dare to libel the queens of France. In this spiritual retreat, let the noble libeller remain. Let him there meditate on his Thalmud, until he learns a conduct more becoming his birth and parts, and not so disgraceful to the antient religion to which he has become a proselyte; or until some persons from your side of the water, to please your new Hebrew brethren, shall ransom him. He may then be enabled to purchase, with the old hoards of the synagogue, and a very small poundage, on the long compound interest of the thirty pieces of silver (Dr Price has shewn us what miracles compound interest will perform in 1790 years) the lands which are lately discovered to have been usurped by the Gallican church. Send us your popish Archbishop of Paris, and we will send you our protestant Rabbin. We shall treat the person you send us in exchange like a gentleman and an honest man, as he is; but pray let him bring with him the fund of his hospitality, bounty, and charity; and, depend upon it, we shall never confiscate a shilling of that honourable and pious fund, nor think of enriching the treasury with the spoils of the poor-box.

To tell you the truth, my dear Sir, I think the honour of our nation to be somewhat concerned in the disclaimer of the proceedings of this society of the Old Jewry and the London Tavern. I have no man's proxy. I speak only from myself; when I disclaim, as I do with all possible earnestness, all communion with the actors in that triumph, or with the admirers of it. When I assert any thing else, as concerning the people of England, I speak from observation not from authority; but I speak from the experience I have had in a pretty extensive and mixed communication with the inhabitants of this kingdom, of all descriptions and ranks, and after a course of attentive observation, began early in life, and continued for near forty years, I have often been astonished, considering that we are divided from you but by a slender dyke of about twenty-four miles, and that the mutual intercourse between the two countries has lately been very great, to find how little you seem to know of us. I suspect that this is owing to your forming a judgment of this nation from certain publications, which do, very erroneously, if they do at all, represent the opinions and dispositions generally prevalent in England. The vanity, restlessness, petulance, and spirit of intrigue of several petty cabals, who attempt to hide their total want of consequence in bustle and noise, and puffing, and mutual quotation of each other, makes you imagine that our contemptuous neglect of their abilities is a mark of general acquiescence in their opinions. No such thing, I assure you. Because half a dozen grashoppers under a fern make the field ring with their importunate chink, whilst thousands of great cattle, reposed beneath the shadow of the British oak, chew the cud and are silent, pray do not imagine, that those who make the noise are the only inhabitants of the field; that of course, they are many in number; or that, after all, they are other than the little shrivelled, meagre, hopping, though loud and troublesome insects of the hour.

I almost venture to affirm, that not one in a hundred amongst us participates in the 'triumph' of the Revolution Society. If the king and queen of France, and their children, were to fall into our hands by the chance of war, in the most acrimonious of all hostilities (I deprecate such an event, I deprecate such hostility) they would be treated with another sort of triumphal entry into London. We formerly have had a king of France in that situation;* you have read how he was treated by the victor in the field; and in what manner he was afterwards received in England. Four hundred years have gone over us; but I believe we are not materially changed since that period. Thanks to our sullen resistancce to innovation, thanks to the cold sluggishness of our national character, we still bear the stamp of our forefathers. We have not (as I conceive) lost the generosity and dignity of thinking of the fourteenth century; nor as yet have we subtilized ourselves into savages. We are not the converts of Rousseau; we are not the disciples of Voltaire; Helvetius has made no progress amongst us. Atheists are not our preachers; madmen are not our lawgivers. We know that *we* have made no discoveries; and we think that no discoveries are to be made, in morality; nor many in the great principles of government, nor in the ideas of liberty, which were understood long before we were born, altogether as well as they will be after the grave has heaped its mould upon our presumption, and the silent tomb shall have imposed its law on our pert loquacity. In England we have not yet been completely embowelled of our natural entrails; we still feel within us, and we cherish and cultivate, those inbred sentiments which are the faithful guardians, the active monitors of our duty, the true supporters of all liberal and manly morals. We have not been drawn and trussed, in order that we may be filled, like stuffed birds in a museum, with chaff and rags, and paltry, blurred shreds of paper about the rights of man. We preserve the whole of our feelings still native and entire, unsophisticated by pedantry and infidelity. We have real hearts of flesh and blood beating in our bosoms. We fear God; we look up with awe to kings; with affection to parliaments; with duty to magistrates; with reverence to priests; and with respect to nobility.[1] Why? Because when such ideas are brought before our minds, it is *natural* to be so

[1] The English are, I conceive, misrepresented in a Letter published in one of the papers, by a gentleman thought to be a dissenting minister. When writing to Dr Price, of the spirit which prevails at Paris, he says, 'The spirit of the people in this place has abolished all the proud *distinctions* which the *king* and *nobles* had usurped in their minds; whether they talk of *the king, the noble, or the priest*, their whole language is that of the most *enlightened and liberal amongst the English*.' If this gentleman means to confine the terms *enlightened and liberal* to one set of men in England, it may be true. It is not generally so.

affected; because all other feelings are false and spurious, and tend to corrupt our minds, to vitiate our primary morals, to render us unfit for rational liberty; and by teaching us a servile, licentious, and abandoned insolence, to be our low sport for a few holidays, to make us perfectly fit for, and justly deserving of slavery, through the whole course of our lives.

You see, Sir, that in this enlightened age I am bold enough to confess, that we are generally men of untaught feelings; that instead of casting away all our old prejudices, we cherish them to a very considerable degree, and, to take more shame to ourselves, we cherish them because they are prejudices; and the longer they have lasted, and the more generally they have prevailed, the more we cherish them. We are afraid to put men to live and trade each on his own private stock of reason; because we suspect that this stock in each man is small, and that the individuals would be better to avail themselves of the general bank and capital of nations, and of ages. Many of our men of speculation, instead of exploding general prejudices, employ their sagacity to discover the latent wisdom which prevails in them. If they find what they seek, and they seldom fail, they think it more wise to continue the prejudice, with the reason involved, than to cast away the coat of prejudice, and to leave nothing but the naked reason; because prejudice, with its reason, has a motive to give action to that reason, and an affection which will give it permanence. Prejudice is of ready application in the emergency; it previously engages the mind in a steady course of wisdom and virtue, and does not leave the man hesitating in the moment of decision, sceptical, puzzled, and unresolved. Prejudice renders a man's virtue his habit; and not a series of unconnected acts. Through just prejudice, his duty becomes a part of his nature.

Your literary men, and your politicans, and so do the whole clan of the enlightened among us, essentially differ in these points. They have no respect for the wisdom of others; but they pay it off by a very full measure of confidence in their own. With them it is a sufficient motive to destroy an old scheme of things, because it is an old one. As to the new, they are in no sort of fear with regard to the duration of a building run up in haste; because duration is no object to those who think little or nothing has been done before their time, and who place all their hopes in discovery. They conceive, very systematically, that all things which give perpetuity are mischievous, and therefore they are at inexpiable war with all establishments. They think that government may vary like modes of dress, and with as little ill effect. That there needs no principle of attachment, except a sense of present conveniency, to any constitution of the state. They always speak as if they were of opinion that there is a singular species of compact between them and their magistrates, which binds the magistrate, but which has nothing reciprocal in it, but that the majesty of the people has a right to dissolve it without any reason, but its will. Their attachment to their country itself, is only so far as it agrees with some of their fleeting projects; it begins and ends with that scheme of polity which falls in with their momentary opinion.

These doctrines, or rather sentiments, seem prevalent with your new statesmen. But they are wholly different from those on which we have always acted in this country.

I hear it is sometimes given out in France, that what is doing among you is after the example of England. I beg leave to affirm, that scarcely any thing done with you has originated from the practice or the prevalent opinions of this people, either in the act or in the spirit of the proceeding. Let me add, that we are as unwilling to learn these lessons from France, as we are sure that we never taught them to that nation. The cabals here who take a sort of share in your transactions as yet consist but of an handful of people. If unfortunately by their intrigues, their sermons, their publications, and by a confidence derived from an expected union with the counsels and forces of the French nation, they should draw considerable numbers into their faction, and in consequence should seriously attempt any thing here in imitation of what has been done with you, the event, I dare venture to prophesy, will be, that, with some trouble to their country, they will soon accomplish their own destruction. This people refused to change their law in remote ages, from respect to the infallibility of popes; and they will not now alter it from a pious implicit faith in the dogmatism of philosophers; though the former was armed with the anathema and crusade, and though the latter should act with the libel and the lamp-iron.

Formerly your affairs were your own concern only. We felt for them as men; but we kept aloof from them, because we were not citizens of France. But when we see the model held up to ourselves, we must feel as Englishmen, and feeling, we must provide as Englishmen. Your affairs, in spite of us, are made a part of our interest; so far at least as to keep at a distance your panacea, or your plague. If it be a panacea, we do not want it. We know the consequences of unnecessary physic. If it be a plague; it is such a plague, that the precautions of the most severe quarantine ought to be established against it.

I hear on all hands that a cabal, calling itself philosophic, receives the glory of many of the late proceedings; and that their opinions and systems are the true actuating spirit of the whole of them. I have heard of no party in England, literary or political, at any time, known by such a description. It is not with you composed of those men, is it? whom the vulgar, in their blunt, homely style, commonly call Atheists and Infidels? If it be, I admit that we too have had writers of that description, who made some noise in their day. At present they repose in lasting oblivion. Who, born within the last forty years, has read one word of Collins, and Toland, and Tindal, and Chubb, and Morgan, and that whole race who called themselves Freethinkers?* Who now reads Bolingbroke?* Who ever read him through? Ask the booksellers of London what is become of all these lights of the world. In as few years their few successors will go to the family vault of 'all the Capulets.'* But whatever they were, or are, with us, they were and are wholly unconnected individuals. With us they kept the common nature of their kind, and were not gregarious. They never acted in corps, nor were known as a faction in the state, nor presumed to influence, in that name or character, or for the purposes of such a faction, on any of our public concerns. Whether they ought so to exist, and so be permitted to act, is another question. As such cabals have not existed in England, so neither has the spirit of them had any influence in establishing the original frame of our constitution, or in any one of the several reparations and improvements it has undergone. The whole has been done under the auspices, and is confirmed by the sanctions of religion and piety. The whole has emanated from the simplicity of our national character, and from a sort of native plainness and directness of understanding, which for a long time characterized those men who have successively obtained authority amongst us. This disposition still remains, at least in the great body of the people.

We know, and what is better we feel inwardly, that religion is the basis of civil society, and the source of all good and of all comfort.[1] In England we are so convinced of this, that there is no rust of superstition, with which the accumulated absurdity of the human mind might have crusted it over in the course of ages, that ninety-nine in an hundred of the people of England would not prefer to impiety. We shall never be such fools as to call in an enemy to the substance of any system to remove its corruptions, to supply its defects, or to perfect its construction. If our religious tenets should ever want a further elucidation, we shall not call on atheism to explain them. We shall not light up our temple from that unhallowed fire. It will be illuminated with other lights. It will be perfumed with other incense, than the infectious stuff which is imported by the smugglers of adulterated metaphysics. If our ecclesiastical establishment should want a revision, it is not avarice or rapacity, public or private, that we shall employ for the audit, or receipt, or application of its consecrated revenue.—Violently condemning neither the Greek nor the Armenian, nor, since heats are subsided, the Roman system of religion, we prefer the Protestant; not because we think it has less of the Christian religion in it, but because, in our judgment, it has more. We are protestants, not from indifference but from zeal.

We know, and it is our pride to know, that man is by his

---

[1] Sit igitur hoc ab initio persuasum civibus, dominos esse omnium rerum ac moderatores, deos; eaque, quae gerantur, eorum geri vi, ditione, ac numine; eosdemque optime de genere hominum mereri; et qualis quisque sit, quid agat, quid in se admittat, qua mente, qua pietate colat religiones intueri: piorum et impiorum habere rationem. His enim rebus imbutae mentes haud sane abhorrebunt ab utili et a vera sententia. Cic. de Legibus, 1. 2.*

constitution a religious animal; that atheism is against, not only our reason but our instincts; and that it cannot prevail long. But if, in the moment of riot, and in a drunken delirium from the hot spirit drawn out of the alembick of hell, which in France is now so furiously boiling, we should uncover our nakedness by throwing off the Christian religion which has hitherto been our boast and comfort, and one great source of civilization amongst us, and among many other nations, we are apprehensive (being well aware that the mind will not endure a void) that some uncouth, pernicious, and degrading superstition, might take place of it.

For that reason, before we take from our establishment the natural human means of estimation, and give it up to contempt, as you have done, and in doing it have incurred the penalties you well deserve to suffer, we desire that some other may be presented to us in the place of it. We shall then form our judgment.

On these ideas, instead of quarrelling with establishments, as some do, who have made a philosophy and a religion of their hostility to such institutions, we cleave closely to them. We are resolved to keep an established church, an established monarchy, an established aristocracy, and an established democracy, each in the degree it exists, and in no greater. I shall shew you presently how much of each of these we possess.

It has been the misfortune (not as these gentlemen think it, the glory) of this age, that every thing is to be discussed, as if the constitution of our country were to be always a subject rather of altercation than enjoyment. For this reason, as well as for the satisfaction of those among you (if any such you have among you) who may wish to profit of examples, I venture to trouble you with a few thoughts upon each of these establishments. I do not think they were unwise in antient Rome, who, when they wished to new-model their laws, sent commissioners to examine the best constituted republics within their reach.

First, I beg leave to speak of our church establishment, which is the first of our prejudices, not a prejudice destitute of reason, but involving in it profound and extensive wisdom. I speak of it first. It is first, and last, and midst in our minds.

For, taking ground on that religious system, of which we are now in possession, we continue to act on the early received, and uniformly continued sense of mankind. That sense not only, like a wise architect, hath built up the august fabric of states, but like a provident proprietor, to preserve the structure from prophanation and ruin, as a sacred temple, purged from all the impurities of fraud, and violence, and injustice, and tyranny, hath solemnly and for ever consecrated the commonwealth, and all that officiate in it. This consecration is made, that all who administer in the government of men, in which they stand in the person of God himself, should have high and worthy notions of their function and destination; that their hope should be full of immortality; that they should not look to the paltry pelf of the moment, nor to the temporary and transient praise of the vulgar, but to a solid, permanent existence, in the permanent part of their nature, and to a permanent fame and glory, in the example they leave as a rich inheritance to the world.

Such sublime principles ought to be infused into persons of exalted situations; and religious establishments provided, that may continually revive and enforce them. Every sort of moral, every sort of civil, every sort of politic institution, aiding the rational and natural ties that connect the human under-standing and affections to the divine, are not more than necessary, in order to build up that wonderful structure, Man; whose prerogative it is, to be in a great degree a creature of his own making, and who when made as he ought to be made, is destined to hold no trivial place in the creation. But whenever man is put over men, as the better nature ought ever to preside, in that case more particularly, he should as nearly as possible be approximated to his perfection.

The consecration of the state, by a state religious establishment, is necessary also to operate with an wholesome awe upon free citizens; because, in order to secure their freedom, they must enjoy some determinate portion of power. To them therefore a religion connected with the state, and with their duty towards it, becomes even more necessary than in such societies, where the people by the terms of their subjection are confined to private sentiments, and the management of their own family concerns. All persons possessing any portion of power ought to be strongly and awefully impressed with an idea that they act in trust; and that they are to account for their conduct in that trust to the one great master; author and founder of society.

This principle ought even to be more strongly impressed upon the minds of those who compose the collective sovereignty than upon those of single princes. Without instruments, these princes can do nothing. Whoever uses instruments, in finding helps, finds also impediments. Their power is therefore by no means compleat; nor are they safe in extreme abuse. Such persons, however elevated by flattery, arrogance, and self-opinion, must be sensible that, whether covered or not by positive law, in some way or other they are accountable even here for the abuse of their trust. If they are not cut off by a rebellion of their people, they may be strangled by the very Janissaries kept for their security against all other rebellion. Thus we have seen the king of France sold by his soldiers for an encrease of pay. But where popular authority is absolute and unrestrained, the people have an infinitely greater, because a far better founded confidence in their own power. They are themselves, in a great measure, their own instruments. They are nearer to their objects. Besides, they are less under responsibility to one of the greatest controlling powers on earth, the sense of fame and estimation. The share of infamy that is likely to fall to the lot of each individual in public acts, is small indeed; the operation of opinion being in the inverse ratio to the number of those who abuse power. Their own approbation of their own acts has to them the appearance of a public judgment in their favour. A perfect democracy is therefore the most shameless thing in the world. As it is the most shameless, it is also the most fearless. No man apprehends in his person he can be made subject to punishment. Certainly the people at large never ought: for as all punishments are for example towards the conservation of the people at large, the people at large can never become the subject of punishment by any human hand.[1] It is therefore of

---

[1] Quicquid multis peccatur inultum.*

infinite importance that they should not be suffered to imagine that their will, any more than that of kings, is the standard of right and wrong. They ought to be persuaded that they are full as little entitled, and far less qualified, with safety to themselves, to use any arbitrary power whatsoever; that therefore they are not, under a false shew of liberty, but, in truth, to exercise an unnatural inverted domination, tyrannically to exact, from those who officiate in the state, not an entire devotion to their interest, which is their right, but an abject submission to their occasional will; extinguishing thereby, in all those who serve them, all moral principle, all sense of dignity, all use of judgment, and all consistency of character, whilst by the very same process they give themselves up a proper, a suitable, but a most contemptible prey to the servile ambition of popular sycophants or courtly flatterers.

When the people have emptied themselves of all the lust of selfish will, which without religion it is utterly impossible they ever should, when they are conscious that they exercise, and exercise perhaps in an higher link of the order of delegation, the power, which to be legitimate must be according to that eternal immutable law, in which will and reason are the same, they will be more careful how they place power in base and incapable hands. In their nomination to office, they will not appoint to the exercise of authority, as to a pitiful job, but as to an holy function; not according to their sordid selfish interest, nor to their wanton caprice, nor to their arbitrary will; but they will confer that power (which any man may well tremble to give or to receive) on those only, in whom they may discern that predominant proportion of active virtue and wisdom, taken together and fitted to the charge, such, as in the great and inevitable mixed mass of human imperfections and infirmities, is to be found.

When they are habitually convinced that no evil can be acceptable, either in the act or the permission, to him whose essence is good, they will be better able to extirpate out of the minds of all magistrates, civil, ecclesiastical, or military, any thing that bears the least resemblance to a proud and lawless domination.

But one of the first and most leading principles on which the commonwealth and the laws are consecrated, is lest the temporary possessors and life-renters in it, unmindful of what they have received from their ancestors, or of what is due to their posterity, should act as if they were the entire masters; that they should not think it amongst their rights to cut off the entail, or commit waste on the inheritance, by destroying at their pleasure the whole original fabric of their society; hazarding to leave to those who come after them, a ruin instead of an habitation—and teaching these successors as little to respect their contrivances, as they had themselves respected the institutions of their forefathers. By this un-principled facility of changing the state as often, and as much, and in as many ways as there are floating fancies or fashions, the whole chain and continuity of the commonwealth would be broken. No one generation could link with the other. Men would become little better than the flies of a summer.

And first of all the science of jurisprudence, the pride of the human intellect, which, with all its defects, redundancies, and errors, is the collected reason of ages, combining the principles of original justice with the infinite variety of human concerns, as a heap of old exploded errors, would be no longer studied. Personal self-sufficiency and arrogance (the certain attendants upon all those who have never experienced a wisdom greater than their own) would usurp the tribunal. Of course, no certain laws, establishing invariable grounds of hope and fear, would keep the actions of men in a certain course, or direct them to a certain end. Nothing stable in the modes of holding property, or exercising function, could form a solid ground on which any parent could speculate in the education of his offspring, or in a choice for their future establishment in the world. No principles would be early worked into the habits. As soon as the most able instructor had completed his laborious course of institution, instead of sending forth his pupil, accomplished in a virtuous discipline, fitted to procure him attention and respect, in his place in society, he would find every thing altered; and that he had turned out a poor creature to the contempt and derision of the world, ignorant of the true grounds of estimation. Who would insure a tender and delicate sense of honour to beat almost with the first pulses of the heart, when no man could know what would be the test of honour in a nation, continually varying the standard of its coin? No part of life would retain its acquisitions. Barbarism with regard to science and literature, unskilfulness with regard to arts and manufactures, would infallibly succeed to the want of a steady education and settled principle; and thus the commonwealth itself would, in a few generations, crumble away, be disconnected into the dust and powder of individuality, and at length dispersed to all the winds of heaven.

To avoid therefore the evils of inconstancy and versatility, ten thousand times worse than those of obstinacy and the blindest prejudice, we have consecrated the state, that no man should approach to look into its defects or corruptions but with due caution; that he should never dream of beginning its reformation by its subversion; that he should approach to the faults of the state as to the wounds of a father, with pious awe and trembling sollicitude. By this wise prejudice we are taught to look with horror on those children of their country who are prompt rashly to hack that aged parent in pieces, and put him into the kettle of magicians, in hopes that by their poisonous weeds, and wild incantations, they may regenerate the paternal constitution, and renovate their father's life.

Society is indeed a contract. Subordinate contracts for objects of mere occasional interest may be dissolved at pleasure—but the state ought not to be considered as nothing better than a partnership agreement in a trade of pepper and coffee, callico or tobacco, or some other such low concern, to be taken up for a little temporary interest, and to be dissolved by the fancy of the parties. It is to be looked on with other reverence; because it is not a partnership in things subservient only to the gross animal existence of a temporary and perishable nature. It is a partnership in all science; a partnership in all art; a partnership in every virtue, and in all perfection. As the ends of such a partnership cannot be obtained in many generations, it becomes a partnership not only between those who are living, but between those who are living, those who are dead, and those who are to be born.

Each contract of each particular state is but a clause in the great primaeval contract of eternal society, linking the lower with the higher natures, connecting the visible and invisible world, according to a fixed compact sanctioned by the inviolable oath which holds all physical and all moral natures, each in their appointed place. This law is not subject to the will of those, who by an obligation above them, and infinitely superior, are bound to submit their will to that law. The municipal corporations of that universal kingdom are not morally at liberty at their pleasure, and on their speculations of a contingent improvement, wholly to separate and tear asunder the bands of their subordinate community, and to dissolve it into an unsocial, uncivil, unconnected chaos of elementary principles. It is the first and supreme necessity only, a necessity that is not chosen but chooses, a necessity paramount to deliberation, that admits no discussion, and demands no evidence, which alone can justify a resort to anarchy. This necessity is not exception to the rule; because this necessity itself is a part too of that moral and physical disposition of things to which man must be obedient by consent or force; but if that which is only submission to necessity should be made the object of choice, the law is broken, nature is disobeyed, and the rebellious are outlawed, cast forth, and exiled, from this world of reason, and order, and peace, and virtue, and fruitful penitence, into the antagonist world of madness, discord, vice, confusion, and unavailing sorrow.

These, my dear Sir, are, were, and I think long will be the sentiments of not the least learned and reflecting part of this kingdom. They who are included in the description, form their opinions on such grounds as such persons ought to form them. The less enquiring receive them from an authority which those whom Providence dooms to live on trust need not be ashamed to rely on. These two sorts of men move in the same direction, tho' in a different place. They both move with the order of the universe. They all know or feel this great antient truth: 'Quod illi principi et praepotenti Deo qui omnem hunc mundum regit, nihil eorum quae quidem fiant in terris acceptius quam concilia et caetus hominum jure sociati quae civitates appellantur.'* They take this tenet of the head and heart, not from the great name which it immediately bears, nor from the greater from whence it is derived; but from that which alone can give true weight and sanction to any learned opinion, the common nature and common relation of men. Persuaded that all things ought to be done with reference, and referring all to the point of reference to which all should be directed, they think themselves bound, not only as individuals in the sanctuary of the heart, or as congregated in that personal capacity, to renew the memory of their high origin and cast; but also in their corporate character to perform their national homage to the institutor, and author and protector of civil society; without which civil society man could not by any possibility arrive at the perfection of which his nature is capable, nor even make a remote and faint approach to it. They conceive that He who gave our nature to be perfected by our virtue, willed also the necessary means of its perfection—He willed therefore the state—He willed its connexion with the source and original archetype of all perfection. They who are convinced of this his will, which is the law of laws and the sovereign of sovereigns, cannot think it reprehensible, that this our corporate fealty and homage, that this our recognition of a signiory paramount, I had almost said this oblation of the state itself, as a worthy offering on the high altar of universal praise, should be performed as all publick solemn acts are performed, in buildings, in musick, in decoration, in speech, in the dignity of persons, according to the customs of mankind, taught by their nature; that is, with modest splendour, with unassuming state, with mild majesty and sober pomp. For those purposes they think some part of the wealth of the country is as usefully employed as it can be, in fomenting the luxury of individuals. It is the publick ornament. It is the publick consolation. It nourishes the publick hope. The poorest man finds his own importance and dignity in it, whilst the wealth and pride of individuals at every moment makes the man of humble rank and fortune sensible of his inferiority, and degrades and vilifies his condition. It is for the man in humble life, and to raise his nature, and to put him in mind of a state in which the privileges of opulence will cease, when he will be equal by nature, and may be more than equal by virtue, that this portion of the general wealth of his country is employed and sanctified.

I assure you I do not aim at singularity. I give you opinions which have been accepted amongst us, from very early times to this moment, with a continued and general approbation, and which indeed are so worked into my mind, that I am unable to distinguish what I have learned from others from the results of my own meditation.

It is on some such principles that the majority of the people of England, far from thinking a religious, national establishment unlawful, hardly think it lawful to be without one. In France you are wholly mistaken if you do not believe us above all other things attached to it, and beyond all other nations; and when this people has acted unwisely and unjustifiably in its favour (as in some instances they have done most certainly) in their very errors you will at least discover their zeal.

This principle runs through the whole system of their polity. They do not consider their church establishment as convenient, but as essential to their state; not as a thing heterogeneous and separable; something added for accommodation; what they may either keep up or lay aside, according to their temporary ideas of convenience. They consider it as the foundation of their whole constitution, with which, and with every part of which, it holds an indissoluble union. Church and state are ideas inseparable in their minds, and scarcely is the one ever mentioned without mentioning the other.

Our education is so formed as to confirm and fix this impression. Our education is in a manner wholly in the hands of ecclesiastics, and in all stages from infancy to manhood. Even when our youth, leaving schools and universities, enter that most important period of life which begins to link experience and study together, and when with that view they visit other countries, instead of old domestics whom we have seen as governors to principal men from other parts, three-fourths of those who go abroad with our young nobility and gentlemen are ecclesiastics; not as austere masters, nor as mere followers; but as friends and companions of a graver character, and not seldom persons as well born as themselves. With them, as relations, they most commonly keep up a close connexion through life. By this connexion we conceive that we attach our gentlemen to the church; and we liberalize the church by an intercourse with the leading characters of the country.

So tenacious are we of the old ecclesiastical modes and fashions of institution, that very little alteration has been made in them since the fourteenth or fifteenth century; adhering in this particular, as in all things else, to our old settled maxim, never entirely nor at once to depart from antiquity. We found these old institutions, on the whole, favourable to morality and discipline; and we thought they were susceptible of amendment, without altering the ground. We thought that they were capable of receiving and meliorating, and above all of preserving the accessions of science and literature, as the order of Providence should successively produce them. And after all, with this Gothic and monkish education (for such it is in the ground-work) we may put in our claim to as ample and as early a share in all the improvements in science, in arts, and in literature, which have illuminated and adorned the modern world, as any other nation in Europe; we think one main cause of this improvement was our not despising the patrimony of knowledge which was left us by our forefathers.

It is from our attachment to a church establishment that the English nation did not think it wise to entrust that great fundamental interest of the whole to what they trust no part of their civil or military public service, that is to the unsteady and precarious contribution of individuals. They go further. They certainly never have suffered and never will suffer the fixed estate of the church to be converted into a pension, to depend on the treasury, and to be delayed, withheld, or perhaps to be extinguished by fiscal difficulties; which difficulties may sometimes be pretended for political purposes, and are in fact often brought on by the extravagance, negligence, and rapacity of politicians. The people of England think that they have constitutional motives, as well as religious, against any project of turning their independent

clergy into ecclesiastical pensioners of state. They tremble for
their liberty, from the influence of a clergy dependent on the
crown; they tremble for the public tranquillity from the
disorders of a factious clergy, if it were made to depend upon
any other than the crown. They therefore made their church,
like their king and their nobility, independent.

From the united considerations of religion and constitutional policy, from their opinion of a duty to make a sure
provision for the consolation of the feeble and the instruction
of the ignorant, they have incorporated and identified the
estate of the church with the mass of *private property*, of
which the state is not the proprietor, either for use or
dominion, but the guardian only and the regulator.* They
have ordained that the provision of this establishment might
be as stable as the earth on which it stands, and should not
fluctuate with the Euripus* of funds and actions.

The men of England, the men, I mean, of light and leading
in England, whose wisdom (if they have any) is open and
direct, would be ashamed, as of a silly deceitful trick, to
profess any religion in name, which by their proceedings they
appeared to contemn. If by their conduct (the only language
that rarely lies) they seemed to regard the great ruling
principle of the moral and natural world, as a mere invention
to keep the vulgar in obedience, they apprehend that by such a
conduct they would defeat the politic purpose they have in
view. They would find it difficult to make others to believe in
a system to which they manifestly gave no credit themselves.
The Christian statesmen of this land would indeed first
provide for the *multitude*; because it is the *multitude*; and is
therefore, as such, the first object in the ecclesiastical
institution, and in all institutions. They have been taught, that
the circumstance of the gospel's being preached to the poor,
was one of the great tests of its true mission. They think,
therefore, that those do not believe it, who do not take care it
should be preached to the poor. But as they know that charity
is not confined to any one description, but ought to apply
itself to all men who have wants, they are not deprived of a
due and anxious sensation of pity to the distresses of the
miserable great. They are not repelled through a fastidious

delicacy, at the stench of their arrogance and presumption, from a medicinal attention to their mental blotches and running sores. They are sensible, that religious instruction is of more consequence to them than to any others; from the greatness of the temptation to which they are exposed; from the important consequences that attend their faults; from the contagion of their ill example; from the necessity of bowing down the stubborn neck of their pride and ambition to the yoke of moderation and virtue; from a consideration of the fat stupidity and gross ignorance concerning what imports men most to know, which prevails at courts, and at the head of armies, and in senates, as much as at the loom and in the field.

The English people are satisfied, that to the great the consolations of religion are as necessary as its instructions. They too are among the unhappy. They feel personal pain and domestic sorrow. In these they have no privilege, but are subject to pay their full contingent to the contributions levied on mortality. They want this sovereign balm under their gnawing cares and anxieties, which being less conversant about the limited wants of animal life, range without limit, and are diversified by infinite combinations in the wild and unbounded regions of imagination. Some charitable dole is wanting to these, our often very unhappy brethren, to fill the gloomy void that reigns in minds which have nothing on earth to hope or fear; something to relieve in the killing languour and over-laboured lassitude of those who have nothing to do; something to excite an appetite to existence in the palled satiety which attends on all pleasures which may be bought, where nature is not left to her own process, where even desire is anticipated, and therefore fruition defeated by meditated schemes and contrivances of delight; and no interval, no obstacle, is interposed between the wish and the accomplishment.

The people of England know how little influence the teachers of religion are likely to have with the wealthy and powerful of long standing, and how much less with the newly fortunate, if they appear in a manner no way assorted to those with whom they must associate, and over whom they must even exercise, in some cases, something like an authority. What must they think of that body of teachers, if they see it in no part above the establishment of their domestic servants? If the poverty were voluntary, there might be some difference. Strong instances of self-denial operate powerfully on our minds; and a man who has no wants has obtained great freedom and firmness, and even dignity. But as the mass of any description of men are but men, and their poverty cannot be voluntary, that disrespect which attends upon all Lay poverty, will not depart from the Ecclesiastical. Our provident constitution has therefore taken care that those who are to instruct presumptuous ignorance, those who are to be censors over insolent vice, should neither incur their contempt, nor live upon their alms; nor will it tempt the rich to a neglect of the true medicine of their minds. For these reasons, whilst we provide first for the poor, and with a parental solicitude, we have not relegated religion (like something we were ashamed to shew) to obscure municipalities or rustic villages. No! We will have her to exalt her mitred front in courts and parliaments. We will have her mixed throughout the whole mass of life, and blended with all the classes of society. The people of England will shew to the haughty potentates of the world, and to their talking sophisters, that a free, a generous, an informed nation, honours the high magistrates of its church; that it will not suffer the insolence of wealth and titles, or any other species of proud pretension, to look down with scorn upon what they look up to with reverence; nor presume to trample on that acquired personal nobility, which they intend always to be, and which often is the fruit, not the reward, (for what can be the reward?) of learning, piety, and virtue. They can see, without pain or grudging, an Archbishop precede a Duke. They can see a Bishop of Durham, or a Bishop of Winchester, in possession of ten thousand pounds a year; and cannot conceive why it is in worse hands than estates to the like amount in the hands of this Earl, or that Squire; although it may be true, that so many dogs and horses are not kept by the former, and fed with the victuals which ought to nourish the children of the people. It is true, the whole church revenue is not always employed, and to every shilling, in charity; nor perhaps ought it; but something is generally so employed. It is better to cherish virtue and humanity, by leaving much to free will, even with some loss to the object, than to attempt to make men mere machines and instruments of a political benevolence. The world on the whole will gain by a liberty, without which virtue cannot exist.

When once the commonwealth has established the estates of the church as property, it can, consistently, hear nothing of the more or the less. Too much and too little are treason against property. What evil can arise from the quantity in any hand, whilst the supreme authority has the full, sovereign superintendance over this, as over all property, to prevent every species of abuse; and, whenever it notably deviates, to give to it a direction agreeable to the purposes of its institution.

In England most of us conceive that it is envy and malignity towards those who are often the beginners of their own fortune, and not a love of the self-denial and mortification of the antient church, that makes some look askance at the distinctions, and honours, and revenues, which, taken from no person, are set apart for virtue. The ears of the people of England are distinguishing. They hear these men speak broad. Their tongue betrays them. Their language is in the *patois* of fraud; in the cant and gibberish of hypocrisy. The people of England must think so, when these praters affect to carry back the clergy to that primitive evangelic poverty which, in the spirit, ought always to exist in them, (and in us too, however we may like it) but in the thing must be varied, when the relation of that body to the state is altered; when manners, when modes of life, when indeed the whole order of human affairs has undergone a total revolution. We shall believe those reformers to be then honest enthusiasts, not as now we think them, cheats and deceivers, when we see them throwing their own goods into common, and submitting their own persons to the austere discipline of the early church.

With these ideas rooted in their minds, the commons of Great Britain, in the national emergencies, will never seek their resource from the confiscation of the estates of the church and poor. Sacrilege and proscription are not among the ways and means in our committee of supply. The Jews in Change Alley have not yet dared to hint their hopes of a mortgage on the revenues belonging to the see of Canterbury. I am not afraid that I shall be disavowed, when I assure you that there is not *one* public man in this kingdom, whom you would wish to quote; no not one of any party or description, who does not reprobate the dishonest, perfidious, and cruel confiscation which the national assembly has been compelled to make of that property which it was their first duty to protect.*

It is with the exultation of a little national pride I tell you, that those amongst us who have wished to pledge the societies of Paris in the cup of their abominations, have been disappointed. The robbery of your church has proved a security to the possessions of ours. It has roused the people. They see with horror and alarm that enormous and shameless act of proscription. It has opened, and will more and more open their eyes upon the selfish enlargement of mind, and the narrow liberality of sentiment of insidious men, which commencing in close hypocrisy and fraud have ended in open violence and rapine. At home we behold similar beginnings. We are on our guard against similar conclusions.

I hope we shall never be so totally lost to all sense of the duties imposed upon us by the law of social union, as, upon any pretext of public service, to confiscate the goods of a single unoffending citizen. Who but a tyrant (a name expressive of every thing which can vitiate and degrade human nature) could think of seizing on the property of men, unaccused, unheard, untried, by whole descriptions, by hundreds and thousands together? who that had not lost every trace of humanity could think of casting down men of exalted rank and sacred function, some of them of an age to call at once for reverence and compassion, of casting them down from the highest situation in the commonwealth, wherein they were maintained by their own landed property, to a state of indigence, depression and contempt?

The confiscators truly have made some allowance to their victims from the scraps and fragments of their own tables from which they have been so harshly driven, and which have been so bountifully spread for a feast to the harpies of usury. But to drive men from independence to live on alms is itself great cruelty. That which might be a tolerable condition to men in one state of life, and not habituated to other things, may, when all these circumstances are altered, be a dreadful revolution; and one to which a virtuous mind would feel pain in condemning any guilt except that which would demand the life of the offender. But to many minds this punishment of *degradation* and *infamy* is worse than death. Undoubtedly it is an infinite aggravation of this cruel suffering, that the persons who were taught a double prejudice in favour of religion, by education and by the place they held in the administration of its functions, are to receive the remnants of their property as alms from the profane and impious hands of those who had plundered them of all the rest; to receive (if they are at all to receive) not from the charitable contributions of the faithful, but from the insolent tenderness of known and avowed Atheism, the maintenance of religion, measured out to them on the standard of the contempt in which it is held; and for the purpose of rendering those who receive the allowance vile and of no estimation in the eyes of mankind.

But this act of seizure of property, it seems, is a judgment in law, and not a confiscation. They have, it seems, found out in the academies of the *Palais Royale*, and the *Jacobins*,* that certain men had no right to the possessions which they held under law, usage, the decisions of courts, and the accumulated prescription of a thousand years. They say that ecclesiastics are fictitious persons, creatures of the state; whom at pleasure they may destroy, and of course limit and modify in every particular; that the goods they possess are not properly theirs, but belong to the state which created the fiction; and we are therefore not to trouble ourselves with what they may suffer in their natural feelings and natural persons, on account of what is done towards them in this their constructive character. Of what import is it, under what names you injure men, and deprive them of the just emoluments of a profession, in which they were not only permitted but encouraged by the state to engage; and upon the supposed certainty of which emoluments they had formed the plan of their lives, contracted debts, and led multitudes to an entire dependence upon them?

You do not imagine, Sir, that I am going to compliment this miserable distinction of persons with any long discussion. The arguments of tyranny are as contemptible as its force is dreadful. Had not your confiscators by their early crimes obtained a power which secures indemnity to all the crimes of which they have since been guilty, or that they can commit, it is not the syllogism of the logician but the lash of the executioner that would have refuted a sophistry which becomes an accomplice of theft and murder. The sophistick tyrants of Paris are loud in their declamations against the departed regal tyrants who in former ages have vexed the world. They are thus bold, because they are safe from the dungeons and iron cages of their old masters. Shall we be more tender of the tyrants of our own time, when we see them acting worse tragedies under our eyes? shall we not use the same liberty that they do, when we can use it with the same safety? when to speak honest truth only requires a contempt of the opinions of those who actions we abhor?

This outrage on all the rights of property was at first covered with what, on the system of their conduct, was the most astonishing of all pretexts—a regard to national faith. The enemies to property at first pretended a most tender, delicate, and scrupulous anxiety for keeping the king's engagements with the public creditor. These professors of the rights of men are so busy in teaching others, that they have not leisure to learn any thing themselves; otherwise they would have known that it is to the property of the citizen, and not to the demands of the creditor of the state, that the first and original faith of civil society is pledged. The claim of the citizen is prior in time, paramount in title, superior in equity. The fortunes of individuals, whether possessed by acquisition, or by descent, or in virtue of a participation in the goods of some community, were no part of the creditor's security, expressed or implied. They never so much as entered into his head when he made his bargain. He well knew that the public, whether represented by a monarch, or by a senate, can pledge nothing but the public estate; and it can have no public estate, except in what it derives from a just and proportioned imposition upon the citizens at large. This was engage, and nothing else could be engaged to the public creditor. No man can mortgage his injustice as a pawn for his fidelity.

It is impossible to avoid some observation on the contradictions caused by the extreme rigour and the extreme laxity of the new public faith, which influenced in this transaction, and which influenced not according to the nature of the obligation, but to the description of the persons to whom it was engaged. No acts of the old government of the kings of France are held valid in the National Assembly, except its pecuniary engagements; acts of all others of the most ambiguous legality. The rest of the acts of that royal government are considered in so odious a light, that to have a claim under its authority is looked on as a sort of crime. A pension, given as a reward for service to the state, is surely as good a ground of property as any security for money advanced to the state. It is a better; for money is paid, and well paid, to obtain that service. We have however seen multitudes of people under this description in France, who never had been deprived of their allowances by the most arbitrary ministers, in the most arbitrary times, by this assembly of the rights of men, robbed without mercy. They were told, in answer to their claim to the bread earned with their blood, that their services had not been rendered to the country that now exists.

This laxity of public faith is not confined to those unfortunate persons. The assembly, with perfect consistency it must be owned, is engaged in a respectable deliberation how far it is bound by the treaties made with other nations under the former government, and their Committee is to report which of them they ought to ratify, and which not. By this means they have put the external fidelity of this virgin state on a par with its internal.

It is not easy to conceive upon what rational principle the royal government should not, of the two, rather have possessed the power of rewarding service, and making treaties, in virtue of its prerogative, than that of pledging to creditors the revenue of the state actual and possible. The treasure of the nation, of all things, has been the least allowed to the preprogative of the king of France, or to the prerogative of any king in Europe. To mortgage the public revenue implies the sovereign dominion, in the fullest sense, over the public purse. It goes far beyond the trust even of a temporary and occasional taxation. The acts however of that dangerous power (the distinctive mark of a boundless despotism) have been alone held sacred. Whence arose this preference given by a democratic assembly to a body of property deriving its title from the most critical and obnoxious of all the exertions of monarchical authority? Reason can furnish nothing to reconcile inconsistency; nor can partial favour be accounted for upon equitable principles. But the contradiction and partiality which admit no justification, are not the less without an adequate cause; and that cause I do not think it difficult to discover.

By the vast debt of France a great monied interest had insensibly grown up, and with it a great power.* By the ancient usages which prevailed in that kingdom, the general circulation of property, and in particular the mutual convertibility of land into money, and of money into land, had always been a matter of difficulty. Family settlements, rather more general and more strict than they are in England, the *jus retractus*,* the great mass of landed property held by the crown, and by a maxim of French law held unalienably, the vast estates of the ecclesiastic corporations,—all these had kept the landed and monied interests more separated in France, less miscible, and the owners of the two distinct species of property not so well disposed to each other as they are in this country.

The monied property was long looked on with rather an evil eye by the people. They saw it connected with their distresses, and aggravating them. It was no less envied by the old landed interests, partly for the same reasons that rendered it obnoxious to the people, but much more so as it eclipsed, by the splendour of an ostentatious luxury, the unendowed pedigrees and naked titles of several among the nobility. Even when the nobility, which represented the more permanent landed interest, united themselves by marriage (which some-times was the case) with the other description, the wealth what saved the family from ruin, was supposed to contaminate and degrade it. Thus the enmities and heart-burnings of these parties were encreased even by the usual means by which discord is made to cease, and quarrels are turned into friendship. In the mean time, the pride of the wealthy men, not noble or newly noble, encreased with its cause. They felt with resentment an inferiority, the grounds of which they did not acknowledge. There was no measure to which they were not willing to lend themselves, in order to be revenged of the outrages of this rival pride, and to exalt their wealth to what they considered as its natural rank and estimation. They struck at the nobility through the crown and the church. They attacked them particularly on the side on which they thought them the most vulnerable, that is, the possessions of the church, which, through the patronage of the crown, generally devolved upon the nobility. The bishopricks, and the great commendatory abbies, were, with few exceptions, held by that order.

In this state of real, though not always perceived warfare between the noble ancient landed interest, and the new monied interest, the greatest because the most applicable strength was in the hands of the latter. The monied interest is in its nature more ready for any adventure; and its possessors more disposed to new enterprizes of any kind. Being of a recent acquisition, it falls in more naturally with any novelties. It is therefore the kind of wealth which will be resorted to by all who wish for change.

Along with the monied interest, a new description of men had grown up, with whom that interest soon formed a close and marked union; I mean the political Men of Letters, Men of Letters, fond of distinguishing themselves, are rarely averse to innovation. Since the decline of the life and greatness of Lewis the XIVth, they were not so much cultivated either by him, or by the regent,* or the successors to the crown; nor were they engaged to the court by favours and emoluments so systematically as during the splendid period of that ostent-atious and not impolitic reign. What they lost in the old court protection, they endeavoured to make up by joining in a sort of incorporation of their own; to which the two academies of France, and afterwards the vast undertaking of the Encyclopaedia,* carried on by a society of these gentlemen, did not a little contribute.

The literary cabal had some years ago formed something like a regular plan for the destruction of the Christian religion. This object they pursued with a degree of zeal which hitherto had been discovered only in the propagators of some system of piety. They were possessed with a spirit of proselytism in the most fanatical degree; and from thence, by an easy progress, with the spirit of persecution according to their means.[1] What was not to be done towards their great end by any direct or immediate act, might be wrought by a longer process through the medium of opinion. To command that opinion, the first step is to establish a dominion over those who direct it. They contrived to possess themselves, with great method and perseverance, of all the avenues to literary fame. Many of them indeed stood high in the ranks of literature and science. The world had done them justice; and in favour of general talents forgave the evil tendency of their peculiar principles. This was true liberality; which they returned by endeavouring to confine the reputation of sense, learning, and taste to themselves or their followers. I will venture to say that this narrow, exclusive spirit has not been less prejudicial to literature and to taste, then to morals and true philosophy. These Atheistical fathers have a bigotry of their own; and they have learnt to talk against monks with the spirit of a monk. But in some things they are men of the world. The resources of intrigue are called in to supply the defects of argument and wit. To this system of literary monopoly was joined an unremitting industry to blacken and discredit in every way, and by every means, all those who did not hold to their faction. To those who have observed the spirit of their conduct, it has long been clear that nothing was wanted but the power of carrying the intolerance of the tongue and of the

[1] This (down to the end of the first sentence in the next paragraph) and some other parts here and there, were inserted, on his reading the manuscript, by my lost son.* [1803]

pen into a persecution which would strike at property, liberty, and life.

The desultory and faint persecution carried on against them, more from compliance with form and decency than with serious resentment, neither weakened their strength, nor relaxed their efforts. The issue of the whole was, that what with opposition, and what with success, a violent and malignant zeal, of a kind hitherto unknown in the world, had taken an entire possession of their minds, and rendered their whole conversation, which otherwise would have been pleasing and instructive, perfectly disgusting. A spirit of cabal, intrigue, and proselytism, pervaded all their thoughts, words, and actions. And, as controversial zeal soon turns its thoughts on force, they began to insinuate themselves into a correspondence with foreign princes; in hopes, through their authority, which at first they flattered, they might bring about the changes they had in view. To them it was indifferent whether these changes were to be accomplished by the thunderbolt of despotism, or by the earthquake of popular commotion. The correspondence between this cabal, and the late king of Prussia,* will throw no small light upon the spirit of all their proceedings.[1] For the same purpose for which they intrigued with princes, they cultivated, in a distinguished manner, the monied interest of France; and partly through the means furnished by those whose peculiar offices gave them the most extensive and certain means of communication, they carefully occupied all the avenues to opinion.

Writers, especially when they act in a body, and with one direction, have great influence on the publick mind; the alliance therefore of these writers with the monied interest[2] had no small effect in removing the popular odium and envy which attended that species of wealth. These writers, like the propagators of all novelties, pretended to a great zeal for the poor, and the lower orders, whilst in their satires they rendered hateful, by every exaggeration, the faults of courts,

[1] I do not chuse to shock the feeling of the moral reader with any quotation of their vulgar, base, and profane language.

[2] Their connection with Turgot* and almost all the people of the finance. [1803]

of nobility, and of priesthood. They became a sort of demagogues. They served as a link to unite, in favour of one object, obnoxious wealth to restless and desperate poverty.

As these two kinds of men appear principal leaders in all the late transactions, their junction and politics will serve to account, not upon any principles of law or of policy, but as a *cause*, for the general fury with which all the landed property of ecclesiastical corporations has been attacked; and the great care which, contrary to their pretended principles, has been taken, of a monied interest originating from the authority of the crown. All the envy against wealth and power, was artificially directed against other descriptions of riches. On what other principle than that which I have stated can we account for an appearance so extraordinary and unnatural as that of the ecclesiastical possessions, which had stood so many successions of ages and shocks of civil violences, and were guarded at once by justice, and by prejudice, being applied to the payment of debts, comparatively recent, invidious, and contracted by a decried and subverted government?

Was the public estate a sufficient stake for the public debts? Assume that it was not, and that a loss *must* be incurred somewhere—When the only estate lawfully possessed, and which the contracting parties had in contemplation at the time in which their bargain was made, happens to fail, who, according to the principles of natural and legal equity, ought to be the sufferer? Certainly it ought to be either the party who trusted; or the party who persuaded him to trust; or both; and not third parties who had no concern with the transaction. Upon any insolvency they ought to suffer who were weak enough to lend upon bad security, or they who fraudulently held out a security that was not valid. Laws are acquainted with no other rules of decision. But by the new institute of the rights of men, the only persons, who in equity ought to suffer, are the only persons who are to be saved harmless: those are to answer the debt who neither were lenders or borrowers, mortgagers or mortgagees.

What had the clergy to do with these transactions? What had they to do with any publick engagement further than the extent of their own debt? To that, to be sure, their estates were bound to the last acre. Nothing can lead more to the true spirit of the assembly, which sits for public confiscation, with its new equity and its new morality, than an attention to their proceeding with regard to this debt of the clergy. The body of confiscators, true to that monied interest for which they were false to every other, have found the clergy competent to incur a legal debt. Of course they declared them legally entitled to the property which their power of incurring the debt and mortgaging the estate implied; recognizing the rights of those persecuted citizens, in the very act in which they were thus grossly violated.

If, as I said, any persons are to make good deficiencies to the public creditor, besides the public at large, they must be those who managed the agreement. Why therefore are not the estates of all the comptrollers general confiscated?[1] Why not those of the long succession of ministers, financiers, and bankers who have been enriched whilst the nation was impoverished by their dealings and their counsels? Why is not the estate of Mr Laborde* declared forfeited rather than of the archbishop of Paris, who has had nothing to do in the creation or in the jobbing of the public funds? Or, if you must confiscate old landed estates in favour of the money-jobbers, why is the penalty confined to one description? I do not know whether the expences of the duke de Choiseul have left any thing of the infinite sums which he had derived from the bounty of his master, during the transactions of a reign which contributed largely, by every species of prodigality in war and peace, to the present debt of France. If any such remains, why is not this confiscated? I remember to have been in Paris during the time of the old government. I was there just after the duke d'Aiguillion had been snatched (as it was generally thought) from the block by the hand of a protecting despotism. He was a minister, and had some concern in the affairs of that prodigal period. Why do I not see his estate delivered up to the municipalities in which it is situated? The noble family of Noailles have long been servants, (meritorious servants I admit) to the crown of France, and have had of

---

[1] All have been confiscated in their turn. [1803]

course some share in its bounties. Why do I hear nothing of
the application of their estates to the public debt? Why is the
estate of the duke de Rochefoucault more sacred than that of
the cardinal de Rochefoucault?* The former is, I doubt not, a
worthy person; and (if it were not a sort of profaneness to talk
of the use, as affecting the title to property) had makes a good
use of his revenues; but it is no disrespect to him to say, what
authentic information well warrants me in saying, that the use
made of a property equally valid, by his brother[1] the cardinal
archbishop of Rouen, was far more laudable and far more
public-spirited. Can one hear of the proscription of such
persons, and the confiscation of their effects, without indignation and horror? He is not a man who does not feel such
emotions on such occasions. He does not deserve the name of
a free man who will not express them.

Few barbarous conquerors have ever made so terrible a
revolution in property. None of the heads of the Roman
factions, when they established '*crudelem illam Hastam*'* in
all their auctions of rapine, have ever set up to sale the goods
of the conquered citizen to such an enormous amount. It must
be allowed in favour of those tyrants of antiquity, that what
was done by them could hardly be said to be done in cold
blood. Their passions were inflamed, their tempers soured,
their understandings confused, with the spirit of revenge, with
the innumerable reciprocated and recent inflictions and
retaliations of blood and rapine. They were driven beyond all
bounds of moderation by the apprehension of the return of
power with the return of property to the families of those they
had injured beyond all hope of forgiveness.

These Roman confiscators, who were yet only in the
elements of tyranny, and were not instructed in the rights of
men to exercise all sorts of cruelties on each other without
provocation, thought it necessary to spread a sort of colour
over their injustice. They considered the vanquished party as
composed of traitors who had borne arms, or otherwise had
acted with hostility against the commonwealth. They regarded

[1] Not his brother, nor any near relation; but this mistake does not affect the
argument. [1803]

them as persons who had forfeited their property by their crimes. With you, in your improved state of the human mind, there was no such formality. You seized upon five millions sterling of annual rent, and turned forty or fifty thousand human creatures out of their houses, because 'such was your pleasure.' The tyrant, Harry the Eighth of England, as he was not better enlightened than the Roman Marius's and Sylla's, and had not studied in your new schools, did not know what an effectual instrument of despotism was to be found in that grand magazine of offensive weapons, the rights of men.* When he resolved to rob the abbies, as the club of the Jacobins have robbed all the ecclesiastics, he began by setting on foot a commission to examine into the crimes and abuses which prevailed in those communities. As it might be expected, his commission reported truths, exaggerations, and falshoods. But truly or falsely it reported abuses and offences. However, as abuses might be corrected, as every crime of persons does not infer a forfeiture with regard to communities, and as property, in that dark age, was not discovered to be a creature of prejudice, all those abuses (and there were enough of them) were hardly thought sufficient ground for such a confiscation as it was for his purposes to make. He therefore procured the formal surrender of these estates. All these operose proceedings were adopted by one of the most decided tyrants in the rolls of history, as necessary preliminaries, before he could venture, by bribing the members of his two servile houses with a share of the spoil, and holding out to them an eternal immunity from taxation, to demand a confirmation of his iniquitous proceedings by an act of parliament. Had fate reserved him to our times, four technical terms would have done his business, and saved him all this trouble; he needed nothing more than one short form of incantation—'*Philosophy, Light, Liberality, the Rights of Men.*'

I can say nothing in praise of these acts of tyranny, which no voice has hitherto ever commended under any of their false colours; yet in these false colours an homage was paid by despotism to justice. The power which was above all fear and all remorse was not set above all shame. Whilst Shame keeps its watch, Virtue is not wholly extinguished in the heart; nor will Moderation be utterly exiled from the minds of tryants.

I believe every honest man sympathizes in his reflections with our political poet on that occasion, and will pray to avert the omen whenever these acts of rapacious despotism present themselves to his view or his imagination:

—— May no such storm
Fall on our times, where ruin must reform.
Tell me (my muse) what monstrous, dire offence,
What crimes could any Christian king incense
To such a rage? Was't luxury, or lust?
Was *he* so temperate, so chaste, so just?
Were these their crimes? they were his own much more;
But wealth is crime enough to him that's poor.[1]

---

[1] The rest of the passage is this——

Who having spent the treasures of his crown,
Condemns their luxury to feed his own.
And yet this act, to varnish o'er the shame
Of sacrilege, must bear Devotion's name.
No crime so bold, but would be understood
A real, or at least a seeming good,
Who fears not to do ill, yet fears the name;
And, free from conscience, is a slave to fame.
Thus he the church at once protects, and spoils:
But princes' swords are sharper than their styles.
And thus to th'ages past he makes amends,
Their charity destroys, their faith defends.
Then did Religion in a lazy cell,
In empty aëry contemplations dwell;
And, like the block, unmoved lay: but ours,
As much too active, like the stork devours.
Is there no temp'rate region can be known,
Betwixt their frigid, and our torrid zone?
Could we not wake from that lethargic dream,
But to be restless in a worse extreme?
And for that lethargy was there no cure,
But to be cast into a calenture?
Can knowledge have no bound, but must advance
So far, to make us wish for ignorance?
And rather in the dark to grope our way,
Than, led by a false guide, to err by day?

This same wealth, which is at all times treason and *lese nation* to indigent and rapacious despotism, under all modes of polity, was your temptation to violate property, law, and religion, united in one object. But was the state of France so wretched and undone, that no other resource but rapine remained to preserve its existence? On this point I wish to receive some information. When the states met, was the condition of the finances of France such, that, after oeconomising on principles of justice and mercy through all departments, no fair repartition of burthens upon all the orders could possibly restore them? If such an equal imposition would have been sufficient, you well know it might easily have been made. Mr Necker,* in the budget which he laid before the Orders assembled at Versailles, made a detailed exposition of the state of the French nation.[1]

If we give credit to him, it was not necessary to have recourse to any new impositions whatsoever, to put the receipts of France on a balance with its expences. He stated the permanent charges of all descriptions, including the interest of a new loan of four hundred millions, at 531,444,000 livres; the fixed revenue at 475,294,000, making the deficiency 56,150,000, or short of 2,200,000 sterling. But to balance it, he brought forward savings and improvements of revenue (considered as entirely certain) to rather more than the amount of that deficiency; and he concludes with these emphatical words (p. 39) 'Quel pays, Messieurs, que celui, ou, *sans impots* et avec de simples objets *inappercus*, on peut faire disparoitre un deficit qui a fait tant de bruit en Europe.'* As to

> Who sees these dismal heaps, but would demand,
> What barbarous invader sack'd the land?
> But when he hears, no Goth, no Turk did bring
> This desolation, but a Christian king;
> When nothing, but the name of zeal, appears
> 'Twixt our best actions, and the worst of theirs,
> What does he think our sacrilege would spare,
> When such th' effects of our Devotion are?

COOPER'S HILL, by SIR JOHN DENHAM

[1] Rapport de Mons. le Directeur général des finances, fait par ordre du Roi à Versailles. Mai 5, 1789.*

the re-imbursement, the sinking of debt, and the other great objects of public credit and political arrangement indicated in Mons. Necker's speech, no doubt could be entertained, but that a very moderate and proportioned assesssment on the citizens without distinction would have provided for all of them to the fullest extent of their demand.

If this representation of Mons. Necker was false, then the assembly are in the highest degree culpable for having forced the king to accept as his minister, and since the king's deposition, for having employed as *their* minister, a man who had been capable of abusing so notoriously the confidence of his master and their own; in a matter too of the highest moment, and directly appertaining to his particular office. But if the representation was exact (as, having always, along with you, conceived a high degree of respect for Mr Necker, I make no doubt it was) then what can be said in favour of those, who, instead of moderate, reasonable, and general contribution, have in cold blood, and impelled by no necessity, had recourse to a partial and cruel confiscation?

Was that contribution refused on a pretext of privilege, either on the part of the clergy or on that of the nobility? No certainly. As to the clergy, they even ran before the wishes of the third order. Previous to the meeting of the states, they had in all their instructions expressly directed their deputies to renounce every immunity, which put them upon a footing distinct from the condition of their fellow-subjects. In this renunciation the clergy were even more explicit than the nobility.

But let us suppose that the deficiency had remained at the 56 millions, (or £.2,200,000 sterling) as at first stated by Mr Necker. Let us allow that all the resources he opposed to that deficiency were impudent and groundless fictions; and that the assembly (or their lords of articles[1] at the Jacobins) were from thence justified in laying the whole burthen of that deficiency on the clergy,—yet allowing all this, a necessity of £.2,200,000 sterling will not support a confiscation to the

---

[1] In the constitution of Scotland during the Stuart reigns, a committee sat for preparing bills; and none could pass, but those previously approved by them. This committee was called lords of articles.

amount of five millions. The imposition of £.2,200,000 on the clergy, as partial, would have been oppressive and unjust, but it would not have been altogether ruinous to those on whom it was imposed; and therefore it would not have answered the real purpose of the managers.

Perhaps persons, unacquainted with the state of France, on hearing the clergy and the noblesse were privileged in point of taxation, may be led to imagine, that previous to the revolution these bodies had contributed nothing to the state. This is a great mistake. They certainly did not contribute equally with each other, nor either of them equally with the commons. They both however contributed largely. Neither nobility nor clergy enjoyed any exemption from the excise on consumable commodities, from duties of custom, or from any of the other numerous *indirect* impositions, which in France as well as here, make so very large a proportion of all payments to the public. The noblesse paid the capitation. They paid also a land-tax, called the twentieth penny, to the height sometimes of three, sometimes of four shillings in the pound; both of them *direct* impositions of no light nature, and no trivial produce. The clergy of the provinces annexed by conquest to France (which in extent make about an eighth part of the whole but in wealth a much larger proportion) paid likewise to the capitation and the twentieth penny, at the rate paid by the nobility. The clergy in the old provinces did not pay the capitation; but they had redeemed themselves at the expence of about 24 millions, or a little more than a million sterling. They were exempted from the twentieths; but then they made free gifts; they contracted debts for the state; and they were subject to some other charges, the whole computed at about a thirteenth part of their clear income. They ought to have paid annually about forty thousand pounds more, to put them on a par with the contribution of the nobility.*

When the terrors of this tremendous proscription hung over the clergy, they made an offer of a contribution, through the archbishop of Aix, which, for its extravagance, ought not to have been accepted. But it was evidently and obviously more advantageous to the public creditor, than any thing which could rationally be promised by the confiscation. Why was it not accepted? The reason is plain—There was no desire that the church should be brought to serve the state. The service of the state was made a pretext to destroy the church. In their way to the destruction of the church they would not scruple to destroy their country: and they have destroyed it. One great end in the project would have been defeated, if the plan of extortion had been adopted in lieu of the scheme of confiscation. The new landed interest connected with the new republic, and connected with it for its very being, could not have been created. This was among the reasons why the extravagant ransom was not accepted.

The madness of the project of confiscation, on the plan that was first pretended, soon became apparent. To bring this unwieldy mass of landed property, enlarged by the confiscation of all the vast landed domain of the crown, at once into market, was obviously to defeat the profits proposed by the confiscation, by depreciating the value of those lands, and indeed of all the landed estates throughout France. Such a sudden diversion of all its circulating money from trade to land, must be an additional mischief. What step was taken? Did the assembly, on becoming sensible of the inevitable ill effects of their projected sale, revert to the offers of the clergy? No distress could oblige them to travel in a course which was disgraced by any appearance of justice. Giving over all hopes from a general immediate sale, another project seems to have succeeded. They proposed to take stock in exchange for the church lands. In that project great difficulties arose in equalizing the objects to be exchanged. Other obstacles also presented themselves, which threw them back again upon some project of sale. The municipalities had taken an alarm. They would not hear of transferring the whole plunder of the kingdom to the stock-holders in Paris. Many of those municipalities had been (upon system) reduced to the most deplorable indigence. Money was no where to been seen. They were therefore led to the point that was so ardently desired. They panted for a currency of any kind which might revive their perishing industry. The municipalities were then to be admitted to a share in the spoil, which evidently rendered the first scheme (if ever it had been seriously entertained) altogether impracticable. Public exigencies pressed upon all sides. The minister of finance reiterated his call for supply with a most urgent, anxious, and boding voice. Thus pressed on all sides, instead of the first plan of converting their bankers into bishops and abbots, instead of paying the old debt, they contracted a new debt, at 3 per cent. creating a new paper currency, founded on an eventual sale of the church lands.* They issued this paper currency to satisfy in the first instance chiefly the demands made upon them by the *Bank of discount*, the great machine, or paper-mill, of their fictitious wealth.

The spoil of the church was now become the only resource of all their operations in finance; the vital principle of all their politics; the sole security for the existence of their power. It was necessary by all, even the most violent means, to put every individual on the same bottom, and to bind the nation in one guilty interest to uphold this act, and the authority of those by whom it was done. In order to force the most reluctant into a participation of their pillage, they rendered their paper circulation compulsory in all payments. Those who consider the general tendency of their schemes to this one object as a centre; and a centre from which afterwards all their measures radiate, will not think that I dwell too long upon this part of the proceedings of the national assembly.

To cut off all appearance of connection between the crown and public justice, and to bring the whole under implicit obedience to the dictators in Paris, the old independent judicature of the parliaments,* with all its merits, and all its faults, was wholly abolished. Whilst the parliaments existed, it was evident that the people might some time or other come to resort to them, and rally under the standard of their antient laws. It became however a matter of consideration that the magistrates and officers, in the courts now abolished, *had purchased their places* at a very high rate, for which, as well as for the duty they performed, they received but a very low return of interest. Simple confiscation is a boon only for the clergy;—to the lawyers some appearances of equity are to be observed; and they are to receive compensation to an immense amount. Their compensation becomes part of the national debt, for the liquidation of which there is the one exhaustless fund. The lawyers are to obtain their compensation in the new church paper, which is to march with the new principles of judicature and legislature. The dismissed magistrates are to take their share of martyrdom with the ecclesiastics, or to receive their own property from such a fund and in such a manner, as all those, who have been seasoned with the antient principles of jurisprudence, and had been the sworn guardians of property, must look upon with horror. Even the clergy are to receive their misereable allowance out of the depreciated paper which is stamped with the indelible character of sacrilege, and with the symbols of their own ruin, or they must starve. So violent an outrage upon credit, property, and liberty, as this compulsory paper currency, has seldom been exhibited by the alliance of bankruptcy and tyranny, at any time, or in any nation.

In the course of all these operations, at length comes out the grand *arcanum*;*—that in reality, and in a fair sense, the lands of the church (so far as any thing certain can be gathered from their proceedings) are not to be sold at all. By the late resolutions of the national assembly, they are indeed to be delivered to the highest bidder. But it is to be observed, that *a certain portion only of the purchase money is to be laid down.* A period of twelve years is to be given for the payment of the rest. The philosophic purchasers are therefore, on payment of a sort of fine, to be put instantly into possession of the estate. It becomes in some respects a sort of gift to them; to be held on the feudal tenure of zeal to the new establishment. This project is evidently to let in a body of purchasers without money. The consequence will be, that these purchasers, or rather grantees, will pay, not only from the rents as they accrue, which might as well be received by the state, but from the spoil of the materials of buildings, from waste in woods, and from whatever money, by hands habituated to the gripings of usury, they can wring from the miserable peasant. He is to be delivered over to the mercenary and arbitrary discretion of men, who will be stimulated to every species of extortion by the growing demands on the growing profits of an estate held under the precarious settlement of a new political system.

When all the frauds, impostures, violences, rapines, burnings, murders, confiscations, compulsory paper currencies, and every description of tyranny and cruelty employed to bring about and to uphold this revolution, have their natural effect, that is, to shock the moral sentiments of all virtuous and sober minds, the abettors of this philosphic system immediately strain their throats in a declamation against the old monarchical government of France. When they have rendered that deposed power sufficiently black, they then proceed in argument, as if all those who disapprove of their new abuses, must of course be partizans of the old; that those who reprobate their crude and violent schemes of liberty ought to be treated as advocates for servitude. I admit that their necessities do compel them to this base and contemptible fraud. Nothing can reconcile men to their proceedings and projects but the supposition that there is no third option between them, and some tyranny as odious as can be furnished by the records of history, or by the invention of poets. This prattling of theirs hardly deserves the name of sophistry. It is nothing but plain impudence. Have these gentlemen never heard, in the whole circle of the worlds of theory and practice, of any thing between the despotism of the monarch and the despotism of the multitude? Have they never heard of a monarchy directed by laws, controlled and balanced by the great hereditary wealth and hereditary dignity of a nation; and both again controlled by a judicious check from the reason and feeling of the people at large acting by a suitable and permanent organ? Is it then impossible that a man may be found who, without criminal ill intention, or pitiable absurdity, shall prefer such a mixed and tempered government to either of the extremes; and who may repute that nation to be destitute of all wisdom and of all virtue, which, having in its choice to obtain such a government with ease, *or rather to confirm it when actually possessed*, thought proper to commit a thousand crimes, and to subject their country to a thousand evils, in order to avoid it? Is it then a truth so universally acknowledged, that a pure democracy is the only tolerable form into which human society can be thrown, that a man is not permitted to hesitate about its merits, without the suspicion of being a friend to tyranny, that is, of being a foe to mankind?

I do not know under what description to class the present ruling authority in France. It affects to be a pure democracy, though I think it in a direct train of becoming shortly a mischievous and ignoble oligarchy. But for the present I admit it to be a contrivance of the nature and effect of what it pretends to. I reprobate no form of government merely upon abstract principles. There may be situations in which the purely democratic form will become necessary. There may be some (very few, and very particularly circumstanced) where it would be clearly desireable. This I do not take to be the case of France, or of any other great country. Until now, we have seen no examples of considerable democracies. The antients were better acquainted with them. Not being wholly unread in the authors, who had seen the most of those constitutions, and who best understood them, I cannot help concurring with their opinion, that an absolute democracy, no more than absolute monarchy, is to be reckoned among the legitimate forms of government. They think it rather the corruption and degeneracy, than the sound constitution of a republic. If I recollect rightly, Aristotle observes, that a democracy has many striking points of resemblance with a tyranny.[1] Of this I am certain, that in a democracy, the majority of the citizens is

---

[1] When I wrote this I quoted from memory, after many years had elapsed from my reading the passage. A learned friend has found it, and it is as follows:

Τὸ ἦθος τὸ αὐτό, καὶ ἄμφω δεσποτικὰ τῶν βελτιόνων, καὶ τὰ ψηφίσματα, ὥσπερ ἐκεῖ τὰ ἐπιτάγματα καὶ ὁ δημαγωγὸς καὶ ὁ κόλαξ οἱ αὐτοὶ καὶ ἀνάλογοι καὶ μάλιστα ἑκάτεροι παρ᾽ ἑκατέροις ἰσχύουσιν, οἱ μὲν κόλακες παρὰ τυράννοις, οἱ δὲ δημαγωγοὶ παρὰ τοῖς δήμοις τοῖς τοιούτοις.—

'The ethical character is the same; both exercise despotism over the better class of citizens; and decrees are in the one, what ordinances and arrêts are in the other; the demagogue too, and the court favourite, are not unfrequently the same identical men, and always bear a close analogy; and these have the principal power, each in their respective forms of government, favourites with the absolute monarchy, and demagogues with a people such as I have described.' Arist. Politic. lib. iv. cap. 4.

capable of exercising the most cruel oppressions upon the minority, whenever strong divisions prevail in that kind of polity, as they often must; and that oppression of the minority will extend to far greater numbers, and will be carried on with much greater fury, than can almost ever be apprehended from the dominion of a single sceptre. In such a popular persecution, individual sufferers are in a much more deplorable condition than in any other. Under a cruel prince they have the balmy compassion of mankind to assuage the smart of their wounds; they have the plaudits of the people to animate their generous constancy under their sufferings; but those who are subjected to wrong under multitudes, are deprived of all external consolation. They seem deserted by mankind; overpowered by a conspiracy of their whole species.

But admitting democracy not to have that inevitable tendency to party tyranny, which I suppose it to have, and admitting it to possess as much good in it when unmixed, as I am sure it possesses when compounded with other forms; does monarchy, on its part, contain nothing at all to recommend it? I do not often quote Bolingbroke, nor have his works in general, left any permanent impression on my mind. He is a presumptuous and a superficial writer. But he has one observation, which, in my opinion, is not without depth and solidity. He says, that he prefers a monarchy to other governments; because you can better ingraft any description of republic on a monarchy than any thing of monarchy upon the republican forms. I think him perfectly in the right. The fact is so historically; and it agrees well with the speculation.*

I know how easy a topic it is to dwell on the faults of departed greatness. By a revolution in the state, the fawning sycophant of yesterday, is converted into the austere critic of the present hour. But steady independent minds, when they have an object of so serious a concern to mankind as government, under their contemplation, will disdain to assume the part of satirists and declaimers. They will judge of human institutions as they do of human characters. They will sort out the good from the evil, which is mixed in mortal institutions as it is in mortal men.

Your government in France, though usually, and I think

justly, reputed the best of the qualified or ill-qualified monarchies, was still full of abuses. These abuses accumulated in a length of time, as they must accumulate in every monarchy not under the constant inspection of a popular representative. I am no stranger to the faults and defects of the subverted government of France; and I think I am not inclined by nature or policy to make a panegyric upon any thing which is a just and natural object of censure. But the question is not now of the vices of that monarchy, but of its existence. Is it then true, that the French government was such as to be incapable or undeserving of reform; so that it was of absolute necessity the whole fabric should be at once pulled down, and the area cleared for the erection of a theoretic experimental edifice in its place? All France was of a different opinion in the beginning of the year 1789. The instructions to the represent-atives to the states-general,* from every district in that kingdom, were filled with projects for the reformation of that government, without the remotest suggestion of a design to destroy it. Had such a design been then even insinuated, I believe there would have been but one voice, and that voice for rejecting it with scorn and horror. Men have been sometimes led by degrees, sometimes hurried into things, of which, if they could have seen the whole together, they never would have permitted the most remote approach. When those instructions were given, there was no question but that abuses existed, and that they demanded a reform; nor is there now. In the interval between the instructions and the revolution, things changed their shape; and in consequence of that change, the true question at present is, Whether those who would have reformed, or those who have destroyed, are in the right?

To hear some men speak of the late monarchy of France, you would imagine that they were talking of Persia bleeding under the ferocious sword of Taehmas Kouli Khân;* or at least describing the barbarous anarchic despotism of Turkey, where the finest countries in the most genial climates in the world are wasted by peace more than any countries have been worried by war; where arts are unknown, where manu-factures languish, where science is extinguished, where agriculture decays, where the human race itself melts away and perishes under the eye of the observer. Was this the case of France? I have no way of determining the question but by a reference to facts. Facts do not support this resemblance. Along with much evil, there is some good in monarchy itself; and some corrective to its evil, from religion, from laws, from manners, from opinions, the French monarchy must have received; which rendered it (though by no means a free, and therefore by no means a good constitution) a despotism rather in appearance than in reality.

Among the standards upon which the effects of government on any country are to be estimated, I must consider the state of its population as not the least certain. No country in which population flourishes, and is in progressive improvement, can be under a *very* mischievous government. About sixty years ago, the Intendants of the generalities* of France made, with other matters, a report of the population of their several districts. I have not the books, which are very voluminous, by me, nor do I know where to procure them (I am obliged to speak by memory, and therefore the less positively) but I think the population of France was by them, even at that period, estimated at twenty-two millions of souls. At the end of the last century it had been generally calculated at eighteen. On either of these estimations France was not ill-peopled. Mr Necker, who is an authority for his own time at least equal to the Intendants for theirs, reckons, and upon apparently sure principles, the people of France, in the year, 1780, at twenty-four millions six hundred and seventy thousand. But was this the probable ultimate term under the old establishment? Dr Price is of opinion, that the growth of population in France was by no means at its *acmé* in that year. I certainly defer to Dr Price's authority a good deal more in these speculations, than I do in his general politics. This gentleman, taking ground on Mr Necker's data, is very confident, that since the period of that minister's calculation, the French population has encreased rapidly; so rapidly that in the year 1789 he will not consent to rate the people of that kindgom at a lower number than thirty millions. After abating much (and much I think ought to be abated) from the sanguine calculations of Dr Price, I have no doubt that the population of France did encrease considerably during this later period: but supposing that it encreased to nothing more than will be sufficient to compleat the 24,670,000 to 25 millions, still a population of 25 millions, and that in an encreasing progress, on a space of about twenty-seven thousand square leagues, is immense. It is, for instance, a good deal more than the proportionable population of this island, or even than that of England, the best-peopled part of the united kingdom.

It is not universally true, that France is a fertile country. Considerable tracts of it are barren, and labour under other natural disadvantages. In the portions of that territory, where things are more favourable, as far as I am able to discover, the numbers of the people correspond to the indulgence of nature.[1] The Generality of Lisle (this I admit is the strongest example) upon an extent of 404½ leagues, about ten years ago, contained 734,600 souls, which is 1772 inhabitants to each square league. The middle term for the rest of France is about 900 inhabitants to the same admeasurement.

I do not attribute this population to the deposed government; because I do not like to compliment the contrivances of men, with what is due in a great degree to the bounty of Providence. But that decried government could not have obstructed, most probably it favoured, the operation of those causes (whatever they were) whether of nature in the soil, or in habits of industry among the people, which has produced so large a number of the species throughout that whole kingdom, and exhibited in some particular places such prodigies of population. I never will suppose that fabrick of a state to be the worst of all political institutions, which, by experience, is found to contain a principle favourable (however latent it may be) to the encrease of mankind.

The wealth of a country is another, and no contemptible standard, by which we may judge whether, on the whole, a government be protecting or destructive. France far exceeds England in the multitude of her people; but I apprehend that

[1] *De l'Administration des Finances de la France,* par Mons. Necker, vol. i. p. 288.

her comparative wealth is much inferior to ours; that it is not so equal in the distribution, nor so ready in the circulation. I believe the difference in the form of the two governments to be amongst the causes of this advantage on the side of England. I speak of England, not of the whole British dominions; which, if compared with those of France, will, in some degree, weaken the comparative rate of wealth upon our side. But that wealth, which will not endure a comparison with the riches of England, may constitute a very respectable degree of opulence. Mr Necker's book published in 1785,[1] contains an accurate and interesting collection of facts relative to public oeconomy and to political arithmetic; and his speculations on the subject are in general wise and liberal. In that work he gives an idea of the state of France, very remote from the portrait of a country whose government was a perfect grievance, an absolute evil, admitting no cure but through the violent and uncertain remedy of a total revolution. He affirms, that from the year 1726 to the year 1784, there was coined at the mint of France, in the species of gold and silver, to the amount of about one hundred millions of pounds sterling.[2]

It is impossible that Mr Necker should be mistaken in the amount of the bullion which has been coined in the mint. It is a matter of official record. The reasonings of this able financier, concerning the quantity of gold and silver which remained for circulation, when he wrote in 1785, that is about four years before the deposition and imprisonment of the French King, are not of equal certainty; but they are laid on grounds so apparently solid, that it is not easy to refuse a considerable degree of assent to his calculation. He calculates the *numeraire*, or what we call *specie*, then actually existing in France, at about eighty-eight millions of the same English money. A great accumulation of wealth for one country, large as that country is! Mr Necker was so far from considering this influx of wealth as likely to cease, when he wrote in 1785, that he presumes upon a future annual increase of two per cent. upon the money brought into France during the periods from which he computed.

[1] De l'Administration des Finances de la France, par M. Necker.
[2] Vol. iii. chap. 8. and chap. 9.

Some adequate cause must have originally introduced all the money coined at its mint into that kingdom; and some cause as operative must have kept at home, or returned into its bosom, such a vast flood of treasure as Mr Necker calculates to remain for domestic circulation. Suppose any reasonable deductions from M. Necker's computation; the remainder must still amount to an immense sum. Causes thus powerful to acquire and to retain, cannot be found in discouraged industry, insecure property, and a positively destructive government. Indeed, when I consider the face of the kingdom of France; the multitude and opulence of her cities; the useful magnificence of her spacious high roads and bridges; the opportunity of her artificial canals and navigations opening the conveniences of maritime communication through a solid continent of so immense an extent; when I turn my eyes to the stupendous works of her ports and harbours, and to her whole naval apparatus, whether for war or trade; when I bring before my view the number of her fortifications, constructed with so bold and masterly a skill, and made and maintained at so prodigious a charge, presenting an armed front and impenetrable barrier to her enemies upon every side; when I recollect how very small a part of that extensive region is without cultivation, and to what complete perfection the culture of many of the best productions of the earth have been brought in France; when I reflect on the excellence of her manufactures and fabrics, second to none but ours, and in some particulars not second; when I contemplate the grand foundations of charity, public and private; when I survey the state of all the arts that beautify and polish life; when I reckon the men she has bred for extending her fame in war, her able statesmen, the multitude of her profound lawyers and theologians, her philosophers, her critics, her historians and antiquaries, her poets, and her orators sacred and profane, I behold in all this something which awes and commands the imagination, which checks the mind on the brink of precipitate and indiscriminate censure, and which demands, that we should very seriously examine, what and how great are the latent vices that could authorise us at once to level so spacious a fabric with the ground. I do not recognize, in this view of things, the despotism of Turkey. Nor do I discern the character of a government, that has been, on the whole, so oppressive, or so corrupt, or so negligent, as to be utterly unfit *for all reformation*. I must think such a government well deserved to have its excellencies heightened; its faults corrected; and its capacities improved into a British constitution.

Whoever has examined into the proceedings of that deposed government for several years back, cannot fail to have observed, amidst the inconstancy and fluctuation natural to courts, an earnest endeavour towards the prosperity and improvement of the country; he must admit, that it had long been employed, in some instances, wholly to remove, in many considerably to correct, the abusive practices and usages that had prevailed in the state; and that even the unlimited power of the sovereign over the persons of his subjects, inconsistent, as undoubtedly it was, with law and liberty, had yet been every day growing more mitigated in the exercise. So far from refusing itself to reformation, that government was open, with a censurable degree of facility, to all sorts of projects and projectors on the subject. Rather too much countenance was given to the spirit of innovation, which soon was turned against those who fostered it, and ended in their ruin. It is but cold, and no very flattering justice to that fallen monarchy, to say, that, for many years, it trespassed more by levity and want of judgment in several of its schemes, than from any defect in diligence or in public spirit. To compare the government of France for the last fifteen or sixteen years with wise and well-constituted establishments, during that, or during any period, is not to act with fairness. But if in point of prodigality in the expenditure of money, or in point of rigour in the exercise of power, it be compared with any of the former reigns, I believe candid judges will give little credit to the good intentions of those who dwell perpetually on the donations to favourites, or on the expences of the court, or on the horrors of the Bastile in the reign of Louis the XVIth.[1]

---

[1] The world is obliged to Mr de Calonne* for the pains he has taken to refute the scandalous exaggerations relative to some of the royal expences, and to detect the fallacious account given of pensions, for the wicked purpose of provoking the populace to all sorts of crimes.

Whether the system, if it deserves such a name, now built on the ruins of that antient monarchy, will be able to give a better account of the population and wealth of the country, which it has taken under its care, is a matter very doubtful. Instead of improving by the change, I apprehend that a long series of years must be told before it can recover in any degree the effects of this philosophic revolution, and before the nation can be replaced on its former footing. If Dr Price should think fit, a few years hence, to favour us with an estimate of the population of France, he will hardly be able to make up his tale of thirty millions of souls, as computed in 1789, or the assembly's computation of twenty-six millions of that year; or even Mr Necker's twenty-five millions in 1780. I hear that there are considerable emigrations from France; and that many quitting that voluptuous climate, and that seductive *Circean* liberty,* have taken refuge in the frozen regions, and under the British despotism, of Canada.

In the present disappearance of coin, no person could think it the same country, in which the present minister of the finances has been able to discover fourscore millions sterling in specie. From its general aspect one would conclude that it had been for some time past under the special direction of the learned academicians of Laputa and Balnibarbi.*[1] Already the population of Paris has so declined, that Mr Necker stated to the national assembly the provision to be made for its subsistence at a fifth less than what had formerly been found requisite.[2] It is said (and I have never heard it contradicted) that an hundred thousand people are out of employment in that city, though it is become the seat of the imprisoned court and national assembly. Nothing, I am credibly informed, can exceed the shocking and disgusting spectacle of mendicancy displayed in that capital. Indeed, the votes of the national assembly leave no doubt of the fact. They have lately appointed a standing committee of mendicancy. They are contriving at once a vigorous police on this subject, and, for the first time, the imposition of a tax to maintain the poor, for

[1] See Gulliver's Travels for the idea of countries governed by philosophers.
[2] Mr de Calonne states the falling off of the population of Paris as far more considerable; and it may be so, since the period of Mr Necker's calculation.

whose present relief great sums appear on the face of the public accounts of the year.[1] In the mean time, the leaders of the legislative clubs and coffee-houses are intoxicated with admiration at their own wisdom and ability. They speak with the most sovereign contempt of the rest of the world. They tell the people, to comfort them in the rags with which they have cloathed them, that they are a nation of philosophers; and, sometimes, by all the arts of quackish parade, by shew, tumult, and bustle, sometimes by the alarms of plots and invasions, they attempt to drown the cries of indigence, and to divert the eyes of the observer from the ruin and wretchedness of the state. A brave people will certainly prefer liberty, accompanied with a virtuous poverty, to a depraved and wealthy servitude. But before the price of comfort and opulence is paid, one ought to be pretty sure it is real liberty which is purchased, and that she is to be purchased at no other price. I shall always, however, consider that liberty as very equivocal in her appearance, which has not wisdom and

[1] Travaux de charité pour

	Liv.		£.		s. d.
subvenir au manque de travail à Paris et dans les provinces	3,866,920	St^g	161,121		13 4
Destruction de vagbondage et de la mendicité	1,671,417		69,642		7 6
Primes pour l'importation de grains	5,671,907		236,329		9 2
Dépenses relatives aux subsistances, deduction fait des récouvremens qui ont eu lieu*	39,871,790		1,661,324		11 8
Total—Liv.	51,082,034	St^g	2,128,418		1 8

When I sent this book to the press I entertained some doubt concerning the nature and extent of the last article in the above accounts, which is only under a general head, without any detail. Since then I have seen M. de Calonne's work. I must think it a great loss to me that I had not that advantage earlier. M. de Calonne thinks this article to be on account of general subsistence: but as he is not able to comprehend how so great a loss as upwards of £.1,661,000 sterling could be sustained on the difference between the price and the sale of grain, he seems to attribute this enormous head of charge to secret expences of the revolution. I cannot say any thing positively on that subject. The reader is capable of judging, by the aggregate of these immense charges, on the state and condition of France; and the system of publick oeconomy adopted in that nation. These articles of account produced no enquiry or discussion in the National Assembly.

justice for her companions; and does not lead prosperity and plenty in her train.

The advocates for this revolution, not satisfied with exaggerating the vices of their antient government, strike at the fame of their country itself, by painting almost all that could have attracted the attention of strangers, I mean their nobility and their clergy, as objects of horror. If this were only a libel, there had not been much in it. But it has practical consequences. Had your nobility and gentry, who formed the great body of your landed men, and the whole of your military officers, resembled those of Germany, at the period when the Hanse-towns* were necessitated to confederate against the nobles in defence of their property—had they been like the *Orsini* and *Vitelli** in Italy, who used to sally from their fortified dens to rob the trader and traveller—had they been such as the *Mamalukes* in Egypt, or the *Nayrs* on the coast of Malabar,* I do admit, that too critical an enquiry might not be adviseable into the means of freeing the world from such a nuisance. The statues of Equity and Mercy might be veiled for a moment. The tenderest minds, confounded with the dreadful exigence in which morality submits to the suspension of its own rules in favour of its own principles, might turn aside whilst fraud and violence were accomplishing the destruction of a pretended nobility which disgraced whilst it persecuted human nature. The persons most abhorrent from blood, and treason, and arbitrary confiscation, might remain silent spectators of this civil war between the vices.

But did the privileged nobility who met under the king's precept at Versailles, in 1789, or their constituents, deserve to be looked on as the *Nayres* or *Mamalukes* of this age, or as the *Orsini* and *Vitelli* of ancient times? If I had then asked the question, I should have passed for a madman. What have they since done that they were to be driven into exile, that their persons should be hunted about, mangled, and tortured, their families dispersed, their houses laid in ashes, that their order should be abolished, and the memory of it, if possible, extinguished, by ordaining them to change the very names by which they were usually known?* Read their instructions to their representatives. They breathe the spirit of liberty as warmly, and they recommend reformation as strongly, as any other order. Their privileges relative to contribution were voluntarily surrendered; as the king, from the beginning, surrendered all pretence to a right of taxation. Upon a free constitution there was but one opinion in France. The absolute monarchy was at an end. It breathed its last, without a groan, without struggle, without convulsion. All the struggle, all the dissension arose afterwards upon the preference of a despotic democracy to a government of reciprocal controul. The triumph of the victorious party was over the principles of a British constitution.

I have observed the affectation, which, for many years past, has prevailed in Paris even to a degree perfectly childish, of idolizing the memory of your Henry the Fourth.* If any thing could put one out of humour with that ornament to the kingly character, it would be this overdone style of insidious panegyric. The persons who have worked this engine the most busily, are those who have ended their panegyrics in dethroning his successor and descendant; a man, as good-natured at the least, as Henry the Fourth; altogether as fond of his people; and who has done infinitely more to correct the antient vices of the state than that great monarch did, or we are sure he ever meant to do. Well it is for his panegyrists that they have not him to deal with. For Henry of Navarre was a resolute, active and politic prince. He possessed indeed great humanity and mildness; but an humanity and mildness that never stood in the way of his interests. He never sought to be loved without putting himself first in a condition to be feared. He used soft language with determined conduct. He asserted and maintained his authority in the gross, and distributed his acts of concession only in the detail. He spent the income of his prerogatives nobly; but he took care not to break in upon the capital; never abandoning for a moment any of the claims, which had made under the fundamental laws, nor sparing to shed the blood of those who opposed him, often in the field, sometimes upon the scaffold. Because he knew how to make his virtues respected by the ungrateful, he has merited the praises of those whom, if they had lived in his time, he would have shut up in the Bastile, and brought to punishment along with the regicides whom he hanged after he had famished Paris into a surrender.

If these panegyrists are in earnest in their admiration of Henry the Fourth, they must remember, that they cannot think more highly of him, than he did of the noblesse of France; whose virtue, honour, courage, patriotism, and loyalty were his constant theme.

But the nobility of France are degenerated since the days of Henry the Fourth.—This is possible. But it is more than I can believe to be true in any great degree. I do not pretend to know France as correctly as some others; but I have endeavoured through my whole life to make myself acquainted with human nature: otherwise I should be unfit to take even my humble part in the service of mankind. In that study I could not pass by a vast portion of our nature, as it appeared modified in a country but twenty-four miles from the shore of this island. On my best observation, compared with my best enquiries, I found your nobility for the greater part composed of men of an high spirit, and of a delicate sense of honour, both with regard to themselves individually, and with regard to their whole corps, over whom they kept, beyond what is common in other countries, a censorial eye. They were tolerably well-bred; very officious, humane, and hospitable; in their conversation frank and open; with a good military tone; and reasonably tinctured with literature, particularly of the authors in their own language. Many had pretensions far above this description. I speak of those who were generally met with.

As to their behaviour to the inferior classes, they appeared to me to comport themselves towards them with good-nature, and with something more nearly approaching to familiarity, than is generally practised with us in the intercourse between the higher and lower ranks of life. To strike any person, even in the most abject condition, was a thing in a manner unknown, and would be highly disgraceful. Instances of other ill-treatment of the humble part of the community were rare; and as to attacks made upon the property or the personal liberty of the commons, I never heard of any whatsoever from *them*; nor, whilst the laws were in vigour under the antient government, would such tyranny in subjects have been permitted. As men of landed estates, I had no fault to find with their conduct, though much to reprehend, and much to wish changed, in many of the old tenures. Where the letting of their land was by rent, I could not discover that their agreements with their farmers were oppressive; nor when they were in partnership with the farmer, as often was the case, have I heard that they had taken the lion's share. The proportions seemed not inequitable. There might be exceptions; but certainly they were exceptions only. I have no reason to believe that in these respects the landed noblesse of France were worse than the landed gentry of this country; certainly in no respect more vexatious than the landholders, not noble, of their own nation. In cities the nobility had no manner of power; in the country very little. You know, Sir, that much of the civil government, and the police in the most essential parts, was not in the hands of that nobility which presents itself first to our consideration. The revenue, the system and collection of which were the most grievous parts of the French government, was not administered by the men of the sword; nor were they answerable for the vices of its principle, or the vexations, where any such existed, in its management.

Denying, as I am well warranted to do, that the nobility had any considerable share in the oppression of the people, in cases in which real oppression existed, I am ready to admit that they were not without considerable faults and errors. A foolish imitation of the worst part of the manners of England, which impaired their natural character without substituting in its place what perhaps they meant to copy, has certainly rendered them worse than formerly they were. Habitual dissoluteness of manners continued beyond the pardonable period of life, was more common amongst them than it is with us; and it reigned with the less hope of remedy, though possibly with something of less mischief, by being covered with more exterior decorum. They countenanced too much that licentious philosophy which has helped to bring on their ruin. There was another error amongst them more fatal. Those of the commons, who approached to or exceeded many of the nobility in point of wealth, were not fully admitted to the rank and estimation which wealth, in reason and good policy, ought to bestow in every country; though I think not equally with that of other nobility. The two kinds of aristocracy were too punctiliously kept asunder; less so, however, than in Germany and some other nations.

This separation, as I have already taken the liberty of suggesting to you, I conceive to be one principal cause of the destruction of the old nobility. The military, particularly, was too exclusively reserved for men of family.* But after all, this was an error of opinion, which a conflicting opinion would have rectified. A permanent assembly, in which the commons had their share of power, would soon abolish whatever was too invidious and insulting in these distinctions; and even the faults in the morals of the nobility would have been probably corrected by the greater varieties of occupation and pursuit to which a constitution by orders would have given rise.

All this violent cry against the nobility I take to be a mere work of art. To be honoured and even privileged by the laws, opinions, and inveterate usages of our country, growing out of the prejudice of ages, has nothing to provoke horror and indignation in any man. Even to be too tenacious of those privileges, is not absolutely a crime. The strong struggle in every individual to preserve possession of what he has found to belong to him and to distinguish him, is one of the securities against injustice and despotism implanted in our nature. It operates as an instinct to secure property, and to preserve communities in a settled state. What is there to shock in this? Nobility is a graceful ornament to the civil order. It is the Corinthian capital of polished society. *Omnes boni nobilitati semper favemus,** was the saying of a wise and good man. It is indeed one sign of a liberal and benevolent mind to incline to it with some sort of partial propensity. He feels no ennobling principle in his own heart who wishes to level all the artifical institutions which have been adopted for giving a body to opinion, and permanence to fugitive esteem. It is a sour, malignant, envious disposition, without taste for the reality, or for any image or representation of virtue, that sees with joy the unmerited fall of what had long flourished in splendour and in honour. I do not like to see any thing destroyed; any void produced in society; any ruin on the face of the land. It was therefore with no disappointment or dissatisfaction that my enquiries and observation did not present to me any incorrigible vices in the noblesse of France, or any abuse which could not be removed by a reform very short of abolition. Your noblesse did not deserve punishment; but to degrade is to punish.

It was with the same satisfaction I found that the result of my enquiry concerning your clergy was not dissimilar. It is no soothing news to my ears, that great bodies of men are incurably corrupt. It is not with much credulity I listen to any, when they speak evil of those whom they are going to plunder. I rather suspect that vices are feigned or exaggerated, when profit is looked for in their punishment. An enemy is a bad witness: a robber is a worse. Vices and abuses there were undoubtedly in that order, and must be. It was an old establishment, and not frequently revised. But I saw no crimes in the individuals that merited confiscation of their substance, nor those cruel insults and degradations, and that unnatural persecution which have been substituted in the place of meliorating regulation.

If there had been any just cause for this new religious persecution, the atheistic libellers, who act as trumpeters to animate the populace to plunder, do not love any body so much as not to dwell with complacence on the vices of the existing clergy. This they have not done. They find themselves obliged to rake into the histories of former ages (which they have ransacked with a malignant and profligate industry) for every instance of oppression and persecution which has been made by that body or in its favour, in order to justify, upon very iniquitous, because very illogical principles of retaliation, their own persecutions, and their own cruelties. After destroying all other genealogies and family distinctions, they invent a sort of pedigree of crimes. It is not very just to chastise men for the offences of their natural ancestors; but to take the fiction of ancestry in a corporate succession, as a ground for punishing men who have no relation to guilty acts, except in names and general descriptions, is a sort of refinement in injustice belonging to the philosophy of this enlightened age. The assembly punishes men, many, if not most, of whom abhor the violent conduct of ecclesiastics in former times as much as their present persecutors can do, and who would be as loud and as strong in the expression of that sense, if they were not well aware of the purposes for which all this declamation is employed.

Corporate bodies are immortal for the good of the members, but not for their punishment. Nations themselves are such corporations. As well might we in England think of waging inexpiable war upon all Frenchmen for the evils which they have brought upon us in the several periods of our mutual hostilities. You might, on your part, think yourselves justified in falling upon all Englishmen on account of the unparalleled calamities brought upon the people of France by the unjust invasions of our Henries and our Edwards. Indeed we should be mutually justified in this exterminatory war upon each other, full as much as you are in the unprovoked persecution of your present countrymen, on account of the conduct of men of the same name in other times.

We do not draw the moral lessons we might from history. On the contrary, without care it may be used to vitiate our minds and to destroy our happiness. In history a great volume is unrolled for our instruction, drawing the materials of future wisdom from the past errors and infirmities of mankind. It may, in the perversion, serve for a magazine, furnishing offensive and defensive weapons for parties in church and state, and supplying the means of keeping alive, or reviving dissensions and animosities, and adding fuel to civil fury. History consists, for the greater part, of the miseries brought upon the world by pride, ambition, avarice, revenge, lust, sedition, hypocrisy, ungoverned zeal, and all the train of disorderly appetites, which shake the public with the same

> ——troublous storms that toss
> The private state, and render life unsweet.*

These vices are the *causes* of those storms. Religion, morals, laws, prerogatives, privileges, liberties, rights of men, are the *pretexts*. The pretexts are always found in some specious appearance of a real good. You would not secure men from tyranny and sedition, by rooting out of the mind the principles to which these fraudulent pretexts apply? If you did, you would root out every thing that is valuable in the human breast. As these are the pretexts, so the ordinary actors and instruments in great public evils are kings, priests, magistrates, senates, parliaments, national assemblies, judges, and captains. You would not cure the evil by resolving, that there should be no more monarchs, nor ministers of state, nor of the gospel; no interpreters of law; no general officers; no public councils. You might change the names. The things in some shape must remain. A certain *quantum* of power must always exist in the community, in some hands, and under some appellation. Wise men will apply their remedies to vices, not to names; to the causes of evil which are permanent, not to the occasional organs by which they act, and the transitory modes in which they appear. Otherwise you will be wise historically, a fool in practice. Seldom have two ages the same fashion in their pretexts and the same modes of mischief. Wickedness is a little more inventive. Whilst you are discussing fashion, the fashion is gone by. The very same vice assumes a new body. The spirit transmigrates; and, far from losing its principle of life by the change of its appearance, it is renovated in its new organs with the fresh vigour of a juvenile activity. It walks abroad; it continues its ravages; whilst you are gibbeting the carcass, or demolishing the tomb. You are terrifying yourself with ghosts and apparitions, whilst your house is the haunt of robbers. It is thus with all those, who, attending only to the shell and husk of history, think they are waging war with intolerance, pride, and cruelty, whilst, under colour of abhorring the ill principles of antiquated parties, they are authorizing and feeding the same odious vices in different factions, and perhaps in worse.

Your citizens of Paris formerly had lent themselves as the ready instruments to slaughter the followers of Calvin, at the infamous massacre of St Bartholomew.* What should we say to those who could think of retaliating on the Parisians of this day the abominations and horrors of that time? They are indeed brought to abhor *that* massacre. Ferocious as they are, it is not difficult to make them dislike it; because the politicians and fashionable teachers have no interest in giving their passions exactly the same direction. Still however they find it their interest to keep the same savage dispositions alive. It was but the other day that they caused this very massacre to be acted on the stage* for the diversion of the descendants of those who committed it. In this tragic farce they produced the cardinal of Lorraine in his robes of function, ordering general slaughter. Was this spectacle intended to make the Parisians abhor persecution, and loath the effusion of blood?—No, it was to teach them to persecute their own pastors; it was to excite them, by raising a disgust and horror of their clergy, to an alacrity in hunting down to destruction an order, which, if it ought to exist at all, ought to exist not only in safety, but in reverence. It was to stimulate their cannibal appetites (which one would think had been gorged sufficiently) by variety and seasoning; and to quicken them to an alertness in new murders and massacres, if it should suit the purpose of the Guises of the day. An assembly, in which sat a multitude of priests and prelates, was obliged to suffer this indignity at its door. The author was not sent to the gallies, nor the players to the house of correction. Not long after this exhibition, those players came forward to the assembly to claim the rites of that very religion which they had dared to expose, and to shew their prostituted faces in the senate, whilst the archbishop of Paris, whose function was known to his people only by his prayers and benedictions, and his wealth only by his alms, is forced to abandon his house, and to fly from his flock (as from ravenous wolves) because, truly, in the sixteenth century, the Cardinal of Lorraine was a rebel and a murderer.[1]

Such is the effect of the perversion of history, by those, who, for the same nefarious purposes, have perverted every other part of learning. But those who will stand upon that elevation of reason, which places centuries under our eye, and brings things to the true point of comparison, which obscures little names, and effaces the colours of little parties, and to which nothing can ascend but the spirit and moral quality of human

---

[1] This is on a supposition of the truth of this story; but he was not in France at the time. One name serves as well as another. [1803]

actions, will say to the teachers of the Palais Royal,—the Cardinal of Lorraine was the murderer of the sixteenth century, you have the glory of being the murderers in the eighteenth; and this is the only difference between you. But history, in the nineteenth century, better understood, and better employed, will, I trust, teach a civilized posterity to abhor the misdeeds of both these barbarous ages. It will teach future priests and magistrates not to retaliate upon the speculative and inactive atheists of future times, the enormities committed by the present practical zealots and furious fanatics of that wretched error, which, in its quiescent state, is more than punished, whenever it is embraced. It will teach posterity not to make war upon either religion or philosophy, for the abuse which the hypocrites of both have made of the two most valuable blessings conferred upon us by the bounty of the universal Patron, who in all things eminently favours and protects the race of man.

If your clergy, or any clergy, should shew themselves vicious beyond the fair bounds allowed to human infirmity, and to those professional faults which can hardly be separated from professional virtues, though their vices never can countenance the exercise of oppression, I do admit, that they would naturally have the effect of abating very much of our indignation against the tyrants who exceed measure and justice in their punishment. I can allow in clergymen, through all their divisions, some tenaciousness of their own opinion; some overflowings of zeal for its propagation; some predilection to their own state and office; some attachment to the interest of their own corps; some preference to those who listen with docility to their doctrines, beyond those who scorn and deride them. I allow all this, because I am a man who have to deal with men, and who would not, through a violence of toleration, run into the greatest of all intolerance. I must bear with infirmities until they fester into crimes.

Undoubtedly, the natural progress of the passions, from frailty to vice, ought to be prevented by a watchful eye and a firm hand. But is it true that the body of your clergy had past those limits of a just allowance? From the general style of your late publications of all sorts, one would be led to believe that your clergy in France were a sort of monsters; an horrible composition of superstition, ignorance, sloth, fraud, avarice, and tyranny. But is this true? Is it true, that the lapse of time, the cessation of conflicting interests, the woful experience of the evils resulting from party rage, have had no sort of influence gradually to meliorate their minds? Is it true, that they were daily renewing invasions on the civil power, troubling the domestic quiet of their country, and rendering the operations of its government feeble and precarious? Is it true, that the clergy of our times have pressed down the laity with an iron hand, and were, in all places, lighting up the fires of a savage persecution? Did they by every fraud endeavour to encrease their estates? Did they use to exceed the due demands on estates that were their own? Or, rigidly screwing up right into wrong, did they convert a legal claim into a vexatious extortion? When not possessed of power, were they filled with the vices of those who envy it? Were they enflamed with a violent litigious spirit of controversy? Goaded on with the ambition of intellectual sovereignty, were they ready to fly in the face of all magistracy, to fire churches, to massacre the priests of other descriptions, to pull down altars, and to make their way over the ruins of subverted governments to an empire of doctrine, sometimes flattering, sometimes forcing the consciences of men from the jurisdiction of public institutions into a submission to their personal authority, beginning with a claim of liberty and ending with an abuse of power?

These, or some of these, were the vices objected, and not wholly without foundation, to several of the churchmen of former times, who belonged to the two great parties which then divided and distracted Europe.

If there was in France, as in other countries there visibly is, a great abatement, rather than any increase of these vices, instead of loading the present clergy with the crimes of other men, and the odious character of other times, in common equity they ought to be praised, encouraged, and supported, in their departure from a spirit which disgraced their predecessors, and for having assumed a temper of mind and manners more suitable to their sacred function.

When my occasions took me into France, towards the close of the late reign, the clergy, under all their forms, engaged a considerable part of my curiosity. So far from finding (except from one set of men, not then very numerous though very active) the complaints and discontents against that body, which some publications had given me reason to expect, I perceived little or no public or private uneasiness on their account. On further examination, I found the clergy in general, persons of moderate minds and decorous manners; I include the seculars, and the regulars of both sexes. I had not the good fortune to know a great many of the parochial clergy; but in general I received a perfectly good account of their morals, and of their attention to their duties. With some of the higher clergy I had a personal acquaintance;* and of the rest in that class, very good means of information. They were, almost all of them, persons of noble birth. They resembled others of their own rank; and where there was any difference, it was in their favour. They were more fully educated than the military noblesse; so as by no means to disgrace their profession by ignorance, or by want of fitness for the exercise of their authority. They seemed to me, beyond the clerical character, liberal and open; with the hearts of gentlemen, and men of honour; neither insolent nor servile in their manners and conduct. They seemed to me rather a superior class; a set of men, amongst whom you would not be surprised to find a *Fenelon*.* I saw among the clergy in Paris (many of the description are not to be met with any where) men of great learning and candour; and I had reason to believe, that this description was not confined to Paris. What I found in other places, I know was accidental; and therefore to be presumed a fair sample. I spent a few days in a provincial town, where, in the absence of the bishop, I passed my evenings with three clergymen, his vicars general, persons who would have done honour to any church. They were all well informed; two of them of deep, general, and extensive erudition, antient and modern, oriental and western; particularly in their own profession. They had a more extensive knowledge of our English divines than I expected; and they entered into the genius of those writers with a critical accuracy. One of these gentlemen is since dead, the Ábbé *Morangis*. I pay this tribute, without reluctance, to the memory of that noble, reverend, learned, and excellent person; and I should do the same, with equal cheerfulness, to the merits of the others, who I believe are still living, if I did not fear to hurt those whom I am unable to serve.

Some of these ecclesiastics of rank, are, by all titles, persons deserving of general respect. They are deserving of gratitude from me, and from many English. If this letter should ever come into their hands, I hope they will believe there are those of our nation who feel for their unmerited fall, and for the cruel confiscation of their fortunes, with no common sensibility. What I say of them is a testimony, as far as one feeble voice can go, which I owe to truth. Whenever the question of this unnatural persecution is concerned, I will pay it. No one shall prevent me from being just and grateful. The time is fitted for the duty; and it is particularly becoming to shew our justice and gratitude, when those who have deserved well of us and of mankind are labouring under popular obloquy and the persecutions of oppressive power.*

You had before your revolution about an hundred and twenty bishops. A few of them were men of eminent sanctity, and charity without limit. When we talk of the heroic, of course we talk of rare, virtue. I believe the instances of eminent depravity may be as rare amongst them as those of transcendent goodness. Examples of avarice and of licentiousness may be picked out, I do not question it, by those who delight in the investigation which leads to such discoveries. A man, as old as I am, will not be astonished that several, in every description, do not lead that perfect life of self-denial, with regard to wealth or to pleasure, which is wished for by all, by some expected, but by none exacted with more rigour, than by those who are the most attentive to their own interests, or the most indulgent to their own passions. When I was in France, I am certain that the number of vicious prelates was not great. Certain individuals among them not distinguishable for the regularity of their lives, made some amends for their want of the severe virtues, in their possession of the liberal; and were endowed with qualitites which made them useful in the church and state. I am told, that with few exceptions, Louis the Sixteenth had been more attentive to character, in his promotions to that rank, than his immediate predecessor; and I believe, (as some spirit of reform has prevailed through the whole reign) that it may be true. But the present ruling power has shewn a disposition only to plunder the church. It has punished *all* prelates; which is to favour the vicious, at least in point of reputation. It has made a degrading pensionary establishment, to which no man of liberal ideas or liberal condition will destine his children. It must settle into the lowest classes of the people. As with you the inferior clergy are not numerous enough for their duties; as these duties are, beyond measure, minute and toilsome; as you have left no middle classes of clergy at their ease, in future nothing of science or erudition can exist in the Gallican church. To complete the project, without the least attention to the rights of patrons, the assembly has provided in future an elective clergy, an arrangement which will drive out of the clerical profession all men of sobriety; all who can pretend to independence in their function or their conduct; and which will throw the whole direction of the public mind into the hands of a set of licentious, bold, crafty, factious, flattering wretches, of such condition and such habits of life as will make their contemptible pensions (in comparison of which the stipend of an exciseman is lucrative and honourable) an object of low and illiberal intrigue. Those officers, whom they still call bishops, are to be elected to a provision comparatively mean, through the same arts, (that is, electioneering arts) by men of all religious tenets that are known or can be invented. The new lawgivers have not ascertained any thing whatsoever concerning their qualifications, relative either to doctrine or to morals; no more than they have done with regard to the subordinate clergy; nor does it appear but that both the higher and the lower may, at their discretion, practise or preach any mode of religion or irreligion that they please. I do not yet see what the jurisdiction of bishops over their subordinates is to be; or whether they are to have any jurisdiction at all.

In short, Sir, it seems to me, that this new ecclesiastical establishment is intended only to be temporary, and preparatory to the utter abolition, under any of its forms, of the Christian religion, whenever the minds of men are prepared for this last stroke against it, by the accomplishment of the plan for bringing its ministers into universal contempt. They who will not believe, that the philosophical fanatics who guide in these matters, have long entertained such a design, are utterly ignorant of their character and proceedings. These enthusiasts do not scruple to avow their opinion, that a state can subsist without any religion better than with one; and that they are able to supply the place of any good which may be in it, by a project of their own—namely, by a sort of education they have imagined, founded in a knowledge of the physical wants of men; progressively carried to an enlightened self-interest, which, when well understood, they tell us will identify with an interest more enlarged and public. The scheme of this education has been long known. Of late they distinguish it (as they have got an entire new nomenclature of technical terms) by the name of a *Civic Education.**

I hope their partizans in England, (to whom I rather attribute very inconsiderate conduct than the ultimate object in this detestable design) will succeed neither in the pillage of the ecclesiastics, nor in the introduction of a principle of popular election to our bishoprics and parochial cures. This, in the present condition of the world, would be the last corruption of the church; the utter ruin of the clerical character; the most dangerous shock that the state ever received through a misunderstood arrangement of religion. I know well enough that the bishoprics and cures, under kingly and seignoral patronage, as now they are in England, and as they have been lately in France, are sometimes acquired by unworthy methods; but the other mode of ecclesiastical canvas subjects them infinitely more surely and more generally to all the evil arts of low ambition, which, operating on and through greater numbers, will produce mischief in proportion.

Those of you who have robbed the clergy, think that they shall easily reconcile their conduct to all protestant nations; because the clergy, whom they have thus plundered, degraded, and given over to mockery and scorn, are of the Roman Catholic, that is, of *their own* pretended persuasion. I have no doubt that some miserable bigots will be found here as well as elsewhere, who hate sects and parties different from their own, more than they love the substance of religion; and who are more angry with those who differ from them in their particular plans and systems, than displeased with those who attack the foundation of our common hope. These men will write and speak on the subject in the manner that is to be expected from their temper and character. Burnet* says, that when he was in France, in the year 1683, 'the method which carried over the men of the finest parts to popery was this—they brought themselves to doubt of the whole Christian religion. When that was once done, it seemed a more indifferent thing of what side or form they continued outwardly.' If this was then the ecclesiastic policy of France, it is what they have since but too much reason to repent of. They preferred atheism to a form of religion not agreeable to their ideas. They succeeded in destroying that form; and atheism has succeeded in destroying them. I can readily given credit to Burnet's story; because I have observed too much of a similar spirit (for a little of it is 'much too much') amongst ourselves. The humour, however, is not general.

The teachers who reformed our religion in England bore no sort of resemblance to your present reforming doctors in Paris. Perhaps they were (like those whom they opposed) rather more than could be wished under the influence of a party spirit; but they were most sincere believers; men of the most fervent and exalted piety; ready to die (as some of them did die) like true heroes in defence of their particular ideas of Christianity; as they would with equal fortitude, and more chearfully, for that stock of general truth, for the branches of which they contended with their blood. These men would have disavowed with horror those wretches who claimed a fellowship with them upon no other titles than those of their having pillaged the persons with whom they maintained controversies, and their having despised the common religion, for the purity of which they exerted themselves with a zeal, which unequivocally bespoke their highest reverence for the substance of that system which they wished to reform. Many of their descendants have retained the same zeal; but, (as less engaged in conflict) with more moderation. They do not forget that justice and mercy are substantial parts of religion. Impious men do not recommend themselves to their communion by iniquity and cruelty towards any description of their fellow creatures.

We hear these new teachers continually boasting of their spirit of toleration.* That those persons should tolerate all opinions, who think none to be of estimation, is a matter of small merit. Equal neglect is not impartial kindness. The species of benevolence, which arises from contempt, is no true charity. There are in England abundance of men who tolerate in the true spirit of toleration. They think the dogmas of religion, though in different degrees, are all of moment; and that amongst them there is, as amongst all things of value, a just ground of preference. They favour, therefore, and they tolerate. They tolerate, not because they despise opinions, but because they respect justice. They would reverently and affectionately protect all religions, because they love and venerate the great principle upon which they all agree, and the great object to which they are all directed. They begin more and more plainly to discern, that we have all a common cause, as against a common enemy. They will not be so misled by the spirit of faction, as not to distinguish what is done in favour of their subdivision, from those acts of hostility, which, through some particular description, are aimed at the whole corps, in which they themselves, under another denomination, are included. It is impossible for me to say what may be the character of every description of men amongst us. But I speak for the greater part; and for them, I must tell you, that sacrilege is no part of their doctrine of good works; that, so far from calling you into their fellowship on such title, if your professors are admitted to their communion, they must carefully conceal their doctrine of the lawfulness of the proscription of innocent men; and that they must make restitution of all stolen goods whatsoever. Till then they are none of ours.

You may suppose that we do not approve your confiscation of the revenues of bishops, and deans, and chapters, and parochial clergy possessing independent estates arising from land, because we have the same sort of establishment in England. That objection, you will say, cannot hold as to the confiscation of the goods of monks and nuns, and the abolition of their order. It is true, that this particular part of your general confiscation does not affect England, as a precedent in point: but the reason applies; and it goes a great way. The long parliament confiscated the lands of deans and chapters in England on the same ideas upon which your assembly set to sale the lands of the monastic orders. But it is in the principle of injustice that the danger lies, and not in the description of persons on whom it is first exercised. I see, in a country very near us, a course of policy pursued, which sets justice, the common concern of mankind, at defiance. With the national assembly of France, possession is nothing; law and usage are nothing. I see the national assembly openly reprobate the doctrine of prescription, which[1] one of the greatest of their own lawyers tells us, with great truth, is a part of the law of nature. He tells us, that the positive ascertainment of its limits, and its security from invasion, were among the causes for which civil society itself has been instituted. If prescription be once shaken, no species of property is secure, when it once becomes an object large enough to tempt the cupidity of indigent power. I see a practice perfectly correspondent to their contempt of this great fundamental part of natural law. I see the confiscators begin with bishops, and chapters, and monasteries; but I do not see them end there. I see the princes of the blood, who, by the oldest usages of that kingdom, held large landed estates, (hardly with the compliment of a debate) deprived of their possessions, and in lieu of their stable independent property, reduced to the hope of some precarious, charitable pension, at the pleasure of an assembly, which of course will pay little regard to the rights of pensioners at pleasure, when it despises those of legal proprietors. Flushed with the insolence of their first inglorious victories, and pressed by the distressed caused by their lust of unhallowed lucre, disappointed but not discouraged, they have at length ventured completely to subvert all property of

[1] Domat.*

all descriptions throughout the extent of a great kingdom. They have compelled all men, in all transactions of commerce, in the disposal of lands, in civil dealing, and through the whole communion of life, to accept as perfect payment and good and lawful tender, the symbols of their speculations on a projected sale of their plunder. What vestiges of liberty or property have they left? The tenant-right of a cabbage-garden, a year's interest in a hovel, the good-will of an alehouse, or a baker's shop, the very shadow of a constructive property, are more ceremoniously treated in our parliament than with you the oldest and most valuable landed possessions, in the hands of the most respectable personages, or than the whole body of the monied and commercial interest of your country. We entertain an high opinion of the legislative authority; but we have never dreamt that parliaments had any right whatever to violate property, to overrule prescription, or to force a currency of their own fiction in the place of that which is real, and recognized by the law of nations. But you, who began with refusing to submit to the most moderate restraints, have ended by establishing an unheard of despotism. I find the ground upon which your confiscators go is this; that indeed their proceedings could not be supported in a court of justice; but that the rules of prescription cannot bind a legislative assembly.[1] So that this legislative assembly of a free nation sits, not for the security, but for the destruction of property, and not of property only, but of every rule and maxim which can give it stability, and of those instruments which can alone give it circulation.

When the Anabaptists of Munster,* in the sixteenth century, had filled Germany with confusion by their system of levelling and their wild opinions concerning property, to what country in Europe did not the progress of their fury furnish just cause of alarm? Of all things, wisdom is the most terrified with epidemical fanaticism, because of all enemies it is that against which she is the least able to furnish any kind of resource. We cannot be ignorant of the spirit of atheistical fanaticism, that is inspired by a multitude of writings,

[1] Speech of Mr Camus,* published by order of the National Assembly.

dispersed with incredible assiduity and expence, and by sermons delivered in all the streets and places of public resort in Paris. These writings and sermons have filled the populace with a black and savage atrocity of mind, which supersedes in them the common feelings of nature, as well as all sentiments of morality and religion; insomuch that these wretches are induced to bear with a sullen patience the intolerable distresses brought upon them by the violent convulsions and permutations that have been made in property?[1] The spirit of proselytism attends this spirit of fanaticism. They have societies to cabal and correspond at home and abroad for the propagation of their tenets. The republic of Berne,* one of the happiest, the most prosperous, and the best governed countries upon earth, is one of the great objects, at the destruction of which they aim. I am told they have in some measure succeeded in sowing there the seeds of discontent. They are busy throughout Germany. Spain and Italy have not been untried. England is not left out of the comprehensive scheme of their malignant charity; and in England we find those who stretch out their arms to them, who recommend their examples from more than one pulpit, and who choose, in more than one periodical meeting, publicly to correspond

[1] Whether the following description is strictly true I know not; but it is what the publishers would have pass for true, in order to animate others. In a letter from Toul, given in one of their papers, is the following passage concerning the people of that district: 'Dans la Révolution actuelle, ils ont résisté à toutes les *séductions du bigotisme, aux persécutions et aux tracasseries* des Ennemis de la Révolution. *Oubliant leurs plus grands intérêts* pour rendre hommage aux vues d'ordre général qui ont determiné l'Assemblée Nationale, ils voient, *sans se plaindre*, supprimer cette foule d'établissemens ecclésiastiques par lesquels *ils subsistoient*; et même, en perdant leur siège épiscopal, la seule de toutes ces ressources qui pouvoit, ou plutôt *qui devoit, en tout équité*, leur être conservée; condamnés *à la plus effrayante misère*, sans avoir *été ni pu être entendus, ils ne murmurent point*, ils restent fidèles aux principes du plus pur patriotisme; ils sont encore prêts à *verser leur sang* pour le maintien de la Constitution, qui va reduire leur Ville *à la plus déplorable nullité.*'* These people are not supposed to have endured those sufferings and injustices in a struggle for liberty, for the same account states truly that they had been always free; their patience in beggary and ruin, and their suffering, without remonstrance, the most flagrant and confessed injustice, if strictly true, can be nothing but the effect of this dire fanaticism. A great multitude all over France is in the same condition and the same temper.

with them, to applaud them, and to hold them up as objects for imitation; who receive from them tokens of confraternity, and standards consecrated amidst their rites and mysteries,[1] who suggest to them leagues of perpetual amity, at the very time when the power, to which our constitution has exclusively delegated the federative capacity of this kingdom, may find it expedient to make war upon them.

It is not the confiscation of our church property from this example in France that I dread, though I think this would be no trifling evil. The great source of my solicitude is, lest it should ever be considered in England as the policy of a state, to seek a resource in confiscations of any kind; or that any one description of citizens should be brought to regard any of the others, as their proper prey.[2] Nations are wading deeper and deeper into an ocean of boundless debt. Public debts, which at first were a security to governments, by interesting many in the public tranquillity, are likely in their excess to become the means of their subversion. If governments provide for these debts by heavy impositions, they perish by becoming odious to the people. If they do not provide for them, they will be undone by the efforts of the most dangerous of all parties; I mean an extensive discontented monied interest, injured and not destroyed. The men who compose this interest look for their security, in the first instance, to the fidelity of government;

[1] See the proceedings of the confederation of *Nantz.**
[2] 'Si plures sunt ii quibus improve datum est, quam illi quibus injuste ademptum est, idcirco plus etiam valent? Non enim numero haec judicantur sed pondere. Quam autem habet aequitatem, ut agrum multis annis, aut etiam saeculis aut possessum, qui nullum habuit habeat; qui autem habuit amittat. Ac, propter hoc injuriae genus, Lacedaemonii Lysandrum Ephorum expulerunt: Agin regem (quod nunquam antea apud eos acciderat) necaverunt: exque eo tempore tantae discordiae secutae sunt, ut et tyranni exsisterint, et optimates exterminarentur, et preclarissime constituta respublica dilaberetur. Nec vero solum ipsa cecidit, sed etiam reliquam Graeciam evertit contagionibus malorum, quae a Lacadaemoniis profectae manarunt latius.'—After speaking of the conduct of the model of true patriots, Aratus of Sycion, which was in a very different spirit, he says, 'Sic par est agere cum civibus; non ut bis jam vidimus, hastam in foro ponere et bona civium voci subjicere praeconis. At ille Graecus (id quod fuit sapientis et praestantis viri) omnibus consulendum esse putavit: eaque est summa ratio et sapientia boni civis, commoda civium non divellere, sed omnes eadem aequitate continere.' Cic. Off. 1. 2.*

in the second, to its power. If they find the old governments effete, worn out, and with their springs relaxed, so as not to be of sufficient vigour for their purposes, they may seek new ones that shall be possessed of more energy; and this energy will be derived, not from an acquisition of resources, but from a contempt of justice. Revolutions are favourable to confiscation; and it is impossible to know under what obnoxious names the next confiscations will be authorised. I am sure that the principles predominant in France extend to very many persons and descriptions of persons in all countries who think their innoxious indolence their security. This kind of innocence in proprietors may be argued into inutility; and inutility into an unfitness for their estates. Many parts of Europe are in open disorder. In many others there is a hollow murmuring under ground; a confused movement is felt, that threatens a general earthquake in the political world. Already confederacies and correspondences of the most extraordinary nature are forming, in several countries.[1] In such a state of things we ought to hold ourselves upon our guard. In all mutations (if mutations must be) the circumstance which will serve most to blunt the edge of their mischief, and to promote what good may be in them, is, that they should find us with our minds tenacious of justice, and tender of property.

But it will be argued, that this confiscation in France ought not to alarm other nations. They say it is not made from wanton rapacity; that it is a great measure of national policy, adopted to remove an extensive inveterate, superstitious mischief. It is with the greatest difficulty that I am able to separate policy from justice. Justice is itself the great standing policy of civil society; and any eminent departure from it, under any circumstances, lies under the suspicion of being no policy at all.

When men are encouraged to go into a certain mode of life by the existing laws, and protected in that mode as in a lawful occupation—when they have accommodated all their ideas, and all their habits to it—when the law had long made their adherence to its rules a ground of reputation, and their

---

[1] See two books intitled, Enige Originalschriften des Illuminatenordens.— System und Folgen des Illuminatenordens. Munchen 1787.*

departure from them a ground of disgrace and even of penalty—I am sure it is unjust in legislature, by an arbitrary act, to offer a sudden violence to their minds and their feelings; forcibly to degrade them from their state and condition, and to stigmatize with shame and infamy that character and those customs which before had been made the measure of their happiness and honour. If to this be added an expulsion from their habitations, and a confiscation of all their goods, I am not sagacious enough to discover how this despotic sport, made of the feelings, consciences, prejudices, and properties of men, can be discriminated from the rankest tyranny.

If the injustice of the course pursued in France be clear, the policy of the measure, that is, the public benefit to be expected from it, ought to be at least as evident, and at least as important. To a man who acts under the influence of no passion, who has nothing in view in his projects but the public good, a great difference will immediately strike him, between what policy would dictate on the original introduction of such institutions, and on a question of their total abolition, where they have cast their roots wide and deep, and where by long habit things more valuable than themselves are so adapted to them, and in a manner interwoven with them, that the one cannot be destroyed without notably impairing the other. He might be embarassed, if the case were really such as sophisters represent it in their paltry style of debating. But in this, as in most questions of state, there is a middle. There is something else than the mere alternative of absolute destruction, or unreformed existence. *Spartam nactus es; hanc exorna.** This is, in my opinion, a rule of profound sense, and ought never to depart from the mind of an honest reformer. I cannot conceive how any man can have brought himself to that pitch of presumption, to consider his country as nothing but *carte blanche*, upon which he may scribble whatever he pleases. A man full of warm speculative benevolence may wish his society otherwise constituted than he finds it; but a good patriot and a true politician, always considers how he shall make the most of the existing materials of his country. A disposition to preserve, and an ability to improve, taken together, would be my standard of a statesman. Every thing else is vulgar in the conception, perilous in the execution.

There are moments in the fortune of states when particular men are called to make improvements by great mental exertion. In those moments, even when they seem to enjoy the confidence of their prince and country, and to be invested with full authority, they have not always apt instruments. A politician, to do great things, looks for a *power*, what our workmen call a *purchase*; and if he finds that power, in politics as in mechanics he cannot be at a loss to apply it. In the monastic institutions, in my opinion, was found a great *power* for the mechanism of politic benevolence. There were revenues with a public direction; there were men wholly set apart and dedicated to public purposes, without any other than public ties and public principles; men without the possibility of converting the estate of the community into a private fortune; men denied to self-interests, whose avarice is for some community; men to whom personal poverty is honour, and implicit obedience stands in the place of freedom. In vain shall a man look to the possibility of making such things when he wants them. The winds blow as they list. These institutions are the products of enthusiasm; they are the instruments of wisdom. Wisdom cannot create materials; they are the gifts of nature or of chance; her pride is in the use. The perennial existence of bodies corporate and their fortunes, are things particularly suited to a man who has long views; who meditates designs that require time in fashioning; and which propose duration when they are accomplished. He is not deserving to rank high, or even to be mentioned in the order of great statesmen, who, having obtained the command and direction of such a power as existed in the wealth, the discipline, and the habits of such corporations, as those which you have rashly destroyed, cannot find any way of converting it to the great and lasting benefit of his country. On the view of this subject a thousand uses suggest themselves to a contriving mind. To destroy any power, growing wild from the rank productive force of the human mind, is almost tantamount, in the moral world, to the destruction of the apparently active properties of bodies in the material. It would be like the attempt to destroy (if it were in our competence to destroy) the expansive force of fixed air in nitre, or the power of steam, or of electricity, or of magnetism. These energies always existed in nature, and they were always discernible. They seemed, some of them unserviceable, some noxious, some no better than a sport to children; until contemplative ability combining with practic skill, tamed their wild nature, subdued them to use, and rendered them at once the most powerful and the most tractable agents, in subservience to the great views and designs of men. Did fifty thousand persons, whose mental and whose bodily labour you might direct, and so many hundred thousand a year of a revenue, which was neither lazy nor superstitious, appear too big for your abilities to wield? Had you no way of using the men but by converting monks into pensioners? Had you no way of turning the revenue to account, but through the improvident resource of a spendthrift sale? If you were thus destitute of mental funds, the proceeding is in its natural course. Your politicians do not understand their trade; and therefore they sell their tools.

But the institutions savour of superstition in their very principle; and they nourish it by a permanent and standing influence. This I do not mean to dispute; but this ought not to hinder you from deriving from superstition itself any resources which may thence be furnished for the public advantage. You derive benefits from many dispositions and many passions of the human mind, which are of as doubtful a colour in the moral eye, as superstition itself. It was your business to correct and mitigate every thing which was noxious in this passion, as in all the passions. But is superstition the greatest of all possible vices? In its possible excess I think it becomes a very great evil. It is, however, a moral subject; and of course admits of all degrees and all modifications. Superstition is the religion of feeble minds; and they must be tolerated in an intermixture of it, in some trifling or some enthusiastic shape or other, else you will deprive weak minds of a resource found necessary to the strongest. The body of all true religion consists, to be sure, in obedience to the will of the sovereign of the world; in a confidence in his declarations; and an imitation of his perfections. The rest is our own. It may be prejudicial to the great end; it may be auxiliary. Wise men, who as such, are not *admirers* (not admirers at least of the *Munera Terrae*)* are not violently attached to these things, not do they violently hate them. Wisdom is not the most severe corrector of folly. They are the rival follies, which mutually wage so unrelenting a war; and which make so cruel a use of their advantages, as they can happen to engage the immoderate vulgar on the one side or the other in their quarrels. Prudence would be neuter; but if, in the contention between fond attachment and fierce antipathy concerning things in their nature not made to produce such heats, a prudent man were obliged to make a choice of what errors and excesses of enthusiasm he would condemn or bear, perhaps he would think the superstition which builds, to be more tolerable than that which demolishes— that which adorns a country, than that which deforms it—that which endows, than that which plunders—that which disposes to mistaken beneficence, than that which stimulates to real injustice—that which leads a man to refuse to himself lawful pleasures, than that which snatches from others the scanty subsistence of their self-denial. Such, I think, is very nearly the state of the question between the ancient founders of monkish superstition, and the superstition of the pretended philosophers of the hour.

For the present I postpone all consideration of the supposed public profit of the sale, which however I conceive to be perfectly delusive. I shall here only consider it as a transfer of property. On the policy of that transfer I shall trouble you with a few thoughts.

In every prosperous community something more is produced than goes to the immediate support of the producer. This surplus forms the income of the landed capitalist. It will be spent by a proprietor who does not labour. But this idleness is itself the spring of labour; this repose the spur to industry. The only concern of the state is, that the capital taken in rent from the land, should be returned again to the industry from whence it came; and that its expenditure should be with the least possible detriment to the morals of those who expend it, and to those of the people to whom it is returned.

In all the views of receipt, expenditure, and personal

employment, a sober legislator would carefully compare the possessor whom he was recommended to expel, with the stranger who was proposed to fill his place. Before the inconveniences are incurred which *must* attend all violent revolutions in property through extensive confiscation, we ought to have some rational assurance that the purchasers of the confiscated property will be in a considerable degree more laborious, more virtuous, more sober, less disposed to extort an unreasonable proportion of the gains of the labourer, or to consume on themselves a larger share than is fit for the measure of an individual, or that they should be qualified to dispense the surplus in a more steady and equal mode, so as to answer the purposes of a politic expenditure, than the old possessors, call those possessors, bishops, or canons, or commendatory abbots, or monks, or what you please. The monks are lazy. Be it so. Suppose them no otherwise employed than by singing in the choir. They are as usefully employed as those who neither sing nor say. As usefully even as those who sing upon the stage. They are as usefully employed as if they worked from dawn to dark in the innumerable servile, degrading, unseemly, unmanly, and often most unwholesome and pestiferous occupations, to which by the social oeconomy so many wretches are inevitably doomed. If it were not generally pernicious to disturb the natural course of things, and to impede, in any degree, the great wheel of circulation which is turned by the strangely directed labour of these unhappy people, I should be infinitely more inclined forcibly to rescue them from their miserable industry, than violently to disturb the tranquil repose of monastic quietude. Humanity, and perhaps policy, might better justify me in the one than in the other. It is a subject on which I have often reflected, and never reflected without feeling from it. I am sure that no consideration, except the necessity of submitting to the yoke of luxury, and the despotism of fancy, who in their own imperious way will distribute the surplus product of the soil, can justify the toleration of such trades and employments in a well-regulated state. But, for this purpose of distribution, it seems to me, that the idle expences of monks are quite as well directed as the idle expences of us lay-loiterers.

When the advantages of the possession, and of the project, are on a par, there is no motive for a change. But in the present case, perhaps they are not upon a par, and the difference is in favour of the possession. It does not appear to me, that the expences of those whom you are going to expel, do, in fact, take a course so directly and so generally leading to vitiate and degrade and render miserable those through whom they pass, as the expences of those favourites whom you are intruding into their houses. Why should the expenditure of a great landed property, which is a dispersion of the surplus product of the soil, appear intolerable to you or to me, when it takes its course through the accumulation of vast libraries, which are the history of the force and weakness of the human mind; through great collections of antient records, medals, and coins, which attest and explain laws and customs; through paintings and statues, that, by imitating nature, seem to extend the limits of creation; through grand monuments of the dead, which continue the regards and connexions of life beyond the grave; through collections of the specimens of nature, which become a representative assembly of all the classes and families of the world, that by disposition facilitate, and, by exciting curiosity, open the avenues to science? If, by great permanent establishments, all these objects of expence are better secured from the inconstant sport of personal caprice and personal extravagance, are they worse than if the same tastes prevailed in scattered individuals? Does not the sweat of the mason and carpenter, who toil in order to partake the sweat of the peasant, flow as pleasantly and as salubriously, in the construction and repair of the majestic edifices of religion, as in the painted booths and sordid sties of vice and luxury; as honourably and as profitably in repairing those sacred works, which grow hoary with innumerable years, as on the momentary receptacles of transient voluptuousness; in opera-houses, and brothels, and gaming-houses, and club-houses, and obelisks in the Champ de Mars?* Is the surplus product of the olive and the vine worse employed in the frugal sustenance of persons, whom the fictions of a pious imagination raise to dignity by construing in the service of God, than in pampering the innumerable multitude of those who are degraded by being made useless domestics subservient to the pride of man? Are the decorations of temples an expenditure less worthy a wise man than ribbons, and laces, and national cockades, and petits maisons, and petit soupers,* and all the innumerable fopperies and follies in which opulence sports away the burthen of its superfluity?

We tolerate even these; not from love of them, but for fear of worse. We tolerate them, because property and liberty, to a degree, require that toleration. But why proscribe the other, and surely, in every point of view, the more laudable use of estates? Why, through the violation of all property, through an outrage upon every principle of liberty, forcibly carry them from the better to the worse?

This comparison between the new individuals and the old corps is made upon a supposition that no reform could be made in the latter. But in a question of reformation, I always consider corporate bodies, whether sole or consisting of many, to be much more susceptible of a public direction by the power of the state, in the use of their property, and in the regulation of modes and habits of life in their members, than private citizens ever can be, or perhaps ought to be; and this seems to me a very material consideration for those who undertake any thing which merits the name of a politic enterprize.—So far as to the estates of monasteries.

With regard to the estates possessed by bishops and canons, and commendatory abbots, I cannot find out for what reason some landed estates may not be held otherwise than by inheritance. Can any philosophic spoiler undertake to demonstrate the positive or the comparative evil, of having a certain, and that too a large portion of landed property, passing in succession thro' persons whose title to it is, always in theory, and often in fact, an eminent degree of piety, morals, and learning; a property which, by its destination, in their turn, and on the score of merit, gives to the noblest families renovation and support, to the lowest the means of dignity and elevation; a property, the tenure of which is the performance of some duty, (whatever value you may choose to set upon that duty) and the character of whose proprietors demands at least an exterior decorum and gravity of manners;

who are to exercise a generous but temperate hospitality; part of whose income they are to consider as a trust for charity; and who, even when they fail in their trust, when they slide from their character, and degenerate into a mere common secular nobleman or gentleman, are in no respect worse than those who may succeed them in their forfeited possessions? Is it better that estates should be held by those who have no duty than by those who have one?—by those whose character and destination point to virtues, than by those who have no rule and direction in the expenditure of their estates but their own will and appetite? Nor are these estates held altogether in the character or with the evils supposed inherent in mortmain. They pass from hand to hand with a more rapid circulation than any other. No excess is good; and therefore too great a proportion of landed property may be held officially for life; but it does not seem to me of material injury to any commonwealth, that there should exist some estates that have a chance of being acquired by other means than the previous acquisition of money.

This letter is grown to a great length, though it is indeed short with regard to the infinite extent of the subject. Various avocations have from time to time called my mind from the subject. I was not sorry to give myself leisure to observe whether, in the proceedings of the national assembly, I might not find reasons to change or to qualify some of my first sentiments. Every thing has confirmed me more strongly in my first opinions. It was my original purpose to take a view of the principles of the national assembly with regard to the great and fundamental establishments; and to compare the whole of what you have substituted in the place of what you have destroyed, with the several members of our British constitution. But this plan is of greater extent than at first I computed, and I find that you have little desire to take the advantage of any examples. At present I must content myself with some remarks upon your establishments; reserving for another time what I proposed to say concerning the spirit of our British monarchy, aristocracy, and democracy, as practically they exist.

I have taken a review of what has been done by the

governing power in France. I have certainly spoke of it with
freedom. Those whose principle it is to despise the antient
permanent sense of mankind, and to set up a scheme of society
on new principles, must naturally expect that such of us who
think better of the judgment of the human race than of theirs,
should consider both them and their devices, as men and
schemes upon their trial. They must take it for granted that we
attend much to their reason, but not at all to their authority.
They have not one of the great influencing prejudices of
mankind in their favour. They avow their hostility to opinion.
Of course they must expect no support from that influence,
which, with every other authority, they have deposed from the
seat of its jurisdiction.

I can never consider this assembly as any thing else than a
voluntary association of men, who have availed themselves of
circumstances, to seize upon the power of the state.* They
have not the sanction and authority of the character under
which they first met. They have assumed another of a very
different nature; and have completely altered and inverted all
the relations in which they originally stood. They do not hold
the authority they exercise under any constitutional law of the
state. They have departed from the instructions of the people
by whom they were sent; which instructions, as the assembly
did not act in virtue of any antient usage or settled law, were
the sole source of their authority. The most considerable of
their acts have not been done by great majorities; and in this
sort of near divisions, which carry only the constructive
authority of the whole, strangers will consider reasons as well
as resolutions.

If they had set up this new experimental government as a
necessary substitute for an expelled tyranny, mankind would
anticipate the time of prescription, which, through long usage,
mellows into legality governments that were violent in their
commencement. All those who have affections which lead
them to the conservation of civil order would recognize, even
in its cradle, the child as legitimate, which has been produced
from those principles of cogent expediency to which all just
governments owe their birth, and on which they justify their
continuance. But they will be late and reluctant in giving any

sort of countenance to the operations of a power, which has derived its birth from no law and no necessity; but which on the contrary has had its origin in those vices and sinister practices by which the social union is often disturbed and sometimes destroyed. This assembly has hardly a year's prescription. We have their own word for it that they have made a revolution. To make a revolution is a measure which, *prima fronte*, requires an apology. To make a revolution is to subvert the antient state of our country; and no common reasons are called for to justify so violent a proceeding. The sense of mankind authorizes us to examine into the mode of acquiring new power, and to criticise on the use that is made of it with less awe and reverence than that which is usually conceded to a settled and recognized authority.

In obtaining and securing their power, the assembly proceeds upon principles the most opposite from those which appear to direct them in the use of it. An observation on this difference will let us into the true spirit of their conduct. Every thing which they have done, or continue to do, in order to obtain and keep their power, is by the most common arts. They proceed exactly as their ancestors of ambition have done before them. Trace them through all their artifices, frauds, and violences, you can find nothing at all that is new. They follow precedents and examples with the punctilious exactness of a pleader. They never depart an iota from the authentic formulas of tyranny and usurpation. But in all the regulations relative to the public good, the spirit has been the very reverse of this. There they commit the whole to the mercy of untried speculations; they abandon the dearest interests of the public to those loose theories, to which none of them would chuse to trust the slightest of his private concerns. They make this difference, because in their desire of obtaining and securing power they are thoroughly in earnest; there they travel in the beaten road. The public interests, because about them they have no real solicitude, they abandon wholly to chance; I say to chance, because their schemes have nothing in experience to prove their tendency beneficial.

We must always see with a pity not unmixed with respect, the errors of those who are timid and doubtful of themselves with regard to points wherein the happiness of mankind is concerned. But in these gentlemen there is nothing of the tender parental solicitude which fears to cut up the infant for the sake of an experiment. In the vastness of their promises, and the confidence of their predictions, they far outdo all the boasting of empirics. The arrogance of their pretensions, in a manner provokes, and challenges us to an enquiry into their foundation.

I am convinced that there are men of considerable parts among the popular leaders in the national assembly. Some of them display eloquence in their speeches and their writings. This cannot be without powerful and cultivated talents. But eloquence may exist without a proportionable degree of wisdom. When I speak of ability, I am obliged to distinguish. What they have done towards the support of their system bespeaks no ordinary men. In the system itself, taken as the scheme of a republic constructed for procuring the prosperity and security of the citizen, and for promoting the strength and grandeur of the state, I confess myself unable to find out any thing which displays, in a single instance, the work of a comprehensive and disposing mind, or even the provisions of a vulgar prudence. Their purpose every where seems to have been to evade and slip aside from *difficulty*. This it has been the glory of the great masters in all the arts to confront, and to overcome; and when they had overcome the first difficulty, to turn it into an instrument for new conquests over new difficulties; thus to enable them to extend the empire of their science; and even to push forward beyond the reach of their original thoughts, the land marks of the human understanding itself. Difficulty is a severe instructor, set over us by the supreme ordinance of a parental guardian and legislator, who knows us better than we know ourselves, as he loves us better too. *Pater ipse colendi haud facilem esse viam voluit.** He that wrestles with us strengthens our nerves, and sharpens our skill. Our antagonist is our helper. This amicable conflict with difficulty obliges us to an intimate acquaintance with our object, and compels us to consider it in all its relations. It will not suffer us to be superficial. It is the want of nerves of understanding for such a task; it is the degenerate fondness for tricking short-cuts, and little fallacious facilities, that has in so many parts of the world created governments with arbitrary powers. They have created the late arbitrary monarchy of France. They have created the arbitrary republic of Paris. With them defects in wisdom are to be supplied by the plenitude of force. They get nothing by it. Commencing their labours on a principle of sloth, they have the common fortune of slothful men. The difficulties which they rather had eluded than escaped, meet them again in their course; they multiply and thicken on them; they are involved, through a labyrinth of confused detail, in an industry without limit, and without direction; and, in conclusion, the whole of their work becomes feeble, vitious, and insecure.

It is this inability to wrestle with difficulty which has obliged the arbitrary assembly of France to commence their schemes of reform with abolition and total destruction.[1] But is it in destroying and pulling down that skill is displayed? Your mob can do this as well at least as your assemblies. The shallowest understanding, the rudest hand, is more than equal to that task. Rage and phrenzy will pull down more in half an hour, than prudence, deliberation, and foresight can build up in an hundred years. The errors and defects of old establishments are visible and palpable. It calls for little ability to point them out; and where absolute power is given, it requires but a word wholly to abolish the vice and the establishment together. The same lazy but restless disposition, which loves sloth and hates quiet, directs these politicians, when they

---

[1] A leading member of the assembly, M. Rabaud de St Etienne,* has expressed the principle of all their proceedings as clearly as possible. Nothing can be more simple:—'*Tous les établissemens en France couronnent le malheur du peuple: pour le rendre heureux il faut le renouveler; changer ses idées; changer ses loix; changer ses moeurs; ... changer les hommes; changer les choses; changer les mots ... tout détruire; oui, tout détruire; puisque tout est à recréer.*'* This gentleman was chosen president in an assembly not sitting at the *Quinze vingt,** or the *Petites Maisons*; and composed of persons giving themselves out to be rational beings; but neither his ideas, language, or conduct, differ in the smallest degree from the discourses, opinions, and actions of those within and without the assembly, who direct the operations of the machine now at work in France.

come to work, for supplying the place of what they have destroyed. To make every thing the reverse of what they have seen is quite as easy as to destroy. No difficulties occur in what has never been tried. Criticism is almost baffled in discovering the defects of what has not existed; and eager enthusiasm, and cheating hope, have all the wide field of imagination in which they may expatiate with little or no opposition.

At once to preserve and to reform is quite another thing. When the useful parts of an old establishment are kept, and what is superadded is to be fitted to what is retained, a vigorous mind, steady persevering attention, various powers of comparison and combination, and the resources of an understanding fruitful in expedients are to be exercised; they are to be exercised in a continued conflict with the combined force of opposite vices; with the obstinacy that rejects all improvement, and the levity that is fatigued and disgusted with every thing of which it is in possession. But you may object—'A process of this kind is slow. It is not fit for an assembly, which glories in performing in a few months the work of ages. Such a mode of reforming, possibly might take up many years.' Without question it might; and it ought. It is one of the excellencies of a method in which time is amongst the assistants, that its operation is slow, and in some cases almost imperceptible. If circumspection and caution are a part of wisdom, when we work only upon inanimate matter, surely they become a part of duty too, when the subject of our demolition and construction is not brick and timber, but sentient beings, by the sudden alteration of whose state, condition, and habits, multitudes may be rendered miserable. But it seems as if it were the prevalent opinion in Paris, that an unfeeling heart, and an undoubting confidence, are the sole qualifications for a perfect legislator. Far different are my ideas of that high office. The true lawgiver ought to have an heart full of sensibility. He ought to love and respect his kind, and to fear himself. It may be allowed to his temperament to catch his ultimate object with an intuitive glance; but his movements towards it ought to be deliberate. Political arrangement, as it is a work for social ends, is to be only wrought by social means. There mind must conspire with mind. Time is required to produce that union of minds which alone can produce all the good we aim at. Our patience will atchieve more than our force. If I might venture to appeal to what is so much out of fashion in Paris, I mean to experience, I should tell you, that in my course I have known, and, according to my measure, have co-operated with great men; and I have never yet seen any plan which has not been mended by the observations of those who were much inferior in understanding to the person who took the lead in the business. By a slow but well-sustained progress, the effect of each step is watched; the good or ill success of the first, gives light to us in the second; and so, from light to light, we are conducted with safety through the whole series. We see, that the parts of the system do not clash. The evils latent in the most promising contrivances are provided for as they arise. One advantage is as little as possible sacrificed to another. We compensate, we reconcile, we balance. We are enabled to unite into a consistent whole the various anomalies and contending principles that are found in the minds and affairs of men. From hence arises, not an excellence in simplicity, but one far superior, an excellence in composition. Where the great interests of mankind are concerned through a long succession of generations, that succession ought to be admitted into some share in the councils which are so deeply to affect them. If justice requires this, the work itself requires the aid of more minds than one age can furnish. It is from this view of things that the best legislators have been often satisfied with the establishment of some sure, solid, and ruling principle in government; a power like that which some of the philosophers have called a plastic nature; and having fixed the principle, they have left it afterwards to its own operation.

To proceed in this manner, that is, to proceed with a presiding principle, and a prolific energy, is with me the criterion of profound wisdom. What your politicians think the marks of a bold, hardy genius, are only proofs of a deplorable want of ability. By their violent haste, and their defiance of the process of nature, they are delivered over blindly to every projector and adventurer, to every alchymist and empiric.

They despair of turning to account any thing that is common. Diet is nothing in their system of remedy. The worst of it is, that this their despair of curing common distempers by regular methods, arises not only from defect of comprehension, but, I fear, from some malignity of disposition. Your legislators seem to have taken their opinions of all professions, ranks, and offices, from the declamations and buffooneries of satirists; who would themselves be astonished if they were held to the letter of their own descriptions. By listening only to these, your leaders regard all things only on the side of their vices and faults, and view those vices and faults under every colour of exaggeration. It is undoubtedly true, though it may seem paradoxical; but in general, those who are habitually employed in finding and displaying faults, are unqualified for the work of reformation: because their minds are not only unfurnished with patterns of the fair and good, but by habit they come to take no delight in the contemplation of those things. By hating vices too much, they come to love men too little. It is therefore not wonderful, that they should be indisposed and unable to serve them. From hence arises the complexional disposition of some of your guides to pull every thing in pieces. At this malicious game they display the whole of their *quadrimanous** activity. As to the rest, the paradoxes of eloquent writers, brought forth purely as a sport of fancy, to try their talents, to rouze attention, and excite surprize, are taken up by these gentlemen, not in the spirit of the original authors, as means of cultivating their taste and improving their style. These paradoxes become with them serious grounds of action, upon which they proceed in regulating the most important concerns of the state. Cicero ludicrously describes Cato as endeavouring to act in the commonwealth upon the school paradoxes which exercised the wits of the junior students in the stoic philosophy.* If this was true of Cato, these gentlemen copy after him in the manner of some persons who lived about his time—*pede nudo Catonem.** Mr Hume told me, that he had from Rousseau himself the secret of his principles of composition.* That acute, though eccentric, observer had perceived, that to strike and interest the public, the marvellous must be produced; that the marvellous of the heathen mythology had long since lost its effect; that giants, magicians, fairies, and heroes of romance which succeeded, had exhausted the portion of credulity which belonged to their age; that now nothing was left to a writer but that species of the marvellous, which might still be produced, and with as great an effect as ever, though in another way; that is, the marvellous in life, in manners, in characters, and in extraordinary situations, giving rise to new and unlooked-for strokes in politics and morals. I believe, that were Rousseau alive, and in one of his lucid intervals, he would be shocked at the practical phrenzy of his scholars, who in their paradoxes are servile imitators; and even in their incredulity discover an implicit faith.

Men who undertake considerable things, even in a regular way, ought to give us ground to presume ability. But the physician of the state, who, not satisfied with the cure of distempers, undertakes to regenerate constitutions, ought to shew uncommon powers. Some very unusual appearances of wisdom ought to display themselves on the face of the designs of those who appeal to no practice, and who copy after no model. Has any such been manifested? I shall take a view (it shall for the subject be a very short one) of what the assembly has done, with regard, first, to the constitution of the legislature; in the next place, to that of the executive power; then to that of the judicature; afterwards to the model of the army; and conclude with the system of finance, to see whether we can discover in any part of their schemes the portentous ability, which may justify these bold undertakers in the superiority which they assume over mankind.

It is in the model of the sovereign and presiding part of this new republic, that we should expect their grand display. Here they were to prove their title to their proud demands. For the plan itself at large, and for the reasons on which it is grounded, I refer to the journals of the assembly of the 29th of September 1789, and to the subsequent proceedings which have made any alterations in the plan. So far as in a matter somewhat confused I can see light, the system remains substantially as it has been originally framed. My few remarks will be such as regard its spirit, its tendency, and its fitness for framing a popular commonwealth, which they profess theirs to be, suited to the ends for which any commonwealth, and particularly such a commonwealth, is made. At the same time, I mean to consider its consistency with itself, and its own principles.

Old establishments are tried by their effects. If the people are happy, united, wealthy, and powerful, we presume the rest. We conclude that to be good from whence good is derived. In old establishments various correctives have been found for their aberrations from theory. Indeed they are the results of various necessities and expediences. They are not often constructed after any theory; theories are rather drawn from them. In them we often see the end best obtained, where the means seem not perfectly reconcileable to what we may fancy was the original scheme. The means taught by experience may be better suited to political ends than those contrived in the original project. They again re-act upon the primitive constitution, and sometimes improve the design itself from which they seem to have departed. I think all this might be curiously exemplified in the British constitution. At worst, the errors and deviations of every kind in reckoning are found and computed, and the ship proceeds in her course. This is the case of old establishments; but in a new and merely theoretic system, it is expected that every contrivance shall appear, on the face of it, to answer its end; especially where the projectors are no way embarassed with an endeavour to accommodate the new building to an old one, either in the walls or on the foundations.

The French builders, clearing away as mere rubbish whatever they found, and, like their ornamental gardeners, forming every thing into an exact level, propose to rest the whole local and general legislature on three bases of three different kinds; one geometrical, one arithmetical, and the third financial; the first of which they call the *basis of territory*; the second, the *basis of population*; and the third, the *basis of contribution*. For the accomplishment of the first of these purposes they divide the area of their country into eighty-three pieces, regularly square, of eighteen leagues by eighteen. These large divisions are called *Departments*. These they portion, proceeding by square measurement, into seventeen hundred and twenty districts called *Communes*. These again they subdivide, still proceeding by square measurement, into smaller districts called *Cantons*, making in all 6,400.

At first view this geometrical basis of theirs presents not much to admire or to blame. It calls for no great legislative talents. Nothing more than an accurate land surveyor, with his chain, sight, and theodolite, is requisite for such a plan as this. In the old divisions of the country various accidents at various times, and the ebb and flow of various properties and jurisdictions, settled their bounds. These bounds were not made upon any fixed system undoubtedly. They were subject to some inconveniencies; but they were inconveniencies for which use had found remedies, and habit had supplied accommodation and patience. In this new pavement of square within square, and this organisation and semiorganisation made on the system of Empedocles and Buffon,* and not upon any politic principle, it is impossible that innumerable local inconveniencies, to which men are not habituated, must not arise. But these I pass over, because it requires an accurate knowledge of the country, which I do not possess, to specify them.

When these state surveyors came to take a view of their work of measurement, they soon found, that in politics, the most fallacious of all things was geometrical demonstration. They had then recourse to another basis (or rather buttress) to support the building which tottered on that false foundation. It was evident, that the goodness of the soil, the number of the people, their wealth, and the largeness of their contribution, made such infinite variations between square and square as to render mensuration a ridiculous standard of power in the commonwealth, and equality in geometry the most unequal of all measures in the distribution of men. However, they could not give it up. But dividing their political and civil representation into three parts, they allotted one of those parts to the square measurement, without a single fact or calculation to ascertain whether this territorial proportion of representation was fairly assigned, and ought upon any principle really to be a third. Having however given to geometry this portion (of a third for her dower) out of compliment I suppose to that sublime science, they left the other two to be scuffled for between the other parts, population and contribution.

When they came to provide for population, they were not able to proceed quite so smoothly as they had done in the field of their geometry. Here their arithmetic came to bear upon their juridical metaphysics. Had they stuck to their metaphysic principles, the arithmetical process would be simple indeed. Men, with them, are strictly equal, and are entitled to equal rights in their own government. Each head, on this system, would have its vote, and every man would vote directly for the person who was to represent him in the legislature. 'But soft— by regular degrees, not yet.'* This metaphysic principle, to which law, custom, usage, policy, reason, were to yield, is to yield itself to their pleasure. There must be many degrees, and some stages, before the representative can come in contact with his constituent. Indeed, as we shall soon see, these two persons are to have no sort of communion with each other. First, the voters in the *Canton*, who compose what they call *primary assemblies*, are to have a *qualification*.* What! a qualification on the indefeasible rights of men? Yes; but it shall be a very small qualification. Our injustice shall be very little oppressive; only the local valuation of three days labour paid to the public. Why, this is not much, I readily admit, for any thing but the utter subversion of your equalising principle. As a qualification it might as well be let alone; for it answers no one purpose for which qualifications are established: and, on your ideas, it excludes from a vote, the man of all others whose natural equality stands the most in need of protection and defence; I mean the man who has nothing else but his natural equality to guard him. You order him to buy the right, which you before told him nature had given to him gratuitously at his birth, and of which no authority on earth could lawfully deprive him. With regard to the person who cannot come up to your market, a tyrannous aristocracy, as against him, is established at the very outset, by you who pretend to be its sworn foe.

The gradation proceeds. These primary assemblies of the *Canton* elect deputies to the *Commune*; one for every two hundred qualified inhabitants. Here is the first medium put between the primary elector and the representative legislator; and here a new turnpike is fixed for taxing the rights of men with a second qualification: for none can be elected into the *Commune* who does not pay the amount of ten days labour. Nor have we yet done. There is still to be another gradation.[1] These *Communes*, chosen by the *Canton*, choose to the *Department*; and the deputies of the *Department* choose their deputies to the *National Assembly*. Here is a third barrier of a senseless qualification. Every deputy to the national assembly must pay, in direct contribution, to the value of a *mark of silver*. Of all these qualifying barriers we must think alike; that they are impotent to secure independence; strong only to destroy the rights of men.*

In all this process, which in its fundamental elements affects to consider only *population* upon a principle of natural right, there is a manifest attention to *property*; which, however just and reasonable on other schemes, is on theirs perfectly unsupportable.

When they come to their third basis, that of *Contribution*, we find that they have more completely lost sight of their rights of men. This last basis rests *entirely* on property. A principle totally different from the equality of men, and utterly irreconcileable to it, is thereby admitted; but no sooner is this principle admitted, than (as usual) it is subverted; and it is not subverted, (as we shall presently see,) to approximate the inequality of riches to the level of nature. The additional share in the third portion of representation, (a portion reserved exclusively for the higher contribution,) is made to regard the *district* only, and not the individuals in it who pay. It is easy to perceive, by the course of their reasonings, how

---

[1] The assembly, in executing the plan of their committee, made some alterations. They have struck out one stage in these gradations; this removes a part of the objection: but the main objection, namely, that in their scheme the first constituent voter has no connection with the representative legislator, remains in all its force. There are other alterations, some possibly for the better, some certainly for the worse; but to the author the merit or demerit of these smaller alterations appear to be of no moment, where the scheme itself is fundamentally vitious and absurd.

much they were embarassed by their contradictory ideas of the rights of men and the privileges of riches. The committee of constitution do as good as admit that they are wholly irreconcileable. 'The relation, with regard to the contributions, is without doubt *null* (say they) when the question is on the balance of the political rights as between individual and individual; without which *personal equality would be destroyed*, and *an aristocracy of the rich* would be established. But this inconvenience entirely disappears when the proportional relation of the contribution is only considered in the *great masses*, and is solely between province and province; it serves in that case only to form a just reciprocal proportion between the cities, without affecting the personal rights of the citizens.'

Here the principle of *contribution*, as taken between man and man, is reprobated as *null*, and destructive to equality; and as pernicious too; because it leads to the establishment of an *aristocracy of the rich*. However, it must not be abandoned. And the way of getting rid of the difficulty is to establish the inequality as between department and department, leaving all the individuals in each department upon an exact par. Observe, that this parity between individuals had been before destroyed when the qualifications within the departments were settled; nor does it seem a matter of great importance whether the equality of men be injured by masses or individually. An individual is not of the same importance in a mass represented by a few, as in a mass represented by many. It would be too much to tell a man jealous of his equality, that the elector has the same franchise who votes for three members as he who votes for ten.

Now take it in the other point of view, and let us suppose their principle of representation according to contribution, that is according to riches, to be well imagined, and to be a necessary basis for their republic. In this their third basis they assume, that riches ought to be respected, and that justice and policy require that they should entitle men, in some mode or other, to a larger share in the administration of public affairs; it is now to be seen, how the assembly provides for the pre-eminence, or even for the security of the rich, by conferring, in virtue of their opulence, that larger measure of power to their district which is denied to them personally. I readily admit (indeed I should lay it down as a fundamental principle) that in a republican government, which has a democratic basis, the rich do require an additional security above what is necessary to them in monarchies. They are subject to envy, and through envy to oppression. On the present scheme, it is impossible to divine what advantage they derive from the aristocratic preference upon which the unequal representation of the masses is founded. The rich cannot feel it, either as a support to dignity, or as security to fortune: for the aristocratic mass is generated from purely democratic principles; and the prevalence given to it in the general representation has no sort of reference to or connexion with the persons, upon account of whose property this superiority of the mass is established. If the contrivers of this scheme meant any sort of favour to the rich in consequence of their contribution, they ought to have conferred the privilege either on the individual rich, or on some class formed of rich persons (as historians represent Servius Tullius* to have done in the early constitution of Rome); because the contest between the rich and the poor is not a struggle between corporation and corporation, but a contest between men and men; a competition not between districts but between descriptions. It would answer its purpose better if the scheme were inverted; that the votes of the masses were rendered equal; and that the votes within each mass were proportioned to property.

Let us suppose one man in a district (it is an easy supposition) to contribute as much as an hundred of his neighbours. Against these he has but one vote. If there were but one representative for the mass, his poor neighbours would outvote him by an hundred to one for that single representative. Bad enough. But amends are to be made him. How? The district, in virtue of his wealth, is to choose, say, ten members instead of one: that is to say, by paying a very large contribution he has the happiness of being outvoted, an hundred to one, by the poor for ten representatives, instead of being outvoted exactly in the same proportion for a single member. In truth, instead of benefitting by this superior quantity of representation, the rich man is subjected to an additional hardship. The encrease of representation within his province sets up nine persons more, and as many more than nine as there may be democratic candidates, to cabal and intrigue, and to flatter the people at his expence and to his oppression. An interest is by this means held out to multitudes of the inferior sort, in obtaining a salary of eighteen livres a day (to them a vast object) besides the pleasure of a residence in Paris and their share in the government of the kingdom. The more the objects of ambition are multiplied and become democratic, just in that proportion the rich are endangered.

Thus it must fare between the poor and the rich in the province deemed aristocratic, which in its internal relation is the very reverse of that character. In its external relation, that is, its relation to the other provinces, I cannot see how the unequal representation, which is given to masses on account of wealth, becomes the means of preserving the equipoise and the tranquillity of the commonwealth. For if it be one of the objects to secure the weak from being crushed by the strong (as in all society undoubtedly it is) how are the smaller and poorer of these masses to be saved from the tyranny of the more wealthy? Is it by adding to the wealthy further and more systematical means of oppressing them. When we come to a balance of representation between corporate bodies, provincial interests, emulations, and jealousies are full as likely to arise among them as among individuals; and their divisions are likely to produce a much hotter spirit of dissention, and something leading much more nearly to a war.

I see that these aristocratic masses are made upon what is called the principle of direct contribution. Nothing can be a more unequal standard than this. The indirect contribution, that which arises from duties on consumption, is in truth a better standard, and follows and discovers wealth more naturally than this of direct contribution. It is difficult indeed to fix a standard of local preference on account of the one, or of the other, or of both, because some provinces may pay the more of either or of both, on account of causes not intrinsic, but originating from those very districts over whom they have obtained a preference in consequence of their ostensible contribution. If the masses were independent sovereign bodies, who were to provide for a federative treasury by distinct contingents, and that the revenue had not (as it has) many impositions running through the whole, which affect men individually, and not corporately, and which, by their nature, confound all territorial limits, something might be said for the basis of contribution as founded on masses. But of all things, this representation, to be measured by contribution, is the most difficult to settle upon principles of equity in a country, which considers its districts as members of an whole. For a great city, such as Bourdeaux or Paris, appears to pay a vast body of duties, almost out of all assignable proportion to other places, and its mass is considered accordingly. But are these cities the true contributors in that proportion? No. The consumers of the commodities imported into Bourdeaux, who are scattered through all France, pay the import duties of Bourdeaux. The produce of the vintage in Guienne and Languedoc give to that city the means of its contribution growing out of an export commerce. The landholders who spend their estates in Paris, and are thereby the creators of that city, contribute for Paris from the provinces out of which their revenues arise. Very nearly the same arguments will apply to the representative share given on account of *direct* contribution: because the direct contribution must be assessed on wealth real or presumed; and that local wealth will itself arise from causes not local, and which therefore in equity ought not to produce a local preference.

It is very remarkable, that in this fundamental regulation, which settles the representation of the mass upon the direct contribution, they have not yet settled how that direct contribution shall be laid, and how apportioned. Perhaps there is some latent policy towards the continuance of the present assembly in this strange procedure. However, until they do this, they can have no certain constitution. It must depend at last upon the system of taxation, and must vary with every variation in that system. As they have contrived matters, their taxation does not so much depend on their constitution, as their constitution on their taxation. This must introduce great confusion among the masses; as the variable qualification for votes within the district must, if ever real contested elections take place, cause infinite internal controversies.

To compare together the three bases, not on their political reason, but on the ideas on which the assembly works, and to try its consistency with itself, we cannot avoid observing, that the principle which the committee call the basis of *population*, does not begin to operate from the same point with the two other principles called the bases of *territory* and of *contribution*, which are both of an aristocratic nature. The consequence is, that where all three begin to operate together, there is the most absurd inequality produced by the operation of the former on the two latter principles. Every canton contains four square leagues, and is estimated to contain, on the average, 4,000 inhabitants, or 680 voters in the *primary assemblies*, which vary in numbers with the population of the canton, and send *one deputy* to the *commune* for every 200 voters. *Nine cantons* make a *commune*.

Now let us take a *canton* containing *a sea-port town of trade*, or *a great manufacturing town*. Let us suppose the population of this canton to be 12,700 inhabitants, or 2,193 voters, forming *three primary assemblies*, and sending *ten deputies* to the *commune*.

Oppose to this *one* canton *two* others of the remaining eight in the same commune. These we may suppose to have their fair population of 4,000 inhabitants, and 680 voters each, or 8,000 inhabitants and 1,360 voters, both together. These will form only *two primary assemblies*, and send only *six* deputies to the *commune*.

When the assembly of the *commune* comes to vote on the *basis of territory*, which principle is first admitted to operate in that assembly, the *single canton* which has *half* the territory of the *other two*, will have *ten* voices to *six* in the election of *three deputies* to the assembly of the department, chosen on the express ground of a representation of territory.

This inequality, striking as it is, will be yet highly aggravated, if we suppose, as we fairly may, the *several* other cantons of the *commune* to fall proportionably short of the average population, as much as the *principal canton* exceeds it. Now, as to *the basis of contribution*, which also is a principle admitted first to operate in the assembly of the *commune*. Let us again take *one* canton, such as is stated above. If the whole of the direct contributions paid by a great trading or manufacturing town be divided equally among the inhabitants, each individual will be found to pay much more than an individual living in the country according to the same average. The whole paid by the inhabitants of the former will be more than the whole paid by the inhabitants of the latter— we may fairly assume one-third more. Then the 12,700 inhabitants, or 2,193 voters of the canton will pay as much as 19,050 inhabitants, or 3,289 voters of the *other cantons*, which are nearly the estimated proportion of inhabitants and voters of *five* other cantons. Now the 2,193 voters will, as I before said, send only *ten* deputies to the assembly; the 3,289 voters will send *sixteen*. Thus, for an *equal* share in the contribution of the whole *commune*, there will be a difference of *sixteen* voices to *ten* in voting for deputies to be chosen on the principle of representing the general contribution of the whole *commune*.

By the same mode of computation we shall find 15,875 inhabitants, or 2,741 voters of the *other* cantons, who pay *one-sixth* LESS to the contribution of the whole *commune*, will have *three* voices MORE than the 12,700 inhabitants, or 2,193 voters of the *one* canton.

Such is the fantastical and unjust inequality between mass and mass, in this curious repartition of the rights of representation arising out of *territory* and *contribution*. The qualifications which these confer are in truth negative qualifications, that give a right in an inverse proportion to the possession of them.

In this whole contrivance of the three bases, consider it in any light you please, I do not see a variety of objects, reconciled in one consistent whole, but several contradictory principles reluctantly and irreconcileably brought and held together by your philosophers, like wild beasts shut up in a cage, to claw and bite each other to their mutual descruction.

I am afraid I have gone too far into their way of considering the formation of a constitution. They have much, but bad, metaphysics; much, but bad, geometry; much, but false, proportionate arithmetic; but if it were all as exact as metaphysics, geometry, and arithmetic ought to be, and if their schemes were perfectly consistent in all their parts, it would make only a more fair and sightly vision. It is remarkable, that in a great arrangement of mankind, not one reference whatsoever is to be found to any thing moral or any thing politic; nothing that relates to the concerns, the actions, the passions, the interests of men. *Hominem non sapiunt.**

You see I only consider this constitution as electoral, and leading by steps to the National Assembly. I do not enter into the internal government of the Departments, and their genealogy through the Communes and Cantons. These local governments are, in the original plan, to be as nearly as possible composed in the same manner and on the same principles with the elective assemblies. They are each of them bodies perfectly compact and rounded in themselves.

You cannot but perceive in this scheme, that it has a direct and immediate tendency to sever France into a variety of republics, and to render them totally independent of each other, without any direct constitutional means of coherence, connection, or subordination, except what may be derived from their acquiescence in the determinations of the general congress of the ambassadors from each independent republic. Such in reality is the National Assembly, and such governments I admit do exist in the world, though in forms infinitely more suitable to the local and habitual circumstances of their people. But such associations, rather than bodies politic, have generally been the effect of necessity, not choice; and I believe the present French power is the very first body of citizens, who, having obtained full authority to do with their country what they pleased, have chosen to dissever it in this barbarous manner.

It is impossible not to observe, that in the spirit of this geometrical distribution, and arithmetical arrangement, these pretended citizens treat France exactly like a country of conquest. Acting as conquerors, they have imitated the policy of the harshest of that harsh race. The policy of such barbarous victors, who contemn a subdued people, and insult their feelings, has ever been, as much as in them lay, to destroy all vestiges of the antient country, in religion, in polity, in laws, and in manners; to confound all territorial limits; to produce a general poverty; to put up their properties to auction; to crush their princes, nobles, and pontiffs; to lay low every thing which had lifted its head above the level, or which could serve to combine or rally, in their distresses, the disbanded people, under the standard of old opinion. They have made France free in the manner in which those sincere friends to the rights of mankind, the Romans, freed Greece, Macedon, and other nations. They destroyed the bonds of their union, under colour of providing for the independence of each of their cities.

When the members who compose these new bodies of cantons, communes, and departments, arrangements purposely produced through the medium of confusion, begin to act, they will find themselves, in a great measure, strangers to one another. The electors and elected throughout, especially in the rural *cantons*, will be frequently without any civil habitudes or connections, or any of that natural discipline which is the soul of a true republic. Magistrates and collectors of revenue are now no longer acquainted with their districts, bishops with their dioceses, or curates with their parishes. These new colonies of the rights of men bear a strong resemblance to that sort of military colonies which Tacitus has observed upon in the declining policy of Rome. In better and wiser days (whatever course they took with foreign nations) they were careful to make the elements of a methodical subordination and settlement to be coeval; and even to lay the foundations of civil discipline in the military.[1] But, when all the good arts had

---

[1] Non, ut olim, universae legiones deducebantur cum tribunis, et centur- ionibus, et sui cujusque ordinis militibus, ut consensu et caritate rempublican afficerent; sed ignoti inter se, diversis manipulis, sine rectore, sine affectibus mutuis, quasi ex alio genere mortalium, repente in unum collecti, numerus magis quam colonia.* Tac. Annal. 1. 14. sect. 27. All this will be still more applicable to the unconnected, rotatory, biennial national assemblies, in this absurd and senseless constitution.

fallen into ruin, they proceeded, as your assembly does, upon the equality of men, and with as little judgment, and as little care for those things which make a republic tolerable or durable. But in this, as well as almost every instance, your new commonwealth is born, and bred, and fed, in those corruptions which mark degenerated and worn out republics. Your child comes into the world with the symptoms of death; the *facies Hippocratica** forms the character of its physiognomy, and the prognostic of its fate.

The legislators who framed the antient republics knew that their business was too arduous to be accomplished with no better apparatus than the metaphysics of an under-graduate, and the mathematics and arithmetic of an exciseman. They had to do with men, and they were obliged to study human nature. They had to do with citizens, and they were obliged to study the effects of those habits which are communicated by the circumstances of civil life. They were sensible that the operation of this second nature on the first produced a new combination; and thence arose many diversities amongst men, according to their birth, their education, their professions, the periods of their lives, their residence in towns or in the country, their several ways of acquiring and of fixing property, and according to the quality of the property itself, all which rendered them as it were so many different species of animals. From hence they thought themselves obliged to dispose their citizens into such classes, and to place them in such situations in the state as their peculiar habits might qualify them to fill, and to allot to them such appropriated privileges as might secure to them what their specific occasions required, and which might furnish to each description such force as might protect it in the conflict caused by the diversity of interests, that must exist, and must contend in all complex society: for the legislator would have been ashamed, that the coarse husbandman should well know how to assort and to use his sheep, horses, and oxen, and should have enough of common sense not to abstract and equalize them all into animals, without providing for each kind an appropriate food, care, and employment; whilst he, the oeconomist, disposer, and shepherd of his own kindred, subliming himself into an airy metaphysician, was resolved to know nothing of his flocks, but as men in general. It is for this reason that Montesquieu* observed very justly, that in their classification of the citizens, the great legislators of antiquity made the greatest display of their powers, and even soared above themselves. It is here that your modern legislators have gone deep into the negative series, and sunk even below their own nothing. As the first sort of legislators attended to the different kinds of citizens, and combined them into one commonwealth, the others, the metaphysical and alchemistical legislators, have taken the direct contrary course. They have attempted to confound all sorts of citizens, as well as they could, into one homogeneous mass; and then they divided this their amalgama into a number of incoherent republics. They reduce men to loose counters merely for the sake of simple telling, and not to figures whose power is to arise from their place in the table. The elements of their own metaphysics might have taught them better lessons. The troll* of their categorical table might have informed them that there was something else in the intellectual world besides *substance* and *quantity*. They might learn from the catechism of metaphysics that there were eight heads more,[1] in every complex deliberation, which they have never thought of, though these, of all the ten, are the subject on which the skill of man can operate any thing at all.

So far from this able disposition of some of the old republican legislators, which follows with a solicitous accuracy, the moral conditions and propensities of men, they have levelled and crushed together all the orders which they found, even under the coarse unartificial arrangement of the monarchy, in which mode of government the classing of the citizens is not of so much importance as in a republic. It is true, however, that every such classification, if properly ordered, is good in all forms of government; and composes a strong barrier against the excesses of despotism, as well as it is the necessary means of giving effect and permanence to a republic. For want of something of this kind, if the present project of a republic should fail, all securities to a moderated freedom fail along

---

[1] Qualitas, Relatio, Actio, Passio, Ubi, Quando, Situs, Habitus.*

with it; all the indirect restraints which mitigate despotism are removed; insomuch that if monarchy should ever again obtain an entire ascendency in France, under this or under any other dynasty, it will probably be, if not voluntarily tempered at setting out, by the wise and virtuous counsels of the prince, and most completely arbitrary power that has ever appeared on earth. This is to play a most desperate game.

The confusion, which attends on all such proceedings, they even declare to be one of their objects, and they hope to secure their constitution by a terror of a return of those evils which attended their making it. 'By this,' say they, 'its destruction will become difficult to authority, which cannot break it up without the entire disorganization of the whole state.' They presume, that if this authority should ever come to the same degree of power that they have acquired, it would make a more moderate and chastised use of it, and would piously tremble entirely to disorganize the state in the savage manner that they have done. They expect, from the virtues of returning despotism, the security which is to be enjoyed by the offspring of their popular vices.

I wish, Sir, that you and my readers would give an attentive perusal to the work of M. de Calonne,* on this subject. It is indeed not only an eloquent but an able and instructive performance. I confine myself to what he says relative to the constitution of the new state, and to the condition of the revenue. As to the disputes of this minister with his rivals,* I do not wish to pronounce upon them. As little do I mean to hazard any opinion concerning his ways and means, financial or political, for taking his country out of its present disgraceful and deplorable situation of servitude, anarchy, bankruptcy, and beggary. I cannot speculate quite so sanguinely as he does: but he is a Frenchman, and has a closer duty relative to those objects, and better means of judging of them, than I can have. I wish that the formal avowal which he refers to, made by one of the principal leaders in the assembly, concerning the tendency of their scheme to bring France not only from a monarchy to a republic, but from a republic to a mere confederacy, may be very particularly attended to. It adds new force to my observations; and indeed M. de

Calonne's work supplies my deficiencies by many new and striking arguments on most of the subjects of this Letter.[1]

It is this resolution, to break their country into separate republics, which has driven them into the greatest number of their difficulties and contradictions. If it were not for this, all the questions of exact equality, and these balances, never to be settled, of individual rights, population, and contribution, would be wholly useless. The representation, though derived from parts, would be a duty which equally regarded the whole. Each deputy to the assembly would be the representative of France, and of all its descriptions, of the many and of the few, of the rich and of the poor, of the great districts and of the small. All these districts would themselves be subordinate to some standing authority, existing independently of them; an authority in which their representation, and every thing that belongs to it, originated, and to which it was pointed. This standing, unalterable, fundamental government would make, and it is the only thing which could make, that territory truly and properly an whole. With us, when we elect popular representatives, we send them to a council, in which each man individually is a subject, and submitted to a government complete in all its ordinary functions. With you the elective assembly is the sovereign, and the sole sovereign: all the members are therefore integral parts of this sole sovereignty. But with us it is totally different. With us the representative, separated from the other parts, can have no action and no existence. The government is the point of reference of the several members and districts of our representation. This is the center of our unity. This government of reference is a trustee for the *whole*,* and not for the parts. So is the other branch of our public council, I mean the house of lords. With us the king and the lords are several and joint securities for the equality of each district, each province, each city. When did you hear in Great Britain of any province suffering from the inequality of its representation; what district from having no representation at all? Not only our monarchy and our peerage

[1] See L'Etat de la France, p. 363.

secure the equality on which our unity depends, but it is the spirit of the house of commons itself. The very inequality of representation, which is so foolishly complained of, is perhaps the very thing which prevents us from thinking or acting as members for districts. Cornwall elects as many members as all Scotland. But is Cornwall better taken care of than Scotland? Few trouble their heads about any of your bases, out of some giddy clubs. Most of those, who wish for any change, upon any plausible grounds, desire it on different ideas.

Your new constitution is the very reverse of ours in its principle; and I am astonished how any persons could dream of holding out any thing done in it as an example for Great Britain. With you there is little, or rather no, connection between the last representative and the first constituent. The member who goes to the national assembly is not chosen by the people, nor accountable to them. There are three elections before he is chosen: two sets of magistracy intervene between him and the primary assembly, so as to render him, as I have said, an ambassador of a state, and not the representative of the people within a state. By this the whole spirit of the election is changed; nor can any corrective your constitution-mongers have devised render him any thing else than what he is. The very attempt to do it would inevitably introduce a confusion, if possible, more horrid than the present. There is no way to make a connexion between the original constituent and the representative, but by the circuitous means which may lead the candidate to apply in the first instance to the primary electors, in order that by their authoritative instructions (and something more perhaps) these primary electors may force the two succeeding bodies of electors to make a choice agreeable to their wishes. But this would plainly subvert the whole scheme. It would be to plunge them back into that tumult and confusion of popular election, which, by their interposed gradation elections, they mean to avoid, and at length to risque the whole fortune of the state with those who have the least knowledge of it, and the least interest in it. This is a perpetual dilemma, into which they are thrown by the vicious, weak, and contradictory principles they have chosen. Unless the people break up and level this gradation, it is plain that they do not at all substantially elect to the assembly; indeed they elect as little in appearance as reality.

What is it we all seek for in an election? To answer its real purposes, you must first possess the means of knowing the fitness of your man; and then you must retain some hold upon him by personal obligation or dependence. For what end are these primary electors complimented, or rather mocked, with a choice? They can never know any thing of the qualities of him that is to serve them, nor has he any obligation whatsoever to them. Of all the powers unfit to be delegated by those who have any real means of judging, that most peculiarly unfit is what relates to a *personal* choice. In case of abuse, that body of primary electors never can call the representative to an account for his conduct. He is too far removed from them in the chain of representation. If he acts improperly at the end of his two years lease, it does not concern him for two years more. By the new French constitution, the best and the wisest representatives go equally with the worst into this *Limbus Patrum*.* Their bottoms are supposed foul, and they must go into dock to be refitted. Every man who has served in an assembly is ineligible for two years after. Just as these magistrates begin to learn their trade, like chimney-sweepers, they are disqualified for exercising it. Superficial, new, petulant acquisition, and interrupted, dronish, broken, ill recollection, is to be the destined character of all your future governors. Your constitution has too much of jealousy to have much of sense in it. You consider the breach of trust in the representative so principally, that you do not at all regard the question of his fitness to execute it.

This purgatory interval is not unfavourable to a faithless representative, who may be as good a canvasser as he was a bad governor. In this time he may cabal himself into a superiority over the wisest and most virtuous. As, in the end, all the members of this elective constitution are equally fugitive, and exist only for the election, they may be no longer the same persons who had chosen him, to whom he is to be responsible when he solicits for a renewal of his trust. To call all the secondary electors of the *Commune* to account, is ridiculous, impracticable, and unjust; they may themselves have been deceived in their choice, as the third set of electors, those of the *Department*, may be in theirs. In your elections responsibility cannot exist.

Finding no sort of principle of coherence with each other in the nature and constitution of the several new republics of France, I considered what cement the legislators had provided for them from any extraneous materials. Their confederations, their *spectacles*, their civic feasts, and their enthusiasm, I take no notice of. They are nothing but mere tricks; but tracing their policy through their actions, I think I can distinguish the arrangements by which they propose to hold these republics together. The first, is the *confiscation*, with the compulsory paper currency annexed to it; the second, is the supreme power of the city of Paris; the third, is the general army of the state. Of this last I shall reserve what I have to say, until I come to consider the army as an head by itself.

As to the operation of the first (the confiscation and paper currency) merely as a cement, I cannot deny that these, the one depending on the other, may for some time compose some sort of cement, if their madness and folly in the management, and in the tempering of the parts together, does not produce a repulsion in the very outset. But allowing to the scheme some coherence and some duration, it appears to me, that if, after a while, the confiscation should not be found sufficient to support the paper coinage (as I am morally certain it will not) then, instead of cementing, it will add infinitely to the dissociation, distraction, and confusion of these confederate republics, both with relation to each other, and to the several parts within themselves. But if the confiscation should so far succeed as to sink the paper currency, the cement is gone with the circulation. In the mean time its binding force will be very uncertain, and it will straiten or relax with every variation in the credit of the paper.

One thing only is certain in this scheme, which is an effect seemingly collateral, but direct, I have no doubt, in the minds of those who conduct this business, that is, its effect in producing an *Oligarchy* in every one of the republics. A paper circulation, not founded on any real money deposited or engaged for, amounting already to four-and-forty millions of

English money, and this currency by force substituted in the place of the coin of the kingdom, becoming thereby the substance of its revenue, as well as the medium of all its commercial and civil intercourse, must put the whole of what power, authority, and influence is left, in any form whatsoever it may assume, into the hands of the managers and conductors of this circulation.

In England we feel the influence of the bank; though it is only the center of a voluntary dealing. He knows little indeed of the influence of money upon mankind, who does not see the force of the management of a monied concern, which is so much more extensive, and in its nature so much more depending on the managers than any of ours. But this is not merely a money concern. There is another member in the system inseparably connected with this money management. It consists in the means of drawing out at discretion portions of the confiscated lands for sale; and carrying on a process of continual transmutation of paper into land, and land into paper. When we follow this process in its effects, we may conceive something of the intensity of the force with which this system must operate. By this means the spirit of money-jobbing and speculation goes into the mass of land itself, and incorporates with it. By this kind of operation, that species of property becomes (as it were) volatilized; it assumes an unnatural and monstrous activity, and thereby throws into the hands of the several managers, principal and subordinate, Parisian and provincial, all the representative of money, and perhaps a full tenth part of all the land in France, which has now acquired the worst and most pernicious part of the evil of a paper circulation, the greatest possible uncertainty in its value. They have reversed the Latonian kindness to the landed property of Delos.* They have sent theirs to be blown about, like the light fragments of a wreck, *oras et littora circum.**

The new dealers being all habitually adventurers, and without any fixed habits or local predilections, will purchase to job out again, as the market of paper, or of money, or of land shall present an advantage. For though an holy bishop thinks that agriculture will derive great advantages from the '*enlightened*' usurers who are to purchase the church confiscations, I, who am not a good, but an old farmer, with great humility beg leave to tell his late lordship, that usury is not a tutor of agriculture; and if the word 'enlightened' be understood according to the new dictionary, as it always is in your new schools, I cannot conceive how a man's not believing in God can teach him to cultivate the earth with the least of any additional skill or encouragement. 'Diis immortalibus sero,' said an old Roman, when he held one handle of the plough, whilst Death held the other.* Though you were to join in the commission all the directors of the two academies to the directors of the *Caisse d'Escompte*,* one old experienced peasant is worth them all. I have got more information, upon a curious and interesting branch of husbandry, in one short conversation with a Carthusian monk, that I have derived from all the Bank directors that I have ever conversed with. However, there is no cause for apprehension from the meddling of money-dealers with rural oeconomy. These gentlemen are too wise in their generation. At first, perhaps, their tender and susceptible imaginations may be captivated with the innocent and unprofitable delights of a pastoral life; but in a little time they will find that agriculture is a trade much more laborious, and much less lucrative than that which they had left. After making its panegyric, they will turn their backs on it like their great precursor and prototype.—They may, like him, begin by singing '*Beatus ille*'—but what will be the end?

> *Haec ubi locutus foenerator Alphius,*
> *Jam jam futurus rusticus*
> *Omnem relegit idibus pecuniam,*
> *Quaerit calendis ponere.* *

They will cultivate the *caisse d'Eglise*, under the sacred auspices of this prelate, with much more profit than its vineyards or its corn-fields. They will employ their talents according to their habits and their interests. They will not follow the plough whilst they can direct treasuries, and govern provinces.

Your legislators, in every thing new, are the very first who have founded a commonwealth upon gaming, and infused this spirit into it as its vital breath. The great object in these politics is to metamorphose France, from a great kingdom into one great play-table; to turn its inhabitants into a nation of gamesters; to make speculation as extensive as life; to mix it with all its concerns; and to divert the whole of the hopes and fears of the people from their usual channels, into the impulses, passions, and superstitions of those who live on chances. They loudly proclaim their opinion, that this their present system of a republic cannot possibly exist without this kind of gaming fund; and that the very thread of its life is spun out of the staple of these speculations. The old gaming in funds was mischievous enough undoubtedly; but it was so only to individuals. Even when it had its greatest extent, in the Mississippi and South Sea,* it affected but few, comparatively; where it extends further, as in lotteries, the spirit has but a single object. But where the law, which in most circumstances forbids, and in none countenances gaming, is itself debauched, so as to reverse its nature and policy, and expressly to force the subject to this destructive table, by bringing the spirit and symbols of gaming into the minutest matters, and engaging every body in it, and in every thing, a more dreadful epidemic distemper of that kind is spread than yet has appeared in the world. With you a man can neither earn nor buy his dinner, without a speculation. What he receives in the morning will not have the same value at night. What he is compelled to take as pay for an old debt, will not be received as the same when he comes to pay a debt contracted by himself; nor will it be the same when by prompt payment he would avoid contracting any debt at all. Industry must wither away. Oeconomy must be driven from your country. Careful provision will have no existence. Who will labour without knowing the amount of his pay? Who will study to encrease what none can estimate? who will accumulate, when he does not know the value of what he saves? If you abstract it from its uses in gaming, to accumulate your paper wealth, would be not the providence of a man, but the distempered instinct of a jackdaw.

The truly melancholy part of the policy of systematically making a nation of gamesters is this; that tho' all are forced to play, few can understand the game; and fewer still are in a condition to avail themselves of the knowledge. The many must be the dupes of the few who conduct the machine of these speculations. What effect it must have on the country-people is visible. The townsman can calculate from day to day: not so the inhabitant of the country. When the peasant first brings his corn to market, the magistrate in the towns obliges him to take the assignat at par; when he goes to the shop with this money, he finds it seven per cent. the worse for crossing the way. This market he will not readily resort to again. The towns-people will be inflamed! they will force the country-people to bring their corn. Resistance will begin, and the murders of Paris and St Dennis* may be renewed through all France.

What signifies the empty compliment paid to the country by giving it perhaps more than its share in the theory of your representation? Where have you placed the real power over monied and landed circulation? Where have you placed the means of raising and falling the value of every man's freehold? Those whose operations can take from, or add ten per cent. to, the possessions of every man in France, must be the masters of every man in France. The whole of the power obtained by this revolution will settle in the towns among the burghers, and the monied directors who lead them. The landed gentleman, the yeoman, and the peasant have, none of them, habits, or inclinations, or experience, which can lead them to any share in this the sole source of power and influence now left in France. The very nature of a country life, the very nature of landed property, in all the occupations, and all the pleasures they afford, render combination and arrangement (the sole way of procuring and exerting influence) in a manner impossible amongst country-people. Combine them by all the art you can, and all the industry, they are always dissolving into individuality. Any thing in the nature of incorporation is almost impracticable amongst them. Hope, fear, alarm, jealousy, the ephemerous tale that does its business and dies in a day, all these things, which are the reins and spurs by which leaders check or urge the minds of followers, are not easily employed, or hardly at all, amongst scattered people. They assemble, they arm, they act with the utmost difficulty, and at the greatest charge. Their efforts, if ever they can be commenced, cannot be sustained. They cannot proceed systematically. If the country gentlemen attempt an influence through the mere income of their property, what is it to that of those who have ten times their income to sell, and who can ruin their property by bringing their plunder to meet it at market. If the landed man wishes to mortgage, he falls the value of his land, and raises the value of assignats. He augments the power of his enemy by the very means he must take to contend with him. The country gentleman therefore, the officer by sea and land, the man of liberal views and habits, attached to no profession, will be as completely excluded from the government of his country as if he were legislatively proscribed. It is obvious, that in the towns, all the things which conspire against the country gentleman, combine in favour of the money manager and director. In towns combination is natural. The habits of burghers, their occupations, their diversion, their business, their idleness, continually bring them into mutual contact. Their virtues and their vices are sociable; they are always in garrison; and they come embodied and half disciplined into the hands of those who mean to form them for civil, or for military action.

All these considerations leave no doubt on my mind, that if this monster of a constitution can continue, France will be wholly governed by the agitators in corporations, by societies in the towns formed of directors of assignats, and trustees for the sale of church lands, attornies, agents, money-jobbers, speculators, and adventurers, composing an ignoble oligarchy founded on the destruction of the crown, the church, the nobility, and the people. Here end all the deceitful dreams and visions of the equality and rights of men. In 'the Serbonian bog'* of this base oligarchy they are all absorbed, sunk, and lost for ever.

Though human eyes cannot trace them, one would be tempted to think some great offences in France must cry to heaven, which has thought fit to punish it with a subjection to a vile and inglorious domination, in which no comfort or compensation is to be found in any, even of those false splendours, which, playing about other tyrannies, prevent mankind from feeling themselves dishonoured even whilst they are oppressed. I must confess I am touched with a sorrow, mixed with some indignation, at the conduct of a few men, once of great rank, and still of great character, who, deluded with specious names, have engaged in a business too deep for the line of their understanding to fathom; who have lent their fair reputation, and the authority of their high-sounding names, to the designs of men with whom they could not be acquainted; and have thereby made their very virtues operate to the ruin of their country.

So far as to the first cementing principle.

The second material of cement for their new republic is the superiority of the city of Paris; and this I admit is strongly connected with the other cementing principle of paper circulation and confiscation. It is in this part of the project we must look for the cause of the destruction of all the old bounds of provinces and jurisdictions, ecclesiastical and secular, and the dissolution of all ancient combinations of things, as well as the formation of so many small unconnected republics. The power of the city of Paris is evidently one great spring of all their politics. It is through the power of Paris, now become the center and focus of jobbing, that the leaders of this faction direct, or rather command the whole legislative and the whole executive government. Every thing therefore must be done which can confirm the authority of that city over the other republics. Paris is compact; she has an enormous strength, wholly disproportioned to the force of any of the square republics; and this strength is collected and condensed within a narrow compass. Paris has a natural and easy connexion of its parts, which will not be affected by any scheme of a geometrical constitution, nor does it much signify whether its proportion of representation be more or less, since it has the whole draft of fishes in its drag-net. The other divisions of the kingdom being hackled and torn to pieces, and separated from all their habitual means, and even principles of union, cannot, for some time at least, confederate against her.* Nothing was to be left in all the subordinate members, but weakness, disconnection, and confusion. To confirm this part of the plan, the assembly has lately come to a resolution, that no two of their republics shall have the same commander in chief.

To a person who takes a view of the whole, the strength of Paris thus formed, will appear a system of general weakness. It is boasted, that the geometrical policy has been adopted, that all local ideas should be sunk, and that the people should no longer be Gascons, Picards, Bretons, Normans, but Frenchmen, with one country, one heart, and one assembly. But instead of being all Frenchmen, the greater likelihood is, that the inhabitants of that region will shortly have no country. No man ever was attached by a sense of pride, partiality, or real affection, to a description of square measurement. He never will glory in belonging to the Checquer, N° 71, or to any other badge-ticket. We begin our public affections in our families. No cold relation is a zealous citizen. We pass on to our neighbourhoods, and our habitual provincial connections. These are inns and resting-places. Such divisions of our country as have been formed by habit, and not by a sudden jerk of authority, were so many little images of the great country in which the heart found something which it could fill. The love to the whole is not extinguished by this subordinate partiality. Perhaps it is a sort of elemental training to those higher and more large regards, by which alone men come to be affected, as with their own concern, in the prosperity of a kingdom so extensive as that of France. In that general territory itself, as in the old name of provinces, the citizens are interested from old prejudices and unreasoned habits, and not on account of the geometric properties of its figure. The power and preeminence of Paris does certainly press down and hold these republics together, as long as it lasts. But, for the reasons I have already given you, I think it cannot last very long.

Passing from the civil creating, and the civil cementing principles of this constitution, to the national assembly, which is to appear and act as sovereign, we see a body in its constitution with every possible power, and no possible external controul. We see a body without fundamental laws, without established maxims, without respected rules of proceeding, which nothing can keep firm to any system whatsoever. Their idea of their powers is always taken at the utmost stretch of legislative competency, and their examples for common cases, from the exceptions of the most urgent necessity. The future is to be in most respects like the present assembly; but, by the mode of the new elections and the tendency of the new circulations, it will be purged of the small degree of internal controul existing in a minority chosen originally from various interests, and preserving something of their spirit. If possible, the next assembly must be worse than the present. The present, by destroying and altering every thing, will leave to their successors apparently nothing popular to do. They will be roused by emulation and example to enterprises the boldest and the most absurd. To suppose such an assembly sitting in perfect quietude is ridiculous.

Your all-sufficient legislators, in their hurry to do every thing at once, have forgot one thing that seems essential, and which, I believe, never has been before, in the theory or the practice, omitted by any projector of a republic. They have forgot to constitute a *Senate*,* or something of that nature and character. Never, before this time, was heard of a body politic composed of one legislative and active assembly, and its executive officers, without such a council; without something to which foreign states might connect themselves; something to which, in the ordinary detail of government, the people could look up; something which might give a bias and steadiness, and preserve something like consistency in the proceedings of state. Such a body kings generally have as a council. A monarchy may exist without it; but it seems to be in the very essence of a republican government. It holds a sort of middle place between the supreme power exercised by the people, or immediately delegated from them, and the mere executive. Of this there are no traces in your constitution; and in providing nothing of this kind, your Solons and Numas* have, as much as in any thing else, discovered a sovereign incapacity.

Let us now turn our eyes to what they have done towards the formation of an executive power. For this they have chosen a degraded king. This their first executive officer is to be a machine, without any sort of deliberative discretion in any one act of his function. At best he is but a channel to convey to the national assembly such matter as may import that body to know. If he had been made the exclusive channel, the power would not have been without its importance; though infinitely perilous to those who would choose to exercise it. But public intelligence and statement of facts may pass to the assembly, with equal authenticity, through any other conveyance. As to the means, therefore, of giving a direction to measures by the statement of an authorized reporter, this office of intelligence is as nothing.

To consider the French scheme of an executive officer in its two natural divisions of civil and political—In the first it must be observed, that, according to the new constitution, the higher parts of judicature, in either of its lines, are not in the king. The king of France is not the fountain of justice. The judges, neither the original nor the appellate, are of his nomination. He neither proposes the candidates, nor has a negative on the choice. He is not even the public prosecutor. He serves only as a notary to authenticate the choice made of the judges in the several districts. By his officers he is to execute their sentence. When we look into the true nature of his authority, he appears to be nothing more than a chief of bumbailiffs, serjeants at mace, catchpoles, jailers, and hangmen. It is impossible to place any thing called royalty in a more degrading point of view. A thousand times better it had been for the dignity of this unhappy prince, that he had nothing at all to do with the administration of justice, deprived as he is of all that is venerable, and all that is consolatory in that function, without power of originating any process; without a power of suspension, mitigation, or pardon. Every thing in justice that is vile and odious is thrown upon him. It was not for nothing that the assembly has been at such pains to remove the stigma from certain offices, when they were resolved to place the person who lately had been their king in a situation but one degree above the executioner, and in an office nearly of the same quality. It is not in nature, that situated as the king of the French now is, he can respect himself, or can be respected by others.

View this new executive officer on the side of his political capacity, as he acts under the orders of the national assembly. To execute laws is a royal office; to execute orders is not to be a king. However, a political executive magistracy, though merely such, is a great trust. It is a trust indeed that has much depending upon its faithful and diligent performance, both in the person presiding in it and in all his subordinates. Means of performing his duty ought to be given by regulation; and dispositions towards it ought to be infused by the circumstances attendant on the trust. It ought to be environed with dignity, authority, and consideration, and it ought to lead to glory. The office of execution is an office of exertion. It is not from impotence we are to expect the tasks of power. What sort of person is a king to command executory service, who has no means whatsoever to reward it? Not in a permanent office; not in a grant of land; no, not in a pension of fifty pounds a year; not in the vainest and most trivial title. In France the king is no more the fountain of honour than he is the fountain of justice. All rewards, all distinctions are in other hands. Those who serve the king can be actuated by no natural motive but fear; by a fear of every thing except their master. His functions of internal coercion are as odious, as those which he exercises in the department of justice. If reflief is to be given to any municipality, the assembly gives it. If troops are to be sent to reduce them to obedience to the assembly, the king is to execute the order; and upon every occasion he is to be spattered over with the blood of his people. He has no negative; yet his name and authority is used to enforce every harsh decree. Nay, he must concur in the butchery of those who shall attempt to free him from his imprisonment, or shew the slightest attachment to his person or to his antient authority.

Executive magistracy ought to be constituted in such a manner, that those who compose it should be disposed to love and to venerate those whom they are bound to obey. A purposed neglect, or, what is worse, a literal but perverse and malignant obedience, must be the ruin of the wisest counsels. In vain will the law attempt to anticipate or to follow such studied neglects and fraudulent attentions. To make men act zealously is not in the competence of law. Kings, even such as are truly kings, may and ought to bear the freedom of subjects that are obnoxious to them. They may too, without derogating from themselves, bear even the authority of such persons if it promotes their service. Louis the XIIIth mortally hated the cardinal de Richlieu: but his support of that minister against his rivals was the source of all the glory of his reign, and the solid foundation of his throne itself. Louis the XIVth, when come to the throne, did not love the cardinal Mazarin,* but for his interests he preserved him in power. When old, he detested Louvois;* but for years, whilst he faithfully served his greatness, he endured his person. When George the IId took Mr Pitt, who certainly was not agreeable to him, into his councils,* he did nothing which could humble a wise sovereign. But these ministers, who were chosen by affairs, not by affections, acted in the name of, and in trust for, kings; and not as their avowed, constitutional, and ostensible masters. I think it impossible that any king, when he has recovered his first terrors, can cordially infuse vivacity and vigour into measures which he knows to be dictated by those who he must be persuaded are in the highest degree ill affected to his person. Will any ministers, who serve such a king (or whatever he may be called) with but a decent appearance of respect, cordially obey the orders of those whom but the other day in his name they had committed to the Bastile? will they obey the orders of those whom, whilst they were exercising despotic justice upon them, they conceived they were treating with lenity; and for whom, in a prison, they thought they had provided an asylum? If you expect such obedience, amongst your other innovations and regenerations, you ought to make a revolution in nature, and provide a new constitution for the human mind. Otherwise, your supreme government cannot harmonize with its executory system. There are cases in which we cannot take up with names and abstractions. You may call half a dozen leading individuals, whom we have reason to fear and hate, the nation. It makes no other difference, than to make us fear and hate them the more. If it had been thought justifiable and expedient to make such a revolution by such means, and through such persons, as you have made yours, it would have been more wise to have completed the business of the fifth and sixth of October. The new executive officer would then owe his situation to those who are his creators as well as his masters; and he might be bound in interest, in the society of crime, and (if in crimes there could be virtues) in gratitude, to serve those who had promoted him to a place of great lucre and great sensual indulgence; and of something more: For more he must have received from those who certainly would not have limited an aggrandized creature, as they have done a submitting antagonist.

A king circumstanced as the present, if he is totally stupified by his misfortunes, so as to think it not the necessity, but the premium and privilege of life, to eat and sleep, without any regard to glory, never can be fit for the office. If he feels as men commonly feel, he must be sensible, that an office so circumstanced is one in which he can obtain no fame or reputation. He has no generous interest that can excite him to action. At best, his conduct will be passive and defensive. To inferior people such an office might be matter of honour. But to be raised to it, and to descend to it, are different things, and suggest different sentiments. Does he *really* name the ministers? They will have a sympathy with him. Are they forced upon him? The whole business between them and the nominal king will be mutual counteraction. In all other countries, the office of ministers of state is of the highest dignity. In France it is full of peril and incapable of glory. Rivals however they will have in their nothingness, whilst shallow ambition exists in the world, or the desire of a miserable salary is an incentive to short-sighted avarice. Those competitors of the ministers are enabled by your constitution to attack them in their vital parts, whilst they have not the means of repelling their charges in any other than the degrading character of culprits. The ministers of state in France are the only persons in that country who are incapable of a share in the national councils. What ministers! What councils! What a nation!—But they are responsible. It is a poor service that is to be had from responsibility. The elevation of mind, to be derived from fear, will never make a nation glorious. Responsibility prevents crimes. It makes all attempts against the laws dangerous. But for a principle of active and zealous service, none but idiots could think of it. Is the conduct of a war to be trusted to a man who may abhor its principle; who, in every step he may take to render it successful, confirms the power of those by whom he is oppressed? Will foreign states seriously treat with him who has no prerogative of peace of war; no, not so much as in a single vote by himself or his ministers, or by any one whom he can possibly influence. A state of contempt is not a state for a prince: better get rid of him at once.

I know it will be said, that these humours in the court and executive government will continue only through this generation; and that the king has been brought to declare the dauphin shall be educated in a conformity to his situation. If he is made to conform to his situation, he will have no education at all. His training must be worse even than that of an arbitrary monarch. If he reads,—whether he reads or not, some good or evil genius will tell him his ancestors were kings. Thenceforward his object must be to assert himself, and to avenge his parents. This you will say is not his duty. That may be; but it is Nature; and whilst you pique Nature against you, you do unwisely to trust to Duty. In this futile scheme of polity, the state nurses in its bosom, for the present, a source of weakness, perplexity, counteraction, inefficiency, and decay; and it prepares the means of its final ruin. In short, I see nothing in the executive force (I cannot call it authority) that has even an appearance of vigour, or that has the smallest degree of just correspondence or symmetry, or amicable relation, with the supreme power, either as it now exists, or as it is planned for the future government.

You have settled, by an oeconomy as perverted as the policy, two[1] establishments of government; one real, one fictitious. Both maintained at a vast expence; but the fictitious at, I think, the greatest. Such a machine as the latter is not worth the grease of its wheels. The expence is exorbitant; and neither the shew nor the use deserve the tenth part of the charge. Oh! but I don't do justice to the talents of the legislators. I don't allow, as I ought to do, for necessity. Their scheme of

---

[1] In reality three, to reckon the provincial republican establishments.

executive force was not their choice. This pageant must be kept. The people would not consent to part with it. Right; I understand you. You do, in spite of your grand theories, to which you would have heaven and earth to bend, you do know how to conform yourselves to the nature and circumstances of things. But when you were obliged to conform thus far to circumstances, you ought to have carried your submission farther, and to have made what you were obliged to take, a proper instrument, and useful to its end. That was in your power. For instance, among many others, it was in your power to leave to your king the right of peace and war. What! to leave to the executive magistrate the most dangerous of all prerogatives? I know none more dangerous; nor any one more necessary to be so trusted. I do not say that this prerogative ought to be trusted to your king, unless he enjoyed other auxiliary trusts along with it, which he does not now hold. But, if he did possess them, hazardous as they are undoubtedly, advantages would arise from such a constitution, more than compensating the risque. There is no other way of keeping the several potentates of Europe from intriguing distinctly and personally with the members of your assembly, from intermeddling in all your concerns, and fomenting, in the heart of your country, the most pernicious of all factions; factions in the interest and under the direction of foreign powers. From that worst of evils, thank God, we are still free. Your skill, if you had any, would be well employed to find out indirect correctives and controls upon this perilous trust. If you did not like those which in England we have chosen, your leaders might have exerted their abilities in contriving better. If it were necessary to exemplify the consequences of such an executive government as yours, in the management of great affairs, I should refer you to the late reports of M. de Montmorin* to the national assembly, and all the other proceedings relative to the differences between Great Britain and Spain.* It would be treating your understanding with disrespect to point them out to you.

I hear that the persons who are called ministers have signified an intention of resigning their places. I am rather astonished that they have not resigned long since. For the universe I would not have stood in the situation in which they have been for this last twelvemonth. They wished well, I take it for granted, to the Revolution. Let this fact be as it may, they could not, placed as they were upon an eminence, though an eminence of humiliation, but be the first to see collectively, and to feel each in his own department, the evils which have been produced by that revolution. In every step which they took, or forbore to take, they must have felt the degraded situation of their country, and their utter incapacity of serving it. They are in a species of subordinate servitude, in which no men before them were ever seen. Without confidence from their sovereign, on whom they were forced, or from the assembly who forced them upon him, all the noble functions of their office are executed by committees of the assembly, without any regard whatsoever to their personal, or their official authority. They are to execute, without power; they are to be responsible, without discretion; they are to deliberate, without choice. In their puzzled situation, under two sovereigns, over neither of whom they have any influence, they must act in such a manner as (in effect, whatever they may intend) sometimes to betray the one, sometimes the other, and always to betray themselves. Such has been their situation; such must be the situation of those who succeed them. I have much respect, and many good wishes, for Mr Necker. I am obliged to him for attentions. I thought when his enemies had driven him from Versailles, that his exile was a subject of most serious congratulation—*sed multae urbes et publica vota vicerunt.** He is now sitting on the ruins of the finances, and of the monarchy of France.

A great deal more might be observed on the strange constitution of the executory part of the new government; but fatigue must give bounds to the discussion of subjects, which in themselves have hardly any limits.

As little genius and talent am I able to perceive in the plan of judicature formed by the national assembly. According to their invariable course, the framers of your constitution have begun with the utter abolition of the parliaments. These venerable bodies, like the rest of the old government, stood in need of reform, even though there should be no change made in the monarchy. They required several more alterations to adapt them to the system of a free constitution. But they had particulars in their constitution, and those not a few, which deserved approbation from the wise. They possessed one fundamental excellence; they were independent. The most doubtful circumstance attendant on their office, that of its being vendible, contributed however to this independency of character. They held for life. Indeed they may be said to have held by inheritance. Appointed by the monarch, they were considered as nearly out of his power. The most determined exertions of that authority against them only shewed their radical independence.* They composed permanent bodies politic, constituted to resist arbitrary innovation; and from that corporate constitution, and from most of their forms, they were well calculated to afford both certainty and stability to the laws. They had been a safe asylum to secure these laws in all the revolutions of humour and opinion. They had saved that sacred deposit of the country during the reigns of arbitrary princes, and the struggles of arbitrary factions. They kept alive the memory and record of the constitution. They were the great security to private property; which might be said (when personal liberty had no existence) to be, in fact, as well guarded in France as in any other country. Whatever is supreme in a state, ought to have, as much as possible, its judicial authority so constituted as not only not to depend upon it, but in some sort to balance it. It ought to give a security to its justice against its power. It ought to make its judicature, as it were, something exterior to the state.

These parliaments had furnished, not the best certainly, but some considerable corrective to the excesses and vices of the monarchy. Such an independent judicature was ten times more necessary when a democracy became the absolute power of the country. In that constitution, elective, temporary, local judges, such as you have contrived, exercising their dependent functions in a narrow society, must be the worst of all tribunals. In them it will be vain to look for any appearance of justice towards strangers, towards the obnoxious rich, towards the minority of routed parties, towards all those who in the election have supported unsuccessful candidates. It will be impossible to keep the new tribunals clear of the worst spirit of faction. All contrivances by ballot, we know experimentally, to be vain and childish to prevent a discovery of inclinations. Where they may the best answer the purposes of concealment, they answer to produce suspicion, and this is a still more mischievous cause of partiality.

If the parliaments had been preserved, instead of being dissolved at so ruinous a change to the nation, they might have served in this new commonwealth, perhaps not precisely the same (I do not mean an exact parallel) but near the same purposes as the court and senate of Areopagus* did in Athens; that is, as one of the balances and correctives to the evils of a light and unjust democracy. Every one knows, that this tribunal was the great stay of that state; every one knows with what care it was upheld, and with what a religious awe it was consecrated. The parliaments were not wholly free from faction, I admit; but this evil was exterior and accidental, and not so much the vice of their constitution itself, as it must be in your new contrivance of sexennial elective judicatories. Several English commend the abolition of the old tribunals, as supposing that they determined every thing by bribery and corruption. But they have stood the test of monarchic and republican scrutiny. The court was well disposed to prove corruption on those bodies when they were dissolved in 1771.—Those who have again dissolved them would have done the same if they could—but both inquisitions having failed, I conclude, that gross pecuniary corruption must have been rather rare amongst them.

It would have been prudent, along with the parliaments, to preserve their antient power of registering, and of remonstrating at least, upon all the decrees of the national assembly, as they did upon those which passed in the time of the monarchy. It would be a means of squaring the occasional decrees of a democracy to some principles of general jurisprudence. The vice of the antient democracies, and one cause of their ruin, was, that they ruled, as you do, by occasional decrees, *psephismata*.* This practice soon broke in upon the tenour and consistency of the laws; it abated the respect of the people towards them; and totally destroyed them in the end.

Your vesting the power of remonstrance, which, in the time of the monarchy, existed in the parliament of Paris, in your principal executive officer, whom, in spite of common sense, you persevere in calling king, is the height of absurdity. You ought never to suffer remonstrance from him who is to execute. This is to understand neither council nor execution; neither authority nor obedience. The person whom you call king, ought not to have this power, or he ought to have more.

Your present arrangement is strictly judicial. Instead of imitating your monarchy, and seating your judges on a bench of independence, your object is to reduce them to the most blind obedience. As you have changed all things, you have invented new principles of order. You first appoint judges, who, I suppose, are to determine according to law, and then you let them know, that, at some time or other, you intend to give them some law by which they are to determine. Any studies which they have made (if any they have made) are to be useless to them. But to supply these studies, they are to be sworn to obey all the rules, orders, and instructions, which from time to time they are to receive from the national assembly. These if they submit to, they leave no ground of law to the subject. They become complete, and most dangerous instruments in the hands of the governing power, which, in the midst of a cause, or on the prospect of it, may wholly change the rule of decision. If these orders of the National Assembly come to be contrary to the will of the people who locally choose those judges, such confusion must happen as is terrible to think of. For the judges owe their place to the local authority; and the commands they are sworn to obey come from those who have no share in their appointment. In the mean time they have the example of the court of *Chatelet** to encourage and guide them in the exercise of their functions. That court is to try criminals sent to it by the National Assembly, or brought before it by other courses of delation. They sit under a guard, to save their own lives. They know not by what law they judge, nor under what authority they act, nor by what tenure they hold. It is thought that they are sometimes obliged to condemn at peril of their lives. This is not perhaps certain, nor can it be ascertained; but when they acquit, we know, they have seen the persons whom they discharge, with perfect impunity to the actors, hanged at the door of their court.

The assembly indeed promises that they will form a body of law, which shall be short, simple, clear, and so forth. That is, by their short laws, they will leave much to the discretion of the judge; whilst they have exploded the authority of all the learning which could make judicial discretion, (a thing perilous at best) deserving the appellation of a *sound* discretion.

It is curious to observe, that the administrative bodies are carefully exempted from the jurisdiction of these new tribunals. That is, those persons are exempted from the power of the laws, who ought to be the most entirely submitted to them. Those who execute public pecuniary trusts, ought of all men to be the most strictly held to their duty. One would have thought, that it must have been among your earliest cares, if you did not mean that those administrative bodies should be real sovereign independent states, to form an awful tribunal, like your late parliaments, or like our king's-bench, where all corporate officers might obtain protection in the legal exercise of their functions, and would find coercion if they trespassed against their legal duty. But the cause of the exemption is plain. These administrative bodies are the great instruments of the present leaders in their progress through democracy to oligarchy. They must therefore be put above the law. It will be said, that the legal tribunals which you have made are unfit to coerce them. They are undoubtedly. They are unfit for any rational purpose. It will be said too, that the administrative bodies will be accountable to the general assembly. This I fear is talking, without much consideration, of the nature of that assembly or of these corporations. However, to be subject to the pleasure of that assembly, is not to be subject to law, either for protection or for constraint.

This establishment of judges as yet wants something to its completion. It is to be crowned by a new tribunal. This is to be a grand state judicature; and it is to judge of crimes committeed against the nation, that is, against the power of the assembly. It seems as if they had something in their view of the nature of the high court of justice erected in England during the time of the great usurpation.* As they have not yet finished this part of the scheme, it is impossible to form a direct judgment upon it. However, if great care is not taken to form it in a spirit very different from that which has guided them in their proceedings relative to state offences, this tribunal, subservient to their inquisition, *the committee of research*,* will extinguish the last sparks of liberty in France, and settle the most dreadful and arbitrary tyranny ever known in any nation. If they wish to give to this tribunal any appearance of liberty and justice, they must not evoke from, or send to it, the causes relative to their own members, at their pleasure. They must also remove the seat of that tribunal out of the republic of Paris.[1]

Has more wisdom been displayed in the constitution of your army than what is discoverable in your plan of judicature? The able arrangement of this part is the more difficult, and requires the greater skill and attention, not only as a great concern in itself, but as it is the third cementing principle in the new body of republics, which you call the French nation. Truly it is not easy to divine what that army may become at last. You have voted a very large one, and on good appointments, at least fully equal to your apparent means of payment. But what is the principle of its discipline? or whom is it to obey? You have got the wolf by the ears, and I wish you joy of the happy position in which you have chosen to place yourselves, and in which you are well circumstanced for a free deliberation, relatively to that army, or to any thing else.

The minister and secretary of state for the war department, is M. de la Tour du Pin.* This gentleman, like his colleagues in administration, is a most zealous assertor of the revolution, and a sanguine admirer of the new constitution, which originated in that event. His statement of facts, relative to the military of France, is important, not only from his official and personal authority, but because it displays very clearly the actual condition of the army in France, and because it throws

---

[1] For further elucidations upon the subject of all these judicatures, and of the committee of research, see M. de Calonne's work.

light on the principles upon which the assembly proceeds in the administration of this critical object. It may enable us to form some judgment how far it may be expedient in this country to imitate the martial policy of France.

M. de la Tour du Pin, on the 4th of last June, comes to give an account of the state of his department, as it exists under the auspices of the national assembly. No man knows it so well; no man can express it better. Addressing himself to the National Assembly, he says, 'His Majesty has *this day* sent me to apprize you of the multiplied disorders of which *every day* he receives the most distressing intelligence. The army (le corps militaire) threatens to fall into the most turbulent anarchy. Entire regiments have dared to violate at once the respect due to the laws, to the King, to the order established by your decrees, and to the oaths which they have taken with the most awful solemnity. Compelled by my duty to give you information of these excesses, my heart bleeds when I consider who they are that have committed them. Those, against whom it is not in my power to withhold the most grievous complaints, are a part of that very soldiery which to this day have been so full of honour and loyalty, and with whom, for fifty years, I have lived the comrade and the friend.*

'What incomprehensible spirit of delirium and delusion has all at once led them astray? Whilst you are indefatigable in establishing uniformity in the empire, and moulding the whole into one coherent and consistent body; whilst the French are taught by you, at once the respect which the laws owe to the rights of man, and that which the citizens owe to the laws, the administration of the army presents nothing but disturbance and confusion. I see in more than one corps the bonds of discipline relaxed or broken; the most unheard-of pretensions avowed directly and without any disguise; the ordinances without force; the chiefs without authority; the military chest and the colours carried off; the authority of the King himself [*risum teneatis*]* proudly defied; the officers despised, degraded, threatened, driven away, and some of them prisoners in the midst of their corps, dragging on a precarious life in the bosom of disgust and humiliation. To fill up the measure of all these horrors, the commandants of places have had their throats cut, under the eyes, and almost in the arms of their own soldiers.

'These evils are great; but they are not the worst consequences which may be produced by such military insurrections. Sooner or later they may menace the nation itself. *The nature of things requires*, that the army should never act but as *an instrument*. The moment that, erecting itself into a deliberative body, it shall act according to its own resolutions, the *government, be it what it may, will immediately degenerate into a military democracy*; a species of political monster, which has always ended by devouring those who have produced it.

'After all this, who must not be alarmed at the irregular consultations, and turbulent committees, formed in some regiments by the common soldiers and non-commissioned officers, without the knowledge, or even in contempt of the authority of their superiors; although the presence and concurrence of those superiors could give no authority to such monstrous democratic assemblies [comices.]'

It is not necessary to add much to this finished picture: finished as far as its canvas admits; but, as I apprehend, not taking in the whole of the nature and complexity of the disorders of this military democracy, which, the minister at war truly and wisely observes, wherever it exists, must be the true constitution of the state, by whatever formal appellation it may pass. For, though he informs the assembly, that the more considerable part of the army have not cast off their obedience, but are still attached to their duty, yet those travellers who have seen the corps whose conduct is the best, rather observe in them the absence of mutiny than the existence of discipline.

I cannot help pausing here for a moment, to reflect upon the expressions of surprise which this Minister has let fall, relative to the excesses he relates. To him the departure of the troops from their antient principles of loyalty and honour seems quite inconceivable. Surely those to whom he addresses himself know the causes of it but too well. They know the doctrines which they have preached, the decrees which they have passed, the practices which they have countenanced. The soldiers remember the 6th of October. They recollect the French guards. They have not forgot the taking of the King's castles in Paris, and at Marseilles. That the governors in both places, were murdered with impunity, is a fact that has not passed out of their minds. They do not abandon the principles laid down so ostentatiously and laboriously of the equality of men. They cannot shut their eyes to the degradation of the whole noblesse of France; and the suppression of the very idea of a gentleman. The total abolition of titles and distinctions is not lost upon them. But Mr du Pin is astonished at their disloyalty, when the doctors of the assembly have taught them at the same time the respect due to laws. It is easy to judge which of the two sorts of lessons men with arms in their hands are likely to learn. As to the authority of the King, we may collect from the minister himself (if any argument on that head were not quite superfluous) that it is not of more consideration with these troops, than it is with every body else. 'The King,' says he, 'has over and over again repeated his orders to put a stop to these excesses: but, in so terrible a crisis *your* [the assembly's] concurrence is become indispensably necessary to prevent the evils which menace the state. *You* unite to the force of the legislative power, *that of opinion* still more important.' To be sure the army can have no opinion of the power or authority of the king. Perhaps the soldier has by this time learned, that the assembly itself does not enjoy a much greater degree of liberty than that royal figure.

It is now to be seen what has been proposed in this exigency, one of the greatest that can happen in a state. The Minister requests the assembly to array itself in all its terrors, and to call forth all its majesty. He desires that the grave and severe principles announced by them may give vigour to the King's proclamation. After this we should have looked for courts civil and martial; breaking of some corps, decimating others, and all the terrible means which necessity has employed in such cases to arrest the progress of the most terrible of all evils; particularly, one might expect, that a serious inquiry would be made into the murder of commandants in the view of their soldiers. Not one word of all this, or of any thing like it. After they had been told that the soldiery trampled upon the decrees of the assembly promulgated by the King, the assembly pass new decrees; and they authorise the King to make new proclamations. After the Secretary at War had stated that the regiments had paid no regard to oaths *prêtés avec la plus imposante solemnité**—they propose— what? More oaths. They renew decrees and proclamations as they experience their insufficiency, and they multiply oaths in proportion as they weaken, in the minds of men, the sanctions of religion. I hope that handy abridgments of the excellent sermons of Voltaire, d'Alembert, Diderot, and Helvetius, on the Immortality of the Soul, on a particular superintending Providence, and on a Future State of Rewards and Punishments, are sent down to the soldiers along with their civic oaths.* Of this I have no doubt; as I understand, that a certain description of reading makes no inconsiderable part of their military exercises, and that they are full as well supplied with the ammunition of pamphlets as of cartridges.

To prevent the mischiefs arising from conspiracies, irregular consultations, seditious committees, and monstrous democratic assemblies ['comitia, comices'] of the soldiers, and all the disorders arising from idleness, luxury, dissipation, and insubordination, I believe the most astonishing means have been used, that ever occurred to men, even in all the inventions of this prolific age. It is no less than this:—The King has promulgated in circular letters to all the regiments his direct authority and encouragement, that the several corps should join themselves with the clubs and confederations in the several municipalities, and mix with them in their feasts and civic entertainments! This jolly discipline, it seems, is to soften the ferocity of their minds; to reconcile them to their bottle companions of other descriptions; and to merge particular conspiracies in more general associations.[1] That

---

[1] Comme sa Majesté y a reconnu, non une système d'associations particulières, mais une réunion de volontés de tous les François pour la liberté et la prosperité communes, ainsi pour le maintien de l'ordre publique; il a pensé qu'il convenoit que chaque regiment prit part a ces fêtes civiques pour multiplier les rapports, et reserrer les liens d'union entre les citoyens et les troupes.*—Lest I should not be credited, I insert the words, authorising the troops to feast with the popular confederacies.*

this remedy would be pleasing to the soldiers, as they are described by Mr de la Tour du Pin, I can readily believe; and that, however mutinous otherwise, they will dutifully submit themselves to *these* royal proclamations. But I should question whether all this civic swearing, clubbing, and feasting, would dispose them more than at present they are disposed, to an obedience to their officers; to teach them better to submit to the austere rules of military discipline. It will make them admirable citizens after the French mode, but not quite so good soldiers after any mode. A doubt might well arise, whether the conversations at these good tables, would fit them a great deal the better for the character of *mere instruments*, which this veteran officer and statesman justly observes, the nature of things always requires an army to be.

Concerning the likelihood of this improvement in discipline, by the free conversation of the soldiers with the municipal festive societies, which is thus officially encouraged by royal authority and sanction, we may judge by the state of the municipalities themselves, furnished to us by the war minister in this very speech. He conceives good hopes of the success of his endeavours towards restoring order *for the present* from the good disposition of certain regiments; but he finds something cloudy with regard to the future. As to preventing the return of confusion 'for this, the administration (says he) cannot be answerable to you, as long as they see the municipalities arrogate to themselves an authority over the troops, which your institutions have reserved wholly to the monarch. You have fixed the limits of the military authority and the municipal authority. You have bounded the action, which you have permitted to the latter over the former, to the right of requisition; but never did the letter or the spirit of your decrees authorise the commons in these municipalities to break the officers, to try them, to give orders to the soldiers, to drive them from the posts committed to their guard, to stop them in their marches ordered by the King, or, in a word, to enslave the troops to the caprice of each of the cities or even market towns through which they are to pass.'

Such is the character and disposition of the municipal society which is to reclaim the soldiery, to bring them back to the true principles of military subordination, and to render them machines in the hands of the supreme power of the country! Such are the distempers of the French troops! Such is their cure! As the army is, so is the navy. The municipalities supersede the orders of the assembly, and the seamen in their turn supersede the orders of the municipalities. From my heart I pity the condition of a respectable servant of the public, like this war minister, obliged in his old age to pledge the assembly in their civic cups, and to enter with an hoary head into all the fantastick vagaries of these juvenile politicians. Such schemes are not like propositions coming from a man of fifty years wear and tear amongst mankind. They seem rather such as ought to be expected from those grand compounders in politics, who shorten the road to their degrees in the state; and have a certain inward fanatical assurance and illumination upon all subjects; upon the credit of which one of their doctors has thought fit, with great applause, and greater success, to caution the assembly not to attend to old men, or to any persons who valued themselves upon their experience. I suppose all the ministers of state must qualify, and take this test; wholly abjuring the errors and heresies of experience and observation. Every man has his own relish. But I think, if I could not attain to the wisdom, I would at least preserve something of the stiff and peremptory dignity of age. These gentlemen deal in regeneration; but at any price I should hardly yield my rigid fibres to be regenerated by them; nor begin, in my grand climacteric, to squall in their new accents, or to stammer, in my second cradle, the elemental sounds of their barbarous metaphysics.[1] *Si isti mihi largiantur ut repueriscam, et in eorum cunis vagiam, valde recuseum!**

The imbecility of any part of the puerile and pedantic system, which they call a constitution, cannot be laid open without discovering the utter insufficiency and mischief of every other part with which it comes in contact, or that bears any the remotest relation to it. You cannot propose a remedy for the incompetence of the crown, without displaying the debility of the assembly. You cannot deliberate on the

[1] This war-minister has since quitted the school and resigned his office.

confusion of the army of the state, without disclosing the worse disorders of the armed municipalities. The military lays open the civil, and the civil betrays the military anarchy. I wish every body carefully to persue the eloquent speech (such it is) of Mons. de la Tour du Pin. He attributes the salvation of the municipalities to the good behaviour of some of the troops. These troops are to preserve the well-disposed part of those municipalities, which is confessed to be the weakest, from the pillage of the worst disposed, which is the strongest. But the municipalities affect a sovereignty and will command those troops which are necessary for their protection. Indeed they must command them or court them. The municipalities, by the necessity of their situation, and by the republican powers they have obtained, must, with relation to the military, be the masters, or the servants, or the confederates, or each successively; or they must make a jumble of all together, according to circumstances. What government is there to coerce the army but the municipality, or the municipality but the army? To preserve concord where authority is extinguished, at the hazard of all consequences, the assembly attempts to cure the distempers by the distempers themselves; and they hope to preserve themselves from a purely military democracy, by giving it a debauched interest in the municipal.

If the soldiers once come to mix for any time in the municipal clubs, cabals, and confederacies, an elective attraction will draw them to the lowest and most desperate part. With them will be their habits, affections, and sympathies. The military conspiracies, which are to be remedied by civic confederacies; the rebellious municipalities, which are to be rendered obedient by furnishing them with the means of seducing the very armies of the state that are to keep them in order; all these chimeras of a monstrous and portentous policy, must aggravate the confusions from which they have arisen. There must be blood. The want of common judgment manifested in the construction of all their descriptions of forces, and in all their kinds of civil and judicial authorities will make it flow. Disorders may be quieted in one time and in one part. They will break out in others; because the evil is radical and intrinsic. All these schemes of mixing mutinous soldiers with seditious citizens, must weaken still more and more the military connection of soldiers with their officers, as well as add military and mutinous audacity to turbulent artificers and peasants. To secure a real army, the officer should be first and last in the eye of the soldier; first and last in his attention, observance, and esteem. Officers it seems there are to be, whose chief qualification must be temper and patience. They are to manage their troops by electioneering arts. They must bear themselves as candidates not as commanders. But as by such means power may be occasionally in their hands, the authority by which they are to be nominated becomes of high importance.*

What you may do finally, does not appear; nor is it of much moment, whilst the strange and contradictory relation between your army and all the parts of your republic, as well as the puzzled relation of those parts to each other and to the whole, remain as they are. You seem to have given the provisional nomination of the officers, in the first instance, to the king, with a reserve of approbation by the National Assembly. Men who have an interest to pursue are extremely sagacious in discovering the true seat of power. They must soon perceive that those who can negative indefinitely, in reality appoint. The officers must therefore look to their intrigues in that assembly, as the sole certain road to promotion. Still, however, by your new constitution they must begin their solicitation at court. This double negotiation for military rank seems to me a contrivance as well adapted, as if it were studied for no other end, to promote faction in the assembly itself, relative to this vast military patronage; and then to poison the corps of officers with factions of a nature still more dangerous to the safety of government, upon any bottom on which it can be placed, and destructive in the end to the efficiency of the army itself. Those officers, who lose the promotions intended for them by the crown, must become of a faction opposite to that of the assembly which has rejected their claims, and must nourish discontents in the heart of the army against the ruling powers. Those officers, on the other hand, who, by carrying their point through an interest in the assembly, feel themselves to be at best only second in the good-will of the crown, though first in that of the assembly, must slight an authority which would not advance, and could not retard their promotion. If to avoid these evils you will have no other rule for command or promotion than seniority, you will have an army of formality; at the same time it will become more independent, and more of a military republic. Not they but the king is the machine. A king is not to be deposed by halves. If he is not every thing in the command of an army, he is nothing. What is the effect of a power placed nominally at the head of the army, who to that army is no object of gratitude, or of fear? Such a cypher is not fit for the administration of an object, of all things the most delicate, the supreme command of military men. They must be constrained (and their inclinations lead them to what their necessities require) by a real, vigorous, effective, decided, personal authority. The authority of the assembly itself suffers by passing through such a debilitating channel as they have chosen. The army will not long look to an assembly acting through the organ of false shew, and palpable imposition. They will not seriously yield obedience to a prisoner. They will either despise a pageant, or they will pity a captive king. This relation of your army to the crown will, if I am not greatly mistaken, become a serious dilemma in your politics. *

It is besides to be considered, whether an assembly like yours, even supposing that it was in possession of another sort of organ through which its orders were to pass, is fit for promoting the obedience and discipline of an army. It is known, that armies have hitherto yielded a very precarious and uncertain obedience to any senate, or popular authority; and they will least of all yield it to an assembly which is to have only a continuance of two years. The officers must totally lose the characteristic disposition of military men, if they see with perfect submission and due admiration, the dominion of pleaders; especially when they find, that they have a new court to pay to an endless succession of those pleaders, whose military policy, and the genius of whose command (if they should have any) must be as uncertain as their duration is transient. In the weakness of one kind of authority, and in the fluctuation of all, the officers of an army will remain for some time mutinous and full of faction, until some popular general, who understands the art of conciliating the soldiery, and who possesses the true spirit of command, shall draw the eyes of all men upon himself. Armies will obey him on his personal account. There is no other way of securing military obedience in this state of things. But the moment in which that event shall happen, the person who really commands the army is your master; the master (that is little) of your king, the master of your assembly, the master of your whole republic.

How came the assembly by their present power over the army? Chiefly, to be sure, by debauching the soldiers from their officers. They have begun by a most terrible operation. They have touched the central point, about which the particles that compose armies are at repose. They have destroyed the principle of obedience in the great essential critical link between the officer and the soldier, just where the chain of military subordination commences, and on which the whole of that system depends. The soldier is told, he is a citizen, and has the rights of man and citizen. The right of a man, he is told, is to be his own governor, and to be ruled only by those to whom he delegates that self-government. It is very natural he should think, that he ought most of all to have his choice where he is to yield the greatest degree of obedience. He will therefore, in all probability, systematically do, what he does at present occasionally; that is, he will exercise at least a negative in the choice of his officers. At present the officers are known at best to be only permissive, and on their good behaviour. In fact, there have been many instances in which they have been cashiered by their corps. Here is a second negative on the choice of the king; a negative as effectual at least as the other of the assembly. The soldiers know already that it has been a question, not ill received in the national assembly, whether they ought not to have the direct choice of their officers, or some proportion of them? When such matters are in deliberation, it is no extravagant supposition that they will incline to the opinion most favourable to their pretensions. They will not bear to be deemed the army of an imprisoned king, whilst another army in the same country, with whom too they are to feast and confederate, is to be considered as the free army of a free constitution. They will cast their eyes on the other and more permanent army; I mean the municipal. That corps, they well know, does actually elect its own officers. They may not be able to discern the grounds of distinction on which they are not to elect a Marquis de la Fayette* (or what is his new name) of their own? If this election of a commander in chief be a part of the rights of men, why not of theirs? They see elective justices of peace, elective judges, elective curates, elective bishops, elective municipalities, and elective commanders of the Parisian army.—Why should they alone be excluded? Are the brave troops of France the only men in that nation who are not the fit judges of military merit, and of the qualifications necessary for a commander in chief? Are they paid by the state, and do they therefore lose the rights of men? They are a part of that nation themselves, and contribute to that pay. And is not the king, is not the national assembly, and are not all who elect the national assembly, likewise paid? Instead of seeing all these forfeit their rights by their receiving a salary, they perceive that in all these cases a salary is given for the exercise of those rights. All your resolutions, all your proceedings, all your debates, all the works of your doctors in religion and politics, have industriously been put into their hands; and you expect that they will apply to their own case just as much of your doctrines and examples as suits your pleasure.

Every thing depends upon the army in such a government as yours; for you have industriously destroyed all the opinions, and prejudices, and, as far as in you lay, all the instincts which support government. Therefore the moment any difference arises between your national assembly and any part of the nation, you must have recourse to force. Nothing else is left to you; or rather you have left nothing else to yourselves. You see by the report of your war minister, that the distribution of the army is in a great measure made with a view of internal coercion.[1] You must rule by an army; and you have infused

---

[1] Courier François, 30 July, 1790. Assemblée Nationale, Numero 210.

into that army by which you rule, as well as into the whole
body of the nation, principles which after a time must disable
you in the use you resolve to make of it. The king is to call out
troops to act against his people, when the world has been told,
and the assertion is still ringing in our ears, that troops ought
not to fire on citizens. The colonies assert to themselves an
independent constitution and a free trade. They must be
constrained by troops. In what chapter of your code of the
rights of men are they able to read, that it is a part of the rights
of men to have their commerce monopolized and restrained
for the benefit of others. As the colonists rise on you, the
negroes rise on them. Troops again—Massacre, torture,
hanging! These are your rights of men! These are the fruits of
metaphysic declarations wantonly made, and shamefully
retracted! It was but the other day that the farmers of land in
one of your provinces refused to pay some sorts of rents to the
lord of the soil. In consequences of this you decree, that the
country people shall pay all rents and dues, except those
which as grievances you have abolished;* and if they refuse,
then you order the king to march troops against them. You lay
down metaphysic propositions which infer universal consequences, and then you attempt to limit logic by despotism.
The leaders of the present system tell them of their rights, as
men, to take fortresses, to murder guards, to seize on kings
without the least appearance of authority even from the
assembly, whilst, as the sovereign legislative body, that
assembly was sitting in the name of the nation—and yet these
leaders presume to order out the troops, which have acted in
these very disorders, to coerce those who shall judge on the
principles, and follow the examples, which have been guaran-
tied by their own approbation.

The leaders teach the people to abhor and reject all
feodality as the barbarism of tyranny, and they tell them
afterwards how much of that barbarous tyranny they are to
bear with patience. As they are prodigal of light with regard to
grievances, so the people find them sparing in the extreme
with regard to redress. They know that not only certain quit-
rents and personal duties, which you have permitted them to
redeem (but have furnished no money for the redemption) are

as nothing to those burthens for which you have made no provision at all. They know, that almost the whole system of landed property in its origin is feudal; that it is the distribution of the possessions of the original proprietors, made by a barbarous conqueror to his barbarous instruments; and that the most grievous effects of the conquest are the land rents of every kind, as without question they are.

The peasants, in all probability, are the descendants of these antient proprietors. Romans or Gauls. But if they fail, in any degree, in the titles which they make on the principles of antiquaries and lawyers, they retreat into the citadel of the rights of men. There they find that men are equal; and the earth, the kind and equal mother of all, ought not to be monopolized to foster the pride and luxury of any men, who by nature are no better than themselves, and who, if they do not labour for their bread, are worse. They find, that by the laws of nature the occupant and subduer of the soil is the true proprietor; that there is no prescription against nature; and that the agreements (where any there are) which have been made with their landlords, during the time of slavery, are only the effect of duresse and force; and that when the people re-entered into the rights of men, those agreements were made as void as every thing else which had been settled under the prevalence of the old feudal and aristocratic tyranny. They will tell you that they see no difference between an idler with a hat and a national cockade, and an idler in a cowl or in a rochet.* If you ground the title to rents on succession and prescription, they tell you, from the speech of Mr *Camus*, published by the national assembly for their information, that things ill begun cannot avail themselves of prescription; that the title of these lords was vicious in its origin; and that force is at least as bad as fraud. As to the title by succession, they will tell you, that the succession of those who have cultivated the soil is the true pedigree of property, and not rotten parchments and silly substitutions; that the lords have enjoyed their usurpation too long; and that if they allow to these lay monks any charitable pension, they ought to be thankful to the bounty of the true proprietor, who is so generous towards a false claimant to his goods.

When the peasants give you back that coin of sophistic reason, on which you have set your image and superscription, you cry it down as base money, and tell them you will pay for the future with French guards, and dragoons, and hussars. You hold up, to chastise them, the second-hand authority of a king, who is only the instrument of destroying, without any power of protecting either the people or his own person. Through him it seems you will make yourselves obeyed. They answer, You have taught us that there are no gentlemen; and which of your principles teach us to bow to kings whom we have not elected? We know, without your teaching, that lands were given for the support of feudal dignities, feudal titles, and feudal offices. When you took down the cause as a grievance, why should the more grievous effect remain? As there are now no hereditary honours, and no distinguished families, why are we taxed to maintain what you tell us ought not to exist? You have sent down our old aristocratic landlords in no other character, and with no other title, but that of exactors under your authority. Have you endeavoured to make these your rent-gatherers respectable to us? No. You have sent them to us with their arms reversed, their shields broken, their impresses defaced; and so displumed, degraded, and metamorphosed, such unfeathered two-legged things, that we no longer know them. They are strangers to us. They do not even go by the names of our ancient lords. Physically they may be the same men; though we are not quite sure of that, on your new philosophic doctrines of personal identity. In all other respects they are totally changed. We do not see why we have not as good a right to refuse them their rents, as you have to abrogate all their honours, titles, and distinctions. This we have never commissioned you to do; and it is one instance, among many indeed, of your assumption of undelegated power. We see the burghers of Paris, through their clubs, their mobs, and their national guards, directing you at their pleasure, and giving that as law to you, which, under your authority, is transmitted as law to us. Through you, these burghers dispose of the lives and fortunes of us all. Why should not you attend as much to the desires of the laborious husbandman wth regard to our rent, by which we are affected in the most serious manner, as you do to the demands of these insolent burghers, relative to distinctions and titles of honour, by which neither they nor we are affected at all? But we find you pay more regard to their fancies than to our necessities. Is it among the rights of man to pay tribute to his equals? Before this measure of yours, we might have thought we were not perfectly equal. We might have entertained some old, habitual, unmeaning prepossession in favour of those landlords; but we cannot conceive with what other view than that of destroying all respect to them, you could have made the law that degrades them. You have forbidden us to treat them with any of the old formalities of respect, and now you send troops to sabre and to bayonet us into a submission to fear and force, which you did not suffer us to yield to the mild authority of opinion.

The ground of some of these arguments is horrid and ridiculous to all rational ears; but to the politicians of metaphysics who have opened schools for sophistry, and made establishments for anarchy, it is solid and conclusive. It is obvious, that on a mere consideration of the right, the leaders in the assembly would not in the least have scrupled to abrogate the rents along with the titles and family ensigns. It would be only to follow up the principle of their reasonings, and to complete the analogy of their conduct. But they had newly possessed themselves of a great body of landed property by confiscation. They had this commodity at market; and the market would have been wholly destroyed, if they were to permit the husbandmen to riot in the speculations with which they so freely intoxicated themselves. The only security which property enjoys in any one of its descriptions, is from the interests of their rapacity with regard to some other. They have left nothing but their own arbitrary pleasure to determine what property is to be protected and what subverted.

Neither have they left any principle by which any of their municipalities can be bound to obedience; or even conscientiously obliged not to separate from the whole, to become independent, or to connect itself with some other state. The people of Lyons, it seems, have refused lately to pay taxes. Why should they not? What lawful authority is there left to exact them? The king imposed some of them. The old states, methodised by orders, settled the more ancient. They may say to the assembly, Who are you, that are not our kings, nor the states we have elected, nor sit on the principles on which we have elected you? And who are we, that when we see the gabelles* which you have ordered to be paid, wholly shaken off, when we see the act of disobedience afterwards ratified by yourselves, who are we, that we are not to judge what taxes we ought or ought not to pay, and who are not to avail ourselves of the same powers, the validity of which you have approved in others? To this the answer is, We will send troops. The last reason of kings, is always the first with your assembly. This military aid may serve for a time, whilst the impression of the increase of pay remains, and the vanity of being umpires in all disputes is flattered. But this weapon will snap short, unfaithful to the hand that employs it. The assembly keep a school where, systematically, and with unremitting perseverance, they teach principles, and form regulations destructive to all spirit of subordination, civil and military—and then they expect that they shall hold in obedience an anarchic people by an anarchic army.

The municipal army, which, according to their new policy, is to balance this national army, if considered in itself only, is of a constitution much more simple, and in every respect less exceptionable. It is a mere democratic body, unconnected with the crown or the kingdom; armed, and trained, and officered at the pleasure of the districts to which the corps severally belong; and the personal service of the individuals, who compose, or the fine in lieu of personal service, are directed by the same authority.[1] Nothing is more uniform. If, however, considered in any relation to the crown, to the national assembly, to the public tribunals, or to the other army, or considered in a view to any coherence or connection

---

[1] I see by Mr Necker's account, that the national guards of Paris have received, over and above the money levied within their own city, about 145,000 *l.* sterling out of the public treasure. Whether this be an actual payment for the nine months of their existence, or an estimate of their yearly charge, I do not clearly perceive. It is of no great importance, as certainly they may take whatever they please.

between its parts, it seems a monster, and can hardly fail to terminate its perplexed movements in some great national calamity. It is a worse preservative of a general constitution, than the systasis of Crete, or the confederation of Poland,* or any other ill-devised corrective which has yet been imagined, in the necessities produced by an ill-constructed system of government.

Having concluded my few remarks on the constitution of the supreme power, the executive, the judicature, the military, and on the reciprocal relation of all these establishments, I shall say something of the ability shewed by your legislators with regard to the revenue.

In their proceedings relative to this object, if possible, still fewer traces appear of political judgment or financial resource. When the states met, it seemed to be the great object to improve the system of revenue, to enlarge its collection, to cleanse it of oppression and vexation, and to establish it on the most solid footing. Great were the expectations entertained on that head throughout Europe. It was by this grand arrangement that France was to stand or fall; and this became, in my opinion, very properly, the test by which the skill and patriotism of those who ruled in that assembly would be tried. The revenue of the state is the state. In effect all depends upon it, whether for support or for reformation. The dignity of every occupation wholly depends upon the quantity and the kind of virtue that may be exerted in it. As all great qualities of the mind which operate in public, and are not merely suffering and passive, require force for their display, I had almost said for their unequivocal existence, the revenue, which is the spring of all power, becomes in its administration the sphere of every active virtue. Public virtue, being of a nature magnificent and splendid, instituted for great things, and conversant about great concerns, requires abundant scope and room, and cannot spread and grow under confinement, and in circumstances straitened, narrow, and sordid. Through the revenue alone the body politic can act in its true genius and character, and therefore it will display just as much of its collective virtue, and as much of that virtue which may characterize those who move it, and are, as it were, its life and guiding principle, as it is possessed of a just revenue. For from hence, not only magnanimity, and liberality, and beneficence, and fortitude, and providence, and the tutelary protection of all good arts, derive their food, and the growth of their organs, but continence, and self-denial, and labour, and vigilance, and frugality, and whatever else there is in which the mind shews itself above the appetite, are no where more in their proper element than in the provision and distribution of the public wealth. It is therefore not without reason that the science of speculative and practical finance, which must take to its aid so many auxiliary branches of knowledge, stands high in the estimation not only of the ordinary sort, but of the wisest and best men; and as this science has grown with the progress of its object, the prosperity and improvement of nations has generally encreased with the encrease of their revenues; and they will both continue to grow and flourish, as long as the balance between what is left to strengthen the efforts of individuals, and what is collected for the common efforts of the state, bear to each other a due reciprocal proportion, and are kept in a close correspondence and communication. And perhaps it may be owing to the greatness of revenues, and to the urgency of state necessities, that old abuses in the constitution of finances are discovered, and their true nature and rational theory comes to be more perfectly understood; insomuch, that a smaller revenue might have been more distressing in one period than a far greater is found to be in another; the proportionate wealth even remaining the same. In this state of things, the French assembly found something in their revenues to preserve, to secure, and wisely to administer, as well as to abrogate and alter. Though their proud assumption might justify the severest tests, yet in trying their abilities on their financial proceedings, I would only consider what is the plain obvious duty of a common finance minister, and try them upon that, and not upon models of ideal perfection.

The objects of a financier are, then, to secure an ample revenue; to impose it with judgment ad equality; to employ it oeconomically; and when necessity obliges him to make use of credit, to secure its foundations in that instance, and for ever, by the clearness and candour of his proceedings, the exactness of his calculations, and the solidity of his funds. On these heads we may take a short and distinct view of the merits and abilities of those in the national assembly, who have taken to themselves the management of this arduous concern. Far from any encrease of revenue in their hands, I find, by a report of M. Vernier,* from the committee of finances, of the second of August last, that the amount of the national revenue, as compared with its produce before the revolution, was diminished by the sum of two hundred millions, or *eight millions sterling* of the annual income, considerably more than one-third of the whole!

If this be the result of great ability, never surely was ability displayed in a more distinguished manner, or with so powerful an effect. No common folly, no vulgar incapacity, no ordinary official negligence, even no official crime, no corruption, no peculation, hardly any direct hostility which we have seen in the modern world, could in so short a time have made so complete an overthrow of the finances, and with them, of the strength of a great kingdom.—*Cedò quî vestram rempublicam tantam amisistis tam cito?**

The sophisters and declaimers, as soon as the assembly met, began with decrying the ancient constitution of the revenue in many of its most essential branches, such as the public monopoly of salt. They charged it, as truly as unwisely, with being ill-contrived, oppressive, and partial. This representation they were not satisfied to make use of in speeches preliminary to some plan of reform; they declared it in a solemn resolution or public sentence, as it were judicially, passed upon it; and this they dispersed throughout the nation. At the time they passed the decree, with the same gravity they ordered this same absurd, oppressive, and partial tax to be paid, until they could find a revenue to replace it. The consequence was inevitable. The provinces which had been always exempted from this salt monopoly, some of whom were charged with other contributions, perhaps equivalent, were totally disinclined to bear any part of the burthen, which by an equal distribution was to redeem the others. As to the assembly, occupied as it was with the declaration and violation of the rights of men, and with their arrangements for general confusion, it had neither leisure nor capacity to contrive, nor authority to enforce any plan of any kind relative to the replacing the tax or equalizing it, or compensating the provinces, or for conducting their minds to any scheme of accommodation with the other districts which were to be relieved.

The people of the salt provinces, impatient under taxes damned by the authority which had directed their payment, very soon found their patience exhausted. They thought themselves as skilful in demolishing as the assembly could be. They relieved themselves by throwing off the whole burthen. Animated by this example, each district, or part of a district, judging of its own grievance by its own feeling, and of its remedy by its own opinion, did as it pleased with other taxes.

We are next to see how they have conducted themselves in contriving equal impositions, proportioned to the means of the citizens, and the least likely to lean heavy on the active capital employed in the generation of that private wealth, from whence the public fortune must be derived. By suffering the several districts, and several of the individuals in each district, to judge of what part of the old revenue they might withhold, instead of better principles of equality, a new inequality was introduced of the most oppressive kind. Payments were regulated by dispositions. The parts of the kingdom which were the most submissive, the most orderly, or the most affectionate to the commonwealth, bore the whole burthen of the state. Nothing turns out to be so oppressive and unjust as a feeble government. To fill up all the deficiencies in the old impositions, and the new deficiencies of every kind which were to be expected, what remained to a state without authority? The national assembly called for a voluntary benevolence; for a fourth part of the income of all the citizens, to be estimated on the honour of those who were to pay. They obtained something more than could be rationally calculated, but what was, far indeed, from answerable to their real necessities, and much less to their fond expectations. Rational people could have hoped for little from this their tax in the disguise of a benevolence; a tax, weak, ineffective, and unequal; a tax by which luxury, avarice, and selfishness were screened, and the load thrown upon productive capital, upon integrity, generosity, and public spirit—a tax of regulation upon virtue. At length the mask is thrown off, and they are now trying means (with little success) of exacting their benevolence by force.

This benevolence, the ricketty offspring of weakness, was to be supported by another resource, the twin brother of the same prolific imbecility. The patriotic donations were to make good the failure of the patriotic contribution. John Doe was to become security for Richard Roe.* By this scheme they took things of much price from the giver, comparatively of small value to the receiver; they ruined several trades; they pillaged the crown of its ornaments, the churches of their plate, and the people of their personal decorations. The invention of these juvenile pretenders to liberty, was in reality nothing more than a servile imitation of one of the poorest resources of doting despotism. They took an old huge full-bottomed perriwig out of the wardrobe of the antiquated frippery of Louis XIV. to cover the premature baldness of the national assembly. They produced this old-fashioned formal folly, though it had been so abundantly exposed in the Memoirs of the Duke de St Simon,* if to reasonable men it had wanted any arguments to display its mischief and insufficiency. A device of the same kind was tried in my memory by Louis XV. but it answered at no time. However, the necessities of ruinous wars were some excuse for desperate projects. The deliberations of calamity are rarely wise. But here was a season for disposition and providence. It was in a time of profound peace, then enjoyed for five years, and promising a much longer continuance, that they had recourse to this desperate trifling. They were sure to lose more reputation by sporting, in their serious situation, with these toys and playthings of finance, which have filled half their journals, than could possibly be compensated by the poor temporary supply which they afforded. It seemed as if those who adopted such projects were wholly ignorant of their circumstances, or wholly unequal to their necessities. Whatever virtue may be in these devices, it is obvious that neither the patriotic gifts, nor the patriotic contribution, can ever be resorted to again. The resources of public folly are soon exhausted. The whole indeed of their scheme of revenue is to make, by any artifice, an appearance of a full reservoir for the hour, whilst at the same time they cut off the springs and living fountains of perennial supply. The account not long since furnished by Mr Necker was meant, without question, to be favourable. He gives a flattering view of the means of getting through the year; but he expresses, as it is natural he should, some apprehension for that which was to succeed. On this last prognostic, instead of entering into the grounds of this apprehension, in order by a proper foresight, to prevent the prognosticated evil, Mr Necker receives a sort of friendly reprimand from the president of the assembly.

As to their other schemes of taxation, it is impossible to say any thing of them with certainty; because they have not yet had their operation; but nobody is so sanguine as to imagine they will fill up any perceptible part of the wide gaping breach which their incapacity has made in their revenues. At present the state of their treasury sinks every day more and more in cash, and swells more and more in fictitious representation. When so little within or without is now found but paper, the representative not of opulence but of want, the creature not of credit but of power, they imagine that our flourishing state in England is owing to that bank-paper, and not the bank-paper to the flourishing condition of our commerce, to the solidity of our credit, and to the total exclusion of all idea of power from any part of the transaction. They forget that, in England, not one shilling of paper-money of any description is received but of choice; that the whole has had its origin in cash actually deposited; and that it is convertible, at pleasure, in an instant, and without the smallest loss, into cash again. Our paper is of value in commerce, because in law it is of none. It is powerful on Change,* because in Westminster-hall it is impotent. In payment of a debt of twenty shillings, a creditor may refuse all the paper of the bank of England. Nor is there amongst us a single public security, of any quality or nature whatsoever, that is enforced by authority. In fact it might be easily shewn, that our paper wealth, instead of lessening the real coin, has a tendency to increase it; instead of being a substitute for money, it only facilitates its entry, its exit, and its circulation; that it is the symbol of prosperity, and not the badge of distress. Never was a scarcity of cash, and an exuberance of paper, a subject of complaint in this nation.

Well! but a lessening of prodigal expences, and the oeconomy which has been introduced by the virtuous and sapient assembly, makes amends for the losses sutained in the receipt of revenue. In this at least they have fulfilled the duty of a financier. Have those, who say so, looked at the expences of the national assembly itself? of the municipalities, of the city of Paris? of the increased pay of the two armies? of the new police? of the new judicatures? Have they even carefully compared the present pension-list with the former? These politicians have been cruel, not oeconomical. Comparing the expences of the former prodigal government and its relation to the then revenues with the expences of this new system as opposed to the state of its new treasury, I believe the present will be found beyond all comparison more chargeable.[1]

It remains only to consider the proofs of financial ability, furnished by the present French managers when they are to raise supplies on credit. Here I am a little at a stand; for credit, properly speaking, they have none. The credit of the antient government was not indeed the best: but they could always, on some terms, command money, not only at home, but from most of the countries of Europe where a surplus capital was

---

[1] The reader will observe, that I have but lightly touched (my plan demanded nothing more) on the condition of the French finances, as connected with the demands upon them. If I had intended to do otherwise, the materials in my hands for such a task are not altogether perfect. On this subject I refer the reader to M. de Calonne's work; and the tremendous display that he has made of the havock and devastation in the public estate, and in all the affairs of France, caused by the presumptuous good intentions of ignorance and incapacity. Such effects, those causes will always produce. Looking over that account with a pretty strict eye, and, with perhaps too much rigour, deducting every thing which may be placed to the account of a financier out of place, who might be supposed by his enemies desirous of making the most of his cause, I believe it will be found, that a more salutary lesson of caution against the daring spirit of innovators than what has been supplied at the expence of France, never was at any time furnished to mankind.

accumulated; and the credit of that government was improving daily. The establishment of a system of liberty would of course be supposed to give it new strength; and so it would actually have done, if a system of liberty had been established. What offers has their government of pretended liberty had from Holland, from Hamburgh, from Switzerland, from Genoa, from England, for a dealing in their paper? Why should these nations of commerce and oeconomy enter into any pecuniary dealings with a people who attempt to reverse the very nature of things; amongst whom they see the debtor prescribing, at the point of the bayonet, the medium of his solvency to the creditor; discharging one of his engagements with another; turning his very penury into his resource; and paying his interest with his rags?

Their fanatical confidence in the omnipotence of church plunder, has induced these philosophers to overlook all care of the public estate, just as the dream of the philosopher's stone induces dupes, under the more plausible delusion of the hermetic art, to neglect all rational means of improving their fortunes. With these philosophic financiers, this universal medicine made of church mummy* is to cure all the evils of the state. These gentlemen perhaps do not believe a great deal in the miracles of piety; but it cannot be questioned, that they have an undoubting faith in the prodigies of sacrilege. Is there a debt which presses them—Issue *assignats*.—Are compensations to be made, or a maintenance decreed to those whom they have robbed of their freehold in their office, or expelled from their profession—*Assignats*. Is a fleet to be fitted out—*Assignats*. If sixteen millions sterling of these *assignats*, forced on the people, leave the wants of the state as urgent as ever—issue, says one, thirty millions sterling of *assignats*—says another, issue fourscore millions more of *assignats*. The only difference among their financial factions is on the greater or the lesser quantity of *assignats* to be imposed on the publick sufferance. They are all professors of *assignats*. Even those, whose natural good sense and knowledge of commerce, not obliterated by philosophy, furnish decisive arguments against this delusion, conclude their arguments, by proposing the emission of *assignats*. I suppose they must talk of *assignats*, as

no other language would be understood. All experience of
their inefficacy does not in the least discourage them. Are the
old *assignats* depreciated at market? What is the remedy?
Issue new *assignats.*—*Mais si maladia, opiniatria, non vult se
garire, quid illi facere? assignare—postea assignare; ensuita
assignare.** The word is a trifle altered. The Latin of your
present doctors may be better than that of your old comedy;
their wisdom, and the variety of their resources, are the same.
They have not more notes in their song than the cuckow;
though, far from the softness of that harbinger of summer and
plenty, their voice is as harsh and as ominous as that of the
raven.

Who but the most desperate adventurerers in philosophy
and finance could at all have thought of destroying the settled
revenue of the state, the sole security for the public credit, in
the hope of rebuilding it with the materials of confiscated
property? If, however, an excessive zeal for the state should
have led a pious and venerable prelate* (by anticipation a
father of the church)[1] to pillage his own order, and, for the
good of the church and people, to take upon himself the place
of grand financier of confiscation, and comptroller general of
sacrilege, he and his coadjutors were, in my opinion, bound to
shew, by their subsequent conduct, that they knew something
of the office they assumed. When they had resolved to
appropriate to the *Fisc,** a certain portion of the landed
property of their conquered country, it was their business to
render their bank a real fund of credit; as far as such a bank
was capable of becoming so.

To establish a current circulating credit upon any *Land-
bank,* under any circumstances whatsoever, has hitherto
proved difficult at the very least.* The attempt has commonly
ended in bankruptcy. But when the assembly were led,
through a contempt of moral, to a defiance of oeconomical
principles, it might at least have been expected, that nothing
would be omitted on their part to lessen this difficulty, to
prevent any aggravation of this bankruptcy. It might be
expected that to render your *Land-bank* tolerable, every

[1] La Bruyere of Bossuet.*

means would be adopted that could display openness and candour in the statement of the security; every thing which could aid the recovery of the demand. To take things in their most favourable point of view, your condition was that of a man of a large landed estate, which he wished to dispose of for the discharge of a debt, and the supply of certain services. Not being able instantly to sell, you wished to mortgage. What would a man of fair intentions, and a commonly clear understanding, do in such circumstances? Ought he not first to ascertain the gross value of the estate; the charges of its management and disposition; the encumbrances perpetual and temporary of all kinds that affect it; then, striking a net surplus, to calculate the just value of the security? When that surplus (the only security to the creditor) had been clearly ascertained, and properly vested in the hands of trustees; then he would indicate the parcels to be sold, and the time, and conditions of sale; after this, he would admit the public creditor, if he chose it, to subscribe his stock into this new fund; or he might receive proposals for an *assignat* from those who would advance money to purchase this species of security.

This would be to proceed like men of business, methodically and rationally; and on the only principles of public and private credit that have an existence. The dealer would then know exactly what he purchased; and the only doubt which could hang upon his mind would be, the dread of the resumption of the spoil, which one day might be made (perhaps with an addition of punishment) from the sacrilegious gripe of those execrable wretches who could become purchasers at the auction of their innocent fellow-citizens.

An open and exact statement of the clear value of the property, and of the time, the circumstances, and the place of sale, were all necessary, to efface as much as possible the stigma that has hitherto been branded on every kind of Land-bank. It became necessary on another principle, that is, on account of a pledge of faith previously given on that subject, that their future fidelity in a slippery concern might be established by their adherence to their first engagement. When they had finally determined on a state resource from church booty, they came, on the 14th of April 1790, to a solemn resolution on the subject; and pledged themselves to their country, 'that in the statement of the public charges for each year there should be brought to account a sum sufficient for defraying the expences of the R. C. A. religion, the support of the ministers at the altars, the relief of the poor, the pensions to the ecclesiastics, secular as well as regular, of the one and of the other sex, *in order that the estates and goods which are at the disposal of the nation may be disengaged of all charges, and employed by the representatives, or the legislative body, to the great and most pressing exigencies of the state.*' They further engaged, on the same day, that the sum necessary for the year 1791 should be forthwith determined.

In this resolution they admit it their duty to show distinctly the expence of the above objects, which, by other resolutions, they had before engaged should be first in the order of provision. They admit that they ought to shew the estate clear and disengaged of all charges, and that they should shew it immediately. Have they done this immediately, or at any time? Have they ever furnished a rent-roll of the immoveable estates, or given in an inventory of the moveable effects which they confiscate to their assignats? In what manner they can fulfil their engagements of holding out to public service 'an estate disengaged of all charges,' without authenticating the value of the estate, or the quantum of the charges. I leave it to their English admirers to explain. Instantly upon this assurance, and previously to any one step towards making it good, they issue, on the credit of so handsome a declaration, sixteen millions sterling of their paper. This was manly. Who, after this masterly stroke, can doubt of their abilities in finance?— But then, before any other emission of these financial *indulgences*, they took care at least to make good their original promise!—If such estimate, either of the value of the estate or the amount of the incumbrances, has been made, it has escaped me. I never heard of it.

At length they have spoken out, and they have made a full discovery of their abominable fraud, in holding out the church lands as a security for any debts or any service whatsoever. They rob only to enable them to cheat; but in a very short time they defeat the ends both of the robbery and the fraud, by making out accounts for other purposes, which blow up their whole apparatus of force and of deception. I am obliged to M. de Calonne for his reference to the document which proves this extraordinary fact: it had, by some means, escaped me. Indeed it was not necessary to make out my assertion as to the breach of faith on the declaration of the 14th of April 1790. By a report of their Committee it now appears, that the charge of keeping up the reduced ecclesiastical establishments, and other expences attendant on religion, and maintaining the religious of both sexes, retained or pensioned, and the other concomitant expences of the same nature, which they have brought upon themselves by this convulsion in property, exceeds the income of the estates acquired by it in the enormous sum of two millions sterling annually; besides a debt of seven millions and upwards. These are the calculating powers of imposture! This is the finance of philosophy! This is the result of all the delusions held out to engage a miserable people in rebellion, murder, and sacrilege, and to make them prompt and zealous instruments in the ruin of their country! Never did a state, in any case, enrich itself by the confiscations of the citizens. This new experiment has succeeded like all the rest. Every honest mind, every true lover of liberty and humanity must rejoice to find that injustice is not always good policy, nor rapine the high road to riches. I subjoin with pleasure, in a note, the able and spirited observations of M. de Calonne on this subject.[1]

---

[1] 'Ce n'est point à l'assemblée entière que je m'adresse ici; je ne parle qu'à ceux qui l'égarent, en lui cachant sous des gazes séduisantes le but où ils l'entraînent. C'est à eux que je dis: votre objet, vous n'en disconviendrez pas, c'est d'ôter tout espoir au clergé, & de consommer sa ruine; c'est-la, en ne vous soupçonnant d'aucune combinaison de cupidité, d'aucun regard sur le jeu des effets publics, c'est-là ce qu'on doit croire que vous avez en vue dans la terrible opération que vous proposez; c'est ce qui doit en être le fruit. Mais le peuple que vous y intéressez, quel avantage peut-il y trouver? En vous servant sans cesse de lui, que faites vous pour lui? Rien, absolument rien; &, au contraire, vous faites ce qui ne conduit qu'à l'accabler de nouvelles charges. Vous avez rejeté, à son prejudice, une offre de 400 millions, dont l'acceptation pouvoit devenir un moyen de soulagement en sa faveur; & à cette ressource, aussi profitable que legitime, vous avez substitué une injustice ruineuse, qui, de votre

In order to persuade the world of the bottomless resource of ecclesiastical confiscation, the assembly have proceeded to other confiscations of estates in offices, which could not be done with any common colour without being compensated out of this grand confiscation of landed property. They have thrown upon this fund, which was to shew a surplus, disengaged of all charges, a new charge; namely, the compensation to the whole body of the disbanded judicature; and of all suppressed offices and estates; a charge which I cannot ascertain, but which unquestionably amounts to many French millions. Another of the new charges, is an annuity of four hundred and eighty thousand pounds sterling, to be paid (if they choose to keep faith) by daily payments, for the interest of the first assignats. Have they ever given themselves the trouble to state fairly the expence of the management of the church lands in the hands of the municipalities, to whose care, skill, and diligence, and that of their legion of unknown under agents, they have chosen to commit the charge of the forfeited estates, and the consequence of which had been so ably pointed out by the bishop of Nancy?*

But it is unnecessary to dwell on these obvious heads of incumbrance. Have they made out any clear state of the grand incumbrance of all, I mean the whole of the general and municipal establishments of all sorts, and compared it with the regular income by revenue? Every deficiency in these becomes a charge on the confiscated estate, before the creditor can plant his cabbages on an acre of church property. There is no other prop than this confiscation to keep the whole state from tumbling to the ground. In this situation they have purposely covered all that they ought industriously to have cleared, with a thick fog; and then, blindfold themselves, like

propre aveu, charge le trésor public, & par conséquent le peuple, d'un surcroît de depense annuelle de 50 millions au moins, & d'un remboursement de 150 millions.

'Malheureux peuple, voilà ce que vous vaut en dernier résultat l'expropriation de l'Eglise, & la dureté des décrets taxateurs du traitement des ministres d'une religion bienfaisante; & deformais ils seront à votre charge: leurs charités soulageoient les pauvres; & vous allez être imposés pour subvenir à leur entretien!'*—*De l'Etat de la France*, p. 81. See also p. 92, and the following pages.

bulls that shut their eyes when they push, they drive, by the point of the bayonets, their slaves, blindfolded indeed no worse than their lords, to take their fictions for currencies, and to swallow down paper pills by thirty-four millions sterling at a dose. Then they proudly lay in their claim to a future credit, on failure of all their past engagements, and at a time when (if in such a matter any thing can be clear) it is clear that the surplus estates will never answer even the first of their mortgages, I mean that of the four hundred million (or sixteen millions sterling) of *assignats*. In all this procedure I can discern neither the solid sense of plain-dealing, nor the subtle dexterity of ingenious fraud. The objection within the assembly to pulling up the flood-gates for this inundation of fraud, are unanswered; but they are thoroughly refuted by an hundred thousand financiers in the street. These are the numbers by which the metaphysic arithmeticians compute. These are the grand calculations on which a philosophical public credit is founded in France. They cannot raise supplies; but they can raise mobs. Let them rejoice in the applauses of the club at Dundee,* for their wisdom and patriotism in having thus applied the plunder of the citizens to the service of the state. I hear of no address upon this subject from the directors of the Bank of England; though their approbation would be of a *little* more weight in the scale of credit than that of the club at Dundee. But, to do justice to the club, I believe the gentlemen who compose it to be wiser than they appear; that they will be less liberal of their money than of their addresses; and that they would not give a dog's-ear of their most rumpled and ragged Scotch paper for twenty of your fairest assignats.

Early in this year the assembly issued paper to the amount of sixteen millions sterling. What must have been the state into which the assembly has brought your affairs, that the relief afforded by so vast a supply has been hardly perceptible? This paper also felt an almost immediate depreciation of five per cent. which in little time came to about seven. The effect of these assignats on the receipt of the revenue is remarkable. Mr Necker found that the collectors of the revenue, who received in coin, paid the treasury in *assignats*. The collectors made seven per cent. by thus receiving in money, and accounting in depreciated paper. It was not very difficult to foresee, that this must be inevitable. It was, however, not the less embarassing. Mr Necker was obliged (I believe, for a considerable part, in the market of London) to buy gold and silver for the mint, which amounted to about twelve thousand pounds above the value of the commodity gained. That minister was of opinion, that whatever their secret nutritive virtue might be, the state could not live upon *assignats* alone; that some real silver was necessary, particularly for the satisfaction of those, who having iron in their hands, were not likely to distinguish themselves for patience, when they should perceive that whilst an encrease of pay was held out to them in real money, it was again to be fraudulently drawn back by depreciated paper. The minister, in this very natural distress, applied to the assembly, that they should order the collectors to pay in specie what in specie they had received. It could not escape him, that if the treasury paid 3 per cent. for the use of a currency, which should be returned seven per cent. worse than the minister issued it, such a dealing could not very greatly tend to enrich the public. The assembly took no notice of his recommendation. They were in this dilemma—If they continued to receive the assignats, cash must become an alien to their treasury: If the treasury should refuse those paper *amulets*, or should discountenance them in any degree, they must destroy the credit of their sole resource. They seem then to have made their option; and to have given some sort of credit to their paper by taking it themselves; at the same time in their speeches they made a sort of swaggering declaration, something, I rather think, above legislative competence; that is, that there is no difference in value between metallic money and their assignats. This was a good stout proof article of faith, pronounced under an anathema, by the venerable fathers of this philosophic synod. *Credat* who will—certainly not *Judaeus Apella.**

A noble indignation rises in the minds of your popular leaders, on hearing the magic lanthorn in their shew of finance compared to the fraudulent exhibitions of Mr Law.* They cannot bear to hear the sands of his Mississippi compared with the rock of the church, on which they build their system. Pray let them suppress this glorious spirit, until they shew to the world what piece of solid ground there is for their assignats, which they have not pre-occupied by other charges. They do injustice to that great, mother fraud, to compare it with their degenerate imitation. It is not true, that Law built solely on a speculation concerning the Mississippi. He added the East India trade; he added the African trade; he added the farms of all the farmed revenue of France. All these together unquestionably could not support the structure which the public enthusiasm, not he, chose to build upon these bases. But these were, however, in comparison, generous delusions. They supposed, and they aimed at an increase of the commerce of France. They opened to it the whole range of the two hemispheres. They did not think of feeding France from its own substance. A grand imagination found in this flight of commerce something to captivate. It was wherewithal to dazzle the eye of an eagle. It was not made to entice the smell of a mole, nuzzling and burying himself in his mother earth, as yours is. Men were not then quite shrunk from their natural dimensions by a degrading and sordid philosophy, and fitted for low and vulgar deceptions. Above all remember, that in imposing on the imagination, the then managers of the system made a compliment to the freedom of men. In their fraud there was no mixture of force. This was reserved to our time, to quench the little glimmerings of reason which might break in upon the solid darkness of this enlightened age.

On recollection, I have said nothing of a scheme of finance which may be urged in favour of the abilities of these gentlemen, and which has been introduced with great pomp, though not yet finally adopted in the national assembly. It comes with something solid in aid of the credit of the paper circulation; and much has been said of its utility and its elegance. I mean the project for coining into money the bells of the suppressed churches. This is their alchymy. There are some follies which baffle argument; which go beyond ridicule; and which excite no feeling in us but disgust; and therefore I say no more upon it.

It is as little worth remarking any farther upon all their

drawing and re-drawing, on their circulation for putting off the evil day, on the play between the treasury and the *Caisse d'Escompte*, and on all these old exploded contrivances of mercantile fraud, now exalted into policy of state. The revenue will not be trifled with. The prattling about the rights of men will not be accepted in payment for a biscuit or a pound of gunpowder. Here then the metaphysicians descend from their airy speculations, and faithfully follow examples. What examples? the examples of bankrupts. But, defeated, baffled, disgraced, when their breath, their strength, their inventions, their fancies desert them, their confidence still maintains its ground. In the manifest failure of their abilities they take credit for their benevolence. When the revenue disappears in their hands, they have the presumption, in some of their late proceedings, to value *themselves* on the relief given to the people. They did not relieve the people. If they entertained such intentions, why did they order the obnoxious taxes to be paid? The people relieved themselves in spite of the assembly.

But waving all discussion on the parties, who may claim the merit of this fallacious relief, has there been, in effect, any relief to the people in any form? Mr Bailly,* one of the grand agents of paper circulation, lets you into the nature of this relief. His speech to the National Assembly contained an high and laboured panegyric on the inhabitants of Paris for the constancy and unbroken resolution with which they have borne their distress and misery. A fine picture of public felicity! What! great courage and unconquerable firmness of mind to endure benefits and sustain redress! One would think from the speech of this learned Lord Mayor, that the Parisians, for this twelvemonth past, has been suffering the straits of some dreadful blockade; that Henry the Fourth had been stopping up the avenues to their supply, and Sully thundering with his ordnance at the gates of Paris; when in reality they are besieged by no other enemies than their own madness and folly, their own credulity and perverseness. But Mr Bailly will sooner thaw the eternal ice of his atlantic regions, than restore the central heat to Paris, whilst it remains 'smitten with the cold, dry, petrifick mace'* of a false and unfeeling philosophy. Some time after this speech, that is, on the thirteenth of last August, the same magistrate, giving an account of his government at the bar of the same assembly, expresses himself as follows: 'In the month of July 1789, [the period of everlasting commemoration] the finances of the city of Paris were *yet* in good order; the expenditure was counterbalanced by the receipt, and she had at that time a million [forty thousand pounds sterling] in bank. The expences which she has been constrained to incur, *subsequent to the revolution*, amount to 2,500,000 livres. From these expences, and the great falling off in the production of the *free gifts*, not only a momentary but a *total* want of money has taken place.' This is the Paris upon whose nourishment, in the course of the last year, such immense sums, drawn from the vitals of all France, has been expended. As long as Paris stands in the place of antient Rome, so long she will be maintained by the subject provinces. It is an evil inevitably attendant on the dominion of sovereign democratic republics. As it happened in Rome, it may survive that republican domination which gave rise to it. In that case despotism itself must submit to the vices of popularity. Rome, under her emperors, united the evils of both systems; and this unnatural combination was one great cause of her ruin.

To tell the people that they are relieved by the dilapidation of their public estate, is a cruel and insolent imposition. Statesmen, before they valued themselves on the relief given to the people, by the destruction of their revenue, ought first to have carefully attended to the solution of this problem:— Whether it be more advantageous to the people to pay considerably, and to gain in proportion; or to gain little or nothing, and to be disburthened of all contribution? My mind is made up to decide in favour of the first proposition. Experience is with me, and, I believe, the best opinions also. To keep a balance between the power of acquisition on the part of the subject, and the demands he is to answer on the part of the state, is a fundamental part of the skill of a true politician. The means of acquisition are prior in time and in arrangement. Good order is the foundation of all good things. To be enabled to acquire, the people, without being servile, must be tractable and obedient. The magistrate must have his reverence, the laws their authority. The body of the people must not find the principles of natural subordination by art rooted out of their minds. They must respect that property of which they cannot partake. They must labour to obtain what by labour can be obtained; and when they find, as they commonly do, the success disproportioned to the endeavour, they must be taught their consolation in the final proportions of eternal justice. Of this consolation, whoever deprives them, deadens their industry, and strikes at the root of all acquisition as of all conservation. He that does this is the cruel oppressor, the merciless enemy of the poor and wretched; at the same time that by his wicked speculations he exposes the fruits of succesful industry, and the accumulations of fortune, to the plunder of the negligent, the disappointed, and the unprosperous.

Too many of the financiers by profession are apt to see nothing in revenue, but banks, and circulations, and annuities on lives, and tontines,* and perpetual rents, and all the small wares of the shop. In a settled order of the state, these things are not to be slighted, nor is the skill in them to be held of trivial estimation. They are good, but then only good, when they assume the effects of that settled order, and are built upon it. But when men think that these beggarly contrivances may supply a resource for the evils which result from breaking up the foundations of public order, and from causing or suffering the principles of property to be subverted, they will, in the ruin of their country, leave a melancholy and lasting monument of the effect of proposterous politics, and presumptuous, short-sighted, narrow-minded wisdom.

The effects of the incapacity shewn by the popular leaders in all the great members of the commonwealth are to be covered with the 'all-atoning name' of liberty. In some people I see great liberty indeed; in many, if not in the most, an oppressive degrading servitude. But what is liberty without wisdom, and without virtue? It is the greatest of all possible evils; for it is folly, vice, and madness, without tuition or restraint. Those who know what virtuous liberty is, cannot bear to see it disgraced by incapable heads, on account of their having high-sounding words in their mouths. Grand, swelling sentiments of liberty, I am sure I do not despise. They warm the heart; they enlarge and liberalise our minds; they animate our courage in a time of conflict. Old as I am, I read the fine raptures of Lucan and Corneille* with pleasure. Neither do I wholly condemn the little arts and devices of popularity. They facilitate the carrying of many points of moment; they keep the people together; they refresh the mind in its exertions; and they diffuse occasional gaiety over the severe brow of moral freedom. Every politician ought to sacrifice to the graces; and to join compliance with reason. But in such an undertaking as that in France, all these subsidiary sentiments and artifices are of little avail. To make a government requires no great prudence. Settle the seat of power; teach obedience: and the work is done. To give freedom is still more easy. It is not necessary to guide; it only requires to let go the rein. But to form a *free government*; that is, to temper together these opposite elements of liberty and restraint in one consistent work, requires much thought, deep reflection, a sagacious, powerful, and combining mind. This I do not find in those who take the lead in the national assembly. Perhaps they are not so miserably deficient as they appear. I rather believe it. It would put them below the common level of human understanding. But when the leaders choose to make themselves bidders at an auction of popularity, their talents, in the construction of the state, will be of no service. They will become flatterers instead of legislators; the instruments, not the guides of the people. If any of them should happen to propose a scheme of liberty, soberly limited, and defined with proper qualifications, he will be immediately outbid by his competitors, who will produce something more splendidly popular. Suspicions will be raised of his fidelity to his cause. Moderation will be stigmatized as the virtue of cowards; and compromise as the prudence of traitors; until, in hopes of preserving the credit which may enable him to temper and moderate on some occasions, the popular leader is obliged to become active in propagating doctrines, and establishing powers, that will afterwards defeat any sober purpose at which he ultimately might have aimed.

But am I so unreasonable as to see nothing at all that deserves commendation in the indefatigable labours of this assembly? I do not deny that among an infinite number of acts of violence and folly, some good may have been done. They who destroy every thing certainly will remove some grievance. They who make every thing new, have a chance that they may establish something beneficial. To give them credit for what they have done in virtue of the authority they have usurped, or which can excuse them in the crimes by which that authority has been acquired, it must appear, that the same things could not have been accomplished without producing such a revolution. Most assuredly they might; because almost every one of the regulations made by them, which is not very equivocal, was either in the cession of the king, voluntarily made at the meeting of the states, or in the concurrent instructions to the orders. Some usages have been abolished on just grounds; but they were such that if they had stood as they were to all eternity, they would little detract from the happiness and prosperity of any state. The improvements of the national assembly are superficial, their errors fundamental.

Whatever they are, I wish my countrymen rather to recommend to our neighbours the example of the British constitution, than to take models from them for the improvement of our own. In the former they have got an invaluable treasure. They are not, I think, without some causes of apprehension and complaint; but these they do not owe to their constitution, but to their own conduct. I think our happy situation owing to our constitution; but owing to the whole of it, and not to any part singly; owing in a great measure to what we have left standing in our several reviews and reformations, as well as to what we have altered or superadded. Our people will find employment enough for a truly patriotic, free, and independent spirit, in guarding what they possess, from violation. I would not exclude alteration neither; but even when I changed, it should be to preserve. I should be led to my remedy by a great grievance. In what I did, I should follow the example of our ancestors. I would make the reparation as nearly as possible in the style of the building. A politic caution, a guarded circumspection, a moral rather than a complexional timidity were among the ruling principles of our forefathers in their most decided conduct. Not being illuminated with the light of which the gentlemen of France tell us they have got so abundant a share, they acted under a strong impression of the ignorance and fallibility of mankind. He that had made them thus fallible, rewarded them for having in their conduct attended to their nature. Let us imitate their caution, if we wish to deserve their fortune, or to retain their bequests. Let us add, if we please, but let us preserve what they have left; and, standing on the firm ground of the British constitution, let us be satisfied to admire rather than attempt to follow in their desperate flights the aëronauts of France.

I have told you candidly my sentiments. I think they are not likely to alter yours. I do not know that they ought. You are young; you cannot guide, but must follow the fortune of your country. But hereafter they may be of some use to you, in some future form which your commonwealth may take. In the present it can hardly remain; but before its final settlement it may be obliged to pass, as one of our poets says, 'through great varieties of untried being,'* and in all its transmigrations to be purified by fire and blood.

I have little to recommend my opinions, but long observation and much impartiality. They come from one who has been no tool of power, no flatterer of greatness; and who in his last acts does not wish to belye the tenour of his life. They come from one, almost the whole of whose public exertion has been a struggle for the liberty of others; from one in whose breast no anger durable or vehement has ever been kindled, but by what he considered as tyranny; and who snatches from his share in the endeavours which are used by good men to discredit opulent oppression, the hours he has employed on your affairs; and who in so doing persuades himself he has not departed from his usual office: they come from one who desires honours, distinctions, and emoluments, but little; and who expects them not at all; who has no contempt for fame, and no fear of obloquy; who shuns contention, though he will hazard an opinion: from one who wishes to preserve consistency; but who would preserve consistency by varying his means to secure the unity of his end; and, when the equipoise of the vessel in which he sails, may be endangered by overloading it upon one side, is desirous of carrying the small weight of his reasons to that which may preserve its equipoise.

FINIS.

APPENDIX

LETTER TO A MEMBER OF THE NATIONAL ASSEMBLY 1791*

REFERRING to the French Revolution, Burke told the Comtesse de Montrond* on 25 January 1791 that he

> certainly never should have written one word more upon the subject, convinced as I am of its utter inutility, if I had not been applied to by a Gentleman at Paris of rank and consideration for an explanation of some sentiments and expressions in my printed letter [the *Reflections*].*

The 'Gentleman' in question was François-Louis-Thibault de Menonville, deputy to the Estates General from Mirecourt in Lorraine. He had written to Burke,* on 17 November 1790, from Paris after reading the *Reflections*. In halting English, he declared it to be 'one of the finest composition of the age', fully fulfilling the expectations of those in France who had 'the greatest impatience, to see the Work who was expected from you'.

Tactfully, Menonville mixed criticism with eulogy. He pointed out one or two factual mistakes in the *Reflections* that stood in need of correction. He defended the conduct of many moderate members of the National Assembly, notably Mounier and Lally-Tollendal, whom Burke had accused of inexperience and dereliction of duty. Above all, he thought that Burke should soften his arguments against the new French constitution. Menonville was not happy with the constitution, but thought matters might become worse if violent men used Burke's words as an excuse to push matters further. Menonville feared that extremists would 'greedily catch every word of yours, that they can, even by the most violent Twarting [*sic*], bring to the support of the measures they seem so fond of. He concluded by specifically asking for a reply and the right to publish it in France: 'I hope the favour of an answer, with the intention of publishing it, if not forbidden by you.'

Burke duly complied with this request by composing *A Letter to a Member of the National Assembly*. It is dated 19 January 1791, but was not despatched to Menonville until 28 January. Burke was apparently entirely content to leave to Menonville the final decision on whether the *Letter* should be published and how it should be published. He told the Comtesse de Montrond that Menonville 'has my leave to publish, or to suppress it, as he thinks may be best for his Cause'.* While waiting for a decision from Menonville, however, Burke made sure that the *Letter*'s contents were at least known in Government circles, by sending copies to Lord Grenville and the King. The first returned his copy, on 23 March 1791, expressing his appreciation of the 'force and eloquence of Mr Burke's observations'. The second 'perused it with much attention, and . . . expressed very great satisfaction at the whole of it.'* The *Letter* was published in Paris by 27 April, when Menonville wrote to Burke enclosing copies of the French edition. This edition was generally available in England by 12 May, and an English edition appeared on 21 May.

Why should Burke have taken so much trouble to answer a reply from a French admirer whom he had never met and who could by no stretch of the imagination be thought of as a leading figure in French politics? Burke addressed this question in a letter to the Chevalier de la Bintinaye in March 1791. He told his friend that

> Some part of the letter was to exculpate myself, (or rather perhaps to apologize) from some faults, which the Gentleman found in my Pamphlet. The rest was to shew, from the actual State of France, (as well as I was able to enter into its condition) the utter impossibility of a counter revolution from any internal Cause.*

As has been noted, one or two elementary errors of fact had been seized on by critics to discredit the *Reflections* as a whole, and had contributed substantially to the disappointing reception of that work. The *Letter* allowed Burke to revise and restate his opinions on these matters. The treatment of electoral arrangements under the new Constitution, for example, is notably modified. Secondly, Burke had already begun by the spring of 1791 to despair of any remedy for the situation in France that did not involve foreign intervention. There was no man or body of men within France that could be given this role. The King had been reduced to a cipher and the Assembly was increasingly led by extremists. If foreign intervention was required, capturing the attention of Menonville and the King made good sense. The *Letter* may perhaps therefore be seen as a postscript to the *Reflections*, a tidying of loose ends, and as the necessary groundwork to launch the argument that England should intervene directly in French affairs, a major theme in Burke's writing over the next two years.

SIR,

I had the honour to receive your letter of the 17th of November last, in which, with some exceptions, you are pleased to consider favourably the letter I have written on the affairs of France. I shall ever accept any mark of approbation, attended with instruction, with more pleasure than general and unqualified praises. The latter can serve only to flatter our vanity; the former, whilst it encourages us to proceed, may help to improve us in our progress.

Some of the errors* you point out to me in my printed letter are really such. One only I find to be material. It is corrected in the edition which I take the liberty of sending to you. As to the cavils which may be made on some part of my remarks, with regard to the *gradations* in your new constitution, you observe justly, that they do not affect the substance of my objections. Whether there be a round more or less in the ladder of representation, by which your workmen ascend from their parochial tyranny to their federal anarchy, when the whole scale is false, appears to me of little or no importance.

I published my thoughts on that constitution, that my countrymen might be enabled to estimate the wisdom of the plans which were held out to their imitation. I conceived that the true character of those plans would be best collected from the committee appointed to prepare them. I thought that the scheme of their building would be better comprehended in the design of the architects than in the execution of the masons. It was not worth my reader's while to occupy himself with the alterations by which bungling practice corrects absurd theory. Such an investigation would be endless: because every day's past experience of impracticability has driven, and every day's future experience will drive, those men to new devices as exceptionable as the old; and which are no otherwise worthy of observation than as they give a daily proof of the delusion of their promises, and the falsehood of their professions. Had I followed all these changes, my letter would have been only a gazette of their wanderings; a journal of their march from error to error, through a dry dreary desart, unguided by the lights of heaven, or by the contrivance which wisdom has invented to supply their place.

I am unalterably persuaded, that the attempt to oppress, degrade, impoverish, confiscate, and extinguish the original gentlemen, and landed property of an whole nation, cannot be justified under any form it may assume. I am satisfied beyond a doubt, that the project of turning a great empire into a vestry, or into a collection of vestries, and of governing it in the spirit of a parochial administration, is senseless and absurd, in any mode, or with any qualifications. I can never be convinced, that the scheme of placing the highest powers of the state in churchwardens and constables, and other such officers, guided by the prudence of litigious attornies and Jew brokers, and set in action by shameless women of the lowest condition, by keepers of hotels, taverns, and brothels, by pert apprentices, by clerks, shop-boys, hair-dressers, fidlers, and dancers on the stage, (who, in such a commonwealth as your's, will in future overbear, as already they have overborne, the sober incapacity of dull uninstructed men, of useful but laborious occupations) can never be put into any shape, that must not be both disgraceful and destructive. The whole of this project, even if it were what it pretends to be, and was not in reality the dominion, through that disgraceful medium, of half a dozen, or perhaps fewer, intriguing politicians, is so mean, so low-minded, so stupid a contrivance, in point of wisdom, as well as so perfectly detestable for its wickedness, that I must always consider the correctives which might make it in any degree practicable, to be so many new objections to it.

In that wretched state of things, some are afraid that the authors of your miseries may be led to precipitate their further designs, by the hints they may receive from the very arguments used to expose the absurdity of their system, to mark the incongruity of its parts, and its consistency with their own principles; and that your masters may be led to render their schemes more consistent, by rendering them more mischievous. Excuse the liberty which your indulgence authorises me to take, when I observe to you, that such apprehensions as these would prevent all exertion of our faculties in this great cause of mankind.

A rash recourse to *force* is not to be justified in a state of real weakness. Such attempts bring on disgrace; and, in their failure, discountenance and discourage more rational endeavours. But *reason* is to be hazarded, though it may be

perverted by craft and sophistry; for reason can suffer no loss
nor shame, nor can it impede any useful plan of future policy.
In the unavoidable uncertainty, as to the effect, which attends
on every measure of human prudence, nothing seems a surer
antidote to the poison of fraud than its detection. It is true the
fraud may be swallowed after this discovery; and perhaps
even swallowed the more greedily for being a detected fraud.
Men sometimes make a point of honour not to be disabused;
and they had rather fall into an hundred errors than confess
one. But after all,—when neither our principles nor our
dispositions, nor, perhaps, our talents, enable us to encounter
delusion with delusion, we must use our best reason to those
that ought to be reasonable creatures, and to take our chance
for the event. We cannot act on these anomalies in the minds
of men. I do not conceive that the persons who have contrived
these things can be made much the better or the worse for any
thing which can be said to them. *They* are reason proof. Here
and there, some men, who were at first carried away by wild
good intentions, may be led, when their first fervors are
abated, to join in a sober survey of the schemes into which
they have been deluded. To those only (and I am sorry to say
they are not likely to make a large description) we apply with
any hope. I may speak it upon an assurance almost approaching
to absolute knowledge, that nothing has been done that has
not been contrived from the beginning, even before the states
had assembled. *Nulla nova mihi res inopinave surgit.** They
are the same men and the same designs that they were from
the first, though varied in their appearance. It was the very
same animal that at first crawled about in the shape of a
caterpillar, that you now see rise into the air, and expand his
wings to the sun.

Proceeding, therefore, as we are obliged to proceed, that is
upon an hypothesis that we address rational men, can false
political principles be more effectually exposed, than by
demonstrating that they lead to consequences directly inconsistent with and subversive of the arrangements grounded upon
them? If this kind of demonstration is not permitted, the
process of reasoning called *deductio ad absurdum*, which even
the severity of geometry does not reject, could not be

employed at all in legislative discussions. One of our strongest weapons against folly acting with authority, would be lost.

You know, Sir, that even the virtuous efforts of your patriots to prevent the ruin of your country have had this very turn given to them. It has been said here, and in France too, that the reigning usurpers would not have carried their tyranny to such destructive lengths, if they had not been stimulated and provoked to it by the acrimony of your opposition. There is a dilemma to which every opposition to successful iniquity must, in the nature of things, be liable. If you lie still, you are considered as an accomplice in the measures in which you silently acquiesce. If you resist, you are accused of provoking irritable power to new excesses. The conduct of a losing party never appears right: at least it never can possess the only infallible criterion of wisdom to vulgar judgments—success.

The indulgence of a sort of undefined hope, an obscure confidence, that some lurking remains of virtue, some degree of shame, might exist in the breasts of the oppressors of France, has been among the causes which have helped to bring on the common ruin of king and people. There is no safety for honest men, but by believing all possible evil of evil men, and by acting with promptitude, decision, and steadiness on that belief. I well remember, at every epocha of this wonderful history, in every scene of this tragic business, that when your sophistic usurpers were laying down mischievous principles, and even applying them in direct resolutions, it was the fashion to say, that they never intended to execute those declarations in their rigour. This made men cautious in their opposition, and remiss in early precaution. By holding out this fallacious hope, the imposters deluded sometimes one description of men, and sometimes another, so that no means of resistance were provided against them, when they came to execute in cruelty what they had planned in fraud.

There are cases in which a man would be ashamed not to have been imposed on. There is a confidence necessary to human intercourse, and without which men are often more injured by their own suspicions than they could be by the perfidy of others. But when men, whom we *know* to be wicked, impose upon us, we are something worse than dupes. When we know them, their fair pretences become new motives for distrust. There is one case, indeed, in which it would be madness not to give the fullest credit to the most deceitful of men, that is, when they make declarations of hostility against us.

I find, that some persons entertain other hopes, which I confess appear more specious than those by which at first so many were deluded and disarmed. They flatter themselves that the extreme misery brought upon the people by their folly, will at last open the eyes of the multitude, if not of their leaders. Much the contrary, I fear. As to the leaders in this system of imposture,—you know, that cheats and deceivers never can repent. The fraudulent have no resource but in fraud. They have no other goods in their magazine. They have no virtue or wisdom in their minds, to which, in a disappointment concerning the profitable effects of fraud and cunning, they can retreat. The wearing out of an old, serves only to put them upon the invention of a new delusion. Unluckily too, the credulity of dupes is an inexhaustible as the invention of knaves. They never give people possession; but they always keep them in hope. Your state doctors do not so much as pretend that any good whatsoever has hitherto been derived from their operations, or that the public has prospered in any one instance, under their management. The nation is sick, very sick, by their medicines. But the *charlatans* tell them that what is past cannot be helped;—they have taken the draught, and they must wait its operation with patience;—that the first effects indeed are unpleasant, but that the very sickness is a proof that the dose is of no sluggish operation;—that sickness is inevitable in all constitutional revolutions;—that the body must pass through pain to ease;—that the prescriber is not an empirick who proceeds by vulgar experience, but one who grounds his practice on[1] the sure rules of art, which cannot possibly fail. You have read Sir, the last Manifesto, or

---

[1] It is said in the last quackish address of the National Assembly to the people of France; that they have not formed their arrangements upon vulgar practice; but on a theory which cannot fail, or something to that effect.

Mountebank's bill, of the National Assembly. You see their presumption in their promises is not lessened by all their failures in the performance. Compare this last address of the Assembly, and the present state of your affairs with the early engagements of that body; engagements which, not content with declaring, they solemnly deposed upon oath, swearing lustily that if they were supported they would make their country glorious and happy; and then judge whether those who can write such things, or those who can bear to read them, are of *themselves* to be brought to any reasonable course of thought or action.

As to the people at large, when once these miserable sheep have broken the fold, and have got themselves loose, not from the restraint, but from the protection of all the principles of natural authority, and legitimate subordination, they became the natural prey of impostors. When they have once tasted of the flattery of knaves, they can no longer endure reason, which appears to them only in the form of censure and reproach. Great distress have never hitherto taught, and whilst the world lasts it never will teach, wise lessons to any part of mankind. Men are as much blinded by the extremes of misery as by the extremes of prosperity. Desperate situations produce desperate councils, and desperate measures. The people of France, almost generally, have been taught to look for other resources than those which can be derived from order, frugality, and industry. They are generally armed; and they are made to expect much from the use of arms. *Nihil non arrogant armis.** Besides this, the retrograde order of society has something flattering to the dispositions of mankind. The life of adventurers, gamesters, gipsies, beggars, and robbers, is not unpleasant. It requires restraint to keep men from falling into that habit. The shifting tides of fear and hope, the flight and pursuit, the peril and escape, the alternate famine and feast, of the savage and the thief, after a time, render all course of slow, steady, progressive, unvaried occupation, and the prospect only of a limited mediocrity at the end of long labour, to the last degree tame, languid, and insipid. Those who have been once intoxicated with power, and have derived any kind of emolument from it, even though but for one year, never can willingly abandon it. They may be distressed in the midst of all their power; but they will never look to any thing but power for their relief. When did distress ever oblige a prince to abdicate his authority? And what effect will it have upon those who are made to believe themselves a people of princes?

The more active and stirring part of the lower orders having got government, and the distribution of plunder, into their hands, they will use its resources in each municipality to form a body of adherents. These rulers, and their adherents, will be strong enough to overpower the discontents of those who have not been able to assert their share of the spoil. The unfortunate adventurers in the cheating lottery of plunder will probably be the least sagacious, or the most inactive and irresolute of the gang. If, on disappointment, they should dare to stir, they will soon be suppressed as rebels and mutineers by their brother rebels. Scantily fed for a while, with the offal of plunder, they will drop off by degrees; they will be driven out of sight, and out of thought; and they will be left to perish obscurely, like rats, in holes and corners.

From the forced repentance of invalid mutineers and disbanded thieves, you can hope for no resource. Government itself, which ought to constrain the more bold and dextrous of these robbers, is their accomplice. Its arms, its treasures, its all, are in their hands. Judicature, which above all things should awe them, is their creature and their instrument. Nothing seems to me to render your internal situation more desperate than this one circumstance of the state of your judicature. Many days are not past since we have seen a set of men brought forth by your rulers for a most critical function.* Your rulers brought forth a set of men, steaming from the sweat and drudgery, and all black with the smoak and soot of the forge of confiscation and robbery—*ardentis massae fuligine lippos,** a set of men brought forth from the trade of hammering arms of proof, offensive and defensive, in aid of the enterprizes, and for the subsequent protection of housebreakers, murderers, traitors, and malefactors; men, who had their minds seasoned with theories perfectly conformable to their practice, and who had always laughed at possession and prescription, and defied all the fundamental maxims of jurisprudence. To the horror and stupefaction of all the honest part of this nation, and indeed of all nations who are spectators, we have seen, on the credit of those very practices and principles, and to carry them further into effect, these very men placed on the sacred seat of justice in the capital city of your late kingdom. We see, that in future, you are to be destroyed with more form and regularity. This is not peace; it is only the introduction of a sort of discipline in their hostility. Their tyranny is complete, in their justice; and their lanthorn is not half so dreadful as their court.

One would think that out of common decency they would have given you men who had not been in the habit of trampling upon law and justice in the assembly, neutral men, or men apparently neutral, for judges, who are to dispose of your lives and fortunes.

Cromwell, when he attempted to legalize his power, and to settle his conquered country in a state of order, did not look for his dispensers of justice in the instruments of his usurpation. Quite the contrary. He sought out with great sollicitude and selection, and even from the party most opposite to his designs, men of weight, and decorum of character; men unstained with the violence of the times, and with hands not fouled with confiscation and sacrilege: for he chose an *Hales** for his chief justice, though he absolutely refused to take his civic oaths, or to make any acknowledgement whatsoever of the legality of his government. Cromwell told this great lawyer, that since he did not approve his title, all he required of him was, to administer, in a manner agreeable to his pure sentiments and unspotted character, that justice without which human society cannot subsist: that it was not his particular government, but civil order itself, which as a judge he wished him to support. Cromwell knew how to separate the institutions expedient to his usurpation from the administration of the public justice of his country. For Cromwell was a man in whom ambition had not wholly suppressed, but only suspended the sentiments of religion, and the love (as far it could consist with his designs) of fair and honourable reputation. Accordingly, we are indebted to this act of his for the preservation of our laws, which some senseless assertors of the rights of men were then on the point of entirely erasing, as relicks of feudality and barbarism. Besides, he gave in the appointment of that man, to that age, and to all posterity, the most brilliant example of sincere and fervent piety, exact justice, and profound jurisprudence.[1] But these are not the things in which your philosophic usurpers choose to follow Cromwell.

One would think, that after an honest and necessary Revolution (if they had a mind that theirs should pass for such) your masters would have imitated the virtuous policy of those who have been at the head of revolutions of that glorious character. Burnet* tells us, that nothing tended to reconcile the English nation to the government of King William so much as the care he took to fill the vacant bishoprics with men who had attracted the public esteem by their learning, eloquence, and piety, and above all, by their known moderation in the state. With you, in your purifying Revolution, whom have you chosen to regulate the church? Mr Mirabeau is a fine speaker—and a fine writer,—and a fine—a very fine man;—but really nothing gave more surprize to every body here, than to find him the supreme head of your ecclesiastical affairs.* The rest is of course. Your Assembly addresses a manifesto to France in which they tell the people, with an insulting irony, that they have brought the church to its primitive condition.* In one respect their declaration is undoubtedly true; for they have brought it to a state of poverty and persecution. What can be hoped for after this? Have not men (if they deserve the name) under this new hope and head of the church, been made bishops, for no other merit than having acted as instruments of atheists; for no other merit than having thrown the children's bread to dogs; and in order to gorge the whole gang of usurers, pedlars, and itinerant Jew-discounters at the corners of streets, starved the poor of their Christian flocks, and their own brother pastors? Have not such men been made bishops to administer in temples, in which (if the patriotic donations have not already

[1] See Burnet's life of Hales.

stripped them of their vessels) the churchwardens ought to take security for the altar plate, and not so much as to trust the chalice in their sacrilegious hands, so long as Jews have assignats on ecclesiastic plunder, to exchange for the silver stolen from churches?

I am told, that the very sons of such Jew-jobbers have been made bishops; persons not to be suspected of any sort of *Christian* superstition, fit colleagues to the holy prelate of Autun;* and bred at the feet of that Gamaliel.* We know who it was that drove the money-changers out of the temple. We see too who it is that brings them in again. We have in London very respectable persons of the Jewish nation, whom we will keep: but we have of the same tribe others of a very different description,—housebreakers, and receivers of stolen goods, and forgers of paper currency, more than we can conveniently hang. These we can spare to France, to fill the new episcopal thrones: men well versed in swearing; and who will scruple no oath which the fertile genius of any of your reformers can devise.

In matters so ridiculous, it is hard to be grave. On a view of their consequences it is almost inhuman to treat them lightly. To what a state of savage, stupid, servile insensibility must your people be reduced, who can endure such proceedings in their church, their state, and their judicature, even for a moment! But the deluded people of France are like other madmen, who, to a miracle, bear hunger, and thirst, and cold, and confinement, and the chains and lash of their keeper, whilst all the while they support themselves by the imagination that they are generals of armies, prophets, kings, and emperors. As to a change of mind in these men, who consider infamy as honour, degradation as preferment, bondage to low tyrants as liberty, and the practical scorn and contumely of their upstart masters, as marks of respect and homage, I look upon it as absolutely impracticable. These madmen, to be cured, must first, like other madmen, be subdued. The sound part of the community, which I believe to be large, but by no means the largest part, has been taken by surprize, and is disjointed, terrified, and disarmed. That sound part of the community must first be put into a better condition, before it can do any thing in the way of deliberation or persuasion. This must be an act of power, as well as wisdom; of power, in the hands of firm, determined patriots, who can distinguish the misled from traitors, who will regulate the state (if such should be their fortune) with a discriminating, manly, and provident mercy; men who are purged of the surfeit and indigestion of systems, if ever they have been admitted into the habit of their minds; men who will lay the foundation of a real reform, in effacing every vestige of that philosophy which pretends to have made discoveries in the *terra australis** of morality; men who will fix the state upon these bases of morals and politics, which are our old, and immemorial, and, I hope, will be our eternal possession.

This power, to such men, must come from *without.** It may be given to you in pity; for surely no nation ever called so pathetically on the compassion of all its neighbours. It may be given by those neighbours on motives of safety to themselves. Never shall I think any country in Europe to be secure, whilst there is established, in the very centre of it, a state (if so it may be called) founded on principles of anarchy, and which is, in reality, a college of armed fanatics, for the propagation of the principles of assassination, robbery, rebellion, fraud, faction, oppression, and impiety. *Mahomet*, hid, as for a time he was, in the bottom of the sands of Arabia,* had his spirit and character been discovered, would have been an object of precaution to provident minds. What if he had erected his fanatic standard for the destruction of the Christian religion in *luce Asiae*,* in the midst of the then noon-day splendour of the then civilized world? The princes of Europe, in the beginning of this century, did well not to suffer the monarchy of France to swallow up the others. They ought not now, in my opinion, to suffer all the monarchies and commonwealths to be swallowed up in the gulph of this polluted anarchy. They may be tolerably safe at present, because the comparative power of France for the present is little. But times and occasions make dangers. Intestine troubles may arise in other countries. There is a power always on the watch, qualified and disposed to profit of every conjucture, to establish its own principles and modes of mischief, wherever it can hope for success. What mercy would these usurpers have on other sovereigns, and on other nations, when they treat their own king with such unparalleled indignities, and so cruelly oppress their own countrymen?

The king of Prussia, in concurrence with us, nobly interfered to save Holland from confusion.* The same power, joined with the rescued Holland and with Great Britain, has put the emperor in the possession of the Netherlands;* and secured, under that prince, from all arbitrary innovation, the antient, hereditary constitution of those provinces. The chamber of Wetzlar has restored the Bishop of Leige, unjustly dispossessed by the rebellion of his subjects.* The king of Prussia was bound by no treaty, nor alliance of blood, nor had any particular reasons for thinking the emperor's government would be more mischievous or more oppressive to human nature than that of the Turk; yet on mere motives of policy that prince has interposed with the threat of all his force, to snatch even the Turk from the pounces of the imperial eagle.* If this is done in favour of a barbarous nation, with a barbarous neglect of police, fatal to the human race, in favour of a nation, by principle in eternal enmity with the Christian name; a nation which will not so much as give the salutation of peace (Salam) to any of us; nor make any pact with any Christian nation beyond a truce;—if this be done in favour of the Turk, shall it be thought either impolitic, or unjust, or uncharitable, to employ the same power, to rescue from captivity a virtuous monarch (by the courtesy of Europe considered as Most Christian)* who, after an intermission of 175 years, had called together the states of his kingdom, to reform abuses, to establish a free government, and to strengthen his throne; a monarch, who at the very outset, without force, even without sollicitation, had given to his people such a Magna Charta of privileges,* as never was given by any king to any subjects?—Is it to be tamely borne by kings who love their subjects, or by subjects who love their kings, that this monarch, in the midst of these gracious acts, was insolently and cruelly torn from his palace, by a gang of traitors and assassins,* and kept in close prison to this very hour, whilst his royal name and sacred character were used for the total ruin of those whom the laws had appointed him to protect?

The only offence of this unhappy monarch towards his people, was his attempt, under a monarchy, to give them a free constitution. For this, by an example hitherto unheard of in the world, he has been deposed. It might well disgrace sovereigns to take part with a deposed tyrant. It would suppose in them a vitious sympathy. But not to make a common cause with a just prince, dethroned by traitors and rebels, who proscribe, plunder, confiscate, and in every way cruelly oppress their fellow citizens, in my opinion is to forget what is due to the honour, and to the rights of all virtuous and legal government.

I think the King of France to be as much an object both of policy and compassion as the Grand Seignor* or his states. I do not conceive, that the total annihilation of France (if that could be effected) is a desirable thing to Europe; or even to this its rival nation. Provident patriots did not think it good for Rome, that even Carthage should be quite destroyed;* and he was a wise Greek, wise for the general Grecian interests, as well as a brave Lacedemonian enemy, and generous conqueror, who did not wish, by the destruction of Athens, to pluck out the other eye of Greece.*

However, Sir, what I have here said of the interference of foreign princes is only the opinion of a private individual; who is neither the representative of any state, nor the organ of any party; but who thinks himself bound to express his own sentiments with freedom and energy in a crisis of such importance to the whole human race.

I am not apprehensive that in speaking freely on the subject of the King and Queen of France, I shall accelerate (as you fear) the execution of traiterous designs against them. You are of opinion, Sir, that the usurpers may, and that they will, gladly lay hold of any pretext to throw off the very name of a king;—assuredly I do not wish ill to your king; but better for him not to live (he does not reign) than to live the passive instrument of tyranny and usurpation.

I certainly meant to shew, to the best of my power, that the existence of such an executive officer, in such a system of republic as theirs, is absurd in the highest degree. But in demonstrating this—to *them*, at least, I can have made no discovery. They only held out the royal name to catch those Frenchmen to whom the name of king is still venerable. They calculate the duration of that sentiment; and when they find it nearly expiring, they will not trouble themselves with excuses for extinguishing the name, as they have the thing. They used it as a sort of navel-string to nourish their unnatural offspring from the bowels of royalty itself. Now that the monster can purvey for its own subsistence, it will only carry the mark about it, as a token of its having torn the womb it came from. Tyrants seldom want pretexts. Fraud is the ready minister of injustice; and whilst the currency of false pretence and sophistic reasoning was expedient to their designs, they were under no necessity of drawing upon me to furnish them with that coin. But pretexts and sophisms have had their day; and have done their work. The usurpation no longer seeks plausibility. It trusts to power.

Nothing that I can say, or that you can say, will hasten them by a single hour, in the execution of a design which they have long since entertained. In spite of their solemn declarations, their soothing addresses, and the multiplied oaths which they have taken, and forced others to take, they will assassinate the king when his name will no longer be necessary to their designs; but not a moment sooner. They will probably first assassinate the queen,* whenever the renewed menace of such an assassination loses its effect upon the anxious mind of an affectionate husband. At present, the advantage which they derive from the daily threats against her life, is her only security for preserving it. They keep their sovereign alive for the purpose of exhibiting him, like some wild beast at a fair; as if they had a Bajazet* in a cage. They choose to make monarchy contemptible by exposing it to derision, in the person of the most benevolent of their kings.

In my opinion, their insolence appears more odious even than their crimes. The horrors of the 5th and 6th of October were less detestable than the festival of the 14th of July.* There are situations (God forbid I should think that of the 5th or 6th of October one of them) in which the best men may be confounded with the worst, and in the darkness and confusion, in the press and medley of such extremities, it may not be so easy to discriminate the one from the other. The necessities created, even by ill designs, have their excuse. They may be forgotten by others, when the guilty themselves do not choose to cherish their recollection, and by ruminating their offences, nourish themselves through the example of their past, to the perpetration of future crimes. It is in the relaxation of security, it is in the expansion of prosperity, it is in the hour of dilatation of the heart, and of its softening into festivity and pleasure, that the real character of men is discerned. If there is any good in them, it appears then or never. Even wolves and tygers, when gorged with their prey, are safe and gentle. It is at such times that noble minds give all the reins to their good-nature. They indulge their genius even to intemperance, in kindness to the afflicted, in generosity to the conquered; forbearing insults, forgiving injuries, overpaying benefits. Full of dignity themselves, they respect dignity in all, but they feel it sacred in the unhappy. But it is then, and basking in the sunshine of unmerited fortune, that low, sordid, ungenerous, and reptile souls swell with their hoarded poisons; it is then that they display their odious splendor, and shine out in the full lustre of their native villainy and baseness. It is in that season that no man of sense or honour can be mistaken for one of them. It was in such a season, for them of political ease and security, tho' their people were but just emerged from actual famine, and were ready to be plunged into a gulph of penury and beggary, that your philosophic lords chose, with an ostentatious pomp and luxury, to feast an incredible number of idle and thoughtless people collected with art and pains, from all quarters of the world. They constructed a vast amphitheatre in which they raised a species of [1]pillory.* On this pillory they set their lawful king and queen, with an insulting figure over their heads. There they exposed these objects of pity and respect to all good minds, to the derision of

---

[1] The pillory (*carcan*) in England is generally made very high, like that raised for exposing the King of France.

an unthinking and unprincipled multitude, degenerated even from the versatile tenderness which marks the irregular and capricious feelings of the populace. That their cruel insult might have nothing wanting to complete it, they chose the anniversary of that day in which they exposed the life of their prince to the most imminent dangers, and the vilest indignities, just following the instant when the assassins, whom they had hired without owning, first openly took up arms against their king, corrupted his guards, surprized his castle, butchered some of the poor invalids of his garrison, murdered his governor, and, like wild beasts, tore to pieces the chief magistrate* of his capital city, on account of his fidelity to his service.

Till the justice of the world is awakened, such as these will go on, without admonition, and without provocation, to every extremity. Those who have made the exhibition of the 14th of July, are capable of every evil. They do not commit crimes for their designs; but they form designs that they may commit crimes. It is not their necessity, but their nature, that impels them. They are modern philosophers, which when you say of them, you express every thing that is ignoble, savage, and hard-hearted.

Besides the sure tokens which are given by the spirit of their particular arrangements, there are some characteristic lineaments in the general policy of your tumultuous despotism, which, in my opinion, indicate beyond a doubt that no revolution whatsoever *in their disposition* is to be expected. I mean their scheme of educating the rising generation, the principles which they intend to instil, and the sympathies which they wish to form in the mind, at the season in which it is the most susceptible. Instead of forming their young minds to that docility, to that modesty, which are the grace and charm of youth, to an admiration of famous examples, and to an averseness to any thing which approaches to pride, petulance, and self-conceit, (distempers to which that time of life is of itself sufficiently liable) they artificially foment these evil dispositions, and even form them into springs of action. Nothing ought to be more weighed than the nature of books recommended by public authority. So recommended, they soon form the character of the age. Uncertain indeed is the efficacy, limited indeed is the extent of a virtuous institution. But if education takes in *vice* as any part of its system, there is no doubt but that it will operate with abundant energy, and to an extent indefinite. The magistrate, who in favour of freedom thinks himself obliged to suffer all sorts of publications, is under a stricter duty than any other, well to consider what sort of writers he shall authorize; and shall recommend, by the strongest of all sanctions, that is, by public honours and rewards. He ought to be cautious how he recommends authors of mixed or ambiguous morality. He ought to be fearful of putting into the hands of youth writers indulgent to the peculiarities of their own complexion, lest they should teach the humours of the professor, rather than the principles of the science. He ought, above all, to be cautious in recommending any writer who has carried marks of a deranged understanding; for where there is no sound reason, there can be no real virtue; and madness is ever vitious and malignant.

The National Assembly proceeds on maxims the very reverse of these. The Assembly recommends to its youth a study of the bold experimenters in morality. Every body knows that there is a great dispute amongst their leaders, which of them is the best resemblance to Rousseau.* In truth, they all resemble him. His blood they transfuse into their minds and into their manners. Him they study; him they meditate; him they turn over in all the time they can spare from the laborious mischief of the day, or the debauches of the night. Rousseau is their canon of holy writ; in his life he is their canon of *Polycletus*;* he is their standard figure of perfection. To this man and this writer, as a pattern to authors and to Frenchmen, the founderies of Paris are now running for statues, with the kettles of their poor and the bells of their churches. If an author had written like a great genius on geometry, though his practical and speculative morals were vitious in the extreme, it might appear that in voting the statue,* they honoured only the geometrician. But Rousseau is a moralist, or he is nothing. It is impossible, therefore, putting the circumstances together, to mistake their design in choosing the author, with whom they have begun to recommend a course of studies.

Their great problem is to find a substitute for all the principles which hitherto have been employed to regulate the human will and action. They find dispositions in the mind, of such force and quality, as may fit men, far better than the old morality, for the purposes of such a state as theirs; and may go much further in supporting their power, and destroying their enemies. They have therefore chosen a selfish, flattering, seductive, ostentatious vice, in the place of plain duty. True humility, the basis of the Christian system, is the low, but deep and firm foundation of all real virtue. But this, as very painful in the practice, and little imposing in the appearance, they have totally discarded. Their object is to merge all natural and all social sentiment in inordinate vanity. In a small degree, and conversant in little things, vanity is of little moment. When full grown, it is the worst of vices, and the occasional mimick of them all. It makes the whole man false. It leaves nothing sincere or trust-worthy about him. His best qualities are poisoned and perverted by it, and operate exactly as the worst. When your lords had many writers as immoral as the object of their statue (such as Voltaire and others) they chose Rousseau; because in him that peculiar vice which they wished to erect into a ruling virtue, was by far the most conspicuous.

We have had the great professor and founder of *the philosophy of vanity* in England.* As I had good opportunities of knowing his proceedings almost from day to day, he left no doubt in my mind, that he entertained no principle either to influence his heart, or to guide his understanding, but *vanity*. With this vice he was possessed to a degree little short of madness. It is from the same deranged eccentric vanity, that this, the insane *Socrates** of the National Assembly, was impelled to publish a mad Confession* of his mad faults, and to attempt a new sort of glory, from bringing hardily to light the obscure and vulgar vices which we know may sometimes be blended with eminent talents. He has not observed on the nature of vanity, who does not know that it is omnivorous; that it has no choice in its food; that it is fond to talk even of its own faults and vices, as what will excite surprize and draw attention, and what will pass at worst for openness and candour. It was this abuse and perversion, which vanity makes even of hypocrisy, which has driven Rousseau to record a life not so much as chequered, or spotted here and there, with virtues, or even distinguished by a single good action. It is such a life he chooses to offer to the attention of mankind. It is such a life, that with a wild defiance, he flings in the face of his Creator, whom he acknowledges only to brave. Your Assembly, knowing how much more powerful example is found than precept, has chosen this man (by his own account without a single virtue) for a model. To him they erect their first statue. From him they commence their series of honours and distinctions.

It is that new-invented virtue which your masters canonize, that led their moral hero constantly to exhaust the stores of his powerful rhetoric in the expression of universal benevolence; whilst his heart was incapable of harbouring one spark of common parental affection.* Benevolence to the whole species, and want of feeling for every individual with whom the professors come in contact, form the character of the new philosophy. Setting up for an unsocial independence, this their hero of vanity refuses the just price of common labour, as well as the tribute which opulence owes to genius, and which, when paid, honours the giver and the receiver; and then he pleads his beggary as an excuse for his crimes. He melts with tenderness for those only who touch him by the remotest relation, and then, without one natural pang, casts away, as a sort of offal and excrement, the spawn of his disgustful amours, and sends his children to the hospital of foundlings. The bear loves, licks, and forms her young; but bears are not philosophers. Vanity, however, finds its account in reversing the train of our natural feelings. Thousands admire the sentimental writer; the affectionate father is hardly known in his parish.

Under this philosophic instructor in the *ethics of vanity*, they have attempted in France a regeneration of the moral constitution of man. Statesmen, like your present rulers, exist by every thing which is spurious, fictitious, and false; by every thing which takes the man from his house, and sets him on a stage, which makes him up an artificial creature, with painted theatric sentiments, fit to be seen by the glare of candlelight, and formed to be contemplated at a due distance. Vanity is too apt to prevail in all of us, and in all countries. To the improvement of Frenchmen it seems not absolutely necessary that it should be taught upon system. But it is plain that the present rebellion was its legitimate offspring, and it is piously fed by that rebellion, with a daily dole.

If the system of institution, recommended by the Assembly, is false and theatric, it is because their system of government is of the same character. To that, and to that alone, it is strictly conformable. To understand either, we must connect the morals with the politics of the legislators. Your practical philosophers, systematic in every thing, have wisely began at the source. As the relation between parents and children is the first among the elements of vulgar, natural morality,[1] they erect statues to a wild, ferocious, low-minded, hard-hearted father, of fine general feelings; a lover of his kind, but a hater of his kindred. Your masters reject the duties of this vulgar relation, as contrary to liberty; as not founded in the social compact; and not binding according to the rights of men; because the relation is not, of course, the result of *free election*; never so on the side of the children, not always on the part of the parents.

The next relation which they regenerate by their statues to Rousseau, is that which is next in sanctity to that of a father. They differ from those old-fashioned thinkers, who considered pedagogues as sober and venerable characters, and allied to the parental. The moralists of the dark times, *preceptorem sancti voluere parentis esse loco.** In this age of light, they teach the people, that preceptors ought to be in the place of gallants. They systematically corrupt a very corruptible race, (for some time a growing nuisance amongst you) a set of pert,

---

[1] Filiola tua te delectari laetor et probari tibi στοργὴν φυσικὴν esse τὴν πρὸς τὰ τέκνα: etenim, si haec non est, nulla potest homini esse ad hominem naturae adjunctio: qua sublata vitae societas tolletur. Valete Patrone [Rousseau] et tui condiscipuli! [L'Assemblée Nationale].
Cic. Ep. ad Atticum.*

petulant, literators, to whom, instead of their proper, but severe, unostentatious duties, they assign the brilliant part of men of wit and pleasure, of gay, young, military sparks, and danglers at toilets. They call on the rising generation in France, to take a sympathy in the adventures and fortunes, and they endeavour to engage their sensibility on the side of pedagogues, who betray the most awful family trusts, and vitiate their female pupils. They teach the people, that the debauchers of virgins, almost in the arms of their parents, may be safe inmates in their house, and even fit guardians of the honour of those husbands who succeed legally to the office which the young literators had pre-occupied, without asking leave of law or conscience.

Thus they dispose of all the family relations of parents and children, husbands and wives. Through this same instructor, by whom they corrupt the morals, they corrupt the taste. Taste and elegance, though they are reckoned only among the smaller and secondary morals, yet are of no mean importance in the regulation of life. A moral taste is not of force to turn vice into virtue; but it recommends virtue with something like the blandishments of pleasure; and it infinitely abates the evils of vice. Rousseau, a writer of great force and vivacity, is totally destitute of taste in any sense of the word. Your masters, who are his scholars, conceive that all refinement has an aristocratic character. The last age had exhausted all its powers in giving a grace and nobleness to our natural appetites, and in raising them into higher class and order than seemed justly to belong to them. Through Rousseau, your masters are resolved to destroy these aristocratic prejudices. The passion called love, has so general and powerful an influence; it makes so much of the entertainment, and indeed so much the occupation of that part of life which decides the character for ever, that the mode and the principles on which it engages the sympathy, and strikes the imagination, become of the utmost importance to the morals and manners of every society. Your rulers were well aware of this; and in their system of changing your manners to accommodate them to their politics, they found nothing so convenient as Rousseau. Through him they teach men to love after the fashion of philosophers; that is, they teach to men, to Frenchmen, a love without gallantry; a love without any thing of that fine flower of youthfulness and gentility, which places it, if not among the virtues, among the ornaments of life. Instead of this passion, naturally allied to grace and manners, they infuse into their youth an unfashioned, indelicate, sour, gloomy, ferocious medley of pedantry and lewdness; of metaphysical speculations, blended with the coarsest sensuality. Such is the general morality of the passions to be found in their famous philosopher, in his famous work of philosophic gallantry, the *Nouvelle Eloise.**

When the fence from the gallantry of perceptors is broken down, and your families are no longer protected by decent pride, and salutary domestic prejudice, there is but one step to a frightful corruption. The rulers in the National Assembly are in good hopes that the females of the first families in France may become an easy prey to dancing-masters, fidlers, pattern-drawers, friseurs, and valets de chambre, and other active citizens of that description,* who having the entry into your houses, and being half-domesticated by their situation, may be blended with you by regular and irregular relations. By a law, they have made these people your equals. By adopting the sentiments of Rousseau, they have made them your rivals. In this manner, these great legislators complete their plan of levelling, and establish their rights of men on a sure foundation.

I am certain that the writings of Rousseau lead directly to this kind of shameful evil. I have often wondered how he comes to be so much more admired and followed on the continent than he is here. Perhaps a secret charm in the language may have its share in this extraordinary difference. We certainly perceive, and to a degree we feel, in this writer, a style glowing, animated, enthusiastic; at the same time that we find it lax, diffuse, and not in the best taste of composition; all the members of the piece being pretty equally laboured and expanded, without any due selection or subordination of parts. He is generally too much on the stretch, and his manner has little variety. We cannot rest upon any of his works, though they contain observations which occasionally discover a considerable insight into human nature. But his doctrines, on the whole, are so inapplicable to real life and manners, that we never dream of drawing from them any rule for laws or conduct, or for fortifying or illustrating any thing by a reference to his opinions. They have with us the fate of older paradoxes,

> Cum ventum ad *verum* est *sensus moresque* repugnant,
> Atque ipsa utilitas justi prope mater et aequi.*

Perhaps bold speculations are more acceptable, because more new to you than to us, who have been long since satiated with them. We continue, as in the two last ages, to read more generally, that I believe is now done on the continent, the authors of sound antiquity. These occupy our minds. They give us another taste and turn; and will not suffer us to be more than transiently amused with paradoxical morality. It is not that I consider this writer as wholly destitute of just notions. Amongst his irregularities, it must be reckoned, that he is sometimes moral, and moral in a very sublime strain. But the *general spirit and tendency* of his works is mischievous; and the more mischievous for this mixture: For, perfect depravity of sentiment is not reconcileable with eloquence; and the mind (though corruptible, not complexionally vitious) would reject and throw off with disgust, a lesson of pure and unmixed evil. These writers make even virtue a pander to vice.

However, I less consider the author, than the system of the Assembly in perverting morality, through his means. This I confess makes me nearly despair of any attempt upon the minds of their followers, through reason, honour, or conscience. The great object of your tyrants, is to destroy the gentlemen of France; and for that purpose they destroy, to the best of their power, all the effect of those relations which may render considerable men powerful or even safe. To destroy that order, they vitiate the whole community. That no means may exist of confederating against their tyranny, by the false sympathies of this Nouvelle Eloise, they endeavour to subvert those principles of domestic trust and fidelity, which form the discipline of social life. They propagate principles by which every servant may think it, if not his duty, at least his privilege,

to betray his master. By these principles, every considerable
father of a family loses the sanctuary of his house. *Debet sua
cuique domus esse perfugium tu tissimum,** says the law,
which your legislators have taken so much pains first to decry,
then to repeal. They destroy all the tranquility and security of
domestic life; turning the asylum of the house into a gloomy
prison, where the father of the family must drag out a
miserable existence, endangered in proportion to the apparent
means of his safety; where he is worse than solitary in a croud
of domestics, and more apprehensive from his servants and
inmates, than from the hired bloodthirsty mob without doors,
who are ready to pull him to the lanterne.

It is thus, and for the same end, that they endeavour to
destroy that tribunal of conscience which exists independently
of edicts and decrees. Your despots govern by terror. They
know, that he who fears God fears nothing else; and therefore
they eradicate from the mind, through their Voltaire, their
Helvetius, and the rest of that infamous gang, that only sort of
fear which generates true courage. Their object is, that their
fellow citizens may be under the dominion of no awe, but that
of their committee of research, and of their lanterne.

Having found the advantage of assassination in the formation
of their tyranny, it is the grand resource in which they trust for
the support of it. Whoever opposes any of their proceedings,
or is suspected of a design to oppose them, is to answer it with
his life, or the lives of his wife and children. This infamous,
cruel, and cowardly practice of assassination, they have the
impudence to call *merciful*. They boast that they have
operated their usurpation rather by terror than by force; and
that a few seasonable murders have prevented the bloodshed
of many battles. There is no doubt they will extend these acts
of mercy whenever they see an occasion. Dreadful, however,
will be the consequences of their attempt to avoid the evils of
war, by the merciful policy of murder. If, by effectual
punishment of the guilty, they do not wholly disavow that
practice, and the threat of it too, as any part of their policy; if
ever a foreign prince enters into France, he must enter it as
into a country of assassins. The mode of civilized war will not
be practised: nor are the French who act on the present system

entitled to expect it. They, whose known policy it is to assassinate every citizen whom they suspect to be discontented by their tyranny, and to corrupt the soldiery of every open enemy, must look for no modified hostility. All war, which is not battle, will be military execution. This will beget acts of retaliation from you; and every retaliation will beget a new revenge. The hell-hounds of war, on all sides, will be uncoupled and unmuzzled. The new school of murder and barbarism, set up in Paris, having destroyed (so far as in it lies) all the other manners and principles which have hitherto civilized Europe, will destroy also the mode of civilized war, which, more than any thing else, had distinguished the Christian world. Such is the approaching golden age, which the [1]Virgil of your Assembly has sung to his Pollios!*

In such a situation of your political, your civil, and your social morals and manners, how can you be hurt by the freedom of any discussion? Caution is for those who have something to lose. What I have said to justify myself in not apprehending any ill consequence from a free discussion of the absurd consequences which flow from the relation of the lawful King to the usurped constitution, will apply to my vindication with regard to the exposure I have made of the state of the army under the same sophistic usurpation. The present tyrants want no arguments to prove, what they must daily feel, that no good army can exist on their principles. They are in no want of a monitor to suggest to them the policy of getting rid of the army, as well as of the King, whenever they are in a condition of effect that measure. What hopes may be entertained of your army for the restoration of your liberties, I know not. At present, yielding obedience to the pretended orders of a King, who, they are perfectly apprised, has no will, and who never can issue a mandate, which is not intended, in the first operation, or in its certain consequences, for his own destruction, your army seems to make one of the principal links in the chain of that servitude of anarchy, by which a cruel usurpation holds an undone people at once in bondage and confusion.

---

[1] Mirabeau's speech concerning universal peace.

You ask me what I think of the conduct of General Monk.*
How this affects your case, I cannot tell. I doubt whether you
possess, in France, any persons of a capacity to serve the
French monarchy in the same manner in which Monk served
the monarchy of England. The army which Monk commanded
had been formed by Cromwell to a perfection of discipline
which perhaps has never been exceeded. That army was
besides of an excellent composition. The soldiers were men of
extraordinary piety after their mode, of the greatest regularity,
and even severity of manners; brave in the field, but modest,
quiet and orderly, in their quarters; men who abhorred the
idea of assassinating their officers or any other persons; and
who (they at least who served in this island) were firmly
attached to those generals, by whom they were well treated
and ably commanded. Such an army, once gained, might be
depended on. I doubt much, if you could now find a Monk,
whether a Monk could find, in France, such an army.

I certainly agree with you, that in all probability we owe our
whole constitution to the restoration of the English monarchy.
The state of things from which Monk relieved England, was
however by no means, at that time, so deplorable in any sense,
as yours is now, and under the present sway is likely to
continue. Cromwell had delivered England from anarchy. His
government, though military and despotic, had been regular
and orderly. Under the iron, and under the yoke, the soil
yielded its produce. After his death, the evils of anarchy were
rather dreaded than felt. Every man was yet safe in his house
and in his property. But it must be admitted, that Monk freed
this nation from great and just apprehensions both of future
anarchy and of probable tyranny in some form or other. The
king whom he gave us was indeed the very reverse of your
benignant sovereign, who in reward for his attempt to bestow
liberty on his subjects, languishes himself in prison. The
person given to us by Monk was a man without any sense of
his duty as a prince; without any regard to the dignity of his
crown; without any love to his people; dissolute, false, venal,
and destitute of any positive good quality whatsoever, except
a pleasant temper, and the manners of a gentleman. Yet the
restoration of our monarchy, even in the person of such a

prince, was every thing to us; for without monarchy in England, most certainly we never can enjoy either peace or liberty. It was under this conviction that the very first regular step which we took on the Revolution of 1688, was to fill the throne with a real king; and even before it could be done in due form, the chiefs of the nation did not attempt themselves to exercise authority so much as by *interim*. They instantly requested the Prince of Orange to take the government on himself. The throne was not effectively vacant for an hour.

Your fundamental laws, as well as ours, suppose a monarchy. Your zeal, Sir, in standing so firmly for it as you have done, shews not only a sacred respect for your honour and fidelity, but a well-informed attachment to the real welfare and true liberties of your country. I have expressed myself ill, if I have given you cause to imagine, that I prefer the conduct of those who have retired from this warfare to your behaviour, who, with a courage and constancy almost supernatural, have struggled against tyranny, and kept the field to the last. You see I have corrected the exceptionable part in the edition which I now send you. Indeed in such terrible extremities as yours, it is not easy to say, in a political view, what line of conduct is the most adviseable. In that state of things, I cannot bring myself severely to condemn persons who are wholly unable to bear so much as the sight of those men in the throne of legislation, who are only fit to be the objects of criminal justice. If fatigue, if disgust, if unsurmountable nausea, drive them away from such spectacles, *ubi miseriarum pars non minima erat, videre et aspici*,* I cannot blame them. He must have an heart of adamant who would hear a set of traitors puffed up with unexpected and undeserved power, obtained by an ignoble, unmanly, and perfidious rebellion, treating their honest fellow citizens as *rebels*, because they refused to bind themselves through their conscience, against the dictates of conscience itself, and had declined to swear an active compliance with their own ruin. How could a man of common flesh and blood endure, that those, who but the other day had skulked unobserved in their antichambers, scornfully insulting men, illustrious in their rank, sacred in their function, and venerable in their character, now in decline of life, and swimming on the wrecks of their fortunes, that those miscreants should tell such men scornfully and outrageously, after they had robbed them of all their property, that it is more than enough if they are allowed what will keep them from absolute famine, and that for the rest, they must let their grey hairs fall over the plough, to make out a scanty subsistence with the labour of their hands! Last, and worst, who could endure to hear this unnatural, insolent, and savage despotism called liberty? If, at this distance, sitting quietly by my fire, I cannot read their decrees and speeches without indignation, shall I condemn those who have fled from the actual sight and hearing of all these horrors? No, no! mankind has no title to demand that we should be slaves to their guilt and insolence; or that we should serve them in spite of themselves. Minds, sore with the poignant sense of insulted virtue, filled with high disdain against the pride of triumphant baseness, often have it not in their choice to stand their ground. Their complexion (which might defy the rack) cannot go through such a trial. Something very high must fortify men to that proof. But when I am driven to comparison, surely I cannot hesitate for a moment to prefer to such men as are common, those heroes, who in the midst of despair perform all the tasks of hope; who subdue their feelings to their duties; who, in the cause of humanity, liberty, and honour, abandon all the satisfactions of life, and every day incur a fresh risque of life itself. Do me the justice to believe that I never can prefer any fastidious virtue (virtue still) to the unconquered persever-ance, to the affectionate patience of those who watch day and night, by the bed-side of their delirious country, who, for their love to that dear and venerable name, bear all the disgusts, and all the buffets they receive from their frantic mother. Sir, I do look on you as true martyrs; I regard you as soldiers who act far more in the spirit of our Commander in chief, and the Captain of our salvation, than those who have left you; though I must first bolt myself very thoroughly, and know that I could do better, before I can censure them. I assure you, Sir, that, when I consider your unconquerable fidelity to your sovereign, and to your country, the courage, fortitude, magnanimity, and long-suffering of yourself, and the Abbé

Maury* and of Mr Cazales,* and of many worthy persons of all orders, in your Assembly, I forget, in the lustre of these great qualities, that on your side has been displayed an eloquence so rational, manly, and convincing, that no time or country, perhaps, has ever excelled. But your talents disappear in my admiration of your virtues.

As to Mr Mounier and Mr Lally,* I have always wished to do justice to their parts, and their eloquence, and the general purity of their motives. Indeed I saw very well from the beginning, the mischiefs which, with all these talents and good intentions, they would do to their country, through their confidence in systems. But their distemper was an epidemic malady. They were young and inexperienced; and when will young and inexperienced men learn caution and distrust of themselves? And when will men, young or old, if suddenly raised to far higher power than that which absolute kings and emperors commonly enjoy, learn any thing like moderation? Monarchs in general respect some settled order of things, which they find it difficult to move from its basis, and to which they are obliged to conform, even when there are no positive limitations to their power. These gentlemen conceived that they were chosen to new model the state, and even the whole order of civil society itself. No wonder that *they* entertained dangerous visions, when the King's ministers, trustees for the sacred deposit of the monarchy, were so infected with the contagion of project and system (I can hardly think it black premeditated treachery) that they publicly advertised for plans and schemes of government, as if they were to provide for the rebuilding of an hospital that had been burned down. What was this, but to unchain the fury of rash speculation amongst a people, of itself but too apt to be guided by a heated imagination, and a wild spirit of adventure?

The fault of Mr Mounier and Mr Lally was very great; but it was very general. If those gentlemen stopped when they came to the brink of the gulph of guilt and public misery, that yawned before them in the abyss of these dark and bottomless speculations, I forgive their first error; in that they were involved with many. Their repentance was their own.

They who consider Mounier and Lally as deserters, must regard themselves as murderers and as traitors: for from what else than murder and treason did they desert? For my part, I honour them for not having carried mistake into crime. If, indeed, I thought that they were not cured by experience, that they were not made sensible that those who would reform a state, ought to assume some actual constitution of government which is to be reformed; if they are not at length satisfied that it is become a necessary preliminary to liberty in France, to commence by the re-establishment of order and property of *every* kind, through the re-establishment of their monarchy, of every one of the old habitual distinctions and classes of the state; if they do not see that these classes are not to be confounded in order to be afterwards revived and separated; if they are not convinced that the scheme of parochial and club governments takes up the state at the wrong end, and is a low and senseless contrivance (as making the sole constitution of a supreme power) I should then allow, that their early rashness ought to be remembered to the last moment of their lives.

You gently reprehend me, because in holding out the picture of your disastrous situation, I suggest no plan for a remedy. Alas! Sir, the proposition of plans, without an attention to circumstances, is the very cause of all your misfortunes; and never shall you find me aggravating, by the infusion of any speculations of mine, the evils which have arisen from the speculations of others. Your malady, in this respect, is a disorder of repletion. You seem to think, that my keeping back my poor ideas, may arise from an indifference to the welfare of a foreign, and sometimes an hostile nation. No, Sir, I faithfully assure you, my reserve is owing to no such causes. Is this letter, swelled to a second book, a mark of national antipathy, or even of national indifference? I should act altogether in the spirit of the same caution, in a similar state of our own domestic affairs. If I were to venture any advice, in any case, it would be my best. The sacred duty of an adviser (one of the most inviolable that exists) would lead me, towards a real enemy, to act as if my best friend were the party concerned. But I dare not risque a speculation with no better view of your affairs than at present I can command; my caution is not from disregard, but from sollicitude for your welfare. It is suggested solely from my dread of becoming the author of inconsiderate counsel.

It is not, that as this strange series of actions has passed before my eyes, I have not indulged my mind in a great variety of political speculations concerning them. But compelled by no such positive duty as does not permit me to evade an opinion; called upon by no ruling power, without authority as I am, and without confidence, I should ill answer my own ideas of what would become myself, or what would be serviceable to others, if I were, as a volunteer, to obtrude any project of mine upon a nation, to whose circumstances I could not be sure it might be applicable.

Permit me to say, that if I were as confident, as I ought to be diffident in my own loose, general ideas, I never should venture to broach them, if but at twenty leagues distance from the centre of your affairs. I must see with my own eyes, I must, in a manner, touch with my own hands, not only the fixed, but the momentary circumstances, before I could venture to suggest any political project whatsoever. I must know the power and disposition to accept, to execute, to persevere. I must see all the aids, and all the obstacles. I must see the means of correcting the plan, where correctives would be wanted. I must see the things; I must see the men. Without a concurrence and adaptation of these to the design, the very best speculative projects might become not only useless, but mischievous. Plans must be made for men. We cannot think of making men, and binding nature to our designs. People at a distance might judge ill of men. They do not always answer to their reputation when you approach them. Nay, the perspective varies, and shews them quite otherwise than you thought them. At a distance, if we judge uncertainly of men, we must judge worse of *opportunities*, which continually vary their shapes and colours, and pass away like clouds. The Eastern politicians never do any thing without the opinion of the astrologers on the *fortunate moment*. They are in the right, if they can do no better; for the opinion of fortune is something towards commanding it. Statesmen of a more judicious prescience, look for the fortunate moment too; but they seek it, not in the conjunctions and oppositions of planets, but in the conjunctions and oppositions of men and things. These form their almanack.

To illustrate the mischief of a wise plan, without any attention to means and circumstances, it is not necessary to go farther than to your recent history. In the condition in which France was found three years ago, what better system could be proposed, what less, even savouring of wild theory, what fitter to provide for all the exigencies, whilst it reformed all the abuses of government, than the convention of the States General? I think nothing better could be imagined. But I have censured, and do still presume to censure your Parliament of Paris, for not having suggested to the King, that this proper measure was of all measures the most critical and arduous; one in which the utmost circumspection, and the greatest number of precautions, were the most absolutely necessary. The very confession that a government wants either amendment in its conformation, or relief to great distress, causes it to lose half its reputation, and as great a proportion of its strength as depends upon that reputation. It was therefore necessary, first to put government out of danger, whilst at its own desire it suffered such an operation, as a general reform at the hands of those who were much more filled with a sense of the disease, than provided with rational means of a cure.

It may be said, that this care, and these precautions, were more naturally the duty of the King's ministers, than that of the Parliament. They were so; but every man must answer in his estimation for the advice he gives, when he puts the conduct of his measure into hands who he does not know will execute his plans according to his ideas. Three or four ministers were not to be trusted with the being of the French monarchy, of all the orders, and of all the distinctions, and all the property of the kingdom. What must be the prudence of those who could think, in the then known temper of the people of Paris, of assembling the states at a place situated as Versailles?*

The Parliament of Paris did worse than to inspire this blind confidence into the King. For, as if names were things, they took no notice of (indeed they rather countenanced) the deviations which were manifest in the execution, from the true antient principles of the plan which they recommended. These deviations (as guardians of the antient laws, usages, and constitution of the kingdom) the Parliament of Paris ought not to have suffered, without the strongest remonstrances to the throne. It ought to have sounded the alarm to the whole nation, as it had often done on things of infinitely less importance. Under pretence of resuscitating the antient constitution, the Parliament saw one of the strongest acts of innovation, and the most leading in its consequences, carried into effect before their eyes; and an innovation through the medium of despotism; that is, they suffered the King's ministers to new model the whole representation of the *Tiers Etat*,* and, in a great measure, that of the clergy too, and to destroy the antient proportions of the orders. These changes, unquestionably the King had no right to make; and here the Parliaments failed in their duty, and along with their country, have perished* by this failure.

What a number of faults have led to this multitude of misfortunes, and almost all from this one source, that of considering certain general maxims, without attending to circumstances, to times, to places, to conjunctures, and to actors! If we do not attend scrupulously to all these, the medicine of to-day becomes the poison of to-morrow. If any measure was in the abstract better than another, it was to call the states—*ea visa salus morientibus una.**—Certainly it had the appearance.—But see the consequences of not attending to critical moments, of not regarding the symptoms which discriminate diseases, and which distinguish constitutions, complexions, and humours.

> ——Mox fuerat hoc ipsum exitio; furiisque refecti,
> Ardebant; ipsique suos, jam morte sub aegra,
> Discissos nudis laniabant dentibus artus.*

Thus the potion which was given to strengthen the constitution, to heal divisions, and to compose the minds of men, became the source of debility, phrenzy, discord, and utter dissolution.

In this, perhaps, I have answered, I think, another of your questions—Whether the British constitution is adapted to your circumstances? When I praised the British constitution, and wished it to be well studied, I did not mean that its exterior form and positive arrangement should become a model for you, or for any people servilely to copy. I meant to recommend the *principles* from which it has grown, and the policy on which it has been progressively improved out of elements common to you and to us. I am sure it is no visionary theory of mine. It is not an advice that subjects you to the hazard of any experiment. I believed the antient principles to be wise in all cases of a large empire that would be free. I thought you possessed our principles in your old forms, in as great a perfection as we did originally. If your states agreed (as I think they did) with your circumstances, they were best for you. As you had a constitution formed upon principles similar to ours, my idea was, that you might have improved them as we have done, conforming them to the state and exigencies of the times, and the condition of property in your country, having the conservation of that property, and the substantial basis of your monarchy, as principal objects in all your reforms.

I do not advise an House of Lords to you. Your antient course by representatives of the Noblesse (in your circumstances) appears to me rather a better institution. I know, that with you, a set of men of rank have betrayed their constituents, their honour, their trust, their King, and their country, and levelled themselves with their footmen,* that through this degradation they might afterwards put themselves above their natural equals. Some of these persons have entertained a project, that in reward of this their black perfidy and corruption, they may be chosen to give rise to a new order, and to establish themselves into an House of Lords. Do you think that, under the name of a British constitution, I mean to recommend to you such Lords, made of such kind of stuff? I do not however include in this description all of those who are fond of this scheme.

If you were now to form such an House of Peers, it would bear, in my opinion, but little resemblance to our's in its origin, character, or the purposes which it might answer, at the same time that it would destroy your true natural nobility.

But if you are not in a condition to frame an House of Lords, still less are you capable, in my opinion, of framing any thing which virtually and substantially could be answerable (for the purposes of a stable, regular government) to our House of Commons. That House is, within itself, a much more subtle and artificial combination of parts and powers, than people are generally aware of. What knits it to the other members of the constitution; what fits it to be at once the great support, and the great controul of government; what makes it of such admirable service to that monarchy which, if it limits, it secures and strengthens, would require a long discourse, belonging to the leisure of a contemplative man, not to one whose duty it is to join in communicating practically to the people the blessings of such a constitution.

Your *Tiers Etat* was not in effect and substance an House of Commons. You stood in absolute need of something else to supply the manifest defects in such a body as your Tiers Etat. On a sober and dispassionate view of your old constitution, as connected with all the present circumstances, I was fully persuaded, that the crown, standing as things have stood (and are likely to stand, if you are to have any monarchy at all) was and is incapable, alone and by itself, of holding a just balance between the two orders, and at the same time of effecting the interior and exterior purposes of a protecting government. I, whose leading principle it is, in a reformation of the state, to make use of existing materials, am of opinion, that the representation of the clergy, as a separate order, was an institution which touched all the orders more nearly than any of them touched the other; that it was well fitted to connect them; and to hold a place in any wise monarchical common-wealth. If I refer you to your original constitution, and think it, as I do, substantially a good one, I do not amuse you in this, more than in other things, with any inventions of mine. A certain intemperance of intellect is the disease of the time, and the source of all its other diseases. I will keep myself as untainted by it as I can. Your architects build without a foundation. I would readily lend an helping hand to any superstructure, when once this is effectually secured—but first I would say δος που στω.*

You think, Sir, and you may think rightly, upon the first view of the theory, that to provide for the exigencies of an empire, so situated and so related as that of France, its King ought to be invested with powers very much superior to those which the King of England possesses under the letter of our constitution. Every degree of power necessary to the state, and not destructive to the rational and moral freedom of individuals, to that personal liberty, and personal security, which contribute so much to the vigour, the prosperity, the happiness, and the dignity of a nation—every degree of power which does not suppose the total absence of all control, and all responsibility on the part of ministers,—a King of France, in common sense, ought to possess. But whether the exact measure of authority, assigned by the letter of the law to the King of Great Britain, can answer to the exterior or interior purposes of the French monarchy, is a point which I cannot venture to judge upon. Here, both in the power given, and its limitations, we have always cautiously felt our way. The parts of our constitution have gradually, and almost insensibly, in a long course of time, accommodated themselves to each other, and to their common, as well as to their separate purposes. But this adaptation of contending parts, as it has not been in our's, so it can never be in your's, or in any country, the effect of a single instantaneous regulation, and no sound heads could ever think of doing it in that manner.

I believe, Sir, that many on the continent altogether mistake the condition of a King of Great Britain. He is a real King, and not an executive officer. If he will not trouble himself with contemptible details, nor wish to degrade himself by becoming a party in little squabbles, I am far from sure, that a King of Great Britain, in whatever concerns him as a King, or indeed as a rational man, who combines his public interest with his personal satisfaction, does not possess a more real, solid, extensive power, than the King of France was possessed of before this miserable Revolution. The direct power of the King of England is considerable. His indirect, and far more certain power, is great indeed. He stands in need of nothing towards dignity; of nothing towards splendour; of nothing towards authority; of nothing at all towards consideration abroad. When was it that a King of England wanted wherewithal to make him respected, courted, or perhaps even feared in every state in Europe?

I am constantly of opinion, that your states, in three orders, on the footing on which they stood in 1614, were capable of being brought into a proper and harmonious combination with royal authority. This constitution by estates, was the natural, and only just representation of France. It grew out of the habitual conditions, relations, and reciprocal claims of men. It grew out of the circumstances of the country, and out of the state of property. The wretched scheme of your present masters, is not to fit the constitution to the people, but wholly to destroy conditions, to dissolve relations, to change the state of the nation, and to subvert property, in order to fit their country to their theory of a constitution.

Until you could make out practically that great work, a combination of opposing forces, 'a work of labour long, and endless praise,' the utmost caution ought to have been used in the reduction of the royal power, which alone was capable of holding together the comparatively heterogeneous mass of your states. But at this day, all these considerations are unseasonable. To what end should we discuss the limitations of royal power? Your king is in prison. Why speculate on the measure and standard of liberty? I doubt much, very much indeed, whether France is at all ripe for liberty on any standard. Men are qualified for civil liberty, in exact proportion to their disposition to put moral chains upon their own appetites; in proportion as their love to justice is above their rapacity; in proportion as their soundness and sobriety of understanding is above their vanity and presumption; in proportion as they are more disposed to listen to the counsels of the wise and good, in preference to the flattery of knaves. Society cannot exist unless a controlling power upon will and appetite be placed somewhere, and the less of it there is within, the more there must be without. It is ordained in the eternal constitution of things, that men of intemperate minds cannot be free. Their passions forge their fetters.

This sentence the prevalent part of your countrymen execute on themselves. They possessed, not long since, what was next to freedom, a mild paternal monarchy. They despised it for its weakness. They were offered a well-poised free constitution. It did not suit their taste or their temper. They carved for themselves; they flew out, murdered, robbed, and rebelled. They have succeeded, and put over their country an insolent tyranny, made up of cruel and inexorable masters, and that too of a description hitherto not known in the world. The powers and policies by which they have succeeded, are not those of great statesmen, or great military commanders, but the practices of incendiaries, assassins, housebreakers, robbers, spreaders of false news, forgers of false orders from authority, and other delinquencies, of which ordinary justice takes cognizance. Accordingly the spirit of their rule is exactly correspondent to the means by which they obtained it. They act more in the manner of thieves who have got possession of an house, than of conquerors who have subdued a nation.

Opposed to these, in appearance, but in appearance only, is another band, who call themselves the *moderate*.* These, if I conceive rightly of their conduct, are a set of men who approve heartily of the whole new constitution, but wish to lay heavy on the most atrocious of those crimes, by which this fine constitution of their's has been obtained. They are a sort of people who affect to proceed as if they thought that men may deceive without fraud, rob without injustice, and overturn every thing without violence. They are men who would usurp the government of their country with decency and moderation. In fact they are nothing more or better, than men engaged in desperate designs, with feeble minds. They are not honest; they are only ineffectual and unsystematic in their iniquity. They are persons who want not the dispositions, but the energy and vigour, that is necessary for great evil machinations. They find that in such designs they fall at best into a secondary rank, and others take the place and lead in usurpation, which they are not qualified to obtain or to hold. They envy to their companions, the natural fruit of their crimes; they join to run them down with the hue and cry of mankind, which pursues their common offences; and then hope to mount into their places on the credit of the sobriety with which they shew themselves disposed to carry on what may seem most plausible in the mischievous projects they pursue in common. But these men naturally are despised by those who have heads to know, and hearts that are able to go through the necessary demands of bold, wicked enterprizes. They are naturally classed below the latter description, and will only be used by them as inferior instruments. They will be only the Fairfaxes* of your Cromwells. If they mean honestly, why do they not strengthen the arms of honest men, to support their antient, legal, wise, and free government, given to them in the spring of 1788, against the inventions of craft, and the theories of ignorance and folly? If they do not, they must continue the scorn of both parties; sometimes the tool, sometimes the incumbrance of that, whose views they approve, whose conduct they decry. These people are only made to be the sport of tyrants. They never can obtain, or communicate freedom.

You ask me too, whether we have a committee of research.* No, Sir,—God forbid! It is the necessary instrument of tyranny and usurpation; and therefore I do not wonder that it has had an early establishment under your present Lords. We do not want it.

Excuse my length. I have been somewhat occupied, since I was honoured with your letter; and I should not have been able to answer it at all, but for the holidays, which have given me means of enjoying the leisure of the country. I am called to duties which I am neither able nor willing to evade. I must soon return to my old conflict with the corruptions and oppressions which have prevailed in our eastern dominions.* I must turn myself wholly from those of France.

In England, we *cannot* work so hard as Frenchmen. Frequent relaxation is necessary to us. You are naturally more intense in your application. I did not know this part of your national character, until I went into France in 1773. At present, this your disposition to labour is rather encreased than lessened. In your Assembly you do not allow yourselves a recess even on Sundays. We have two days in the week, besides the festivals; and besides five or six months of the summer and autumn. This continued unremitted effort of the members of your Assembly, I take to be one among the causes of the mischief they have done. They who always labour, can have no true judgment. You never give yourselves time to cool. You can never survey, from its proper point of sight, the work you have finished, before you decree its final execution. You can never plan the future by the past. You never go into the country, soberly and dispassionately to observe the effect of your measures on their objects. You cannot feel distinctly how far the people are rendered better and improved, or more miserable and depraved, by what you have done. You cannot see with your own eyes the sufferings and afflictions you cause. You know them but at a distance, on the statements of those who always flatter the reigning power, and who, amidst their representations of the grievances, inflame your minds against those who are oppressed. These are amongst the effects of unremitted labour, when men exhaust their attention, burn out their candles, and are left in the dark.—*Malo meorum negligentiam, quam istorum obscuram diligentiam.**

BEACONSFIELD,
JANUARY 19TH 1791.

I HAVE THE HONOR, &C.
(SIGNED) *EDMUND BURKE.*

EXPLANATORY NOTES

3 *the author's sentiments*: Charles-Jean-François Depont (1767–96) was a young Frenchman who had met Burke on a visit to England in 1785. In two letters of 4 November and 29 December 1789, he had invited Burke to express views on what was happening in France. *The Correspondence of Edmund Burke* (Cambridge, 1967), vi. 31–2, 59–61.

4 Constitutional Society . . . Revolution Society: the Society for Constitutional Information had been founded in 1780 to press for parliamentary reform. Its very respectable membership included Richard Sheridan and other leading Whigs. The Revolution Society was founded in 1788 to celebrate the Glorious Revolution of 1688.

5 *Your National Assembly*: in May 1789, the Estates General had been convened to address the imminent possibility of a national bankruptcy. In this body, the French were represented in three Orders sitting separately; nobility, clergy and commoners. On 27 June 1789 the three Orders reconstituted themselves as one institution known as the National Assembly.

5 *a committee . . . the National Assembly*: messages of support and encouragement had passed between the National Assembly and various reforming societies in England.

6 *a congratulatory address . . . France*: at the revolution Society Dinner on 4 November 1789, a leading Dissenting minister Richard Price had congratulated the French on becoming participants in the blessings of representative government and religious toleration. It was this initiative that prompted Burke to take up his pen.

8 *Knight of the Sorrowful Countenance*: the name given by Miguel Cervantes to his hero, Don Quixote. Ironically, Burke was often portrayed as Don Quixote by cartoonists in the period of the French Revolution.

8 *fixed air*: early name for carbonic acid.

9 *Dr Price . . . Duke de Rochefaucault . . . Archbishop of Aix*: Dr Richard Price (1723–91), a leading member of Lord Lansdowne's Bowood Circle, was a prominent member of a number of reform movements. Louis-Alexandre, Duc de la

Roche Guyon et de la Rochefoucauld d'Anville (1743–92) had presented the Revolution Society's good wishes to the National Assembly. Jean de Dieu-Raymond de Cucé Boisgelin Archbishop of Aix (1732–1804) was President of the National Assembly at the time.

10 *French revolution . . . world*: in this diagnosis at least, Burke found himself in agreement with other members of the Whig party. Fox described the fall of the Bastille as follows: 'It is I think by much the greatest Event that has ever happened in the world, and will in all probability have the most extensive good consequences.' L. G. Mitchell, *Charles James Fox* (Oxford, 1992), 110.

10 *Old Jewry*: an area in London between Aldgate and the Minories.

11 *Earl Stanhope*: Charles, 3rd Earl Stanhope (1753–1816), though closely related to William Pitt, was so radical in his politics that he was known as 'Citizen Stanhope'.

11 *sermon . . . implied*: Price's text was taken from Psalm 122: 6–7, 'Pray for the peace of Jerusalem: they shall prosper that love thee. Peace be within thy walls, and prosperity within thy palaces.'

11 *man . . . philosophers*: Burke is here referring to Lord Lansdowne's Bowood Circle, a salon frequented by, among others, Richard Price, Joseph Priestley, and Jeremy Bentham. For many years it had prided itself on its contacts with French writers.

11 *Reverend Hugh Peters*: (1598–1660) a Dissenting minister who was executed for having assisted at the beheading of Charles I.

11 *league in France . . . England*: The Catholic League was formed in France in 1576 to co-ordinate Catholic activity in the French Wars of Religion. The Solemn League and Covenant was agreed in March 1643 between Parliament and Scots Presbyterians. Both groups hoped to impose a religious settlement on their fellow-country men.

12 *reverend lay-divine*: Augustus Henry Fitzroy, 3rd Duke of Grafton (1735–1811), Chancellor of Cambridge University, who had recently published *Hints Submitted to the Serious Attention of the Clergy, Nobility and Gentry, by a Layman*.

12 *Seekers*: religious sect whose aim was to seek the true Church.

13 *hortus siccus*: literally 'a dry garden'.

13 *Mess-Johns*: or Mas Johns, a humorous term for ministers of the Scottish Presbyterian Church.

13 *in former . . . artillery*: during the English Civil War, ministers had travelled with Cromwell's armies.

13 *utinam . . . saevitiae*: 'and would that he had devoted all that time to these trifles rather than to cruelty', Juvenal, *Satires*, iv. 150–1.

14 *Condo . . . possim*: 'I put together and collect things which I will soon be able to draw upon'; Horace, *Epistles*, i.i.12.

16 'To choose . . . ourselves': Price actually describes these rights as follows:
    'First; The right to liberty of conscience in religious matters. Secondly; The right to resist power when abused. And Thirdly; The right to chuse our own governors; to cashier them for misconduct; and to frame a government for ourselves.'
    A Discourse on the Love of our Country (London, 1790), 34.

16 *Declaration of Right*: this measure is usually known as the Bill of Rights (1 Will. and Mary Sess. 2, c. 2).

17 *the consideration . . . legislature*: the Act of Settlement, 1701 (12 and 13 Will. II, c. 2).

17 *deviation . . . succession*: when James II left England in 1688, he was succeeded not only by his eldest daughter Mary, but also by her husband William III, who continued to reign after his wife's death in 1694. His claim to the throne therefore was unprecedented in English history.

17 *Privilegium non transit in exemplum*: 'an individual's right does not translate into a general rule' is a maxim in Roman law.

18 *undoubtedly his*: James II's son, 'James III' or the Old Pretender, was debarred from the succession on the grounds that he was illegitimate.

18 *Lord Somers*: John, 1st Baron Somers (1651–1716), leading Whig statesman. Lord Chancellor, 1697.

22 *per capita . . . per stirpes*: phrases in the law relating to the succession to an estate, determining the share which each beneficiary shall take. If '*per capita*', all individuals share

equally. If '*per stirpes*', each branch of a family takes a share, irrespective of the number of individuals involved.

22 *multosque . . . avorum*: 'Through many years, the fortune of the house stands, and the grandfathers of grandfathers are counted', Virgil, *Georgics*, iv. 8–9.

23 *de tallagio . . . habeas corpus*: De Tallagio non Concedendo (1297), the Petition of Right (1628), and Habeas Corpus (1679) were all viewed as major steps in the history of guaranteeing the rights and liberties of the individual.

23 *electress Sophia*: the Electress Sophia of Hanover (1630–1714), granddaughter of James I and mother of the future George I, was, at the time of drafting the Act of Settlement, the (Protestant) person with the strongest claim to the throne.

24 *act of . . . King William*: the Act of Settlement 1701.

24 *Princess Elizabeth*: (1596–1662), daughter of James I, had married Frederick, Elector Palatine, in 1613.

28 *the act . . . crown*: more usually known as the Bill of Rights (1 Will. and Mary, Sess. 2, c. 2).

28 *act . . . King William*: the Act of Settlement, 1701.

28 *Haec commemoratio est quasi exprobatio*: 'For this reminder is as it were a rebuke'; Terence, *Andria*, 43–4.

29 *one calling himself . . . 'the Fisherman'*: the Pope commonly used the title 'Servant of Servants', and, as the successor to St Peter as Bishop of Rome, could be said to be 'the Fisherman', that having been the Saint's trade.

29 *the Justicia of Arragon*: the Justicia was the supreme judge in the medieval kingdom of Aragon. He could determine disputes between nobles, and even between the king and his nobility.

30 *'Justa bella quibus necessaria'*: this is a paraphrase of a sentence in Livy, ix.i.10. 'War is just, Samnites, to those for whom it is necessary.'

31 *Cyon*: an obsolete spelling of scion.

31 *Sir Edward Coke*: (1552–1634), the leading constitutional lawyer of the reign of James I. His *Institutes of the Laws of England* appeared between 1628 and 1644.

31 *Sir William Blackstone*: (1723–80), was the leading authority on English law in the eighteenth century. His *Commentaries on the Laws of England* appeared between 1765 and 1769.

32 *Magna Charta . . . Henry I*: the Magna Carta of 1215 and Henry I's Coronation Oath of 1101 were thought to set out the nature of feudal ties and obligations.

32 *Selden*: John Selden (1584–1654) was an eminent lawyer, politically allied to those in opposition to James I and Charles I.

32 *Abbé Seyes*: Abbé Emmanuel-Joseph Sieyès (1748–1836), priest and influential author in the early stages of the French Revolution.

33 *mortmain*: a legal term describing the condition of land held inalienably by an ecclesiastical or other corporation.

34 *Your constitution . . . perfected*: Burke is here referring to the fact that the Estates General was not called in France between 1614 and 1789.

36 *Maroon slaves*: a term applied to fugitive slaves in the West Indies.

38 *parliament of Paris*: the Parlement of Paris was a court of law with jurisdiction over nearly one-third of France.

39 *This was unnatural . . . subverted*: this paragraph introduces one of Burke's major preoccupations. On 2 November 1790, at the suggestion of Mirabeau, all ecclesiastical property was placed 'at the disposal of the nation'. On the security of this property the national debt was guaranteed and a paper currency issued under the name of *assignats*.

40 *shoe-buckles*: patriotic citizens contributed to the financing of the Revolution by offering objects of value, even silver shoe buckles.

41 *Third Estate composed of six hundred persons*: normally, each of the three Orders making up an Estates General had 300 representatives. In December 1788, Louis XVI had agreed that the Third Estate should have 600.

42 *A very small desertion . . . third*: on 22 June 1789 250 members of the First Estate, led by the Archbishops of Vienne and Bordeaux, broke ranks to join the Third. Three days later nearly fifty aristocrats, members of the Second Estate, did the same. The new body called itself the National Assembly.

45 *breakers of law in India*: Warren Hastings, Governor of Bengal, was impeached for misdemeanours in India. The affair lasted from 1786 to 1794, and Burke was one of the principal prosecutors.

45 '*fools rush in ... tread*': Alexander Pope, *An Essay on Criticism*, 625.

46 *who, immersed in hopeless poverty ... scramble*: under the Revolution's plans for the Church, parish priests would be guaranteed regular salaries by the state, an idea that would offer many of them the promise of a much enhanced standard of living.

47 *the then Earl of Holland*: Henry Rich, 1st Earl of Holland (1590–1649), the protégé of Charles I and Henrietta Maria. In spite of receiving much royal favour, he fought for Parliament on the outbreak of Civil War in 1642.

48 *Still ... destroys*: Edmund Waller, *A Panegyric to My Lord Protector*, v. 36. Waller was a near relative of Oliver Cromwell.

48 *Guises, Condés, and Colignis*: during the French Wars of Religion in the late sixteenth century, Henri, Duc de Guise (1550–88) and Louis de Guise (1555–88) had been leaders of the Catholics, while Admiral Gaspard de Coligny had been prominent among the Protestants.

48 *the Richlieus*: Armand-Jean du Plessis, Cardinal de Richelieu (1585–1642), principal minister of Louis XIII, undertook a policy of harassment towards Protestants in the early seventeenth century.

48 *Sully*: Maximilien de Béthune, Duc de Sully (1560–1641), principal minister of Henri IV, attempted to pursue conciliatory policies in religious matters.

49 *the chancellor ... honourable*: the Chancellor here mentioned was the Marquis de Barentin, who made this remark in a speech at the opening of the Estates General on 5 May 1789.

52 *shallow speculations ... philosophy*: Burke disliked the Enlightenment and the *philosophes* who preached it. He once advised a French friend that, 'It were better to forget once and for all, the *Encyclopédie* and the whole body of Economists and to revert to those old rules and principles which have hitherto made princes great and nations happy.' Burke to C.-F. de Rivarol, 1 June 1791; *Corresp.* vi. 267–8.

52 *with the lamp-post for its second*: in the disturbances of the summer of 1789, one or two officials had been hanged from lamp-posts.

57 *A man ... of great talents*: the man in question is Joseph

Priestley, a close friend and associate of Richard Price. This passage is taken from his *History of the Conceptions of Christianity*, published in 1782. Priestley was accorded French citizenship in 1792.

58 '*Illa . . . regnet*': 'Let him flaunt himself in that hall—Aeolus, and let him rule the winds in his confined prison.' Virgil, *Aeneid*, i. 140–1.

58 *Levanter*: in the Mediterranean, a Levanter was a strong wind blowing from the east.

62 *Liceat perire poetis . . . Ardentem frigidus Aetnam insiluit*: these two phrases, 'poets may be permitted to die' and 'the cool-headed man jumped into fiery Etna', relate to a story in Horace, *De Arte Poetica*, 464–6, about the poet Empedocles, who committed suicide by leaping into the volcano. Burke by implication accused the French revolutionaries of doing the same.

63 *cantharides*: a genus of insects. Prepared as a drug they were thought to have diuretic properties.

63 *cum perimit saevos classis numerosa tyrranos*: 'while a crowded class kills savage tyrants'; Juvenal, *Satires*, vii. 150–1.

65 *Pisgah*: a mountain range in contemporary Jordan; from the summit of one of its peaks Moses was afforded a first glimpse of the Promised Land.

65 *Another of these reverend gentlemen*: Burke is here referring to Pierre-Étienne-Louis Dumont (1759–1829), a Genevan pastor, who, as a visitor to Bowood, was known to Price and the Bowood Circle generally.

67 *Onondaga*: a Jesuit mission to the south of Lake Ontario.

68 *hundreds of the members*: by October 1789, nearly three hundred members of the National Assembly had resigned, emigrated, or abandoned their seats. The Assembly debated in the presence of a vociferous public gallery, and was endlessly pressurized by petitions and delegations.

68 *Catiline . . . Cethegus*: Lucius Sergius Catiline (?–62 BC) became famous for the conspiracy that bears his name. Publius Cornelius Cethegus, another leading politician of the first century BC, had an unenviable reputation for intrigue.

69 *nec color imperii, nec frons erat ulla senatus*: 'nor will there be the external form of government nor any appearance of a legislative authority'; Lucan, *Pharsalia*, ix. 207.

69 *'that the vessel ... than ever'*: this phrase was used by Mirabeau in the National Assembly.

70 *'the blood spilled was not the most pure'*: an expression used by Barnave to describe the murder, in July 1789, of Foullon and Berthier, two Parisian officials.

70 *ordinary of Newgate*: the chaplain of Newgate, which was one of the largest prisons in London.

70 *the persons ... leze nation*: Lese-majesty in English law was treason against the sovereign. In this fabricated expression, Burke is trying to adapt this concept into treason against the nation.

71 *History will record ... moment*: Burke's account of the invasion of the palace of Versailles by a mob on 6 October is highly coloured and, as some contemporaries noted, simply inaccurate. It encouraged men like Tom Paine to dismiss the work as a 'dramatic performance'; T. Paine, *The Rights of Man* (London, 1791), i. 39.

72 *one of the old palaces of Paris*: the Palace of the Tuileries.

72 *Theban and Thracian Orgies*: religious festivals associated with the cult of Dionysius at Thebes and of Artemis at Samothrace.

72 *Io Paean*: a hymn of praise to Apollo.

73 *fifth monarchy*: Fifth Monarchy Men were a Puritan sect of the seventeenth century, who believed that the 'monarchies' of Assyria, Persia, Greece, and Rome would be succeeded by a 'fifth monarchy' of Christ reigning on earth.

73 *M. de Lally Tollendal*: Trophime-Gérard, Marquis de Lally-Tollendal (1751–1830), was a leading moderate royalist who wrote two pamphlets to defend himself against Burke's charge that he had deserted his post; *Lettre Écrite au très-honorable Edmund Burke* (London, 1792) and *Seconde Lettre à M. Burke* (London, 1792).

74 *M. Mirabeau*: Honoré-Gabriel-Victor Riqueti, Comte de Mirabeau (1749–91), was a nobleman of considerable notoriety before the Revolution, but who was employed by Louis XVI as an adviser in 1790–1.

74 *M. Barnave*: Antoine-Pierre-Joseph-Marie Barnave (1761–93), leading proponent of constitutional monarchy in the National Assembly.

74   *Parlons du parti . . . eu tort de la leur donner*: 'let us speak of
the side I have taken; my conscience justifies it. Neither this
guilty city, nor this still more guilty assembly has any right to
ask me to justify myself; but I am anxious that you, and people
who think like you, should not condemn me.—My health, I
swear, made it impossible for me to undertake public functions;
but even putting that aside, it has been beyond my resources to
put up with the horror which, for a long time, was brought to
me by this blood—these heads—this Queen whose throat was
nearly cut—this King—lead like a slave—entering Paris, in the
middle of his murderers, and preceded by the head of his poor
guards.—These faithless Janissaries; these murderers, these
cannibalistic women, this cry of ALL BISHOPS TO THE GALLOWS
at the moment when the King entered his capital with two
episcopal members of his council in his coach. A rifle shot
which I saw fired into one of the Queen's coaches. M. Bailley
calling this a wonderful day. The assembly having coldly
declared that morning that it would be undignified to go as a
body to protect the King. M. Mirabeau impudently saying in
this assembly that the ship of state, far from being halted in its
tracks, would go forward more quickly than ever towards its
refitting. M. Barnave, laughing with Mirabeau, when rivers of
blood were flowing around us. The virtuous Mounier escaping
by a miracle from twenty assassins, who would have liked to
make his head yet one more trophy.

This is what made me swear never again to set foot *in this
cave of cannibals* [the National Assembly], where I lacked the
energy to raise my voice, where, for six weeks, I had raised it in
vain. I, Mounier, and all honest men, thought that the last
thing to be done for the public good was to leave it. There was
no suggestion of my being afraid. I would blush to defend
myself against such a charge. On my journey, I have received
from people, less guilty than those made drunk by anger,
acclamations and applause, which would have made some
people feel flattered, but which made me shiver. I have
surrendered only to the indignation, horror and physical
convulsions that I have experienced at the sight of blood. One
puts up with a single death; one puts up with it several times,
when it is useful to do so. But no power under Heaven, no
private or public opinion has the right to condemn me to suffer
uselessly a thousand murders a minute, and to perish in
despair, in anger, in the middle of triumphant crime which I
could not stop. They will proscribe me and they will confiscate

> my property. I worked my land and I will never see it again.— There is my justification. You will be able to read, distribute and copy it; it will be just too bad if people will not understand; I will not be in the wrong for giving it to them.'

74 *Mons. Mounier's narrative of these transactions*: Jean Joseph Mounier (1758–1806) was a royalist deputy who abandoned the Assembly after October 1789. Burke could be referring to one of two works; *Exposé de la conduite de M. Mounier, dans l'Assemblée nationale, et des motifs de son retour en Dauphiné* (Paris, 1789), or to *Nouvelles Observations sur les États-Genereaux de France* (Paris, 1789).

75 *It is now . . . vision*: in this celebrated passage Burke gave a description of Marie Antoinette that infuriated many contemporaries. In private correspondence Burke was much more critical of the Queen's political judgement, and expressed the fear that she would be destroyed by her own 'intrigues', Burke to R. Burke, 13 December 1791, *Corresp.* vi. 340.

78 *Non satis . . . dulcia sunto*: 'It is not enough for poems to be beautiful; they must also be sweet', Horace, *De Arte Poetica*, 99–100.

80 *gentis incunabula nostrae*: 'the cradle of our people', Virgil, *Aeneid*, iii. 105.

81 *Garrick . . . Siddons*: David Garrick (1717–79) and Sarah Siddons (1755–1831) were two of the greatest performers on the English stage of their day.

83 *insinuated in certain publications*: just before the attack on the Bastille, it was widely reported that Louis XVI had decided on a recourse to armed force.

83 *Nero . . . Christina*: these monarchs were high in the Whig demonology of rulers who wished to be despots.

83 *French King, or King of the French*: the change from 'King of France' to 'King of the French' was significant in indicating that the monarch, so far from owning a country, was in fact in some contractual arrangement with the French people.

84 *flower-de-luce on their shoulder*: prostitutes in France were branded with the mark of a *fleur de luce*, or lily. The *Mémoires* of the Comtesse de la Motte, who had been so branded, contained many scabrous stories about Marie Antoinette.

84 *Lord George Gordon fast in Newgate*: Lord George Gordon (1751–93), President of the Protestant Association, had been

imprisoned in 1780 for instigating anti-Catholic riots. He was imprisoned again in 1788 for libelling the French Queen.

85 *king of France in that situation*: John II of France (1319–64) was a prisoner in London during the Hundred Years' War.

89 *Collins . . . Freethinkers*: Anthony Collins (1676–1729), John Toland (1670–1722), Matthew Tindal (1657–1733), Thomas Chubb (1679–1747), and Thomas Morgan (?–1743) were all writers who advocated deism.

89 *Bolingbroke*: Henry St John, 1st Visc. Bolingbroke (1678–1751), Jacobite statesman, whom Burke took to represent the exploded idea of divine-right monarchy.

89 *'all the Capulets'*: *Romeo and Juliet*, IV. i. 111–12.

90 *Sit . . . sententia*: 'So at the outset, citizens must be persuaded that the gods are the lords and the rulers of all things, and that what is done is done by their will and authority; that they are likewise great benefactors of men, noticing the character of every individual, what he does, of what wrong he is guilty, and with what intentions and with what piety he fulfils his religious duties; and that they take note of the pious and the impious. For surely minds which are imbued with such ideas will not spurn what is useful and what is true'; Cicero, *De Legibus*, II. vii.

93 *Quicquid multis peccatur inultum*: 'Whatever is secret harms the many.' Attribution unknown.

98 *Quod . . . appellantur*: Burke here slightly misquotes the original text, but without substantially changing its meaning. 'For there is nothing that happens on earth that is more welcome to that supreme God who rules the whole universe than the institutions and congregations of men united by a sense of right which are called states', Cicero, *De Republica*, VI. xiii.

101 *they have incorporated . . . regulator*: Burke's insistence that the property of a corporation like the Church within a state was of the same order as the property of an individual, and therefore to be defended in law on the same terms, provides the basis for the long section on state–Church relations that follows.

101 *Euripus*: a channel between the island of Euboea and the Greek mainland well-known for its strong currents.

104 *dishonest . . . protect*: in November 1789, the property of the

French Church had been declared 'at the disposal of the nation'. Proceeds from its sale were to be used to fund the National Debt.

106 *Palais Royale ... Jacobins*: the Palais Royale was the Paris home of the Duc d'Orléans. The Jacobins, very early in the Revolution, established themselves as one of the leading clubs of Paris, meeting in a former Dominican establishment in the Rue St Honoré.

109 *a great monied interest ... power*: Burke was insistent that a large number of those supporting the Revolution were, as public creditors, motivated less by ideals than by the desire to be assured of their money.

109 *Jus retractus*: a device in Roman Law by which an alienated inheritance might be recovered.

110 *the regent*: Philippe II d'Orléans (1674–1723) was Regent of France from 1715 to 1723 during the minority of Louis XV.

111 *the Encyclopaedia*: the *Encyclopédie*, the first volume of which appeared in 1751, called on the talents of many of the greatest writers of the Enlightenment, who aimed to provide a complete dictionary for the arts and sciences.

111 *my lost son*: Burke's only son, Richard, died in August 1794.

112 *The correspondence ... Prussia*: Frederick II (1712–86) had been the correspondent of a number of French writers.

112 *Turgot*: Anne-Robert-Jacques Turgot (1727–81) was both a leading *philosophe* and, as a minister in the last years of the *ancien régime*, was intimately involved with the management of government debt. In his own person, therefore, he provided Burke with an excellent example of a political man of letters who was also the friend of investors and stockjobbers.

114 *Mr Laborde*: the Contrôleur-Général was the first minister of France, supervising the financial and economic life of the country. The Laborde family was heavily involved in royal finance. François-Louis-Joseph Laborde de Méréville (?–1801) succeeded his uncle as Keeper of the Royal Treasury in 1785. His assistant was his father Jean Joseph de Laborde (1724–94).

115 *duke de Choiseul ... duke d'Aiguillon ... Noailles ... duke de Rochefoucault ... cardinal de Rochefoucault*: Étienne-François, Duc de Choiseul (1719–85), and Emmanuel-Armand de Vignoret du Plessis-Richelieu, Duc d'Aiguillon (1720–88), had both been ministers of the Crown under Louis XV. Louis-

Marie, Vicomte de Noailles (1756–1804), François-Alexandre-Frédéric, Duc de la Rochefoucauld-Liancourt (1747–1827), and Dominique de la Rochefoucauld (1713–1800), Cardinal Archbishop of Rouen, while supporting the Revolution in its early stages, all came from great families caught up in court patronage and intrigue.

115 *crudelem illam Hastam*: 'that bloody spear'; Cicero, *De Officiis*, II. viii. 29. It was customary for Roman auctions to be conducted around a spear buried in the ground.

116 *The tyrant . . . men*: Henry VIII of England (1509–47), Gaius Marius (155–86 BC), and Lucius Cornelius Sulla (138–78 BC) are held up by Burke as examples of men greedy for despotic power. Henry, in the early stages of the Reformation in England, confiscated monastic property.

118 *Mr Necker*: Jacques Necker (1732–1804), Genevan banker and the leading finance minister of the last years of the *ancien régime*.

118 *Quel pays . . . tant de bruit en Europe*: What a country, Gentlemen, is that in which, *without taxes* and with simple *unnoticed* objectives, one can make a deficit disappear that created such a stir in Europe.

118 *Rapport . . . Mai 5, 1789*: report of the director-general of finance, made by order of the King at Versailles. 5 May 1789.

120 *contribution of the nobility*: for details of the taxation of the privileged Orders in the *ancien régime*, see C. B. A. Behrens, *Economic History Review*, 15 (1963) and *French Historical Studies*, 8–9 (1974–6).

122 *a new . . . lands*: the new paper currency was called an *assignat*. Since it was, as Burke indicates, backed by the sales of Church land, its value rose and fell with the fortunes of the Revolution.

122 *the old . . . parliaments*: there were thirteen Parlements in France in 1789, the largest, that of Paris, having jurisdiction over nearly a third of the country. As law courts, they were staffed by magistrates enjoying noble status. They were abolished on 7 September 1790.

123 *arcanum*: literally something hidden or secret, but the term was used in alchemy to mean a miraculous power or elixir, and this is the likely meaning here.

126 *I do not . . . speculation*: the point is made in Bolingbroke's

Letters on the Spirit of Patriotism, on the Idea of a Patriot King and on the State of Parties at the Accession of King George the First (London, 1749), 92–3.

127 *representative to the states-general*: deputies to the Estates General brought with them *cahiers de doléances*, notebooks containing grievances and plans for reform put forward by their constituents.

127 *Taehmus Kouli Khân*: more usually known as Nadir Shah, ruler of Persia from 1736 to 1747.

128 *generalities*: the *généralités*, each presided over by an *intendant*, were the main administrative units of the *ancien régime*.

132 *Mr de Calonne*: Charles-Alexandre de Calonne (1734–1802), after fleeing to England in 1787, wrote a number of works on the state of French governmental finances.

133 *Circean liberty*: Circe, in Greek legend, was a sorceress who lived on the island of Aeaea.

133 *Laputa and Balnibarib*: two mythical states described in *Gulliver's Travels* as having come under the influence of philosophers.

134 *Travaux de charité … qui ont eu lieu*: public works to combat unemployment in Paris and the provinces; elimination of vagrancy and begging; premiums for grain imports; expenses relating to poor relief, deduction made for the recovery of funds that has taken place.

135 *Hanse-towns*: the Hanseatic League, of which Hamburg and Lübeck were the principal partners, was a defensive alliance of north German towns against the pretences of local princes.

135 *Orsini and Vitelli*: the Orsini were a princely Roman family from which several Popes had been drawn. The Vitelli were a fifteenth-century family of mercenaries.

135 *the Mamalukes … Malabar*: Mameluke was a name used to describe the Sultans of Egypt. The Nayrs were a warlike race living on the Malabar Coast in India.

135 *ordaining … known*: by a decree of 19 June 1790, the National Assembly abolished all the titles and insignia of nobility.

136 *your Henry the Fourth*: Henri IV (1553–1610) was revered throughout the Revolution as the promoter of good government and religious toleration. His statue on the Pont Neuf was

one of the few monarchical symbols in Paris to emerge unscathed.

139   *exclusively reserved for men of family*: the Ségur Decree of 22 May 1781 effectively required evidence of four generations of nobility as a qualification to rise above a certain rank in the army.

139   *Omnes boni nobilitati semper favemus*: 'All good people always take the part of the highborn', Cicero, *Pro Sestio*, ix. 21.

141   *troublous . . . unsweet*: 'Long were to tell the troublous stormes, that tosse | The private state, and make the life unsweet.' Edmund Spenser, *The Faerie Queene*, ii. vii. 14.

142   *massacre of St Bartholomew*: took place on St Bartholomew's Day 1572, when perhaps 2,000 French Protestants were murdered in Paris.

143   *on the stage*: the play in question was *Charles IX* by Marc-Joseph de Chénier (1764–1811).

146   *a personal acquaintance*: on his visit to France in 1773 Burke had spent a lot of time with the clergy of Auxerre, including the bishop Jean-Baptiste-Marie Champion de Cicé.

146   *a Fenelon*: refers to François de Salignac de la Mothe-Fénelon (1651–1715), Archbishop of Cambrai, author of a number of important political and theological works.

147   *persecutions of oppressive power*: the sharpness of the poignancy of Burke's remarks on the plight of the French Church was blunted by the fact that the reforms of 1790 had been welcomed by half the French clergy.

149   *a civic education*: a civic, or secular, educational system was particularly associated with two men who were much disliked by Burke, namely Jean-Jacques Rousseau and the Marquis de Condorcet.

150   *Burnet*: Gilbert Burnet (1643–1715), Bishop of Salisbury, theologian and proponent of moderate Whig views in politics.

151   *spirit of toleration*: on 24 December 1789, French Jews and Protestants had been accorded full civil rights by a decree of the National Assembly.

152   *Domat*: Jean Domat (1625–96), jurist and author of *Les Lois Civiles dans leur Ordre Naturel*.

153   *Mr Camus*: Armand-Gaston Camus (1740–1804), lawyer

who played a large part in drafting the Civil Constitution of the Clergy. He argued vigorously that the state had every right to regulate Church affairs, in *Code de l'administration et de l'aliénation des biens nationaux rédigé par ordre de l'Assemblée nationale* (Paris, 1791).

153 *Anabaptists of Munster*: Anabaptists were a sixteenth-century sect who denied the validity of infant baptism. As a result of their excesses when ruling the German town of Munster between 1532 and 1535, their name became synonymous with everything outrageous.

154 *Dans la Révolution actuelle ... la plus déplorable nullité*: in the actual Revolution, they have resisted all the *seductive qualities of the religious bigotry of the Enemies of the Revolution, their wish to persecute and cause a fuss. Forgetting their own greatest interests* in order to render homage to the views of general good order determined by the National Assembly, they see, *without complaining*, the suppression of this crowd of ecclesiastical establishments which offered them subsistence; they even agreed to lose their episcopal status, the only one of these resources which could, or rather *which ought, in all justice*, to be preserved for them; condemned *to the most appalling poverty*, without having *been heard, nor able to be heard, they do not complain*, but remain faithful to the principles of the purest patriotism; they are still ready to *spill their blood* to uphold the Constitution, which is going to reduce their town to the most deplorable nothingness.

154 *Berne*: in 1790 the Club Helvétique, operating from Paris, had sent propagandists to the canton of Berne, whose government had formally protested to the French about their activities.

155 *proceedings of the confederation of Nantz*: on 23 August and 4 November 1790, Anglo-French fêtes had been held at Nantes, whose Jacobin Club was also in correspondence with the Revolution Society in London. A delegation from Nantes visited London in September 1790.

155 *Si plures sunt ... latius. ... Sic par ... continere*: Burke's quotation from the *De Officiis* differs in small points from that offered in modern editions: 'If those to whom things have been wrongly given are more numerous than those from whom things have been unjustly taken, are they on that account also more powerful? No! For things are judged not by numbers but by weight. But what fairness is there in a man who held no land

holding land that has been owned [by another] for many years, generations even, and in the man who held it losing it? Indeed, it was on account of just this sort of injustice that that Spartans expelled Lysander the Ephor and (what had never before happened among them) they put to death their king, Agis. From that time, such great dissensions ensued that tyrants emerged, the upper orders were exiled, and the State, although constituted most gloriously, slid into ruin. But not only did Sparta herself fall; she also overthrew the rest of Greece by the contagion of the evils which, taking their beginning from the Spartans, spread further abroad. . . . In this way it is fair to deal with citizens; not, as we have already seen happen twice, to plant a spear in the forum and subject the goods of citizens to the cry of the auctioneer. But that Greek believed that everybody's interests should be considered (the sign of a wise and excellent man); and this is the best possible policy and wisdom of a good citizen, not violently to divide the interests of citizens but to unite all men together with the same principle of impartial justice', Cicero, *De Officiis*, II. xxii. 79–II. xxiii. 80 and 83.

156 *See two books . . . Munchen 1787*: both books refer to the Illuminati, a secret society with a strong anti-clerical bias.

157 *Spartam nactus es; hanc exorna*: 'Now that Sparta has fallen to your lot, adorn it.' Cicero, *Letters to Atticus*, iv. 6.

160 *the Munera Terrae*: 'the gifts of the Earth'; Horace, *Odes*, II. xiv. 10.

162 *Champ de Mars*: reference is here being made to the Fête de la Fédération that took place on the Champ de Mars on 14 July 1790. Designed by the painter David, it was a ceremony of national reconciliation.

163 *petits maisons, and petit soupers*: *petites-maisons* could mean either lunatic asylums or houses in which mistresses were kept; *petits soupers* are supper parties.

165 *I can never . . . state*: Burke's critics countered this argument by claiming that, in the summer of 1789, 'Every other species of authority was annihilated by popular acts, but that of the States General.'; Sir J. Mackintosh, *Vindiciae Gallicae* (London, 1791), 24–5.

167 *Pater ipse . . . voluit*: 'God himself wished that the farmer's life should not be an easy one'; Virgil, *Georgics*, i. 121–2.

168 *M. Rabaud de St Etienne*: Jean-Paul Rabaut de St Étienne

(1743–93), a Protestant pastor, who often spoke on religious affairs in the National Assembly.

168 *Tous les établissemens . . . tout est á recréer*: all the existing establishments of France crown the unhappiness of the people; in order to make them happy it is necessary to renew them; to change ideas; to change laws; to change habits . . . to change men; to change things; to change words . . . to destroy everything; yes, to destroy everything; since everything is to be recreated.

168 *the Quinze vingt*: Les Quinze-Vingts was a hospital for the blind in Paris.

171 *quadrimanous*: literally 'four-handed'. The likely meaning is a reference to an argument or institution being pulled apart from four different directions.

171 *Cicero . . . philosophy*: Cicero, *Pro Murena*, xxix–xxxi.

171 *pede nudo Catonem*: Horace, *Epistles*, i. xix. 12–14, 'If anyone imitates Cato, stern of face, barefooted and wearing mean clothes, does he also exemplify the morals and virtue of Cato?'

171 *Mr Hume . . . composition*: while Rousseau was an exile in England, he was often entertained by the philosopher David Hume.

174 *Empedocles and Buffon*: Burke was uniformly hostile to what he describes as the Revolution's attempts to squeeze diversity in geography and political temperament into geometrical or mechanical shapes. Empodocles (*c*.490–430 BC) believed that all matter was simply a combination of four basics elements— earth, air, fire, and water. Georges Louis Leclerc Buffon (1707–88) was author of the *Histoire naturelle, générale et particulière*.

175 *'But soft—by regular degrees, not yet'*: 'But soft—by regular approach—not yet', Alexander Pope, *Epistle to Richard Boyle, Earl of Burlington*, 129.

175 *qualification*: a distinction was made between 'active' and 'passive' citizens. All citizens were accorded 'civic rights', such as equality before the law and religious toleration. Only 'active' citizens also enjoyed 'political rights', such as the vote and the role of juror. The distinction rested on the payment of a certain sum in taxation. This provision disfranchised some two million out of six million adult Frenchmen.

176 *These primary . . . destroy the rights of men*: this description of the electoral process is defective. As a number of critics pointed out, Burke confused the electoral system with the system of local government.

178 *Servius Tullius*: the sixth king of Rome (578–543 BC).

183 *Hominem non sapiunt*: 'hominem pagina nostra sapit', Martial, *Epigrammata*, x. iv. 10. 'Our pages smack of man.'

184 *Non, ut olim . . . colonia*: 'For the days had passed when entire legions—with tribunes, centurions, privates in their proper divisions—were so transplanted as to create, by their unanimity, and their comradeship, a little commonwealth. The settlers now were strangers among strangers; men from totally different companies; leaderless; mutually indifferent; suddenly, as if they were anything in the world except soldiers, massed in one place to compose an aggregate rather than a colony', Tacitus, *Annals*, XIV. xxvii.

185 *facies Hippocratica*: a medical term used to describe the shrunken and livid appearance of the face immediately before death.

186 *Montesquieu*: Charles-Louis de Secondat, Baron de Montesquieu (1689–1755), major authority on politics and the law, whose *L'Esprit des Lois* was much admired on both sides of the Channel.

186 *troll*: a round in singing or something repetitious.

186 *Qualitas . . . Habitus*: these are eight of Aristotle's ten categories in the study of Logic; Quality, Relation, Action, Passivity, Place, Date, Situation, Disposition. See W. D. Ross, *Aristotle* (London, 1956), 21.

187 *M. de Calonne*: Charles-Alexandre de Calonne, *De l'état de la France présent et à venir* (London, 1790).

187 *rivals*: in the years before 1789, Calonne had become embroiled in bitter disputes with Necker and Loménie de Brienne, rivals for the office of Contrôleur-Général.

188 *the whole*: Burke insisted that a Member of Parliament, though elected by a particular constituency, was constitutionally the representative of all citizens, and not the mandated delegate of a particular area.

190 *Limbus Patrum*: or Limbo, was, in Catholic theology, a state between heaven and hell inhabited by the virtuous who lived before Christ's death.

192 *reversed ... Delos*: Latona was the mother of Artemis and
      Apollo. As a birthplace for her children, she anchored the
      island of Delos to the sea-bed. By contrast, Burke accuses the
      French of being less interested in anchorage than in destabiliza-
      tion.

192 *oras et littora circum*: 'around the shores and coasts', Virgil,
      Aeneid, iii. 75.

193 '*Diis immortalibus sero*' ... *other*: this is a paraphrase of
      Cicero, *De Senectute*, vii. 25. 'A farmer, however old, will not
      hesitate to reply to one who asks for whom he sows: "for the
      immortal gods, who willed it that I should not only receive
      these things from my forebears but should also produce for
      posterity".'

193 *Caisse d'Escompte*: discount bank.

193 *Haec ubi locutus ... ponere*: 'With these words, the money-
      lender Alfius, who was always on the point of becoming a
      farmer, has called in all his money in the middle of the month
      and seeks to lend it out again at the beginning of the month',
      Horace *Epodes*, ii.

194 *Mississippi and South Sea*: the Mississippi Company in France
      and the South Sea Company in England were two joint-stock
      companies that foundered amid a welter of scandal in the early
      1720s.

195 *St Dennis*: it was not unusual for wagons carrying foodstuffs
      to be intercepted at one of the customs-posts, or *barrières* (such
      as that at Saint-Denis), which surrounded Paris.

196 '*the Serbonian bog*': 'A gulf profound as that Serbonian bog |
      Betwixt Damiata and Mount Casius old, | Where Armies whole
      have sunk' John Milton, *Paradise Lost*, ii. 592–4.

197 *The other divisions ... against her*: this remark was prophetic:
      in the spring and summer of 1793, many parts of France were
      to a lesser or greater extent involved in counter-revolution, but
      there was no co-ordination between these movements.

199 *Senate*: the absence of a second chamber was a major
      deviation from the model of the American constitution, which
      was otherwise much admired. The French idea of popular
      sovereignty insisted that the will of the people, as expressed by
      elected representatives, should not be constrained by any other
      body.

199 *Solons and Numas*: Solon (*c.*630–*c.*560 BC) and Numa

Pompilius (715–672 BC) were lawgivers to the Greek and Roman worlds.

202 *cardinal Mazarin*: Jules Mazarin (1602–61), French cardinal and protégé of Richelieu.

202 *Louvois*: François-Michel Le Tellier, Marquis de Louvois (1641–91).

202 *George . . . councils*: in 1756, George II accepted William Pitt (1708–78) as a Cabinet Minister, though disliking him intensely.

205 *M. de Montmorin*: Armand-Marc, Comte de Montmorin de Saint-Hérem (1745–92), career diplomat and Minister for Foreign Affairs.

205 *differences . . . Spain*: in 1790 a diplomatic crisis was provoked between England and Spain over a settlement called Nootka Sound on Vancouver Island.

206 *sed multae . . . vicerunt*: 'Many cities and public acclamations were his downfall', Juvenal, *Satires* x. 284.

207 *radical independence*: on a number of occasions during the eighteenth century the Parlements, as law courts, had been able to thwart royal policy. Their capacity to resist provoked Louis XV to abolish them in 1771. Louis XVI restored them in 1775.

208 *Areopagus*: a hill in Athens, on which sat councils of elders.

208 *psephismata*: decrees promulgated in the Athenian assembly after a vote.

209 *Chatelet*: the Châtelet was one of the principal courts of Paris and the name of the building in which it sat. In the summer of 1789 it was empowered by the Assembly to try royalist conspirators.

211 *high court . . . usurpation*: Burke is probably thinking of the special court that was set up to try Charles I in 1649.

211 *committee of research*: in order to combat disorder and to unmask royalist plots, the Paris authorities set up a special committee, the *Comité des Recherches*, which very quickly acquired the reputation of being inquisitorial.

211 *M. de la Tour du Pin*: Jean-Frédéric, Comte de la Tour du Pin (1727–94), expert on military affairs; guillotined in 1794.

212 *His Majesty . . . the friend*: in the summer and autumn of 1790 there were a number of disturbances within army units, where morale and discipline had been undermined by the

emigration of royalist officers. In August there was a much-publicized mutiny at Nancy.

212 *[risum teneatis]*: 'please refrain from laughter'.

215 *Prêtés avec ... imposante solemnité*: sworn with the most imposing solemnity.

215 *I hope ... civic oaths*: Burke, with heavy-handed irony, is making the point that since men like François-Marie-Arouet de Voltaire (1694–1778), Jean Le Rond d'Alembert (1717–83), Denis Diderot (1713–84), and Claude-Adrien Helvétius (1715–71) had taught the French to disbelieve in God, oaths were of little value.

215 *Comme sa Majesté ... citoyens et les troupes*: as his Majesty has recognized, this is not a system of individual associations, but a uniting of the wills of all the French for their common liberty and prosperity, and thus for the maintaining of public order; he has thought it proper for each regiment to take part in these civic festivals to increase the sense of rapport between citizens and soldiers and to draw tighter the bonds of union.

215 *Comme sa Majesté ... confederacies*: *Discours de M. de la Tour du Pin* (Paris, 1790).

217 *Si ... recusem*: 'If someone allowed me to return to boyhood, and to bawl in my cradle, I would emphatically refuse', Cicero, *De Senectute*, xxiii. 83.

219 *the authority ... importance*: officers in the National Guard were elected by their men.

220 *This relation ... politics*: this is one of the most prophetic of Burke's remarks. The French were themselves acutely aware that the Revolution might be terminated by some kind of military coup. Lafayette and Dumouriez were early candidates for a role that was ultimately to be filled by Napoleon.

222 *Marquis de la Fayette*: Marie-Joseph-Paul-Yves-Roch-Gilbert Du Motier, Marquis de Lafayette (1757–1834). After a distinguished career in the American War of Independence, Lafayette was a leading liberal among the French aristocracy, and well-known in English, Whig circles.

223 *abolished*: feudal dues were abolished on 4 August 1789. Later a distinction was made between rights that were attached to the person of the landlord and those which were attached to the ownership of land. The first were abolished outright. The second had to be bought out. The reason for this distinction

was that many members of the bourgeoisie, including members of the National Assembly, were themselves owners of land on which dues of various sorts were levied.

224   *rochet*: a type of surplice worn by bishops and abbots.

227   *gabelles*: the *gabelle* was a tax on salt levied in the *ancien régime*. Burke here uses the word to describe arbitrary taxation in general.

228   *systasis of Crete ... Poland*: the systasis of Crete, a loose defensive alliance of Cretan cities, and the Polish Confederation of the eighteenth century were constitutional arrangements that were notoriously unworkable.

230   *M. Vernier*: Théodore Vernier, Comte de Mont-Orient (1731–1818).

230   *Cedò ... cito*: 'Come tell me how you ruined your great state so quickly', Cicero, *De Senectute*, vi. 20.

232   *John Doe ... Richard Roe*: names given to fictitious characters in legal pleadings.

232   *Duke de St Simon*: Louis de Rouvroy, Duc de St Simon (1675–1755), soldier, diplomat, and author of a celebrated set of memoirs.

233   *Change*: the London money market,

235   *church mummy*: a gum used in medicine.

236   *Mais ... assignare*: Burke is here attempting to be humorous by lapsing into schoolboy Latin: 'But if diseased opinion does not wish to cure itself, what's to be done? Issue assignats—and then more assignats; and yet more assignats.'

236   *prelate*: Talleyrand, bishop of Autun, had taken a leading part in the financial debates of the autumn of 1789.

236   *Fisc*: the public exchequer.

236   *To establish ... least*: such a project had been tried in England in the reign of William III and had failed miserably.

236   *La Bruyere of Bossuet*: Jean de la Bruyère (1645–96), the essayist, had used this expression of Jacques-Bénigne Bossuet (1627–1704), Bishop of Meaux.

240   *Ce n'est point ... subvenir à leur entretien*: here, I am not talking to the whole assembly; I am only speaking to those who are leading it astray, by hiding the goal to which they are aiming it beneath seductive veils. It is to these that I speak: your

aim, and you will not dispute the fact, is to deprive the clergy of all hope, and to bring about their ruin; this is your objective, although you are not suspected of any conspiracy based on greed; this is it, without any regard to its effect on daily life; this is believed to be what you have in mind in the terrible operation you propose; this must be its outcome. But the people whose interests you represent, what advantage will they find in it? In serving you without interruption, what are you doing for them? Nothing, absolutely nothing; on the contrary, you are enacting that which leads to them being overwhelmed with new obligations. To their detriment, you have rejected an offer of 400 millions, the acceptance of which could become a way of helping them; and you have substituted for this help, as profitable as legitimate, a ruinous injustice, which, by your own admission, is a charge on the public exchequer, and as a consequence on the people, an increase in annual expenditure of at least 50 millions and a reimbursement of 150 millions.

Unhappy people, here is what in the last resort the expropriation of the Church is worth to you, and the severity of taxing decrees has taken over from the attention of ministers of a kindly religion; and henceforth you will pay for them; their charities relieve the poor; and you are going to be taxed for their upkeep.

240 *bishop of Nancy*: Anne-Louis-Henri de La Fare (1752–1829), Bishop of Nancy; emigrated 1791; became a cardinal in 1823.

241 *club at Dundee*: the Dundee club known as 'The Friends of Liberty'.

242 *Judaeus Apella*: 'Let the Jew Apella believe it, not me', Horace, *Satires*, I. v. 100. Judaeus Apella was a general name for anyone credulous.

242 *Mr Law*: John Law (1671–1729), the promoter of the Mississippi Company, fled France after the Company's bankruptcy.

244 *Mr Bailly*: Jean Sylvain Bailly (1736–93), as Mayor of Paris, frequently addressed the Assembly on the special needs of the capital.

244 *'smitten . . . mace'*: 'The aggregated Soyle | Death with Mace petrific, cold and dry', John Milton, *Paradise Lost*, x. 293–4.

246 *tontines*: financial devices whereby subscribers to a fund each receive an annuity, which increases as their numbers are reduced by death, the last survivor enjoying the whole.

247   *Lucan and Corneille*: Marcus Annaeus Lucanus (AD 39–65), Roman poet. Pierre Corneille (1606–1684), French dramatist.

249   *'through . . . being'*: 'Through what variety of untry'd being', J. Addison, *Cato*, v. i. 11.

251   *Letter . . . 1791: A letter from Mr Burke, to a Member of the National Assembly: in Answer to Some Objections to his Book on French Affairs*, 1st edn., Paris, reprinted J. Dodsley (London, 1791).

251   *Comtesse de Montrond*: Angélique-Marie Dorlus du Tailles, Comtesse de Montrond. (*c*.1745–1827).

251   *certainly . . . [the Reflections]*: *Correspondence*, vi. 212.

251   *He had written to Burke*: ibid, vi. 162–9.

252   *'has my leave . . . Cause'*: ibid, vi. 212.

252   *'perused it . . . whole of it'*: ibid. 252–3.

252   *Some part . . . Cause*: ibid. 241.

253   *errors*: Menonville had pointed out defects in Burke's description of the system of representation in France.

255   *Nulla nova mihi res inopinave surgit*: 'Nothing confronts me which is new or unexpected', Virgil, *Aeneid*, vi. 103–4.

258   *Nihil non arrogant armis*: 'They think that everything must yield to the force of arms', Horace, *De Arte Poetica*, 122.

259   *a set of men . . . function*: for the judicial provisions of the Revolution, see J. Godechot, *Les Institutions de la France* (Paris, 1951). Burke may here be referring to the principle of judges being subject to popular election.

259   *ardentis massae fuligine lippos*: 'Blinded by the smoke of burning matter', Juvenal, *Satires*, x. 130.

260   *Hales*: Sir Matthew Hale (1609–76), became Cromwell's Justice of Common Pleas in 1653, in spite of undertaking the defence of a number of leading Royalists.

261   *Burnet*: Gilbert Burnet (1643–1715), Bishop of Salisbury, was a biographer of Hales, and was himself promoted to a bishopric by William III.

261   *Mr Mirabeau . . . affairs*: Burke is here indulging in heavy-handed irony. Mirabeau, before the Revolution, was almost a byword for immorality and corruption.

261   *primitive condition*: the Church's 'primitive condition' was its

structure and organization in the first two or three centuries after Christ's death.

262 *prelate of Autun*: Talleyrand had been bishop of Autun before the Revolution.

262 *Gamaliel*: one of the great masters of Jewish law in the first century AD. His name is invoked to indicate extraordinary powers of advocacy.

263 *Terra australis*: or 'southern land', had been used by classical authors to indicate unexplored, fabulous lands.

263 *from without*: this is one of the first indications in Burke's writings on France that, in his view, the Revolution could only be checked if other Powers intervened.

263 *Mahomet . . . sands of Arabia*: Burke could be referring either to the story that, as a child, Mahomet was sent into the desert to learn the ways of the Bedouin, or to the fact that, during the Hegira, he took refuge in the oasis of Taif.

263 *luce Asiae*: literally 'by the light of Asia'. It is a term used in classical writing to indicate that something had been done very publicly.

264 *The king . . . confusion*: in the autumn of 1787 Frederick William II of Prussia had sent an army into Holland to restore William V, the Dutch king, who was his brother-in-law. The action had England's blessing.

264 *emperor . . . Netherlands*: the Austrian Netherlands, contemporary Belgium, had been in revolt against government from Vienna for a number of years. With the assistance of her allies, Austria was able to restore her authority in 1790.

264 *restored . . . subjects*: Wetzlar, near Frankfurt am Main, was the city within which the judicial institutions of the Holy Roman Empire was situated. The Prince-Bishop of Liège had been deposed by a revolution in August 1789. He was restored by Austrian troops in December 1790.

264 *prince . . . eagle*: Austria, in alliance with Russia, had been at war with Turkey since 1787. In May 1790, at the Covention of Reichenbach, Prussia compelled Austria to return to Turkey territorial gains that had been made in the conflict.

264 *Most Christian*: in 1469, the title of Most Christian had been conferred on Louis XI of France by Pope Paul II, and was held by his successors.

264 *Magna Charta of privileges*: Burke is probably referring to the Declaration of the Rights of Man of 1789, to which Louis XVI had agreed, though hardly willingly.

264 *torn from his palace . . . assassins*: on the night of 5–6 October 1789, a Parisian mob broke into the Palace of Versailles, secured the Royal family, and brought them to Paris, where they were lodged in the Tuileries.

265 *Grand Seignor*: Grand Seignor was one of the titles of the Sultan of Turkey.

265 *Carthage . . . destroyed*: in 146 BC Rome dispatched an expeditionary force to destroy Carthage. Some Romans, notably Nasica, argued that such destruction would be against Rome's long-term interests.

265 *did not wish . . . Greece*: in 403 BC Pausanias of Sparta failed to capitalize on the divided politics of Athens to destroy the city's influence.

266 *probably first assassinate the queen*: Louis XVI was guillotined on 21 January 1793 and Marie Antoinette on 16 October 1793.

266 *Bajazet*: the younger brother of the Sultan Murad IV of Turkey, who had him executed.

266 *festival of the 14th of July*: on 14 July 1790 the first anniversary of the fall of the Bastille was celebrated on the Champ de Mars in Paris by a national fête.

267 *pillory*: the word 'pillory' may be contrasted with 'throne', the term employed by many eyewitnesses to describe the structure in question.

268 *governor . . . chief magistrate*: Louis-Bénigne-François de Bertier de Sauvigny, the last Intendant of Paris, and de Launay, last Governor of the Bastille.

269 *Rousseau*: Burke was firmly of the opinion that Rousseau was mad, and that his writings on education, notably *Émile*, were pernicious.

269 *Polycletus*: Polyclitus, a sculptor of the fifth century BC produced works that became models for future generations.

269 *statue*: on 22 December 1790, the National Assembly agreed to erect a statue to Rousseau.

270 *in England*: Rousseau visited England in 1766, at the invitation of David Hume. In the event, the two men quarrelled.

270 *Socrates*: the Athenian philosopher (*c*.470–399 BC), put to death for denying the gods and corrupting the young.

270 *Confession*: Rousseau's *Confessions* was published in Geneva in 1782.

271 *incapable . . . parental affection*: it was widely known that Rousseau had abandoned his own children, who were lodged in a foundling hospital.

272 *Filiola . . . [L'Assemblée Nationale]*: 'I am delighted you take pleasure in your daughter, and see the proof that the love of children is nature itself. Indeed, if that is not true, there cannot be any natural bond of one human to another; remove that, and you remove life's fellowship and communion', Cicero, *Letters to Atticus*, vii. 2. Burke then adds a line of his own, 'Farewell Master [Rousseau] and your disciples! [the National Assembly].'

272 *preceptorem . . . loco*: 'They thought that the teacher had the role of a parent', Juvenal, *Satires*, vii. 207–10.

274 *Nouvelle Eloise*: *Julie, ou la Nouvelle Héloise* was published in Amsterdam in 1761.

274 *dancing-masters . . . description*: it is unlikely that any people of this description would have qualified, as active citizens, for the vote under the Constitution of 1791.

275 *Cum ventum . . . aequi*: 'When it comes to the truth, one's character revolts, and expediency itself is the mother of justice and equity', Horace *Satires*, I. iii. 98–9.

276 *Debet . . . tissimum*: 'home ought to be a refuge where you are safest', this is a paraphrase of a remark in Cicero, *In Catilinam*, iv. 2.

277 *Pollios*: the fourth and eighth Eclogues of Virgil are addressed to Gaius Asinius Pollio (*c*.76 BC–*c*.AD 5), a soldier and patron of the arts.

278 *General Monk*: George Monk, 1st Duke of Albemarle (1608–70), prime mover in the Restoration of Charles II in 1660.

279 *ubi . . . aspici*: 'Not the smallest part of one's misery was to see and be seen'; this is a paraphrase of an expression in Tacitus, *Agricola*, xlv. 2.

281 *Abbé Maury*: Jean-Siffrein Maury (1746–1817), vigorous defender of the *ancien régime*; Archbishop of Paris, 1810.

281   *Mr Cazales*: Jacques-Antoine-Marie de Cazalès (1758–1805), arrived in England as a refugee in 1793.

281   *Mr Mounier and Mr Lally*: Joseph Mounier and the Comte de Lally were both leaders of the monarchical party, who had fled France by December 1789.

284   *What . . . Versailles*: calling the Estates General at Versailles, only a few miles from Paris, was controversial because, after the harvest failure of 1788, it was predictable that urban centres would be very disturbed in the summer of 1789.

285   *new model . . . Tiers Etat*: instead of sitting in three distinct Orders on the traditional model (300 clergy in the First Estate; 300 aristocrats in the Second Estate; and 300 commoners in the Third Estate), Louis allowed the Third Estate 600 representatives. Equally, he agreed that voting should be by head rather than by Order.

285   *perished*: the Parlements were abolished on 6 September 1790.

285   *ea visa salus morientibus una*: the only hope of safety for the defeated is to give up the hope of safety; this is an adaptation of lines in Virgil, *Aeneid*, ii. 353–4.

285   *Mox fuerat . . . artus*: 'Soon this very thing proved their destruction, and they burnt with fever restored by the furies, and, close to a painful death, they tore at their dismembered limbs with their bare teeth', Virgil, *Georgics* iii. 511–14.

286   *levelled themselves with their footmen*: on 25 June 1789 nearly fifty members of the aristocracy, led by the Duc d'Orléans, had deserted their Order to join the Third Estate.

287   δος που οτω: give me a place to stand and I can move the earth; an expression used by Archimedes to explain the principles of leverage.

290   *the moderate*: Burke is referring to the Feuillant party of moderate royalists led by Adrian Duport (1759–89) and Charles and Alexandre de Lameth (1757–1832) and (1760–1829).

291   *Fairfaxes*: Thomas Fairfax, 3rd Baron Fairfax (1612–71) was appointed commander of the Parliamentary forces in the English Civil War in 1645 and was succeeded by Cromwell a year later.

291   *committee of research*: the comité des recherches was a body set up by the National Assembly to investigate conspiracy and subversion.

291   *corruptions . . . dominions*: Burke is referring to the supposed mismanagement of the government of India by Warren Hastings.

292   *Malo meorum . . . diligentiam*: I prefer the carelessness of my people to the dark diligence of yours; this is an adaptation of Terence, *Andria*, Prologue 18–21.

INDEX

THE WORLD'S CLASSICS

A Select List

JANE AUSTEN: Emma
Edited by James Kinsley and David Lodge

J. M. BARRIE: Peter Pan in Kensington Gardens & Peter and Wendy
Edited by Peter Hollindale

WILLIAM BECKFORD: Vathek
Edited by Roger Lonsdale

JOHN BUNYAN: The Pilgrim's Progress
Edited by N. H. Keeble

THOMAS CARLYLE: The French Revolution
Edited by K. J. Fielding and David Sorensen

GEOFFREY CHAUCER: The Canterbury Tales
Translated by David Wright

CHARLES DICKENS: Christmas Books
Edited by Ruth Glancy

MARIA EDGEWORTH: Castle Rackrent
Edited by George Watson

ELIZABETH GASKELL: Cousin Phillis and Other Tales
Edited by Angus Easson

THOMAS HARDY: A Pair of Blue Eyes
Edited by Alan Manford

HOMER: The Iliad
Translated by Robert Fitzgerald
Introduction by G. S. Kirk

HENRIK IBSEN: An Enemy of the People, The Wild Duck,
Rosmersholm
Edited and Translated by James McFarlane

HENRY JAMES: The Ambassadors
Edited by Christopher Butler

JOCELIN OF BRAKELOND:
Chronicle of the Abbey of Bury St. Edmunds
Translated by Diana Greenway and Jane Sayers

BEN JONSON: Five Plays
Edited by G. A. Wilkes

LEONARDO DA VINCI: Notebooks
Edited by Irma A. Richter

HERMAN MELVILLE: The Confidence-Man
Edited by Tony Tanner

PROSPER MÉRIMÉE: Carmen and Other Stories
Translated by Nicholas Jotcham

EDGAR ALLAN POE: Selected Tales
Edited by Julian Symons

MARY SHELLEY: Frankenstein
Edited by M. K. Joseph

BRAM STOKER: Dracula
Edited by A. N. Wilson

ANTHONY TROLLOPE: The American Senator
Edited by John Halperin

OSCAR WILDE: Complete Shorter Fiction
Edited by Isobel Murray

VIRGINIA WOOLF: Mrs Dalloway
Edited by Claire Tomalin

A complete list of Oxford Paperbacks, including The World's Classics, OPUS, Past Masters, Oxford Authors, Oxford Shakespeare, and Oxford Paperback Reference, is available in the UK from the Arts and Reference Publicity Department (BH), Oxford University Press, Walton Street, Oxford OX2 6DP.

In the USA, complete lists are available from the Paperbacks Marketing Manager, Oxford University Press, 200 Madison Avenue, New York, NY 10016.

Oxford Paperbacks are available from all good bookshops. In case of difficulty, customers in the UK can order direct from Oxford University Press Bookshop, Freepost, 116 High Street, Oxford, OX1 4BR, enclosing full payment. Please add 10 per cent of published price for postage and packing.